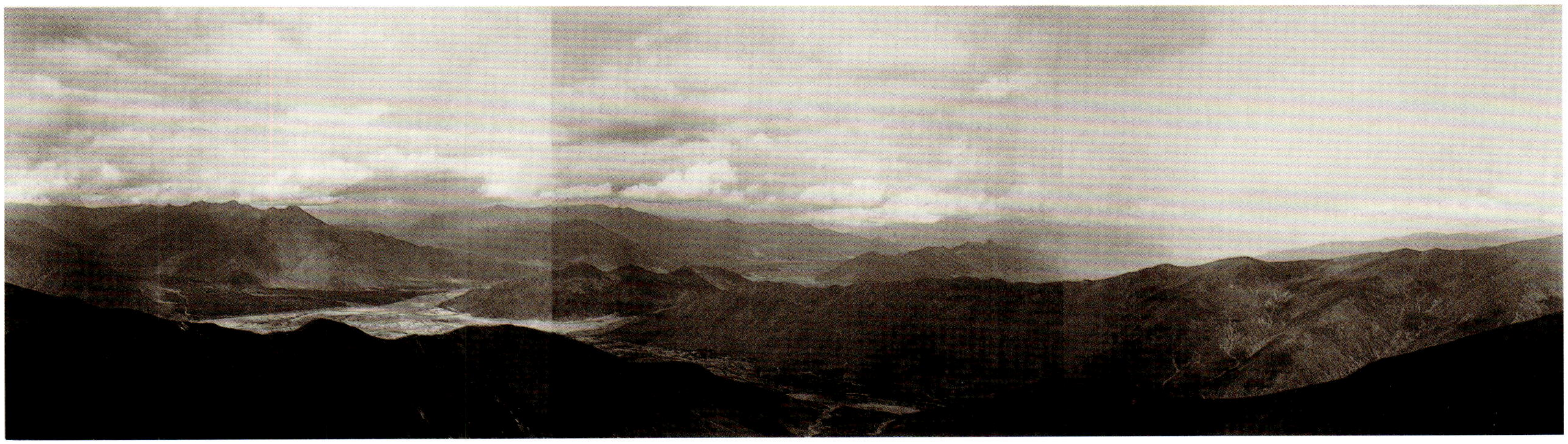

INDIA THROUGH THE LENS

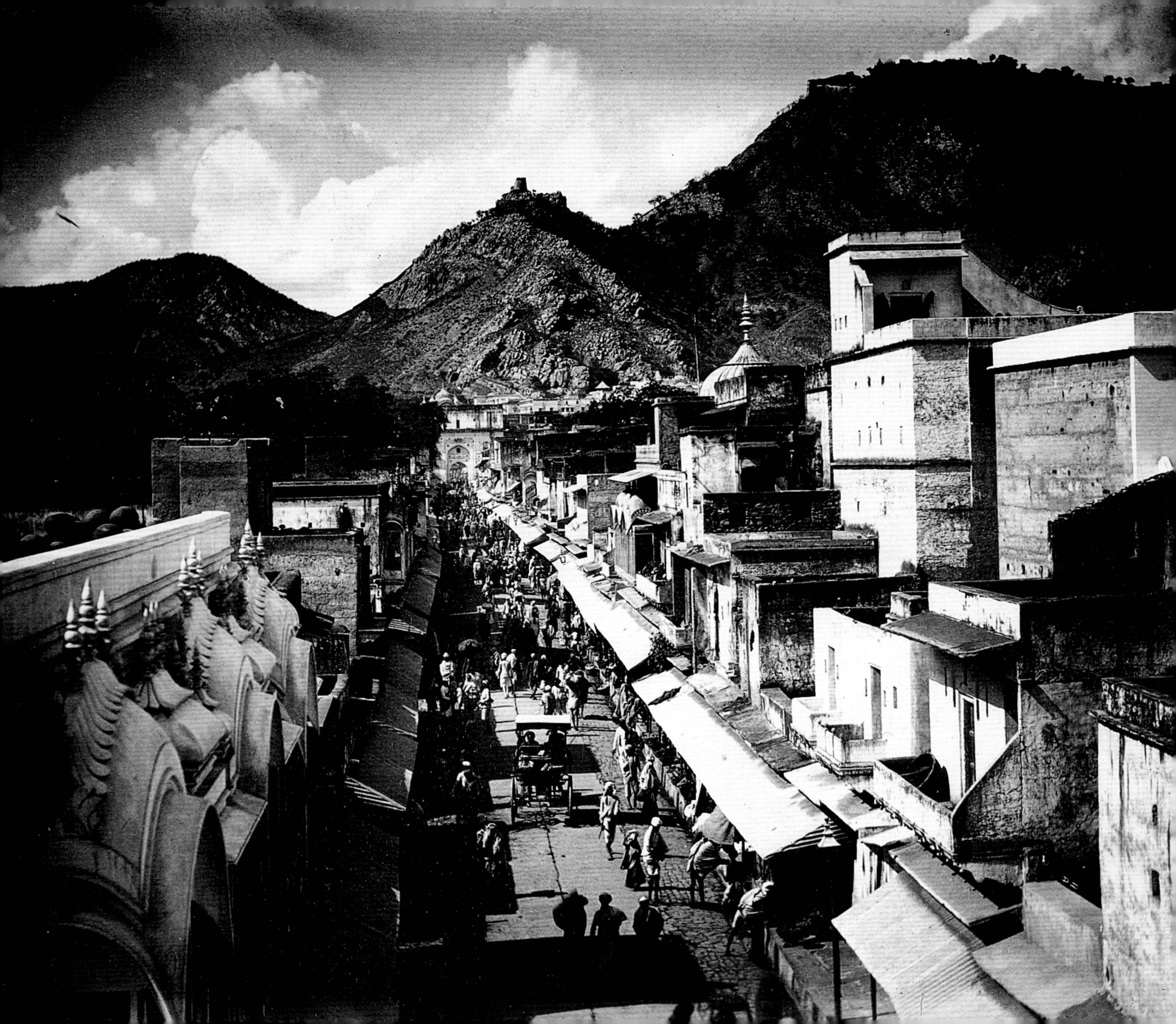

INDIA

THROUGH THE LENS

Photography 1840–1911

VIDYA DEHEJIA

with contributions by

CHARLES ALLEN

JOHN FALCONER

MICHAEL GRAY

DAVID HARRIS

JANE RICKETTS

GARY D. SAMPSON

Published by the FREER GALLERY OF ART *and* ARTHUR M. SACKLER GALLERY

Smithsonian Institution, Washington, D.C.

in association with MAPIN PUBLISHING Ahmedabad *and* MANDALA PUBLISHING San Rafael, California

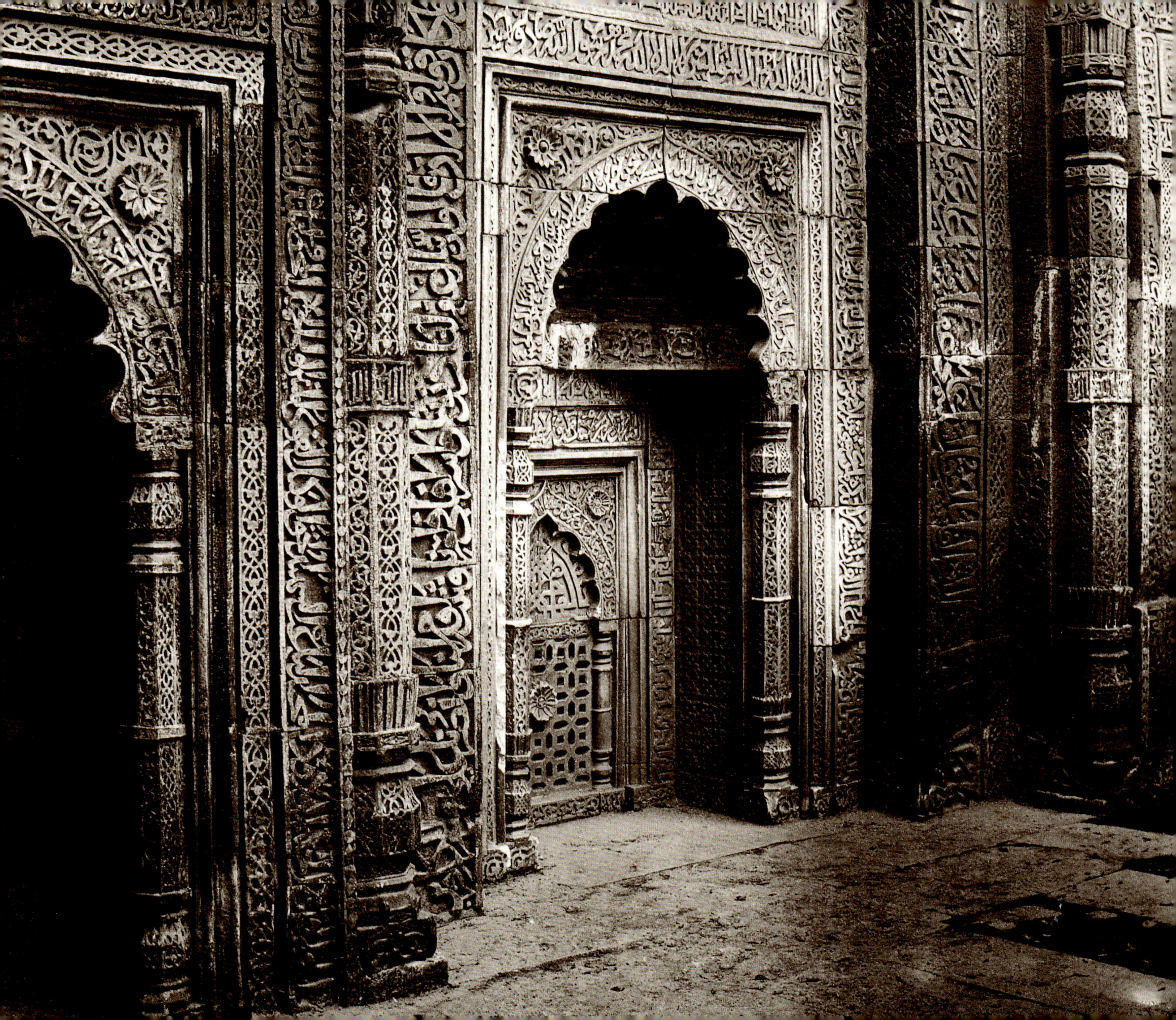

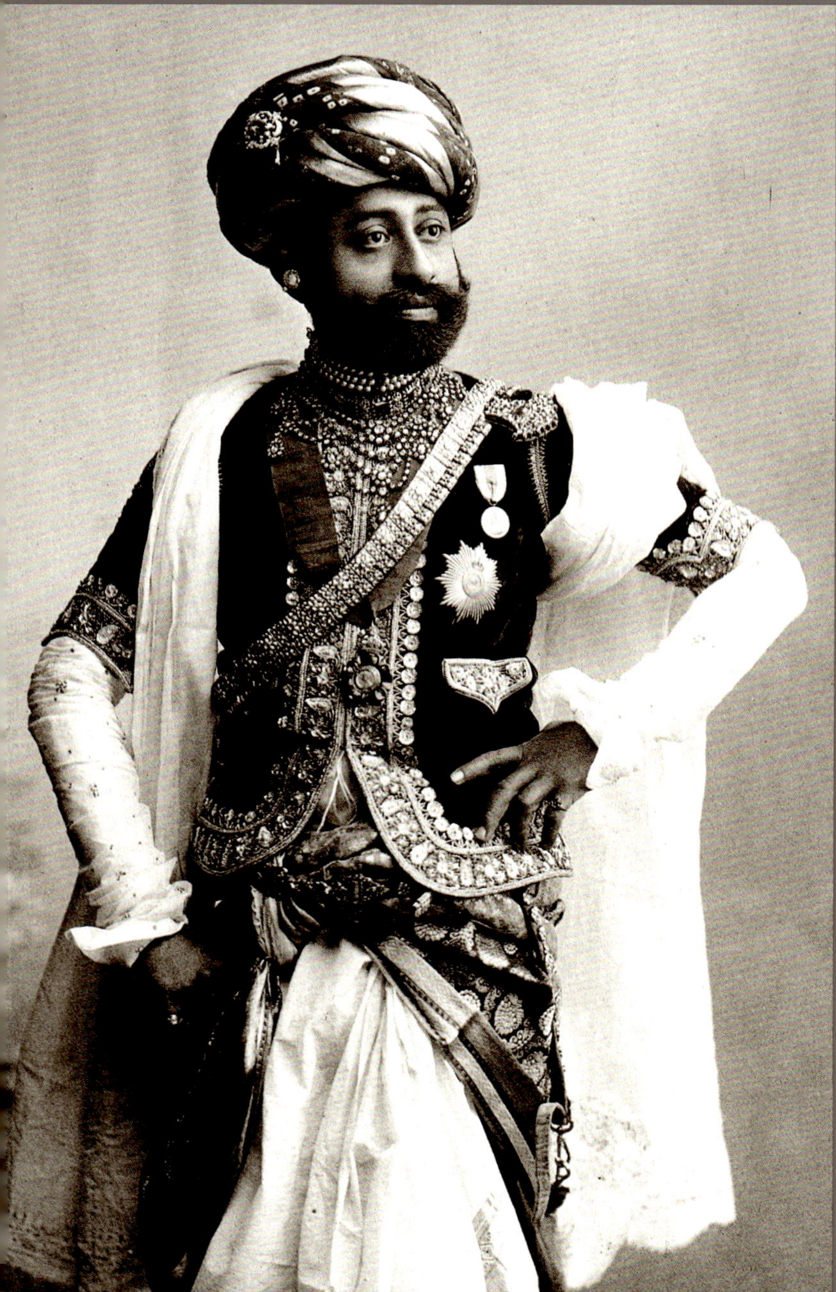

Reprinted in 2006

Published by the Freer Gallery of Art and Arthur M. Sackler Gallery in association with Mapin Publishing Pvt. Ltd., Ahmedabad and Mandala Publishing, San Rafael, California

The publication of this book is supported by a major grant from the E. Rhodes and Leona B. Carpenter Foundation. It is published on the occasion of the exhibition *India through the Lens: Photography 1840-1911,* which is made possible in part by generous grants from Hughes Network Systems and an anonymous donor, with additional support from Sigrid and Vinton Cerf.

Head of Publications: Karen Sagstetter
Edited by Lynne Shaner
Designed by Carol Beehler
Typeset in Monotype Centaur by General Typographers, Inc., Washington, D.C.
Color separations by Reproscan
Printed by Tien Wah Press, Singapore

Library of Congress Cataloging-in-Publication Data
India through the lens: photography 1840–1911/[edited by] Vidya Dehejia.
p. cm.
Includes bibliographical references and index.
1. Photography—India—History—19th century—Exhibitions.
2. Photography—India—History—20th century—Exhibitions. 1. Dehejia, Vidya.
TR103.153 2000
770'.954'09034—dc21

ISBN: 81-85822-73-5 (hc. Mapin)
ISBN: 1-932771-91-3 (sc. Mandala)

The paper used in this publication meets the minimum requirements of the American National Standards for Permanence of Paper for Printed Library Materials.

Mapin Publishing Pvt. Ltd.
Usmanpura, Ahmedabad 380 013
mapin@mapinpub.com
www.mapinpub.com

MANDALA
PUBLISHING
17 Paul Drive
San Rafael, CA 94903
800-688-2218
www.mandala.org

Cover: detail, cat. no. 84 *The Palace in the Lake, Oodeypore,* by Colin Murray; back cover, cat. no. 63, *Cocoa Nuts,* by Donald Horne Macfarlane; half title page, cat. no. 14, *Tsangpo Valley, Tibet,* by Jean Claude White; title page, cat. no. 122, *Street View of Ulwar,* by Lala Deen Dayal; frontispiece, cat. no. 120, *Interior of the Tomb of Shumshudeen at the Kutub, Delhi,* by Lala Deen Dayal; at left, cat. no. 97, *Sir Waghji Ravaji, Thakur Sahib of Morvi,* by Walery

Smithsonian
Freer Gallery of Art and
Arthur M. Sackler Gallery

CONTENTS

FOREWORD

Milo Cleveland Beach

Director, Freer Gallery of Art and Arthur M. Sackler Gallery

INDIA — a nation with a tradition of small-scale paintings with closely observed details created by meticulous perfectionists — proved fertile ground indeed for the advent of photography in the second half of the nineteenth century. It was a new, exciting, and rapidly evolving medium, and India was at the vanguard of that explosion of creativity. While the arrival of the camera brought a new tool for the careful documentation of people, events, and landscape, for centuries these subjects had been of interest to artists in India. Photography therefore provided a stimulating new means to explore India, not a radical change of vision. Perhaps nothing indicates this smooth transition better than the good service medal of 1911 awarded by H. H. Venkat Raman Singh, maharaja of Rewah, to favored courtiers. The image of the ruler was printed on porcelain from an albumen photograph, but it immediately recalls the gold portrait medallions produced for the Mughal emperors three centuries earlier.

This book as well as the exhibition it accompanies recognizes a substantial body of photographs from India as works of art and provides a thematic organization, rescuing them from their status (and occasionally their intended purpose) as mere documentary aids for research. This approach further opens up the topic initially explored in an exhibition organized in 1976 for the Asia Society, New York. In *The Last Empire: Photography in British India, 1855–1911,* scholar Clark Worswick first introduced a broad public to the power of photographic images made in India.

While aesthetics has been the deciding factor here in the choice of images, this project also recognizes the mediated nature of photography and explores the intertwined roles of photography and colonialism. This is evident in several contexts, including the extensive documentation of architectural monuments, the capture of Indian scenery in terms of the picturesque, and the choice of images of the uprising of 1857-58 that the British termed the Indian Mutiny. Such images were made and presented, in their day, as illustrations of the success of the colonial enterprise.

This project was devised and directed by Vidya Dehejia, deputy director and chief curator of the Arthur M. Sackler Gallery and the Freer Gallery of Art; she has spent many years in the study of Indian art. This project especially draws on her familiarity with British Indian photography and continues the research she began nearly fifteen years ago for an essay on the subject in *From Merchants to Emperors: British Artists and India, 1757-1930* (Cornell, 1986). In addition to gathering together strategically important loans, Dr. Dehejia has drawn from the rich (and virtually unknown) group of photographs in the archives of the Freer Gallery of Art and the Arthur M. Sackler Gallery to produce an exhibition and book that stimulates both mind and eye. We are grateful as well to the other contributors: Charles Allen, John Falconer, Michael Gray, David Harris, Jane Ricketts, and Gary Sampson. We are grateful to Hughes Network Systems for its grant for this exhibition, and thank Pradman Kaul, chairman and CEO, and his wife, Sunita, for their personal interest. We also appreciate the support of Mr. and Mrs. Michael R. Sonnenreich for this and numerous other projects at the galleries. Additional funding was provided by Sigrid and Vinton Cerf, new friends of the galleries who are wonderfully curious and enthusiastic about Asian art, and a grant for initial research was made by the J. Watumull Fund. We are particularly grateful to the E. Rhodes and Leona B. Carpenter Foundation for its generous grant for the production of this book.

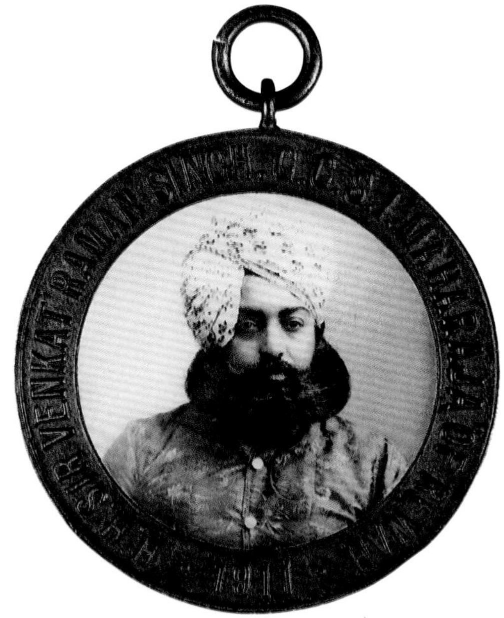

Good service medal. India, 1911. Photograph printed on porcelain mounted in silver.

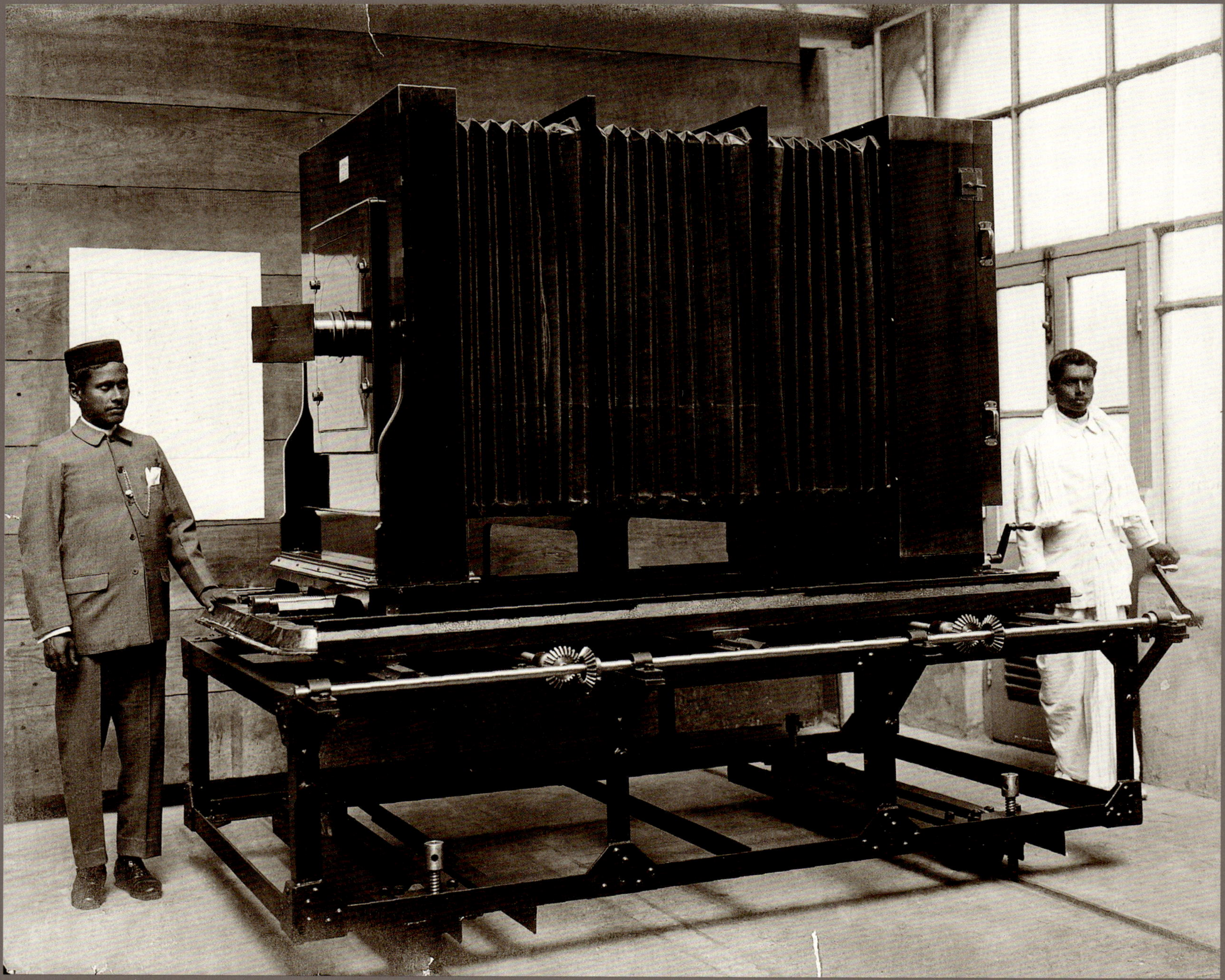

Vidya Dehejia

Fixing a Shadow

At the turn of the millennium, it appears a self-evident truth that silver salts darken upon exposure to light so that shaded areas remain white while the rest blackens. The current generation, accustomed to the marvels of modern technology, treats the "light-box" named a camera as a commonplace acquisition and photography as a routine activity. In this context a special effort of imagination is required to recapture the early days of photography when "the art of fixing a shadow"[1] was a wondrous achievement. Today we scrutinize the aims of photography, pronouncing that "to photograph is to appropriate the thing being photographed," that "photographic recording is always, potentially, a matter of control," or that contemporary photography's favored subjects are the offbeat and the trivial.[2] A century and a half ago, however, the simple ability to produce a photograph was in itself a marvel. The awestruck response to this achievement is evident in a remark published in an 1864 issue of the *Quarterly Review,* which declared that photography "forced the sun . . . to write down his record in enduring characters, so that those who are far away or those who are yet unborn may read it."[3]

The early decades of the nineteenth century witnessed the pursuit of a dream, an obsession with cajoling nature into a miraculous reflection upon a surface where it could be captured and retained for all time. Many believed that such faithful reproduction would be superior to anything created by man with pencil, ink, or paintbrush. Enterprising individuals experimented with a variety of chemicals—nitrates of silver, iodine, mercury, sodium sulphates—on a range of surfaces that included metal plates, glass, and paper. As early as 1826, Frenchman Nicéphore Niépce (1765–1833) produced what amounted to a paper negative, although it did not occur to him that he could print a positive image from it. In 1835,

Henry Fox Talbot (1800–1877) used sensitized paper to capture hazy pictures of his English country house, proclaiming dramatically that this building was "the first that was ever yet known to have drawn its own picture."[4] But he, too, failed to capitalize on these early steps so that the formal announcement of the new invention was made in 1839 by Frenchman Louis Daguerre (1787–1851), who produced sharp and precise "sun pictures" on the mirrorlike surface of a silvered copperplate. By 1850 this miraculous invention came to be known as a photograph, a word coined by the eminent British astronomer Sir John Herschel from Greek *photos* (light) and *graphos* (drawing).

Several problems were inherent in the very nature of Daguerre's eponymous daguerreotype. The silvered plate had to be tilted to discover an appropriate viewing angle, its fragility required it to be kept in a protective case, its laterally inverted mirror-image was disconcerting, its pictures could not be duplicated, and it was expensive to produce. In addition, exposure times could extend to as long as half an hour—an extraordinary length of time for sitters to remain stationary. Several photographers turned instead to Talbot's paper process, which he publicized in a book entitled *Pencil of Nature,* produced between 1844 and 1846, with twenty-four original photographs, making it the first book thus illustrated. The Talbotype, from the name of its inventor, more often known as the calotype (from the Greek root meaning beautiful), used paper for both its negative and its positive print, with exposure times reduced to between four and seven minutes.

By the mid-1850s, Frederick Scott Archer's (1813–1857) newly introduced wet-collodion process, with its accompanying glass plates, became more standard and would dominate the photographic scene for the next thirty years. So named because the plates had to be coated, exposed, and developed while the chemical solution of collodion was still wet, the wet-collodion process yielded images of a sharpness that has not been bettered by today's "film." Prints from glass plates were made on paper coated with albumen (egg white) and salts. Skillful manipulation of the proportions in the bath of albumen salts, as also in the fixing bath of gold toning, led to the varying and subtle shades of coloration seen in the prints produced during the nineteenth century. The rich sepia tones of these albumen prints made from collodion negatives rapidly became the preferred look, and their exposure time of one to three minutes was a further improvement on the time required by the paper negative process.

Page 10: Unknown photographer, copy camera in the photographic department of the Archaeological Survey of India, Calcutta, 1910, silver printing out-paper, 25.3 x 35.4. The British Library, Oriental & India Office Collection photo 527/1 (132)

The year 1871 marked the introduction of the new silver gelatin dry plate. Photographers were now freed from having to be in close proximity to a developing tent because the presensitized plate could be processed a considerable length of time after exposure. An anonymous jingle heralded the new technique:

> Onward still, and onward still
> it runs its sticky way
> And Gelatine you're bound to use
> if you mean to make things pay;
> Collodion—slow old fogey!—
> your palmy days have been
> You must give place in future
> to plates of Gelatine![5]

Finally, in 1888, when George Eastman (1854–1932) introduced his hand-held camera, a box three inches square, which he named the Kodak, accompanied by gelatin-coated paper "film" to be sent back to the manufacturer for processing, he revolutionized the entire process of taking photographs. The camera, sometimes described in the media of the 1880s as the "witch machine," lost its early mystique and became a gadget available to all.

The advent of photography created a crisis in the European world of art. While French painter Paul Delaroche (1797–1856) declared with some alarm, "From today, painting is dead,"[6] most critics refused to give photography the status of an art form. Writer and critic Charles Baudelaire (1821–1867), for instance, labeled it "a refuge for failed painters,"[7] while painter Jean-Auguste-Dominique Ingres (1780–1867) raged, "We do not want this industry."[8] Heated debate ensued over whether photography could be considered an art; after all, was it not nature, albeit with mechanical assistance from man, that created the image? Conversely, in India, British photographer Samuel Bourne (1834–1912) felt that the painter often had an edge over the photographer. When confronted with the vast expanses of Himalayan mountain scenery, Bourne observed: "If the immensity and impressiveness of such scenes could be transferred to canvas, what would such a picture not be worth! How often have I lamented that the camera was powerless to cope with these almost ideal scenes."[9]

In a thoughtful essay on the art of photography, contemporary American writer Susan Sontag points out that photography is not, in essence, an art form at all. Rather, like language, it has the capacity to produce both mundane and artistic forms. Language not only produces works of literary art, but also grocery lists and bureaucratic memos; so, too, photography produces works of artistic beauty, but also passport photographs, X-rays, or satellite pictures. It is curious that the vocabulary of photographic criticism remains as meager as it is. When it moves away from language close to that used to evaluate painting—composition, lighting, focus, and clarity—it uses inexact terms such as subtle, powerful, complex, or simple. Sontag sees contemporary photography's adoption by museums of modern art as having resulted in its being "firmly associated with those important modernist conceits: the 'nominal subject' and the 'profoundly banal.' "[10] Nineteenth-century photographs, too, have taken their place in museum collections, but a degree of ambiguity regarding their status continues to persist into the year 2000. Current discussion among museum professionals centers around whether the rightful place for such works is in collections storage (where art objects reside) or in archives (home to documentary material).

Barely a year after photography was introduced in Europe, the Calcutta firm of Thacker & Company advertised the availability of the daguerreotype camera in a January 1840 issue of the daily paper, *Friend of India.* The very first photographs created on the subcontinent were probably produced in Calcutta, though it is unlikely that we will ever be able to pinpoint them. Artists who had thus far created aquatints and lithographs—printing processes that made use of metal and stone respectively—switched professions and turned to photography. One such was Frederick Fiebig, called an "obstinately mysterious figure," whose 1847 hand-colored lithographic panorama of Calcutta in six parts is reproduced in this volume (no. 1). In 1856, he approached the East India Company with a comprehensive portfolio of small hand-colored calotypes, from which the directors purchased over four hundred views of varying parts of India including Calcutta, Madras, and the Coromandel coast.[11] While the title of "father of photography in India"[12] was given by some to Calcutta surveyor Josiah Rowe (dates not known, but described in 1857 as the oldest photographer in Calcutta), his earliest surviving pictures, including the eight-part Calcutta panorama reproduced in this volume (no. 5), belong to the late 1850s. A few small albums with photographs taken during the mid-1840s still exist, but the corpus of the earliest existing Indian photographs belongs to the 1850s, when photography became the rage.

Groups of enthusiasts came together early on to form photographic societies. The first such society in India was established in Bombay in 1854, lagging behind London by just one year, while two years later photographic societies were formed also in Calcutta and Madras. The Bombay photographic society was ambitious enough to attempt publication of a monthly journal entitled *Indian Amateurs' Photographic Album.* Twenty-four issues were published between December 1856 and October 1858, after which the project was abandoned. From the start, Indians from all walks of life joined the British as members of these societies; for instance, three Indians were elected founding members of the Council of the Photographic Society of Bombay.[13] At the Bengal Photographic Society, the renowned Indologist Rajendralal Mitra (1824–1891) was appointed secretary and treasurer. Unfortunately, Mitra's 1857 public speech denouncing British maltreatment of Indian indigo workers resulted in his expulsion, whereupon the remaining thirty Indian members of the society resigned in protest.[14]

One of the earliest Indian photographers whose work has survived is Ahmed Ali Khan, who was active in Lucknow before the uprising that the British termed "The Indian Mutiny of 1857." He photographed the British officers who became involved in the uprising as well as future Indian rebel leaders, so that his Lucknow albums of salt-print portraits constitute a fascinating historical record. Ahmed Ali Khan had problems with the collodion that was required to coat glass plates, and it was reported at the October 1856 meeting of the Bengal Photographic Society that he "was obliged to doctor it after some plan of his own to make it serviceable."[15]

The status and reliability of photography grew so quickly that in 1855 the East India Company decided to replace its draftsmen with photographers, stating in a letter from London: "We have recently desired the Government of Bombay to discontinue the employment of draughtsmen in the delineation of the antiquities of Western India and to employ photography instead, and it is our desire that this method be generally substituted throughout India."[16] By 1863 photography had become so popular on the subcontinent that it was possible for the visiting British photographer Samuel Bourne to write:

"From the untrodden snows of the Himalayas to the burning shores of Madras the camera is now a familiar sight."[17] Bourne attended a meeting of the Bengal Photographic Society in Calcutta and was surprised to find an attendance of fifty enthusiasts from a total membership of 243. The society had a balance in hand of 1,500 rupees, a respectable sum in those days, and it published a quarterly journal, with each issue featuring a photograph taken by one of its members. Bourne also remarked that it was not uncommon in Calcutta to see portrait studios run by Indians. However, the only Indian photographic establishment that competed on equal terms with European-owned studios was the firm of Deen Dayal and Sons, founded in the mid-1870s. The year 1899 marked the publication of the first Indian book on photography—H. M. Ibrahim's Urdu *Rahno-ma-I-Photography-ya-Usil-I-Musawery,* or *A guide to photography or Rules for taking photographs.* A favorable review in *The Journal of the Photographic Society of India* explained that "every year increasing numbers of the more advanced natives of this country . . . are anxious to learn the art of photography, either as a profession, or for their own pleasure and this has induced him [H. M. Ibrahim] to compile a work which should find him a very large circulation."[18]

In the artistic milieu of India, the European debate on the status of photography as an art was irrelevant. Samuel Bourne declared himself pleasantly surprised to find photographs displayed in an 1864 exhibition of the arts in Lahore (today Pakistan). "Unlike the treatment which photography received last year at the hands of the Commissioners in London," he wrote, "it is here classified as one of the fine arts. Are we then more enlightened, or simply more just and unprejudiced in this land of rising British enterprise than the would-be patrons of art in professedly free but somewhat clique-ridden England?"[19] Several nineteenth-century artists used photographs as aids to painting. Indian miniature painters, however, added an intriguing twist to the relationship between photography and painting by tracing photographs onto sheets of ivory and applying strong opaque watercolors and gold leaf to completely conceal the traced image. The practice was criticized by visiting British artist Val Prinsep (1838–1904), who had been commissioned to paint the 1877 imperial assembly at Delhi for presentation to Queen Victoria on her proclamation as empress of India. He deplored local artists for working "from photographs, and never by any chance from nature."[20] Such painted portraits are distinct from the unique genre of painted photographs in which the photographic image below remains clearly visible and color is judiciously added for extra effect. In India, daguerreotypes, too, were delicately hand-tinted by Indian miniature painters, who added colored powder with a brush and fixed the color to the copperplate with gum arabic. An 1850s daguerreotype portrait of Jaswant Rao Ponwar, the raja of the small principality of Dhar, reveals blue tints added to the robe, maroon to the turban, and gold and silver accents to his many items of decorative jewelry (fig. 1).

One of the challenges faced by early photographers in India was to ensure regular supplies of collodion, which was an essential ingredient in the wet-plate process, but which also happened to be the explosive ingredient used in the manufacture of gunpowder. The Peninsular and Orient Steamship Line (P&O), the only commercial line that plied the waters between England and India, refused to transport it, resulting in either the smuggling of collodion or its local manufacture. Glass plates also presented problems in that they were both bulky and heavy to carry on photographic trips across the Indian subcontinent. Proposed alternatives for glass, such as inexpensive sheets of talc, a soft whitish material much like mica, found to be "portable, easily worked with and the collodion film adheres very firmly to it,"[21] did not prove practical. Because glass plates had to be exposed and developed while they were still wet—postponement was not possible—photographic travel equipment routinely comprised a developing tent, chests full of solutions, and an entire array of accompanying paraphernalia. Samuel Bourne records that thirty porters accompanied him on his travels in the Himalayas in order to carry his ten-foot-high tent; 650 glass plates; two cameras and several lenses; numerous bottles of chemical solutions for coating, sensitizing, developing, and fixing the glass plates; funnels, pails, and baths in which the plates had to be immersed; and of course, his personal baggage.[22]

Photographers in India encountered difficulties particular to the tropics. During the months of torrential monsoon rain, exceedingly damp conditions led to the equipment and materials being subjected to fungus, rust, and mildew. The summer months were too hot for the stability of the chemicals, while rising dust settled on the plates and spotted the resultant work. One English photographer wrote back home in despair about the heat "which dries up the plate, rendering it more and more insensitive every moment, and also communicates to the operator a lassitude which almost wholly unfits him for the duties of the day."[23] Water was frequently in short supply and often impure. Papers presented by members at the regular meetings of the various photographic societies quite often focused on experimental

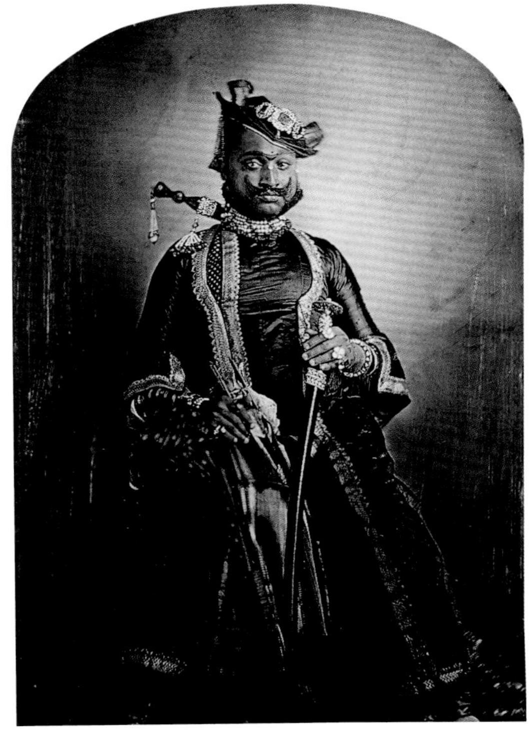

FIGURE 1 Unknown photographer, *Jaswant Rao Ponwar, Raja of Dhar*, ca. 1850, hand-tinted daguerreotype, 18 x 13. The British Library, Oriental & India Office Collection photo 67/1

methods to overcome local problems. For instance, in March 1858, W. E. Underwood told members of the Madras photographic society the secret of how "to make an iodizing mixture for collodion suited to the climate of Madras."[24]

Early cameras were made of wood and were cumbersome appliances. Dr. John McCosh (1805–1885), a pioneer photographer and a surgeon with the Bengal group of the East India Company, cautioned against flimsy portable cameras, which, though initially seductive, soon became useless. He stipulated that the camera "be made of substantial mahogany, clamped with brass, to stand extremes of heat."[25] In a similar vein, photographer John Blees (dates not known) spoke of the need to use well-seasoned wood in the construction of cameras. In 1859, the inimitable Lewis Carroll (1832–1898) wrote a long tongue-in-cheek poem on the trials and tribulations of the early photographer. Titled "Hiawatha's Photographing," it begins:

> From his shoulder Hiawatha
> Took the camera of rosewood,
> Made of sliding, folding rosewood;
> Neatly put it all together.
> In its case it lay compactly,
> Folded into nearly nothing;
> But he opened out the hinges,
> Till it looked all squares and oblongs,
> Like a complicated figure
> In the Second Book of Euclid.
> This he perched upon a tripod—
> Crouched beneath its dusky cover—
> Stretched his hand, enforcing silence—
> Said, "Be motionless, I beg you!"
> Mystic, awful was the process.

The poem narrates how each portrait was a failure because sitters moved, talked, or squinted, and how the final group picture, thought to be perfect by the photographer, was denounced:

> Giving one such strange expressions—
> Sullen, stupid, pert expressions.
> Really anyone would take us
> (Anyone that did not know us)
> For the most unpleasant people! [26]

Even today, this continues to be a common experience, often laughable, often frustrating. So many of us regret the angle or lighting when a photograph does not match up to our somewhat idealized visions of ourselves.

By 1895, as evidenced in the Calcutta publication of George Ewing's substantial technical volume, *Handbook of Photography for Amateurs in India,* advances in technology made camera equipment more reliable and usable in local climatic conditions. And yet, from our vantage point in the year 2000, when cameras decrease in size as rapidly as they increase in power (even in the 1960s, the film *Roman Holiday* had one concealed in a cigarette lighter), it is intriguing to consider the monumental copy camera, over eight feet in length, in use in the Calcutta offices of the Archaeological Survey of India in 1910 (see page 10).

A unique feature of early photography in India was the establishment of *zenana,* or women's, studios to accommodate the prevailing Indian custom that required women to be protected from the gaze of an unknown male photographer. Because Indian families desired photographs of their wives, daughters, and mothers, zenana studios run by British female photographers were introduced. Indian photographer Deen Dayal added one such to his establishment in Hyderabad. The *Journal of the Photographic Society of India* reported: "As this studio is for photographing native ladies only, special arrangements had to be made to protect them from the gaze of the profane and the stern. So the place is surrounded by high walls, and all day long within this charmed enclosure, Mrs. Kenny-Levick, aided by three native female assistants, takes the photographs of the high-born native ladies of the Deccan."[27] By 1885, Indian women had taken to photography, though perhaps as no more than a pleasant diversion.

In an advertisement in the April issue of the Bengali weekly *Bama Bodhini,* a certain Mrs. Wince offered to give lessons in the art of photography to women in their own homes. The first commercial studio opened by an Indian woman dates to 1899, when Sarojini Ghosh advertised "a thoroughly secluded studio for ladies" in Calcutta.[28]

The period 1840–1911, an exciting phase of photographic experimentation and achievement, may be considered the golden age of photography on the Indian subcontinent. The Kodak box camera with its "film" of gelatin-coated paper was introduced in 1888 with the enticing slogan "You press the button, we do the rest"—after 1911, it was available everywhere. In a little over fifty years, photography had moved from the arena of specialized professionals to that of amateurs who looked upon photography as a social pastime closely associated with family life. The process, no longer awe-inspiring, had indeed become quick and easy as suggested by the term "snapshots" used to describe its products. In India, to move from the domain of the commonplace and acquire once again the status of a form of artistic expression, photography had to travel forward a period of nearly seventy-five years.

Ways of Seeing through a Lens

Early ideas about the truthfulness of the lens have given place to widespread agreement that it is as false to state "The camera never lies" as it is to maintain "The paintbrush never lies." Over the years photographs have been manipulated to promote a range of ideas (ignoring the manipulations made possible today by the computer). Often photography was employed to idealize and thereby misrepresent its subjects, whether human beings or nature. One need only look at Edward Curtis's (1868–1954) idealized studies of the North American Indian in which, ignoring their actual condition, he used deliberate poses, theatrical lighting, and dramatic backdrops to highlight their ancient and noble character. When the camera moved away from a mere recording of its subjects, it frequently chose to produce lyrical images, presenting its subjects, whether individuals or landscapes, as visual poems rather than as direct replicas of reality.

From the perspective of postcolonial thinking, nineteenth-century photographs have been analyzed and dissected to reveal how they function as "an influential form of Orientalist discourse."[29] There is no such thing, of course, as an innocent historical eye. Photographs of India taken by early British photographers certainly reveal much about the world of India; but they reveal to an equal degree British attitudes toward that world. In practice imperialism involves much more than governance and geographical expansion; it is also a set of cultural attitudes toward a people under such imperial control. Even an apparently innocent technique like applying the principles of the "picturesque" to India's scenery merits a closer look. When Samuel Bourne applied the aesthetic principles of the picturesque to his landscape photographs of India, he was able to tame, organize, and capture that territory within the boundaries of his carefully chosen frame (nos. 65–74). It has been argued that he was thereby "familiarising and domesticating a potentially hostile landscape."[30]

In recent years, a great deal of emphasis has been placed on analogies between the camera and the gun. In both pursuits, one speaks of "loading," "aiming," and "shooting," so that the camera has arguably become a "sublimation of the gun."[31] This is not merely an example of postcolonial thinking; in writing about the power of photography in 1863, Samuel Bourne himself pointedly referred to the British inventors of photography also as inventors of guns. "From the earliest days of the calotype," he wrote, "the curious tripod, with its mysterious chamber and mouth of brass, taught the natives of this country that their conquerors were the inventors of other instruments besides the formidable guns of their artillery, which, though as suspicious perhaps in appearance, attained their object with less noise and smoke."[32] The rhetoric of light and dark also plays a part in this imperialist discourse. Photography is based on the power of light and it may thus be seen as representing "a transference of 'light' into the 'dark' recesses of the globe."[33]

It is one thing to accept the notion that the camera presents a mediated view of reality, that the photographer may use manipulative skills, and that a colonialist agenda may underlie much of the photography that was undertaken in India. It is quite another, however, to maintain that there is a way of seeing through a lens that is special to the aesthetic of India. "Indian photographers (not Europeans in India) picked up the camera and adapted its use—bent its will—to their conception of life," says

Judith Gutman, who propounds this thesis in a series of assertions in her 1982 publication, *Through Indian Eyes.*[34] In a book that is as much an anecdotal travelogue as a study of photographic practices (and one that surprisingly seems to have found unquestioning acceptance), she proposes that some Indian photographs "match paintings from the same region. Still others match paintings from different regions. But most photographs match paintings that were made seventy-five to one hundred years before the introduction of photography."[35] This forceful claim does not hold up to serious scrutiny.

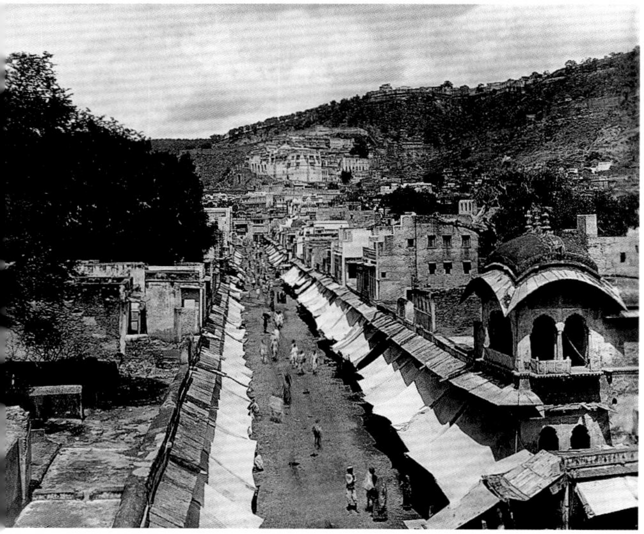

FIGURE 2 Ganpatrao Abajee Kale, *City Bazaar, Bundi,* ca. 1900, albumen print, 23.5. x 29.3. The British Library, Oriental & India Office Collection photo 17/1 (4)

To support her theory Gutman presents a set of small photographs devoted to road-building activities taken by Abdhul Qadir and Adam Khan, two Indians employed by the Indian photographic firm of Deen Dayal and Sons. She suggests a comparison with the paintings of the seventeenth and eighteenth centuries in the state of Mewar in western India. These are often divided somewhat arbitrarily into two blocks of solid color, with an occasional river or pathway running through the center of such compositions, the effect being not unlike that of the photographs that depict deep channels being cut through embankments. Gutman concludes: "When Qadir and Khan created their photograph of the road-building crew, they started where the [Mewar] painter . . . left off."[36]

A brief examination soon demonstrates the superficiality of the comparison. First, roadworks alone are presented to support the argument about photographs matching paintings; second, the idiosyncratic painting style of Mewar alone is presented for comparative discussion. There never was a single universal painted view of reality in the intricate world of Indian painting; rather, painters had choices available to them. Some conceptualized a landscape in the tradition of Mewar or Malwa; others used a lyrical, perspectival style, portraying gently rolling hills and softly flowing rivers, as in the hill states of Kangra or Guler. It is an oversimplification to speak in universal terms of the aesthetic tradition of the Indian artist-turned-photographer.

FIGURE 3 Babu Jageswar Prasad, *The Ghats at Benares,* 1883, albumen print, 21.4 x 27. The British Library, Oriental & India Office Collection photo 177 (29)

That the use of sharply juxtaposed areas and shapes is not exclusively an Indian trait is demonstrated by an abruptly terminated lake at the end of a two-part panoramic view of Mt. Abu (no. 12). The Abu photograph is not the work of an Indian photographer, but was produced in 1902 by Herzog & Higgins, two European photographers who started their careers as assistants to the British concern of Johnston & Hoffman in Calcutta but established an independent firm by 1894. On the other hand, we

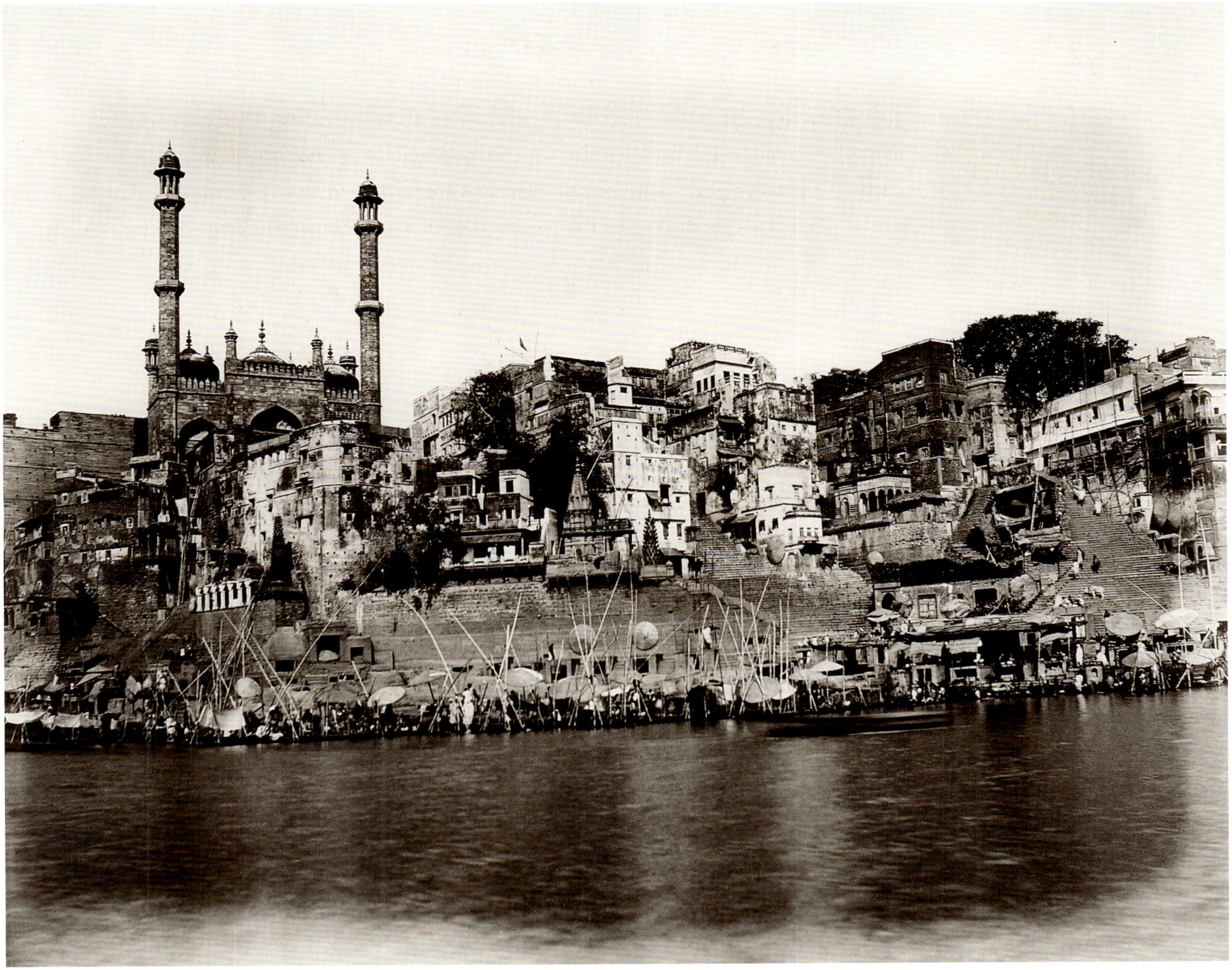

FIGURE 4 Dewan Alim Chand, *Campsite in a Forest Clearing, Kashmir,* 1890s, albumen print, 19.8 x 27.7. The British Library, Oriental & India Office Collection photo 761.1 (105)

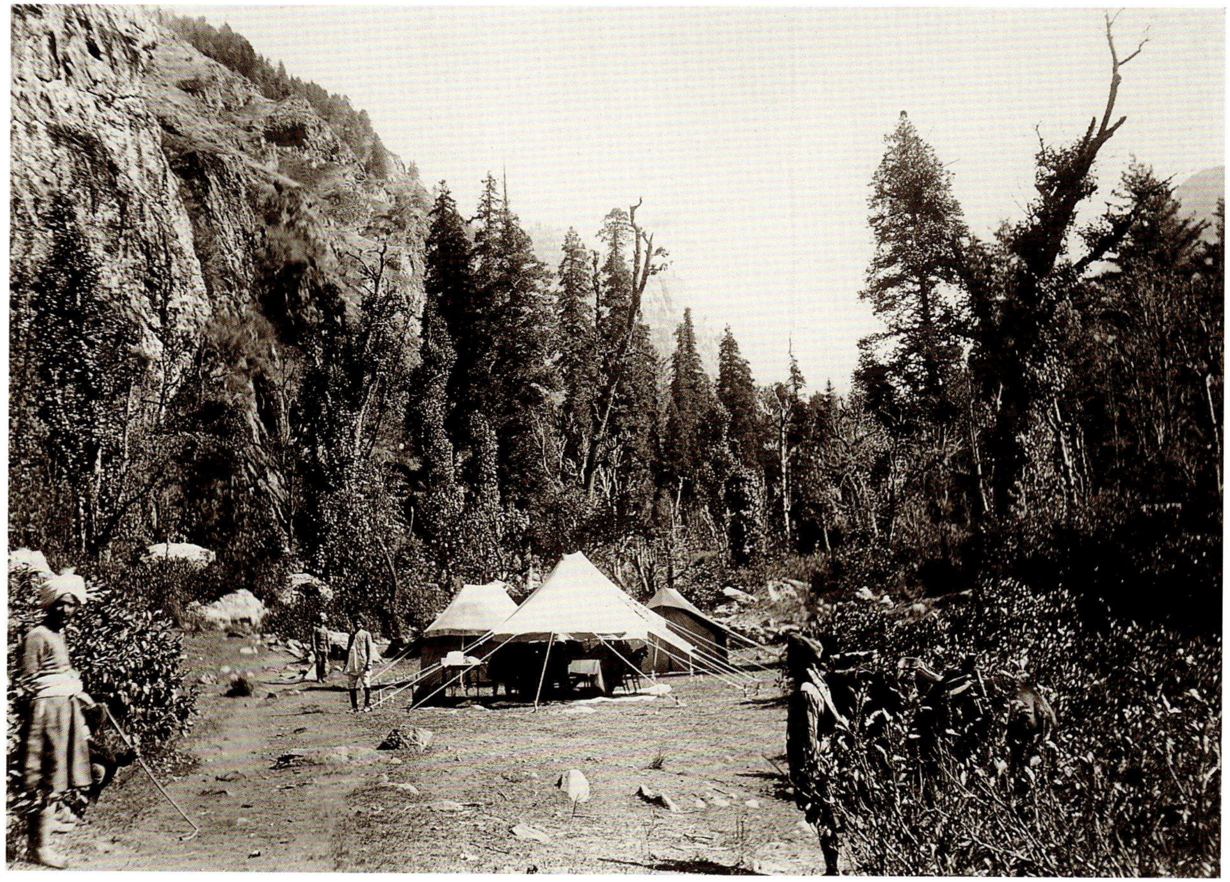

see that the "picturesque" is not exclusive to the tradition of British landscape photography as implied by Gutman.[37] This is evident from the works of four lesser-known Indian photographers, from four different parts of the subcontinent—Ganpatrao Abajee Kale, photographer to the maharao of Bundi around 1900; Babu Jageswar Prasad, photographer to the maharaja of Benares (Varanasi) in the 1880s; Dewan Alim Chand who worked in Kashmir in the 1890s; and Zachariah D'Cruz, a Goan court photographer to the maharaja of Travancore around 1900.

The accompanying reproductions of their landscapes and city scenes reveal little that is specifically "Indian" (figs. 2–5); in fact, it is difficult to place them in a category distinct from the works

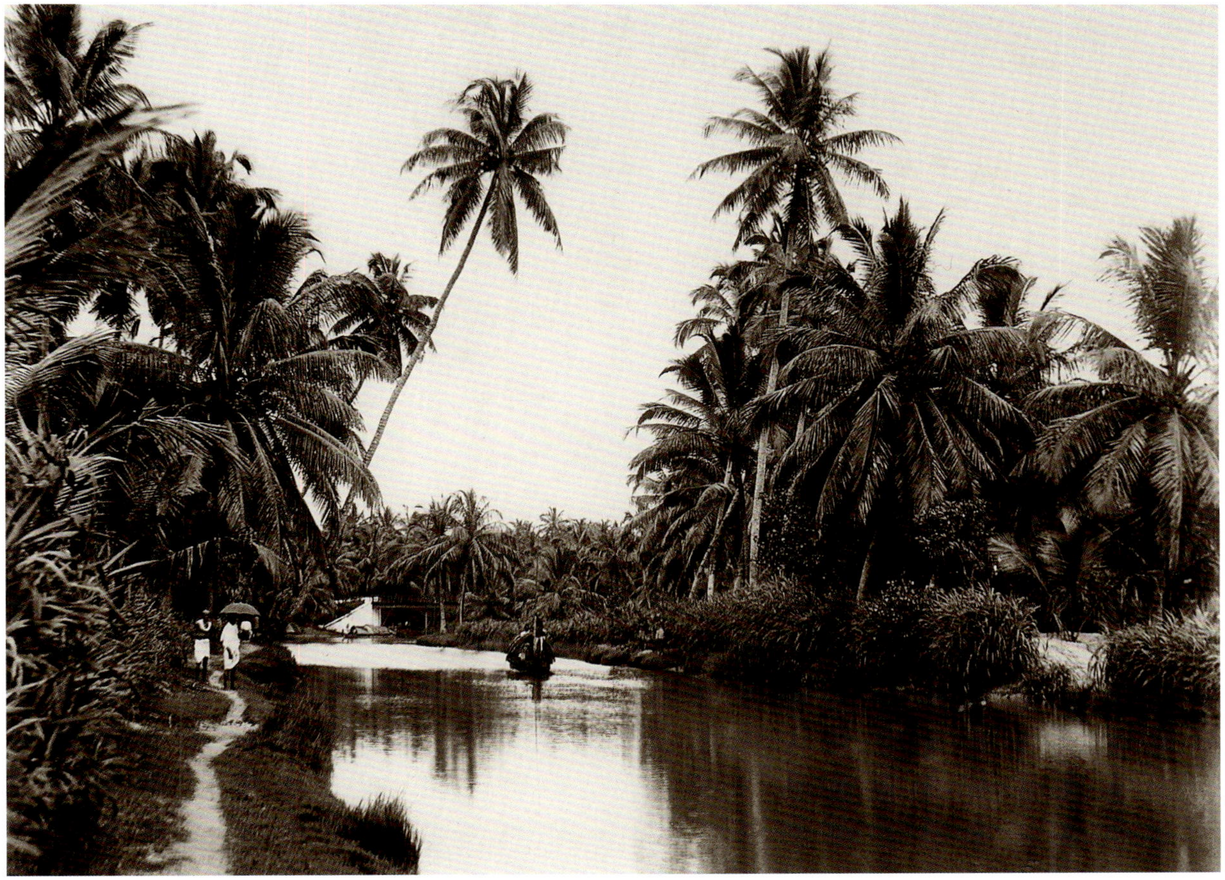

FIGURE 5 Zachariah D'Cruz, *View near Chavray, Kerala,* ca. 1900, albumen print, 18.7 x 23.5. The British Library, Oriental & India Office Collection photo 430/45 (40)

of their British counterparts, be they photographers like John Murray and Samuel Bourne, or artists in oils and watercolors like Thomas and William Daniell or Edward Lear.

The realm of portrait photography reveals a comparable scenario. It is difficult, for instance, to decide which of two portraits of the maharao of Bundi is taken by an Indian photographer and which is the product of a Western aesthetic. The only difference seems to be that Ganpatrao Abajee Kale's portrait from about 1911 (no. 98) places the monarch against a bolster cushion on the floor, while the 1902 photograph by Herzog & Higgins (fig. 6) seats him against a bolster cushion on a chair. Otherwise, the pose and treatment of the ruler are closely similar, and both photographs may be judged to be stiff, formal, and contrived. One may conclude with the notion that there were successful photographers and those who were not so successful; many of the tiny photographs presented by Gutman as examples of views "through Indian eyes" may be classed as little more than indifferent photography.

Today photographs are matted, framed, and displayed on walls, and are frequently intended for viewers unfamiliar with their contextual reference. Originally, however, nineteenth- and early twentieth-century photographs were pasted into scrapbooks and albums that were hand-held and examined at leisure. When Bourne and Shepherd issued a catalogue of photographs that could be ordered for purchase, they presented a choice of over two thousand pictures to the many British men and women who might be keen on recapturing their years in India. The preface to this catalogue, *A Permanent Record of India,* declared, "If you want to take a record of the places you have seen, this selection cannot be surpassed." Formal albums, bound in rich leather covers, were produced for presentation to visiting dignitaries and commonly bore gold-embossed titles such as:

> Autumn Tour of His Excellency
> Lord Curzon of Kedleston
> Viceroy & Governor-General of India
> in
> Central India & Rajputana, 1902

In presenting to the reader a volume of full-page photographs preceded by introductory essays, *India through the Lens: Photography 1840–1911* attempts to recapture the experience of browsing through a photo album. Though original photographs have not been included, the pictures are reprints of the exhibition photographs, themselves originals in that they were prints made at the time the photographs were taken. Thus Samuel Bourne's characteristic manipulations of the fixing bath and toning solutions give his work an individual quality evident even in the reproductions in this volume. His prizewinning view of Dal Lake in Srinagar (no. 67) is qualitatively distinct from other copies of the same photograph made in subsequent generations, even from those produced in the 1880s by his own Calcutta firm of Bourne and Shepherd.

India through the Lens begins with an essay on the appeal of the panoramic photograph, whose theatricality was achieved by manipulation of the image through a deliberate choice of vantage point, occasionally at eye-level but more often than not a bird's-eye view. John Falconer highlights the prephotography popularity of the panorama as a public entertainment spectacle. He points out that while photographers experimented with special revolving cameras, the most popular method of producing panoramas was to piece together pictures taken with a regular camera. Once the first plate had been exposed, the camera was revolved so that the next view would slightly overlap the first. Special attention had to be paid to exposure and development so that each print matched the next in image and tone. The sections were pasted together to create the final dramatic panorama in which the field of vision is frequently so expanded that it is rarely possible to comprehend the whole at a single glance. The panorama found popularity in India in a diverse range of subject areas, from the relatively prosaic documentation of development projects to the capture of the grand sweep of natural scenery, and especially to recording cityscapes that justified the commercial expansion of the British Empire.

John Falconer's second essay, "A Passion for Documentation: Architecture and Ethnography," focuses on the British compulsion to document and conserve the ancient monuments of which they found themselves the custodians, and to record the racial types of the people they governed. Much of this documentation was the work of British officers in the military, civil, or medical services of the three British presidencies of Madras, Bombay, and Bengal, while the balance was contributed by talented amateurs. The inevitable duplication of sites, arising from sporadic bouts of activity on the part of independent photographers, indicates an initial lack of planning. John Falconer points out that several photographers who produced fine architectural documentation nevertheless judged the "indecent" Hindu sculptures to be an indication of India's "headlong and downward tendency," and thus indirectly justified the British presence in India. Documentation was also occasionally used to further the colonial agenda; Captain Linnaeus Tripe's handsome photographs of south India were published in a series of volumes together with text suggesting that under the British "a brighter day has already dawned in India." By 1871, when photography became an accepted part of the duties of officers of the recently formed Archaeological Survey of India, a strong body of work of high aesthetic quality had been amassed. The

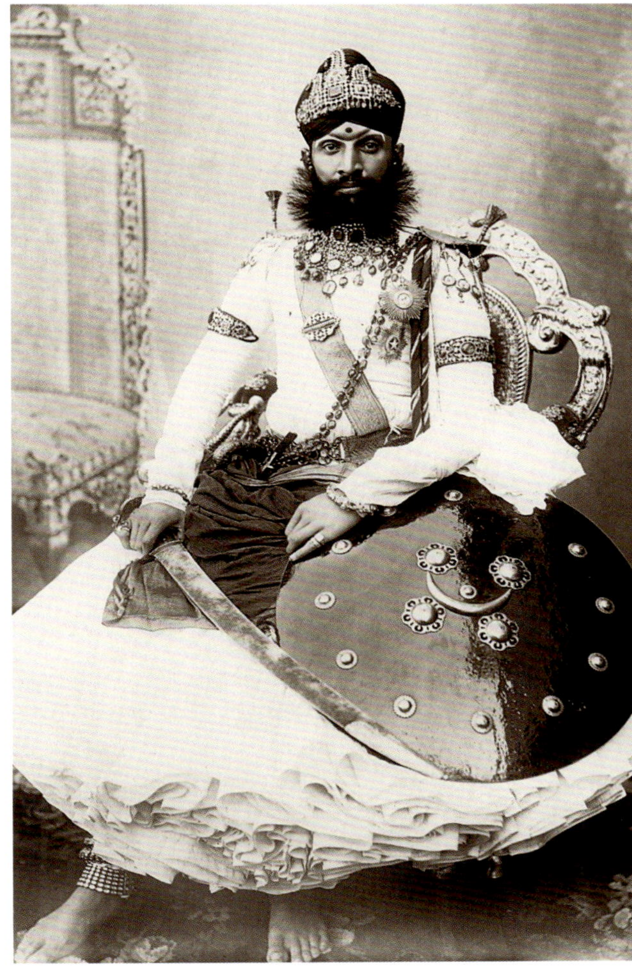

FIGURE 6 Herzog & Higgins, *HH the Maharao of Bundi*, ca. 1902, albumen print, 32 x 22.4. The British Library, Oriental & India Office Collection photo 430/20 (36)

ethnographic project, by contrast, appeared to have a strong start with the 1868–75 publication of *The People of India,* an eight-volume work containing close to five hundred images. This area, too, witnessed an absence of systematic planning that resulted in isolated, intense coverage. One such series of portraits of the Andaman islanders, produced in multiple volumes, depicted them posed in disturbing starkness against a grid of two-inch squares, in frontal, right, and left views.

In his essay "Topography and Memory," David Harris analyzes Felice Beato's images of the 1857–58 uprising that the British termed a "mutiny." These views, once seen as suppliers of factual, objective information, are reexamined in the context of British colonial ideology. Beato arrived in India in February 1858 and worked in the aftermath of what has been called "a terrible war," seeking the advice of British army officers to produce coherent and related groups of views for his prospective customers. We need to remind ourselves that these fine war photographs, displaying a perfection of photographic technique, were taken long after the 1857 sieges and assaults upon Delhi and Kanpur, and immediately after the final British reoccupation of Lucknow in March 1858. The photograph of the interior of Lucknow's Secunderabad, where two thousand Indians were slaughtered, is a case in point. The horse, the Indians, and the disinterred bones scattered in the foreground, were specifically brought together for the restaging of the scene so as to create what Harris terms "a constructed image of military triumph and celebration."

A complete change of mood is introduced by the next two essays, which explore the world of landscape photography, focusing on two British photographers, one amateur and the other professional, who had both mastered the art of the picturesque. In her essay titled "Undiscovered Amateur: Macfarlane and the Picturesque," Jane Ricketts examines the landscape photographs of Donald Macfarlane, who was active in India between 1859 and 1863. Considering the fact that the largest single body of his work was part of an album owned by Sir Bartle Frere, patron of the Bengal Photographic Society and a person of influence, it is somewhat ironic that he remained unknown for over a hundred years. The 1982 discovery of this album led Jane Ricketts to investigate and identify Macfarlane's idiosyncratic style. Free from commercial imperatives, he produced a personal record of the surroundings of Calcutta, proving himself to be a master of the picturesque. But Macfarlane moved beyond recognized categories to produce dazzling semiabstract photographs like *Rocks, Darjeeling* (no. 64), which proved too radical for the critics of his day.

British photographer Samuel Bourne arrived in India in 1863 "perfectly convinced that no scenery in the world is better, or so well adapted to photography, on the whole, as that of Great Britain."[38] His immediate venture into the mountain ranges of the Himalayas in search of the picturesque left him disappointed with the vast expanses of stark magnificence that confronted him. However, he was enormously pleased with the brilliant light in India and produced more than two thousand pictures during his seven-year sojourn in the country. Gary Sampson's essay traces Bourne's career in India, commenting upon his artistic ideals, his determination to chart the natural as well as built environment of the country, and his consummate technical skill that produced photographs exquisite in the delicacy of detail, of nuance, and of careful, studied composition. In many photographs of India's British institution, the hill-station, Bourne's mastery of the art of the picturesque is so apparent that Sampson says "one might well forget that they were actually taken in India, save for an Indian or two placed informally within the composition." He concludes by suggesting that Bourne's use of the picturesque may have furthered a colonial agenda by producing "a deceptively benign representation of India as a relatively safe and exotically scenic land for favorable cultural and commercial exploit."

The colorful world of India's many "princes"—*maharajas, maharanas, maharaos, thakurs, nizams, nawabs,* and *begums*—is the subject of Charles Allen's enquiry. Refuting the commonly held view that princely India was a "protected species," foisted on India by the British, Allen traces the origins of kingship and the rajas all the way back to the Vedic Aryas in the second millennium B.C. From the start, Indian kingship was a two-way contract between ruler and ruled, and Allen points to the astonishing durability of this model throughout India's history. It was only in the nineteenth century, when the British divested the princes of their duty to protect their people, that the more than 3,000-year-old model collapsed. With the breaking of the two-way linkage between ruler and ruled, the only function left to the princes was, in the sardonic words of British writer Rudyard Kipling, to "offer mankind a spectacle." It is this spectacle of pomp and royal trappings that is so splendidly captured in the photographs that follow the essay—a world that the princes were understandably loathe to forgo upon India's independence. The charismatic hold of these erstwhile royals over those they once ruled remains apparent to this day in their role as elected politicians in the world's most complex, and most populous, democracy.

Charles Allen's second essay traces the series of "image-building exercises" undertaken by the British to project an imperial image and to proclaim tacitly their sovereignty over India. The most striking of these exercises was the ceremonial *durbar,* based on the model popularized by the Mughal emperors, in which prominent subjects were required to offer publicly tokens of their submission. The most spectacular of British durbars, one that outdid those of the Mughals in pomp and pageantry, was staged by Viceroy Lord Curzon in Delhi during the winter of 1902–03. To house the princely heads of over five hundred "native states," together with their accompanying retinues, it was necessary to build an entire city of canvas capable of housing 150,000 persons. For the spectacle of the durbar itself, an amphitheater was erected with domes and pillars coated with plaster of Paris that, in Curzon's gratified words, "shone like some fairy palace of marble in the fierce light of the Indian sun." With the British crown represented by a minor royal, the duke of Connaught, it was Lord and Lady Curzon, the quintessential figures of the Raj, who were the focal point of this durbar in which Curzon proclaimed that "the entire continent has acknowledged a single ruler." For ceremonial splendor, it far outshone the succeeding 1911 durbar attended by King George v and Queen Mary.

The final essay is devoted to Indian photographer Lala (or Raja) Deen Dayal, who rose to prominence during the 1870s and 1880s and became the leading Indian professional on the subcontinent. Gary Sampson points out that Deen Dayal functioned in two very different worlds—the world of India's princes, which was coming to a close, and the newly dominant world of the Raj and imperial India. Deen Dayal was equally at ease in and patronized by both. On the one hand he photographed Viceroy and Lady Curzon; on the other, he was official court photographer to one of the most powerful remaining rulers of India, the sixth nizam of Hyderabad. Indeed the prefix "Raja" that is sometimes attached to Deen Dayal's name comes from the title "Raja Musawir Jung," or "Bold Photographic Warrior," bestowed upon him by the nizam.

An appendix by Michael Gray illuminates early photographic processes. It enables the reader to understand the extent and nature of the achievement of the early photographers who had to begin at the beginning. They prepared the paper or glass used for negatives, took the pictures, developed them, and finally printed the pictures on paper they had previously readied and set aside. Commencing with the daguerreotype, Gray moves through the era of paper and glass negatives, and their accompanying salt, albumen, and carbon prints, ending with the era still prevalent today of silver gelatin prints.

Color photography, first introduced in 1907, became the norm in the 1930s when it was embraced by amateurs and the world of advertising and fashion, but largely ignored in the realm of art photography. To this day, color remains suspect in the art milieu, being regarded with a mixture of distrust and disdain. It appears that the human mind and eye are comfortably able to perceive images devoid of color as realistic, though one may yet wonder at the increase in color in the U.S. newspapers, which suggests a reversal of that trend. The photographs reproduced in this volume are all in varying tonal hues of "sepia," ranging from deep chocolate through purplish brown to black-and-white, with the exception of one image of a maharaja in which an artist has applied colored pigments over the photographic portrait. Such enhancement of photographs was extremely popular in India at the turn of the century, and it was customary for photographic studios to retain painters to add color to the black-and-white images produced by them.

This returns us to the question of the relevance that can be ascribed to the mid-nineteenth-century debate on photography versus painting and their claims for supremacy. Painters, it might be pointed out, have the luxury of time which allows them to add, alter, and delete lines and colors at will, and also to create light and shade where nature does not dictate their existence. Photographers are permitted no such indulgence, but must capture the chosen image once and for all, in an instant. These considerations apart, the question still arises as to exactly wherein lies the attraction of photography versus painting. It is not merely a result of the realistic reproduction of images or scenes, although photography certainly recaptures past eras or bygone events. Rather, its intrinsic ability to evoke a response lies elsewhere. As Roland Barthes points out, we look straight through the photograph, ignoring its status as a signifier, and seeing only the signified—the image itself.[39] The photograph, like the footprint, is treated as an actual "trace"—an artifact of the scene it reveals.

NOTES

1. William Henry Fox Talbot, "Some Account of the Art of Photogenic Drawing," 1839, in Vicki Goldberg, ed., *Photography in Print: Writings from 1816 to the Present* (New York: Simon & Schuster, 1981), 40.

2. Susan Sontag, *On Photography* (Harmondsworth: Penguin Books, 1973), 4, 156, 137.

3. "Photography," *The Quarterly Review* 116, no. 232 (July–August 1864): 482–83.

4. Talbot, "Some Account of the Art of Photogenic Drawing," 46.

5. Anonymous poem quoted in Beaumont Newhall, *The History of Photography from 1839 to the Present Day* (New York: Museum of Modern Art, 1964), 88.

6. Goldberg, ed., *Photography in Print,* 20.

7. Charles Baudelaire, "The Salon of 1859," tr. Jonathan Mayne, 1859, an excerpt in Goldberg, ed., *Photography in Print,* 124.

8. Walter Kahmen, *Art History of Photography,* tr. Evan Tubb (New York: Viking, 1974), 14.

9. Samuel Bourne, "Narrative of a Photographic Trip to Kashmir (Cashmere) and Adjacent Districts," *British Journal of Photography* (23 November 1866): 560.

10. Susan Sontag, "Photographic Evangels," in *On Photography,* 113–49.

11. These may be seen in the Oriental and India Office Collections of the British Library.

12. Ray Desmond, "19th Century Indian Photographers in India," *History of Photography* 1 (1977): 313, states that this claim is made by Dr. F. J. Mouat, the first president of the Bengal Photographic Society.

13. Ibid., 314.

14. Siddhartha Ghosh, "Early Photography in Calcutta," in Pratapaditya Pal, ed., *Changing Visions, Lasting Images: Calcutta through 300 Years* (Bombay: Marg Publications, 1990), 150–51.

15. Desmond, "19th Century Indian Photographers in India," 314.

16. Ibid.

17. Samuel Bourne, "Photography in the East," *British Journal of Photography,* (1 July 1863): 268.

18. John Falconer, *A Shifting Focus: Photography in India 1850–1900* (London: The British Council, 1995), 18.

19. Samuel Bourne, "Ten weeks With the Camera in the Himalayas," *British Journal of Photography,* (15 February 1864): 70.

20. Val C. Prinsep, *Imperial India* (London: Chapman and Hall, 1879), 47.

21 Mr. Fosberg's proposal at a Calcutta meeting of the Bengal Photographic Society in October 1856.

22. Samuel Bourne, "Narrative of Photographic Trip to Kashmir (Cashmere) and Adjacent Districts," *British Journal of Photography,* (5 October 1866): 474.

23. W. H. Warner, *British Journal of Photography,* (16 November 1863): 444–45.

24. G. Thomas, "The First Four Decades of Photography in India," *History of Photography* 3 (3 July 1979): 221.

25. Ray Desmond, "Photography in India during the Nineteenth Century," in *India Office Library and Research, Report for the Year 1974* (London: India Office Library, 1976), 31.

26. Lewis Carroll, "Hiawatha's Photographing," 1859, in Goldberg, ed., *Photography in Print,"* 119.

27. *Journal of the Photographic Society of India* 5 (January 1892): 10.

28. Ghosh, "Early Photography in Calcutta," 158.

29. James R. Ryan, *Picturing Empire: Photography and the Visualization of the British Empire* (Chicago: University of Chicago Press, 1997), 26.

30. Ibid., 51.

31. Sontag, *On Photography,* 14–15.

32. Bourne, in "Photography in the East" *British Journal of Photography,* (1 July 1863): 268.

33. Ryan, *Picturing Empire,* 26.

34. Judith Mara Gutman, *Through Indian Eyes: 19th and Early 20th Century Photography from India* (New York: Oxford University Press & International Center of Photography, 1982), 2,

35. Ibid., 69.

36. Ibid., 70. Why two Muslim photographers from Hyderabad in the Deccan region of south-central India should have any links with Mewar paintings of Hindu myth, is not explained.

37. Judith Gutman makes an exception of Deen Dayal, whom she sees as a photographer able to use, as he thought fit, both an Indian and a European vision.

38. Bourne, "Photography in the East," *British Journal of Photography,* (1 July 1863): 268, where he continues thus: "Its mountain streams and lovely fertile valleys—its rustic cottages, overhung with thickly-foliaged trees—its cascades and water falls—its lakes, rivers and verdure-are especially suited for and often so combined as to meet the peculiar requirements of the camera."

39. Roland Barthes, "Rhetoric of the Image," in Alan Trachtenberg ed. *Classic Essays on Photography* (New Haven: Leete's Island Books, 1980), 269–85. See also Michael Charlesworth, "Fox Talbot and the 'White Mythology' of Photography," *Word and Image* 2, no. 3 (July–September, 1995), 208f.

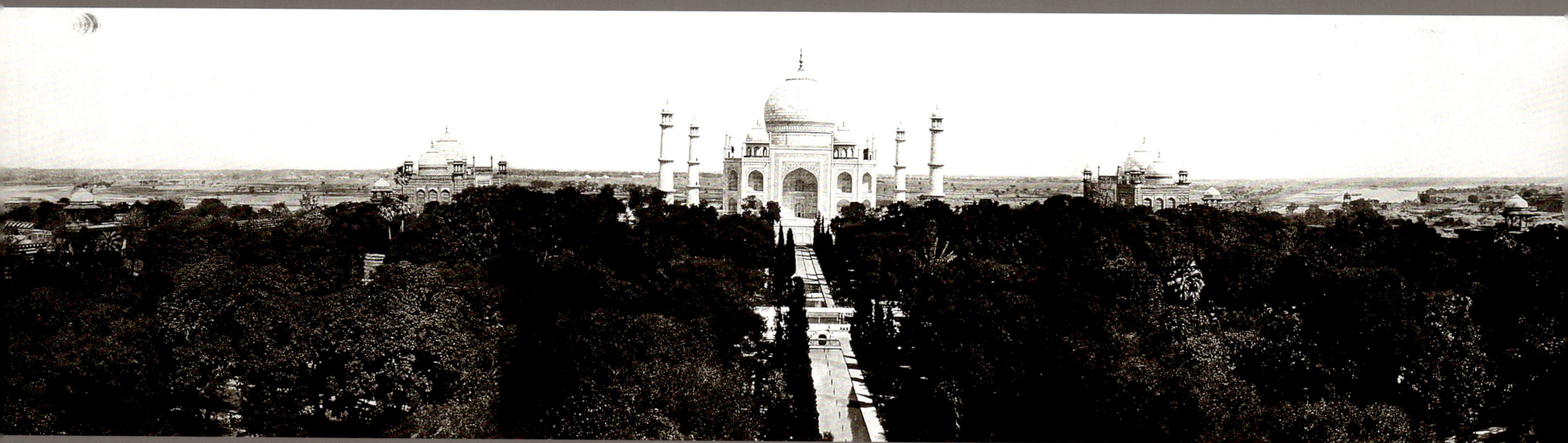

John Falconer

The Appeal of the Panorama

In 1842, some three years after the public announcement of photography, Britain's first pictorial newspaper, the *Illustrated London News,* was founded. As a promotional inducement, it offered early subscribers a panoramic view of London. This appeared on 7 January 1843 in the form of two wood-engraved views, one looking north, one south. Although the technological means were not yet at hand to reproduce photographs directly, the original images from which these engravings were made were daguerreotypes taken by Antoine Claudet from the top of the Duke of York's column in Pall Mall. This early collaboration between the art of the engraver and the photographer heralded the coming primacy of the new medium as a means of topographical documentation. Its use in the compilation of a panoramic view supplies further evidence of the enduring fascination with a form of visual representation whose origins as a public spectacle and entertainment reached back to the 1790s and were to be enthusiastically taken up by photography.

The newly coined term "panorama" had first appeared in an advertisement in the London *Times* of 10 January 1792 to describe the patented invention of the artist Robert Barker, who promised in his representation of London and its river a single painting "which appears as large and in every respect the same as reality." Barker's first panorama, a vista of Edinburgh, which had opened to the public in March 1779, surrounded the viewer (who stood on a platform at its center) with a circular painting taking in a full 360 degrees. Although these and subsequent panoramas incorporated novel elements both in their construction and in the solution of the problems of creating an accurate sense of perspective on a curved plane, they were essentially a continuation of the artist's age-old attempt to escape the limitations of two-dimensional representation with an image that expanded the visual field of the viewer's eye while maintaining the illusion of optical accuracy. Perhaps their most unique attribute was the fact that since the whole of the painted view could not be seen in its entirety at any one moment, they introduced the element of time and narrative into the visual illusion.

Barker's panorama, displayed near London's Leicester Square, survived until 1863 and fed the public with dramatic scenic views and accounts of the historical dramas and military events of the day, but its heyday lasted only until the late 1820s. Photography, with its more trustworthy replication of reality, no doubt played a part in its final demise, and by the time the medium appropriated the term "panorama" for its own productions, the word itself had come to mean any wide-ranging and inclusive overview, used indiscriminately by both writers and artists. And it was in this broader sense that photographers throughout the nineteenth century were to offer their customers panoramic views, ranging from no more than a slightly wider-than-normal angle of view to large ambitious productions that required special production techniques. No sooner had photography been made public than attempts to escape the limited field of view imposed by standard format camera lenses began to exercise the ingenuity of photographers and camera makers.

At its simplest, such attempts to extend the visual range of the image can be seen in multipart prints made by William Henry Fox Talbot in the early 1840s, and for the remainder of the century and beyond much ingenuity was lavished on capturing the extended perspectives and inclusiveness of the panoramic view. For the photographer, more limited than the painter or engraver by the mechanical and optical constraints of the camera in the manipulation of the physical world, there were essentially two methods available for the creation of photographic panoramas. The first and most obvious approach, employed by Talbot and many of his successors, was simply to photograph the scene on a series of overlapping negatives and then to join the prints manually, or in the case of the daguerreotype, to display them in sequence. A more demanding approach was to design and build cameras in which either the lens or the film (sometimes both) revolved in the course of the exposure to take in a wider field of view than would be possible with a fixed lens. In the same year as the appearance of the *Illustrated London News* panorama, the optician Wenzel Pokesch had constructed a panoramic camera; and by 1844 Friedrich von

Page 34: no. 7. *The Taj Mahal from the Gateway*, John Murray

Martens in Paris had successfully designed a rotating-lens camera called the Megaskop for producing daguerreotypes covering an angle of about 150 degrees on a curved metal plate. The following decades saw a great deal of ingenuity devoted more or less successfully to the design of panoramic cameras. The Indian subcontinent was not immune to this novelty; in 1863 the engineer S. A. Stewart proudly displayed his patented panoramic camera to members of the Bengal Photographic Society, where it was decided that he "deserves much credit for his panoramic views as a mechanical engineer and inventor, if not as a photographer," although doubts were expressed as to how original a design it was.[1]

Despite the technical ingenuity that had gone into developing special panoramic cameras, the vast majority of photographers throughout the world continued to create panoramas by the simplest method; they joined prints made from separately photographed, overlapping images. The reasons for this are clear: despite the advantages of cameras that could incorporate a wide angle of view in a single image, the resulting photograph inevitably produced an image whose height was small in relation to its breadth and that often diminished rather than accentuated the sense of grandeur and scale, which was for many the main attraction of the panoramic view. Additionally, many of these inventions produced negatives that were curved or otherwise difficult to print. While in theory the joining together of separate prints was a simple solution to extending the camera's field of view, it did in fact demand considerable skill to create a successful final product. In addition to the necessity for the very precise horizontal alignment of each successive image, differing intensities of light in various parts of a scene at any one time made it difficult to produce prints of precisely matching tonal values. In all but the most carefully made photographic panoramas, there is generally some degree of tonal imbalance between the prints, which detracts from the final result.

For many photographers the panorama represented a challenge to capture public attention by the dramatic exhibition of size for its own sake. Early on, photographers competed in trading boasts of the technical difficulties that had been overcome in their creation. Bernhard Holtermann's thirty-foot panorama of Sydney Harbor, for instance, made from wet-plate negatives each measuring 5 x 3½ feet and shown at the Philadelphia Centennial Exhibition of 1876, required the construction of a special camera within which the processing took place.[2] Contemporaneous reporters of many of the most extreme of these creations were clearly overwhelmed by the sheer spectacle of the display, whether Francis Frith's eight-foot panorama of Cairo, first exhibited in London in 1858, or the thirty-five-foot long panorama of Krupp's steelworks (the largest such works in the world at the time) shown in 1867. Notwithstanding the element of showmanship inherent in some of these more extreme examples, however, the range of uses to which panoramic photography was put from the early years of the medium clearly indicates both its power as a documentary tool and the fascination for the viewer of this extension of the visual range of the eye. Undoubtedly the best and most popular use to which the photographic panorama was put during the course of the nineteenth century was the urban view, advertisements for which appear in the catalogues of almost every established photographer from all over the world. In an age of imperial and commercial expansion, which saw phenomenal urban growth, the panorama proved a means both of grasping the extent of such development and of celebrating it in images whose breadth mirrored the spread of the city itself.

The multifarious subject areas to which the panorama could be applied can be seen in the variety of such work produced in India during the latter half of the nineteenth century. Even in relatively prosaic fields such as the need to record Bombay's development in the 1860s though a process of reclamation from the ocean, (no. 8) the panorama produced images possessing a visual impact beyond their immediate documentary function, while a view of the East Indian Railway works at Jamalpur, (no. 13) made on the occasion of the earl of Elgin's visit in 1896, hold a fascination both in the wealth of observable detail they contain and their ability to portray the immensity of the industrial enterprise. The panorama was also the ideal tool to capture the grandeur of nature, both through the size of the image itself and its ability to reflect the great sweep of open space, an effect captured with remarkable beauty in John Claude White's interpretations of the mountainous and desolate terrain of Tibet, (no. 14) taken while accompanying the Younghusband Mission of 1903–04.[3]

Many photographers were less ambitious in their use of the medium, seeing it as no more than a means of including in a unified composition a scene that overran the bounds of a single image. Deen Dayal's view from the nizam's palace at Hyderabad (no. 116) falls into this more mundane category, and while the panoramic studies of Mughal architecture made by Robert and Harriet Tytler could be similarly categorized, the results they achieved working with large-format paper negatives make a powerful impact. Their initial interest in photography had come about following Harriet Tytler's idea of producing a panoramic painting of the fort at Delhi after the Indian Mutiny of 1857. This led to Robert Tytler's taking up photography in order to assist her, and within six months the couple had produced over five hundred views, which the Bengal Photographic Society considered "unquestionably the finest ever exhibited in Calcutta," embracing "every scene of the mutiny of 1857, from the cavalry lines at Meerut to the Residency at Lucknow."[4] The Tytler's magnificent two-part vertical panorama of the Qutb Minar—the tallest extant minaret in the world—was praised as "remarkably fine," and it is indeed a powerful image of the monument (no. 6). It was produced as a panorama presumably for purely technical reasons, since a single image of the tower—a common view in the catalogue of most commercial photographers—inevitably requires the photographer to be some distance from the subject and diminishes the architectural mass of the structure. Other panoramas by the Tytlers, of the Moti Masjid (Pearl Mosque) at Agra, were "taken in three pieces. Major Tytler is the first who has taken this building in a single panorama."[5] The Tytler Taj Mahal received similar commendation. While the technical and aesthetic impact of the composition is an undeniable achievement—particularly from photographers with only a few months' experience—some credit for the work should probably also be directed toward Felice Beato who, together with John Murray, had assisted their early efforts. Indeed, a number of their views, including the Qutb Minar panorama, are almost identical to Beato's own studies, which might suggest a collaborative venture in their making.

Robert Burford, the owner of the Leicester Square panorama started by Robert Barker, displayed a number of Indian subjects over the years, many of which were clearly painted in response to historical events. While the pamphlets accompanying his painted panoramas of Calcutta and Bombay (both 1831) seek merely to paint a picture of the increasing material prosperity brought about by British rule, those of Kabul (1842) and Lucknow (1858) were clearly intended to capitalize on recent dramatic events. But while such painted interpretations gave a spectacular version of the conflict, they could not supply the verisimilitude of the photographic image, and it is Felice Beato's panoramas that remain the most compelling and historically valuable visual records of the event. Beato's photographs of the Indian

Mutiny of 1857 and of China's Opium Wars were specially featured at Hering's Regent Street premises in London in 1862.[6] The panoramic views were specifically singled out for praise by *The Athenaeum,* for their technical excellence, for their documentation of the glories of Indian architecture, and for their evocation of recent events. As the reviewer pointed out, "As photographs, these leave nothing to be desired; while some of the panoramas, especially those of Lucknow, which are in no less than six pieces each, must have taken extraordinary care in preparation," singling out in particular the view from the Kaiser Bagh, which "gives an idea of the splendour of the building itself and the extent of the city, which is most impressive" and which it would have been impossible to achieve within the confines of a single image.[7] An even larger panorama of Delhi taken from the Jami Masjid in eight sections received similar commendation.

While the two- and three-part panoramas of individual monuments produced by Tytler and Murray were conceived as a practical means of including complete monuments in a single composition and were intended for viewing as a single image, (no. 7) the larger panoramas of the period evoke a more complex visual response as the viewer's eye moves from section to section. In the panoramic views of Calcutta made during the nineteenth century, the photographs reveal something approaching a narrative exposition of the city laid out before the camera. Calcutta, with its open maidan, or esplanade, situated in the heart of the expanding European quarter of the city, was the subject of numerous panoramic delineations from the 1830s through to the age of photography, and the grouping of the most architecturally distinguished buildings around this open area made it a natural focal point from which to view the finest architectural sites of the city. Unlike most later attempts, the first comprehensive panoramic record of the area was not taken from a single vantage point, but favored a shifting view that permitted a closer and more accurate head-on view for each section. This was William Woods's *A Series of Twenty-Eight Panoramic Views of Calcutta,* published as a series of lithographs in London in 1833, from views made by Woods in around 1831. Taken as a whole, the panorama stretches from the River Hugli in the west to Fort William in the south. Woods's method allowed him to give detailed views of individual houses and groups of buildings, but most later panoramas took advantage of the Ochterlony Monument, erected in the center of the maidan in 1828, to give a more comprehensive view of the city. The Prussian artist

Jacob Janssen, resident in Calcutta in the early 1830s, also succumbed to the popularity of the panorama from the maidan, producing versions made both from ground level and from the top of the monument.[8] The use of this single bird's-eye viewpoint by artists and photographers over a period of time offers the viewer a fascinating insight into the developing city. Surviving examples indicate the fascination of this unfamiliar sweeping view of the city, which, as the eye moves from section to section, creates a narrative momentum within the picture.

The first panoramic view of the city taken from the top of the Ochterlony Monument appears to have been that made by the German artist and lithographer Frederick Fiebig, who was active in Calcutta from the mid-1840s and whose very first panoramic attempt appears to have been a now-lost view of Singapore, which he visited in 1846. In the following year the Asiatic Lithographic Press published his panoramic view of Calcutta, made in six sections and taking in almost the full 360 degrees (no. 1). Starting from the south toward the curve of the Hugli with shipping at anchor, the eye is taken around to the north and east, embracing the classical splendors of Government House and Esplanade Row before moving on to the classical mansions lining Chowringhee Road. Apart from the topographical and documentary significance of his work, Fiebig possesses additional significance as a figure straddling the period at which the earlier visual media were being slowly superseded by photography as the prime vehicle of topographical and architectural documentation. This trend is graphically demonstrated in Fiebig's own work: soon after the creation of his Calcutta panorama, Fiebig himself took up photography. By the early years of the following decade he had produced the first extensive photographic documentation of the city and its surroundings, a record comprising some 250 hand-colored calotypes that, together with views of Madras, Ceylon, Mauritius, and the Cape of Good Hope, he sold to the East India Company in 1856. He does not appear, however, to have attempted a photographic panorama of Calcutta. Although Fiebig produced an extensive range of views—the collection now held in the Oriental and India Office Collections of the British Library comprises some 600 prints—the photographer himself remains an obstinately mysterious figure. His photographic work appears to have been undertaken, at least initially, as an amateur, and after a brief correspondence with the East India Company, he fades into obscurity.

But the use of the Ochterlony Monument as a focal point from which to encompass the grandeur and commercial expansion of the "second city of empire" (as Calcutta was commonly known) is continued into the period of photography's dominance. One of the finest surviving examples is the eight-part panorama made by Josiah Rowe in about 1859 (no. 5); this takes in a view similar to Fiebig's lithographic series of the previous decade. Rowe is an important, if little-known, figure in the development of amateur photography in Calcutta. He arrived in the city in around 1835 and was employed as a surveyor before later becoming professor of drawing and surveying at the Presidency College, and while most of his surviving work dates from the late 1850s and early 1860s, he was clearly active before this, for in 1857 the *Journal of the Photographic Society of Bengal* commended "the rare skill of the oldest photographer in Calcutta."[9] The panorama of 1859 may well be the one later shown at the 1862 exhibition of the Bengal Photographic Society and that, while praised by the jurors as "a fine photograph," also attracted some criticism for "the absence of moving life in so extended a space crowded with houses."[10] However, it is also possible that this was a later view, for it was a subject that clearly attracted Rowe, and he appears to have used the same viewpoint to record the cityscape over a number of years. At the society's meeting of 21 January 1857, for instance, his now-lost daguerreotype panorama from the top of the monument, taken on five plates and shown at the society's 1857 exhibition, was much praised for its "minute accuracy and beauty."[11] The attraction of the panoramic view to the surveyor is clear, allowing the relationships of parts of the city to be viewed as an integrated whole, particularly in a series taken over time and charting the growth of the city. The appeal to the commercial photographer is also evident, for such a view supplied the resident or visiting customer with the most easily "readable" visual account of the city, allowing individual views to be placed within their urban context. It is unsurprising therefore that Samuel Bourne should have produced a view almost identical to Rowe's for commercial sale a few years later (no. 2). Starting with the source of Calcutta's wealth as a trading metropolis in the curve of the river with its forest of bristling masts, the eye is then directed over the significant topographical and architectural landmarks of the city, past the concrete symbols of urban organization and imperial rule symbolized by the town hall and Government House, and thence to the rewards of successful trade epitomized by the substantial mansions of Chowringhee Road.

The photographic panorama continued to be produced throughout the nineteenth century, in India as elsewhere, to illustrate landscape, urban topography, archaeological sites, engineering installations, and military subjects. But in the subcontinent, it perhaps reached its apogee with the great Delhi durbar of 1911, where a single photograph could not hope to encompass the vast pageant in celebration of imperial rule. Unlike the multipart panoramas of Calcutta, in which each section unfolds in a cumulative narrative over which the eye might linger, the views of the great amphitheater and the massed guards of honor drawn up to celebrate the coronation of George v are clearly constructed to provide a single image of imperial self-confidence and ordered splendor, whose impact could only be fully illustrated by the breadth of the panoramic image.

NOTES

1. *Journal of the Bengal Photographic Society* 2, no. 7 (March 1864): 83.

2. At least one of these negatives, the largest ever made using the wet-collodion process, is on display at the Mitchell Library, Sydney.

3. This was a mission in which a British military force under Francis Younghusband marched to Lhasa to enforce the signing of the Anglo-Tibetan treaty.

4. *Bengal Hurkaru and India Gazette,* (28 May 1859).

5. Ibid.

6. Henry Hering, a commercial photographer himself, had a gallery at 137 Regent Street.

7. *The Athenaeum,* no. 1807 (14 June 1862): 794.

8. His ground-level view is illustrated in the Christie's *Visions of India* sale catalogue (June 1998), lot 98. His panorama from the top of the Ochterlony Monument is held by the Mitchell Library, Sydney.

9. *Journal of the Photographic Society of Bengal* 2 (21 January 1857): 26.

10. *Journal of the Bengal Photographic Society* 1, no. 2 (1 September 1862): 46. [Note that the society called itself the Photographic Society of Bengal for a short, initial period, after which it renamed itself the Bengal Photographic Society. To avoid confusion we have referred to the society throughout the text as the Bengal Photographic Society. Ed.]

11 *Journal of the Photcgraphic Society of Bengal* 3 (20 May 1857): 53.

NOTE TO THE READER

Dimensions are in centimeters; height precedes width unless otherwise noted.

The British in India anglicized the names of towns, cities, and people to conform to English pronunciation (e.g., Cawnpore). India has today adopted a more accurate rendering of these names (e.g., Kanpur). This book retains the nineteenth-century spellings in the titles of the photographs, but the current spellings are used throughout the rest of the text.

THE APPEAL OF THE PANORAMA

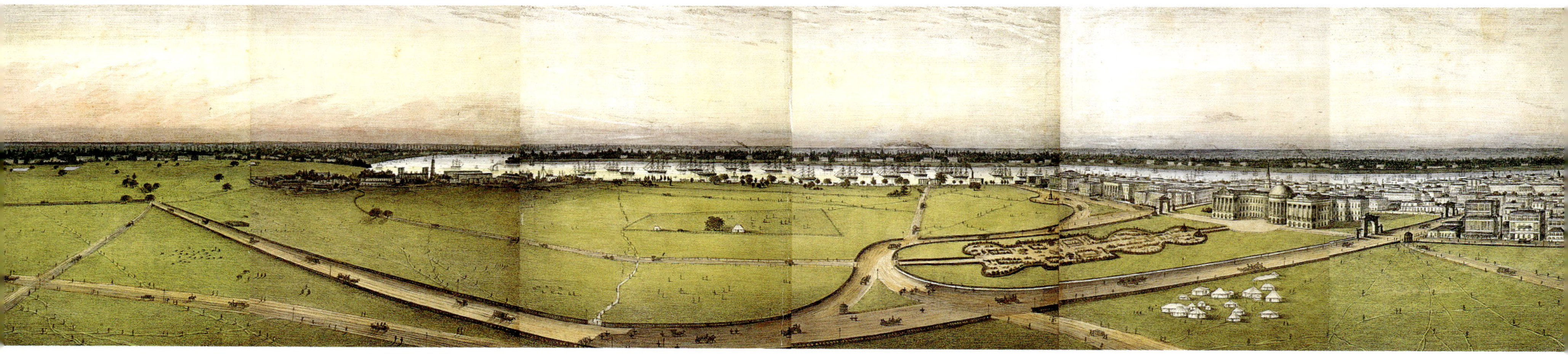

1 *Calcutta*

Frederick Fiebig

6-part panorama, 1847, colored lithograph

23.8 x 198.3

The British Library, Oriental & India Office Collection V12765

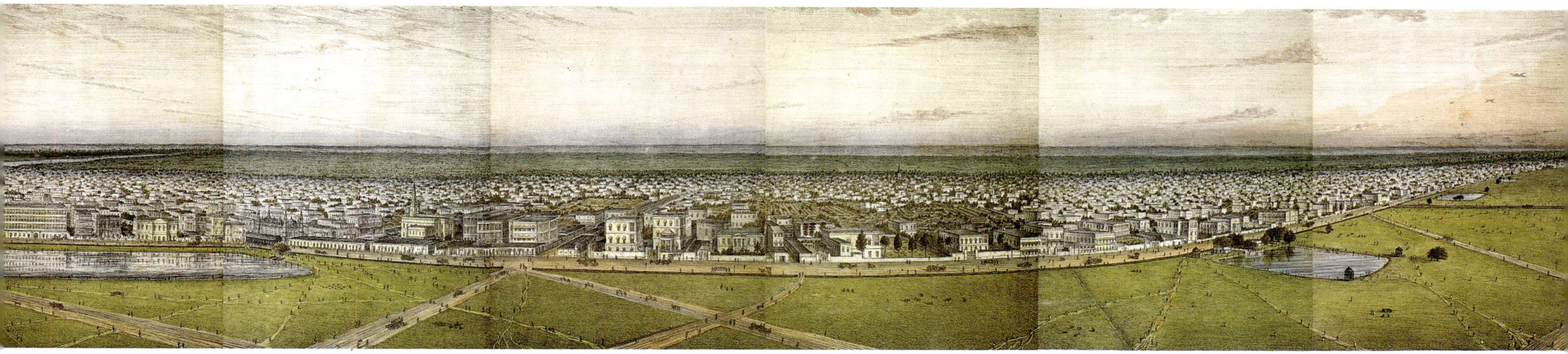

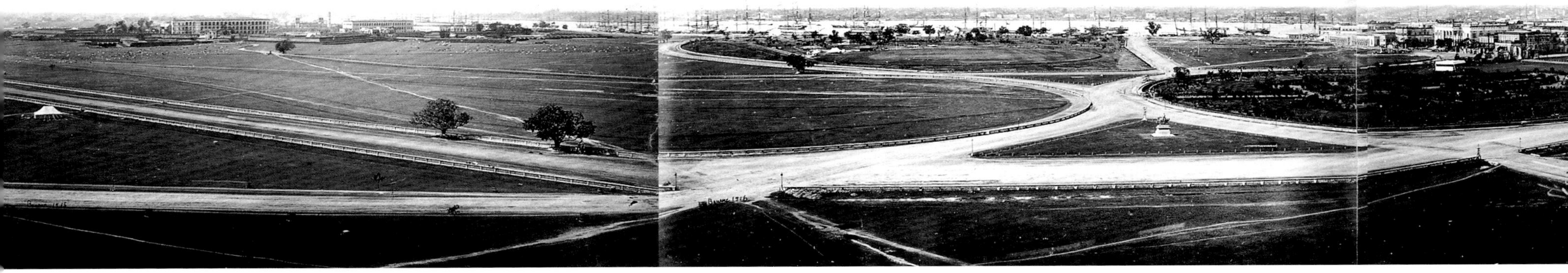

2 *Fort William, Calcutta*

Samuel Bourne

7-part panorama, 1868–69, albumen print

17.8 x 216.1

The British Library, Oriental & India Office

Collection photo 29 (18)–(24)

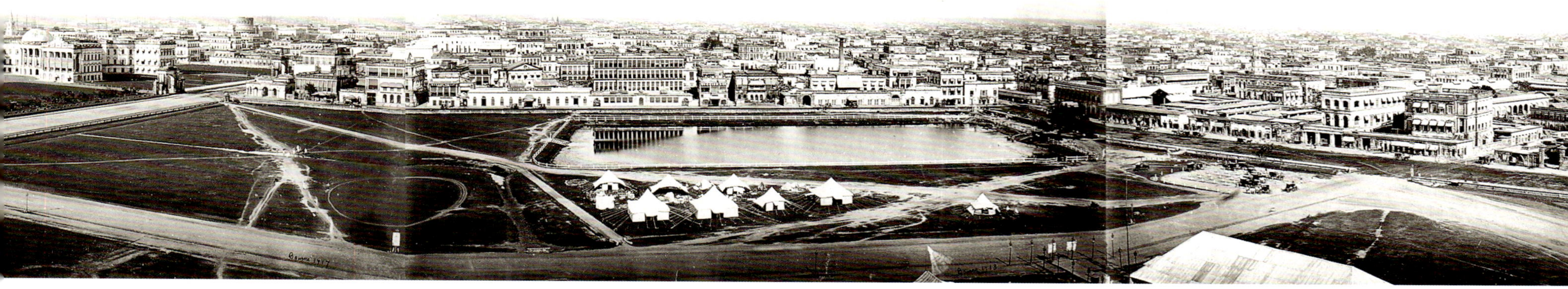

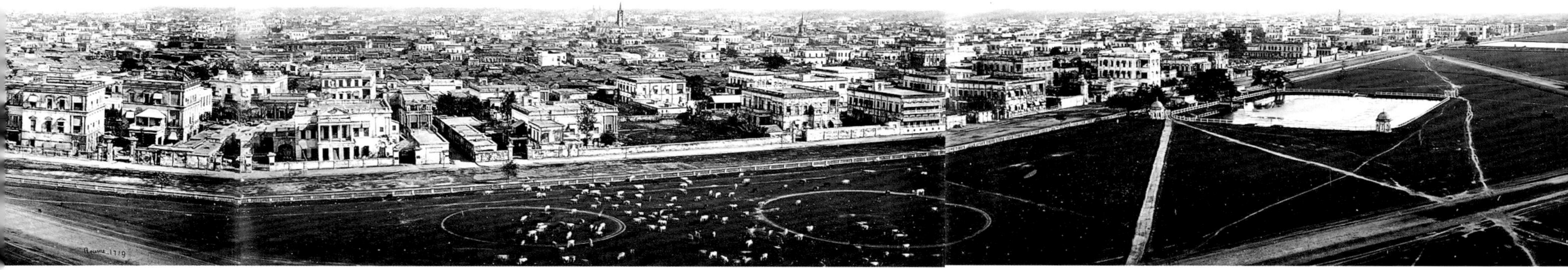
Bourne 1719

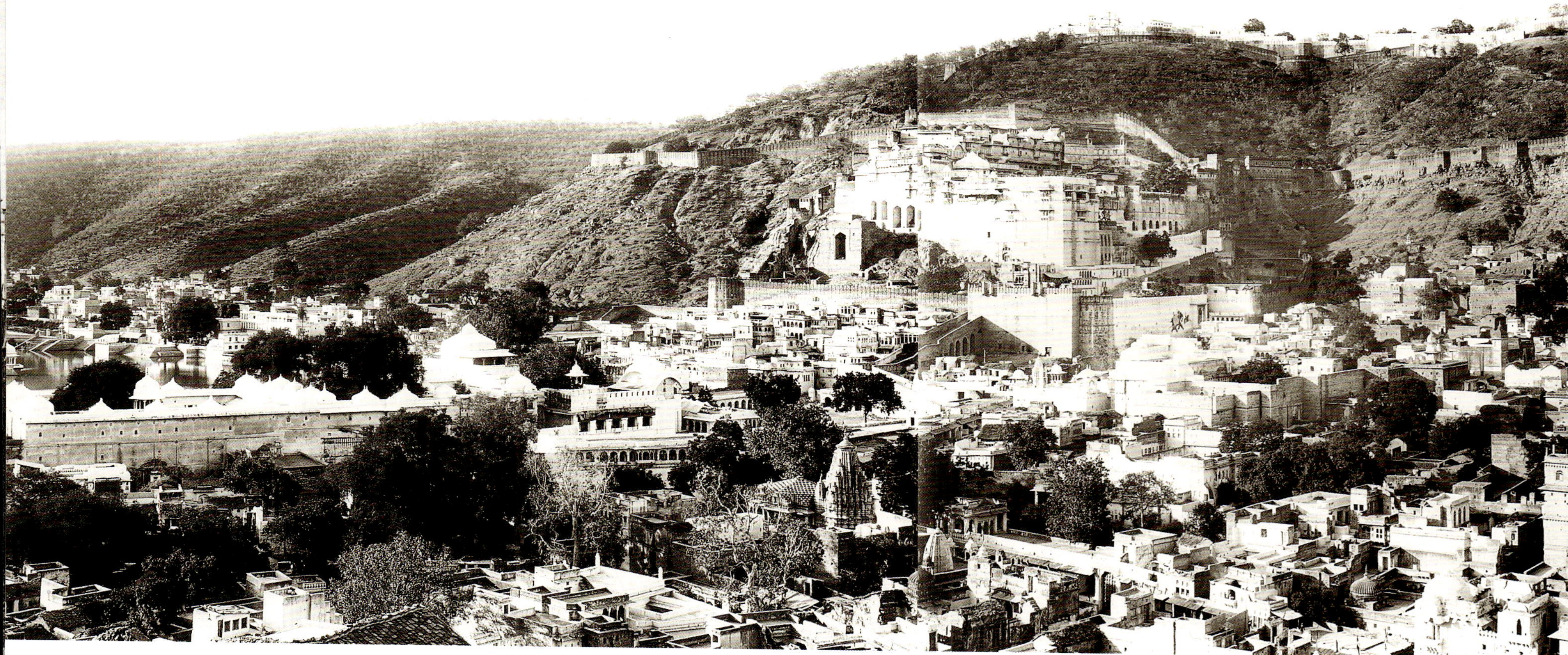

4 *Bundi*

Herzog & Higgins

5-part panorama, 1902, collodion printing-out paper, 21.3 x 144.6

The British Library, Oriental & India Office Collection photo 430/20 (49)

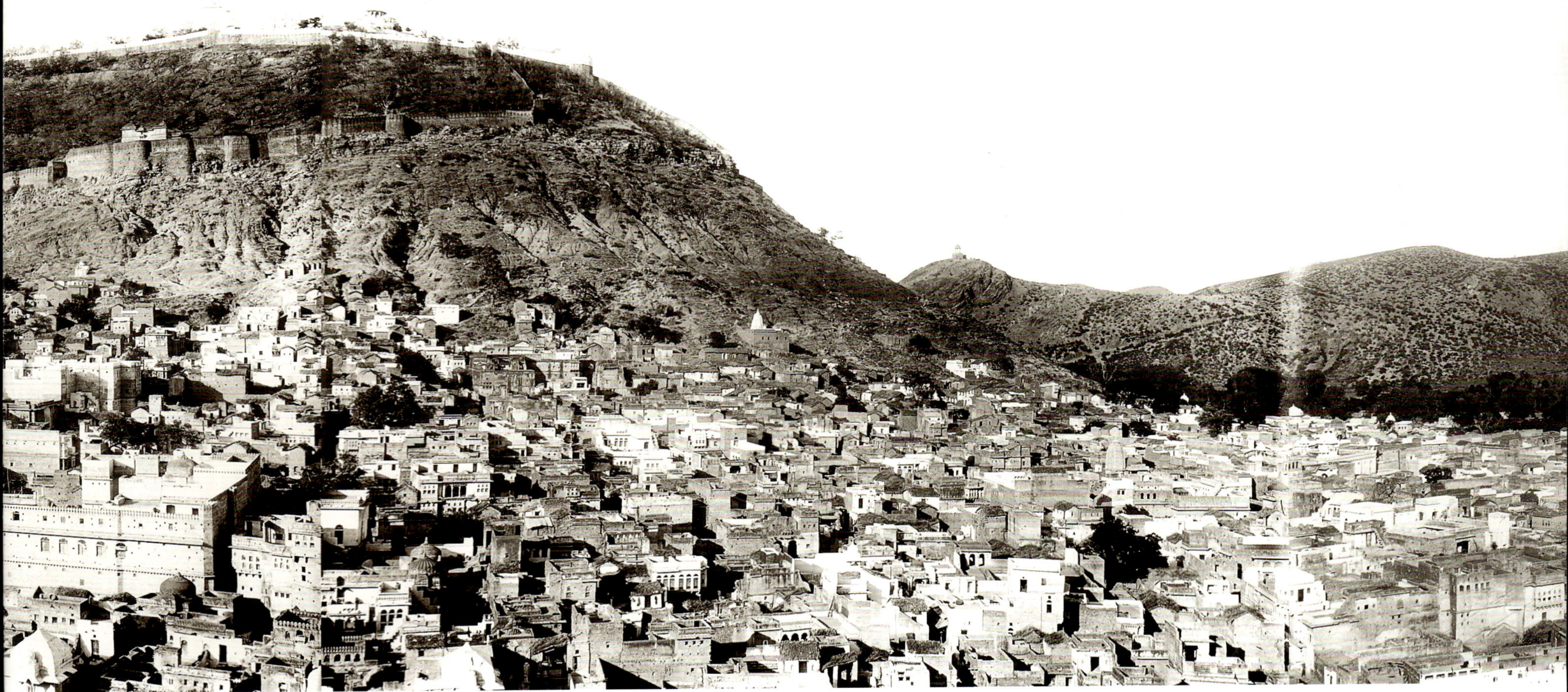

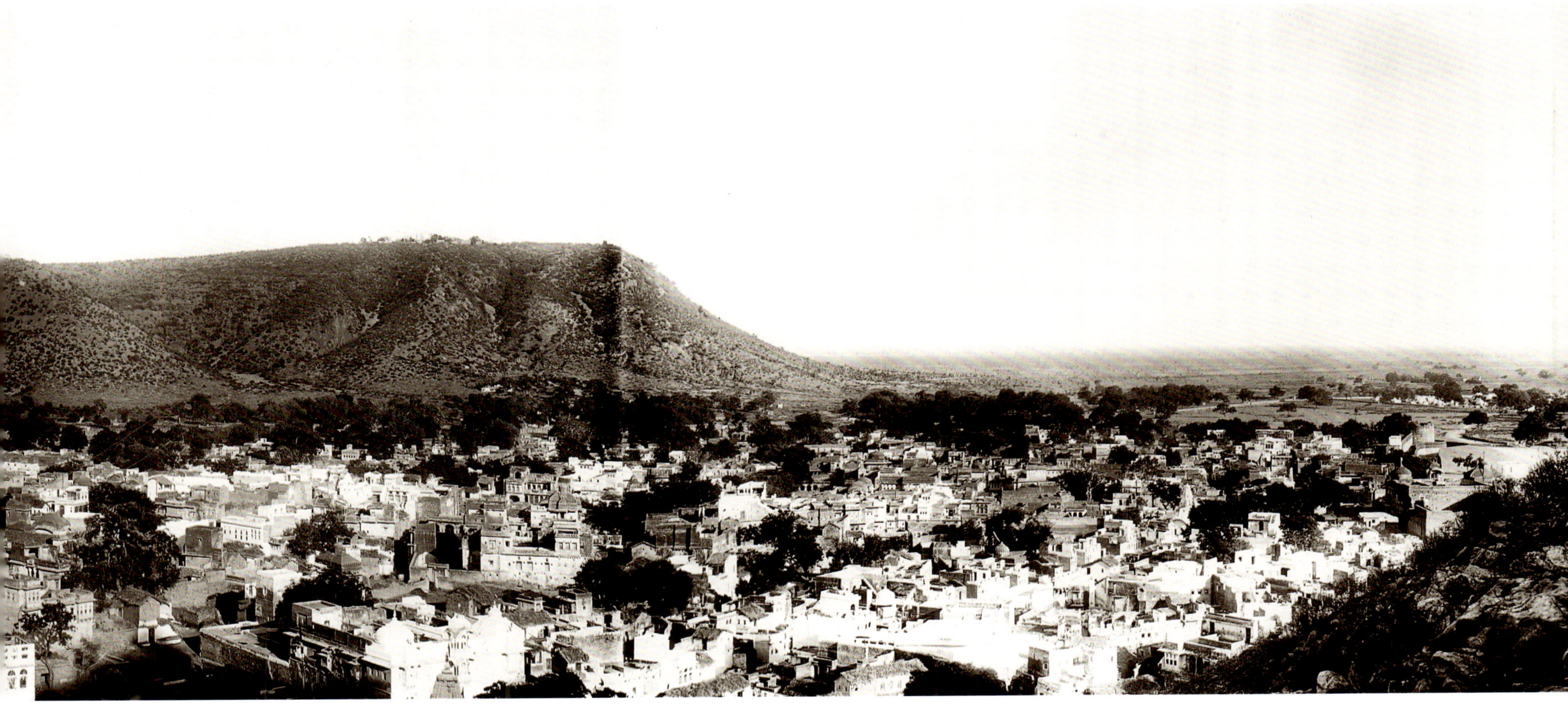

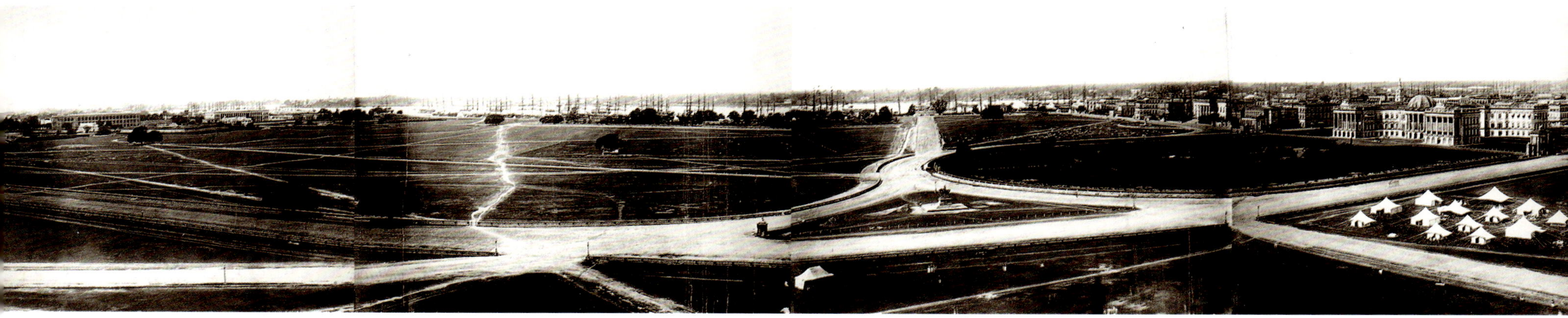

5 *Calcutta*

Josiah Rowe

8-part panorama, 1859, albumen print

16 x 175

The British Library, Oriental & India Office

Collection photo 147/1 (49)

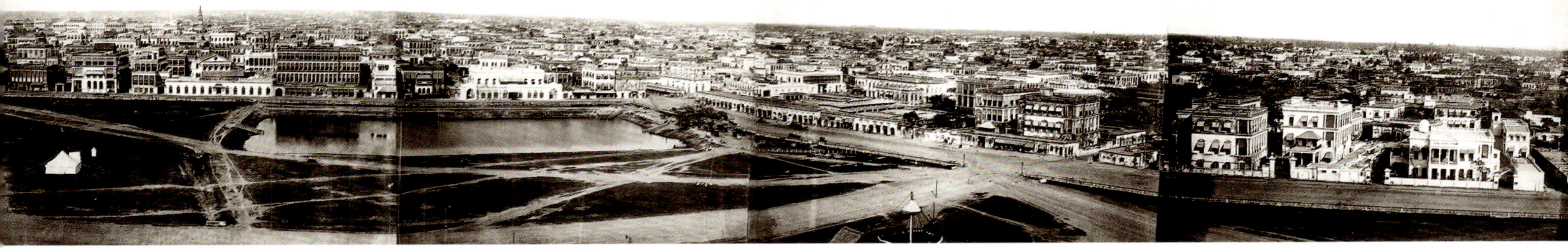

6 *The Kootub, Delhi*

Robert and Harriet Tytler

2-part vertical panorama, 1858, albumen print, 108.4 x 40.2

The British Library, Oriental & India Office Collection photo 193 (18)–(19)

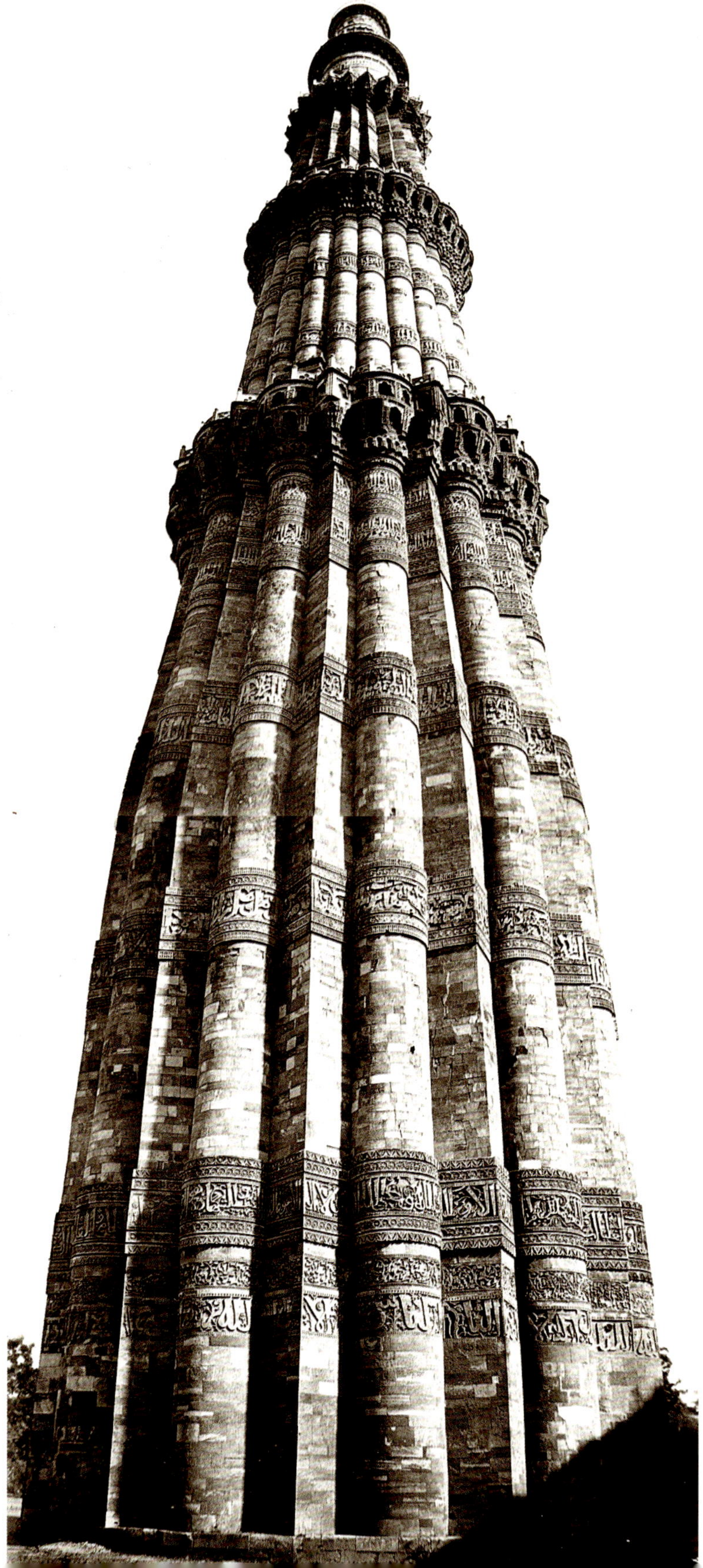

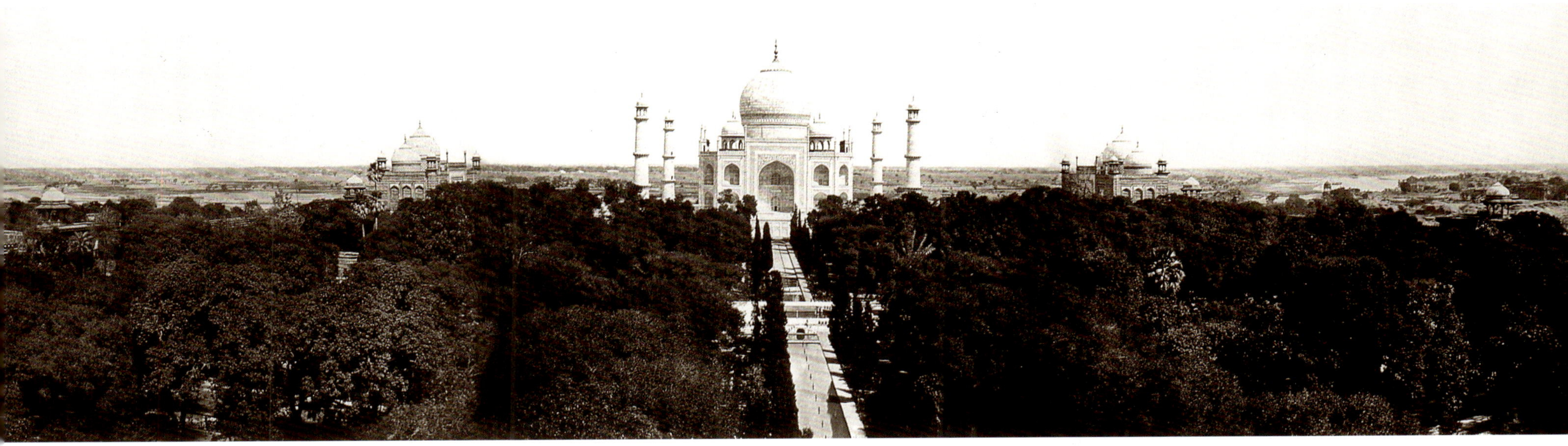

7 *The Taj Mahal from the Gateway*

John Murray

3-part panorama, late 1850s, albumen silver print, 34.5 x 131.7

Gilman Paper Company Collection

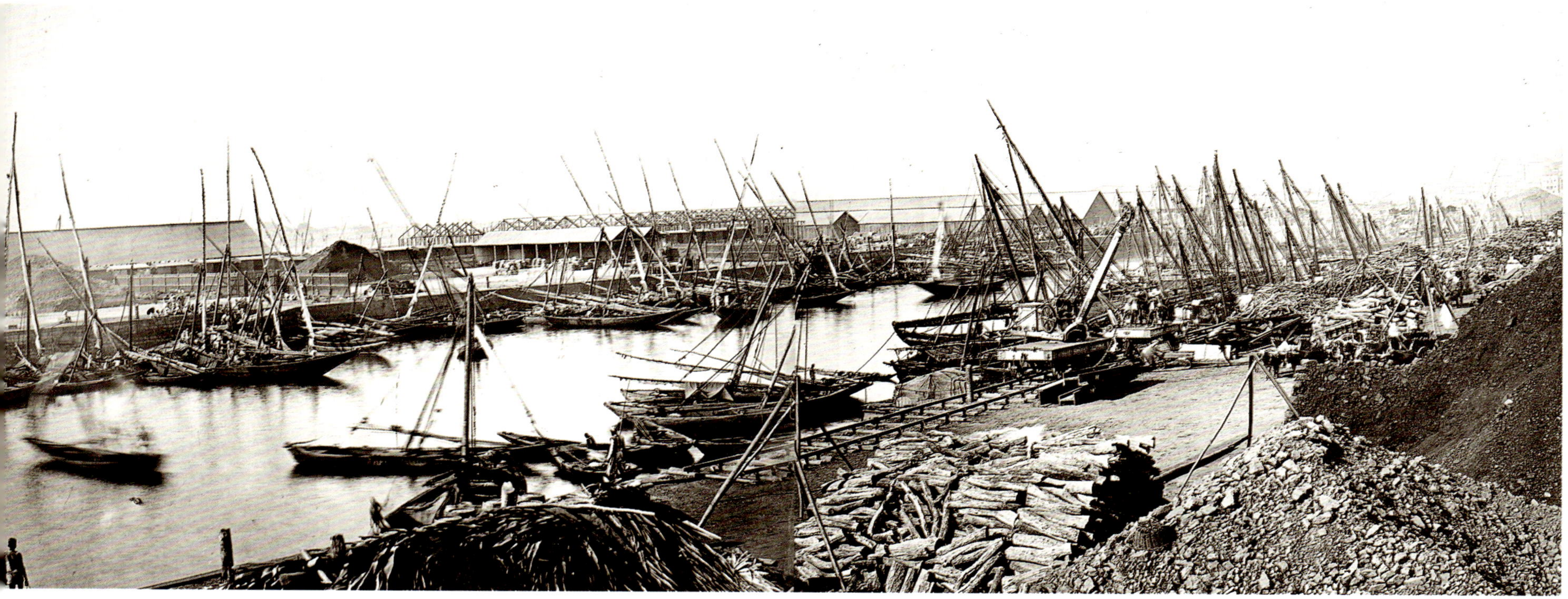

8 *View of Elphinstone Reclamation, Bombay*

Unknown photographer

2-part panorama, early 1860s, albumen print

20.3 x 54.5

The British Library, Oriental & India Office Collection photo 697 (7)

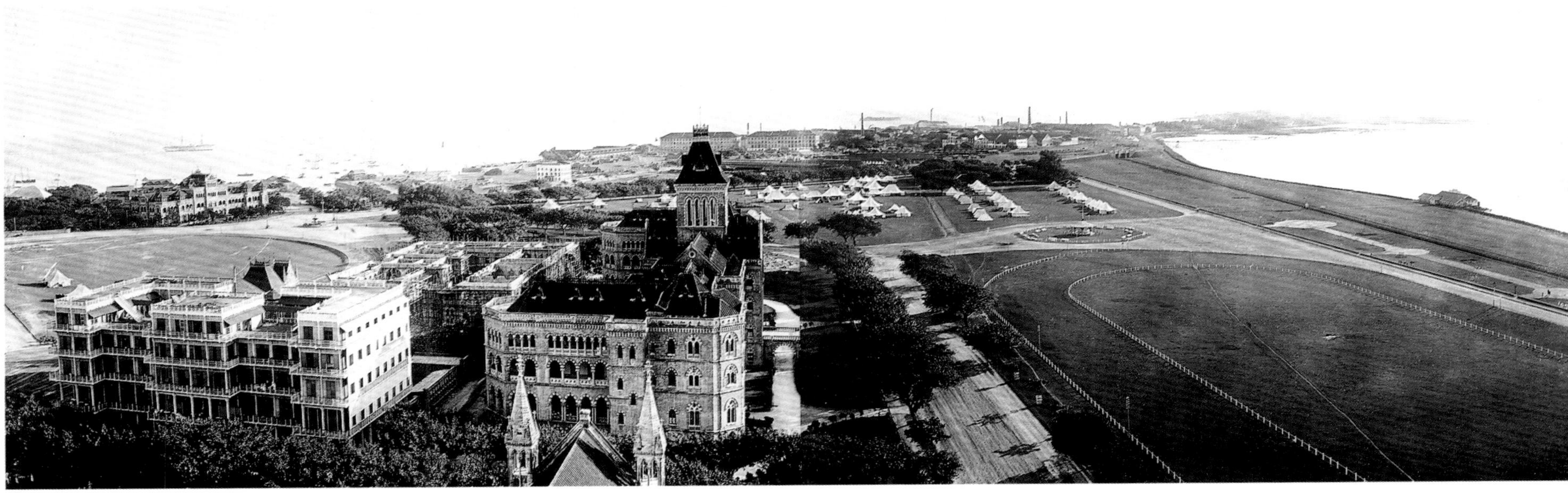

9 *View of Bombay from Rajabai Tower*

Lala Deen Dayal

2-part panorama, ca. 1890, printing-out paper, 15.2 x 51.8
The British Library, Oriental & India Office Collection photo 784 / 1 (35)

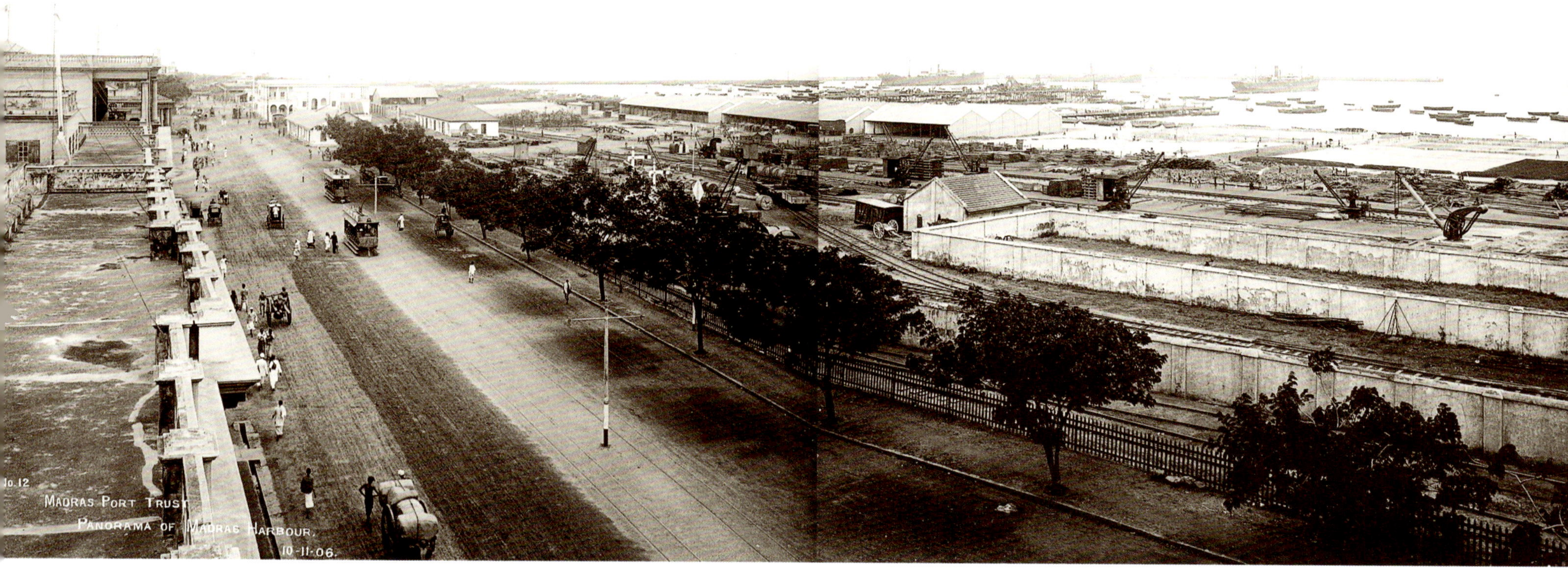

10 *Madras Harbor*

Unknown photographer

4-part panorama, 1906, matte collodion printing-out paper, 22.2 x 113

The British Library, Oriental & India Office Collection photo 384 (4)

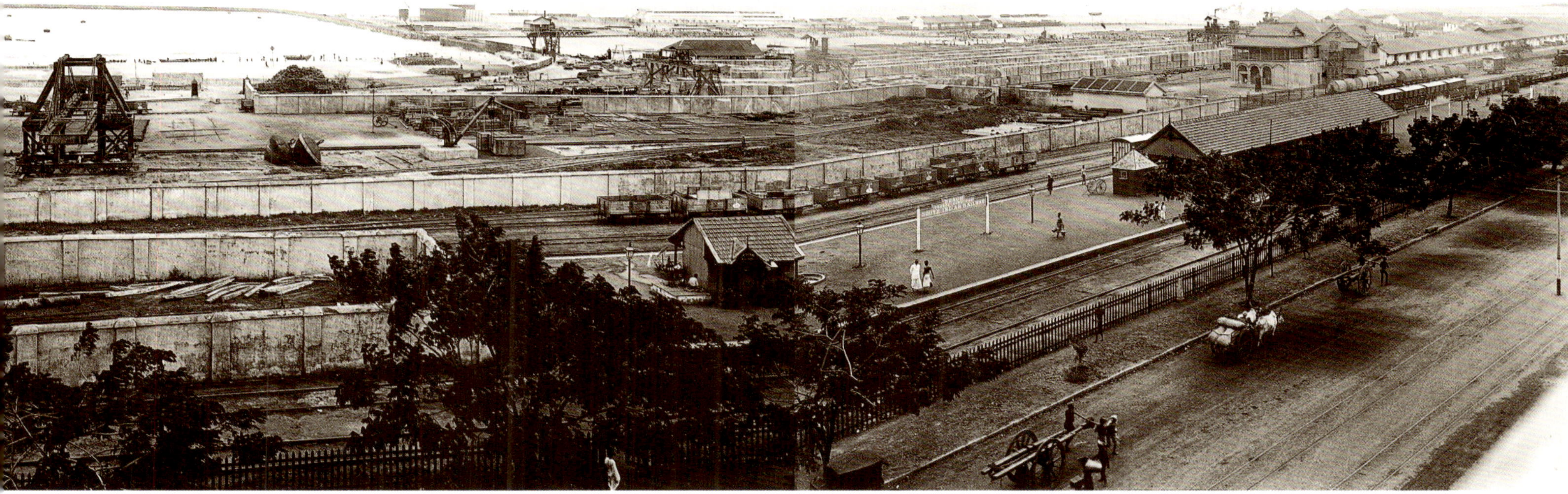

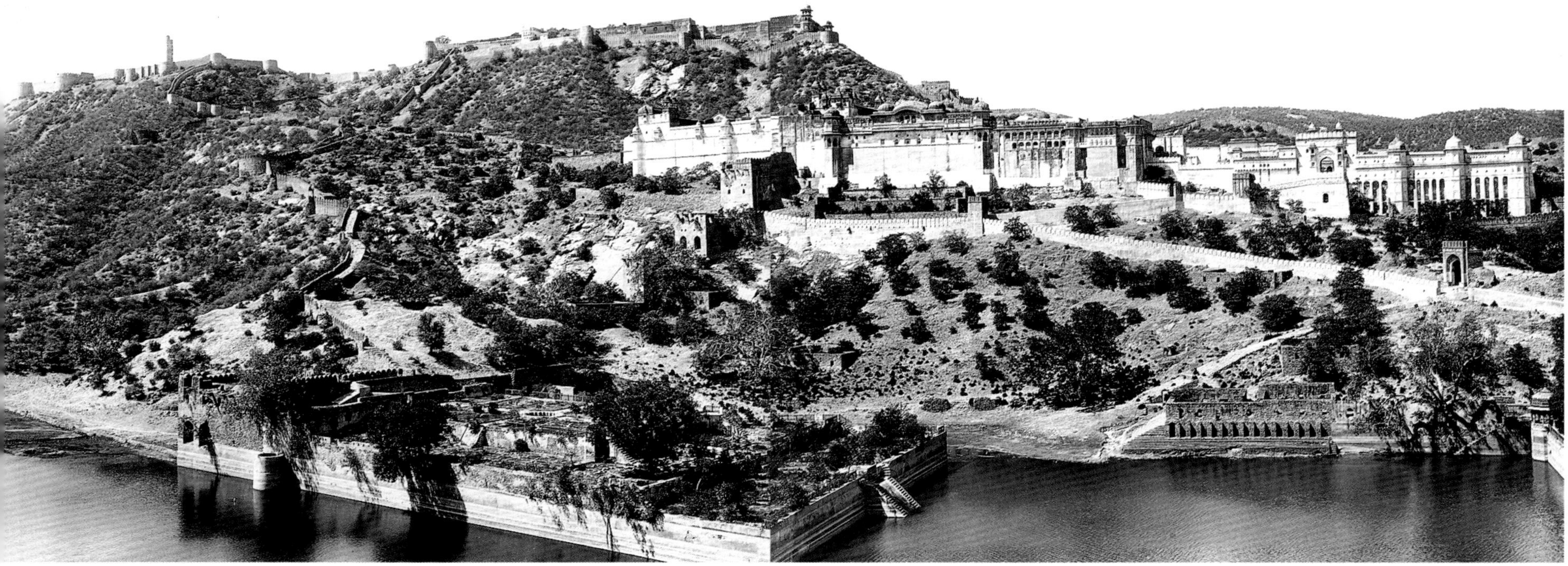

11 *View of Amber Palaces & Fort*

Herzog & Higgins

2-part panorama, 1902, collodion printing-out paper, 23.2 x 54.7
The British Library, Oriental & India Office Collection photo 430/20 (188)

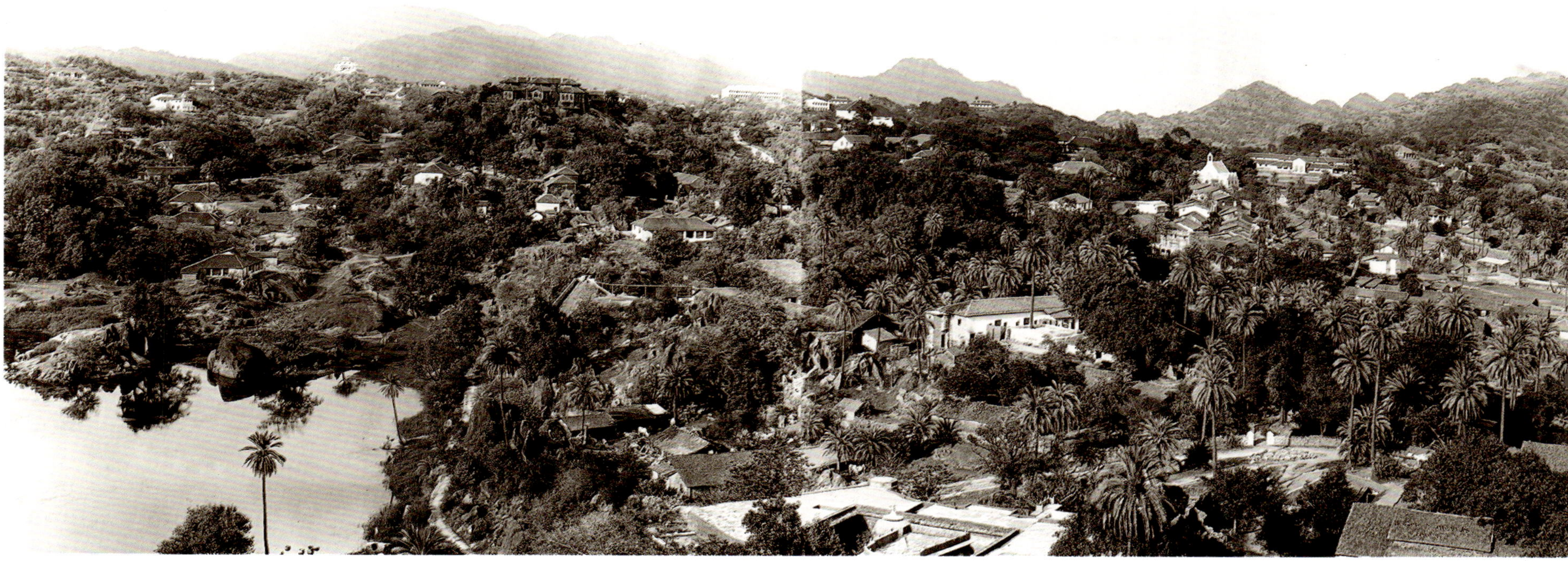

12 *View of Abu Looking North from Jaipur House*

Herzog & Higgins

2-part panorama, 1902, collodion printing-out paper, 19.5 x 54.8
The British Library, Oriental & India Office Collection photo 430/20 (102)

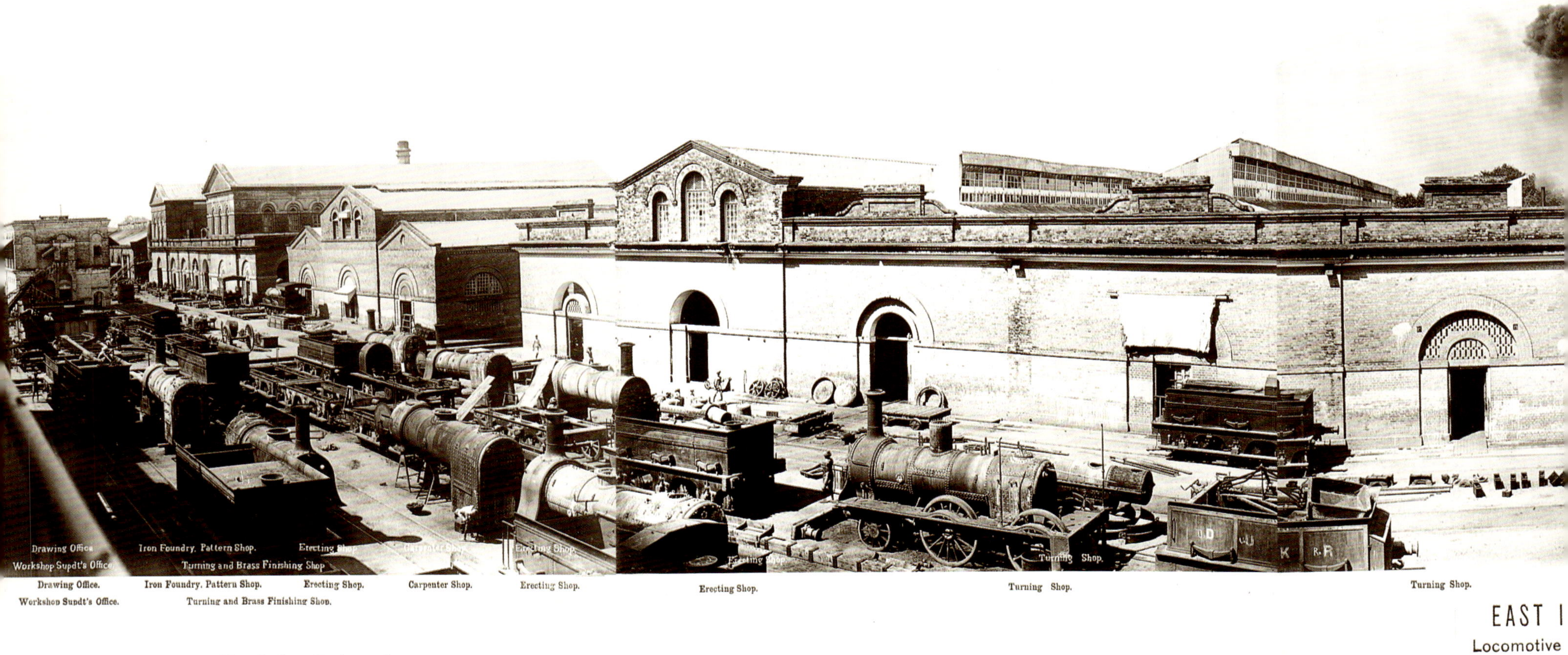

13 *East Indian Railway, Locomotive Department Workshops, Jamalpur*

Unknown photographer

5-part panorama, 1896, printing-out paper

25 x 137.8

The British Library, Oriental & India Office Collection photo 15/8 (1)

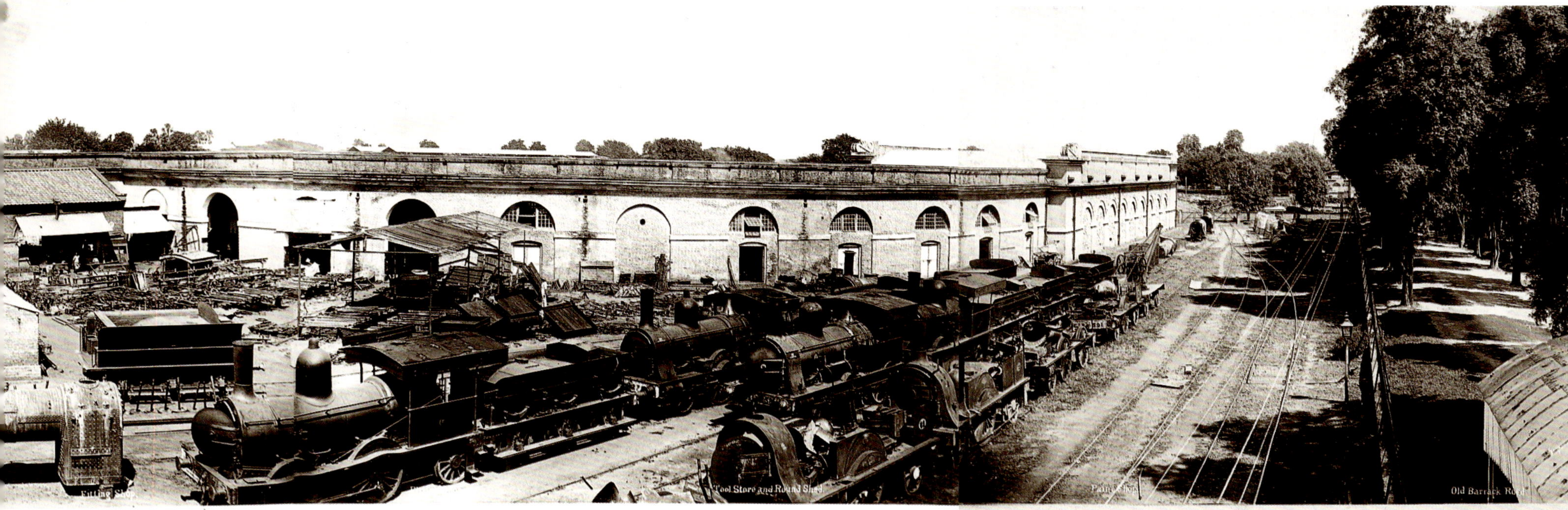

Fitting Shop. Fitting Shop. Tool Store and Round Shed. Paint Shop. Old Barrack Road.

AILWAY.

t Workshops

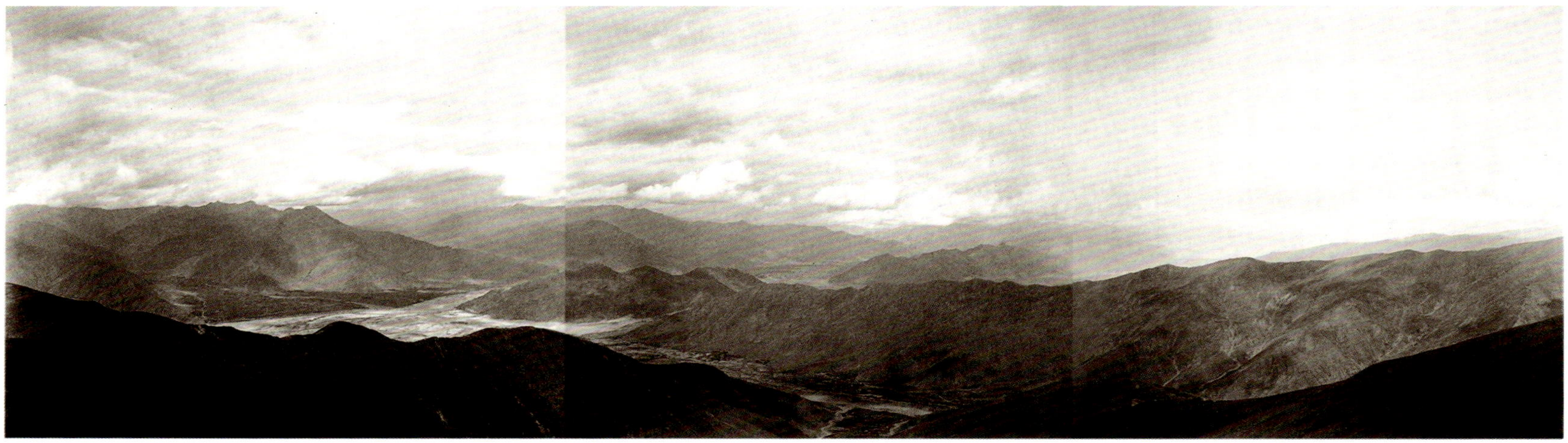

14 *Tsangpo Valley, Tibet*

John Claude White

3-part panorama, ca. 1904, carbon print
22.4 x 81.5
Smithsonian Institution, Freer Gallery of
Art and Arthur M. Sackler Gallery Archives

Detail, no. 14. *Tsangpo Valley, Tibet*

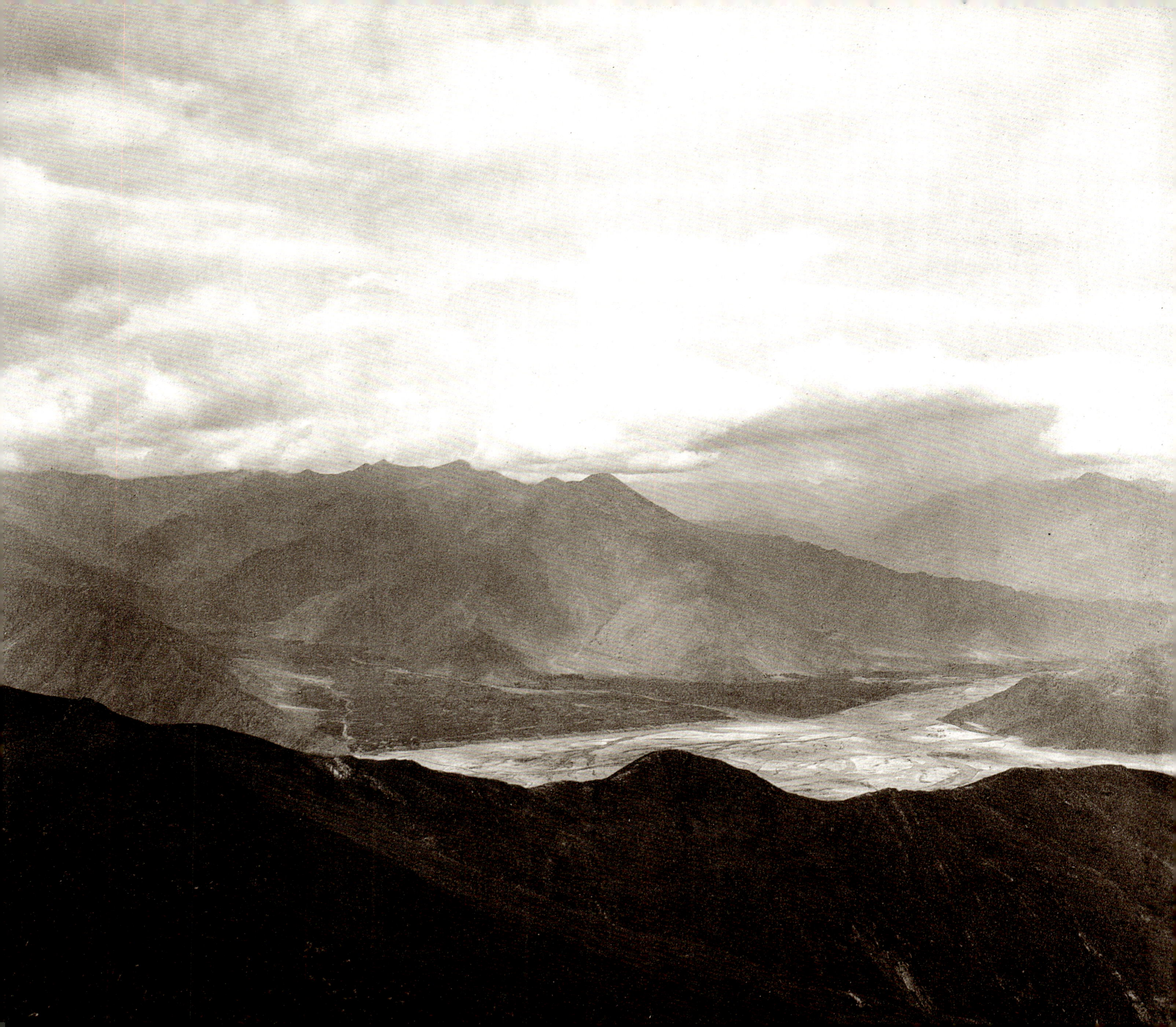

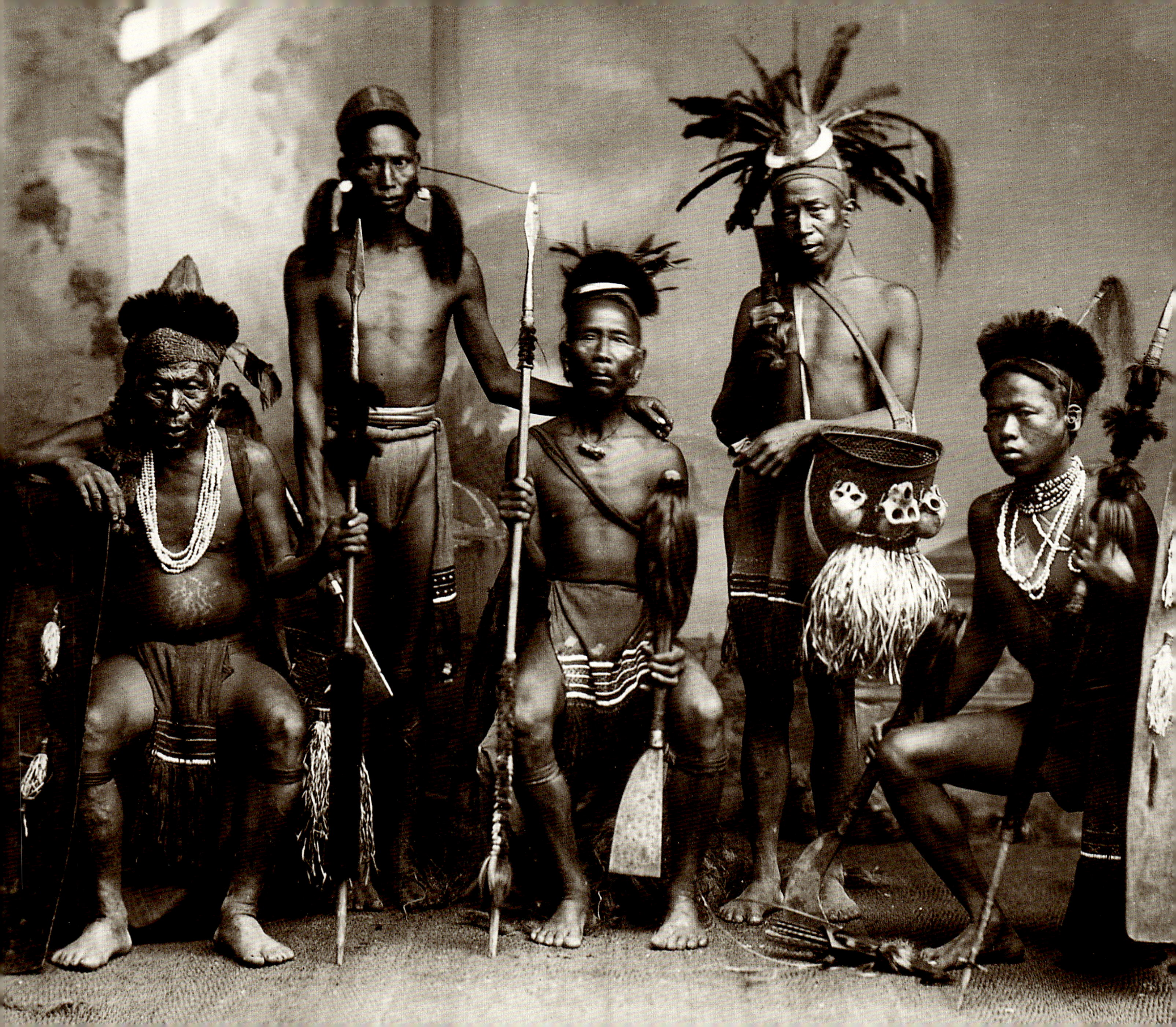

John Falconer

A Passion for Documentation: Architecture and Ethnography

> There are now very few . . . buildings in India—of any importance at least—which have not been photographed with more or less completeness; and for the purposes of comparison such collections . . . are simply invaluable. For detecting similarities, or distinguishing differences between specimens . . . photographs are almost equal to actual personal inspection. . . .[1]

When James Fergusson wrote these words in the introduction to his influential synthesis, *History of Indian and Eastern Architecture* (London, 1876), architectural photography had been well established in India for two decades. Fergusson's endorsement of photography's importance in the study of a subcontinent whose size and architectural variety no single scholar could hope to encompass was a perceptive expression of photography's unique aptitude for such a subject; it also was to some degree the result of his own proselytizing on the medium's behalf. While today his contention that photography's task in India had been largely completed by 1876 seems absurdly optimistic, Indian photographers of the age had indeed produced a body of work, particularly in architectural and ethnographical fields, of both lasting documentary value and high aesthetic quality. This photographic record also shows how colonial rulers used the images to legitimize imperial domination.

In India of the mid-1850s, amateur photographic societies had been active in all three presidencies (administrative units)—Madras, Bombay, and Bengal. Their members, whose cultural interests often coincided with their photographic enthusiasms, had already produced an impressive body of work, much of it in the field of architectural illustration; however, one member, Reverend Joseph Mullins, bemoaned "the want of purpose" of these photographers in India when he delivered his lecture "On the Applications of Photography in India" to the Bengal Photographic Society in October 1856.[2] In an attempt to remedy this shortcoming, Mullins outlined a range of subjects that members might address in order to capture "all the minute varieties of Oriental Life; of Oriental Scenery, Oriental nations and Oriental manners," which India offered in such bewildering abundance. He argued that such work, in addition to its intrinsic value, might also "serve higher interests, in the political and commercial world." Medicine, surveys, public works, portraiture, criminal justice, commercial productions, and industry were among the topics listed. Architecture, racial types, and dress received particular note, especially the last, for in the accurate recording of costume "our English artists are dreadfully at fault."

In architectural matters, the legacy of research into the peoples and culture of the subcontinent by such scholars as Sir William Jones, a moving spirit in the foundation of the Asiatic Society in Calcutta in the last quarter of the eighteenth century, had by the mid-nineteenth century grown to the extent that the East India Company could no longer entirely avoid its responsibility for documenting and conserving the monuments under its charge. Thus, in 1844, a *camera lucida*—a prism fitted with a viewfinder through which an image was cast onto a sheet of paper and could then be traced—was sent out to each of the three presidencies to help draftsmen and artists make records. In 1847 a dispatch was issued by the governor-general, calling for "the collection in each of the three Presidencies of really accurate, minute, and well classified information as to the nature, extent, and state of existing monuments."[3]

At this stage, however, it was felt that a few suitable medical service and military officers and other government officials with antiquarian interests and artistic talents would be able to achieve what was required on a more or less casual basis. Underestimation of the sheer scale of the task, coupled with a lack of any systematic central organization, resulted in few immediately worthwhile results.

In isolated cases some official funding was made available, but the magnitude of the undertaking was highlighted in 1851, when the Bombay artist William Armstrong Fallon was commissioned to make studies of the sculptures at Elephanta and to prepare drawings and measurements of the caves themselves. Fallon was initially employed for a year, and after his efforts were well received in London, his

Page 68: Detail, no. 36. *Members of the Naga Tribe*, unknown photographer

contract was extended. After some time, the East India Company began to grow restive at what was beginning to appear an open-ended commitment. In 1854, in response to further requests for funds, the company pointed out that Fallon's one-year contract had now extended to three and a half years, with no end in sight. In a short statement that would have important implications for photography in India, the company wrote: "We take this opportunity of directing your attention to photography on paper, which, with a view to economy, and in order to shorten the time of Mr. Fallon's employment, should in our opinion, be used for obtaining copies of the sculptures in the caves."[4]

In December 1854 a further dispatch on the subject arrived in India, recommending the employment of Thomas Biggs of the Bombay Artillery, who while in England "has satisfied us of his competency to undertake photographic works of the required description,"[5] and who in consequence had been presented by the company with a set of photographic apparatus for that purpose. There is some suggestion, at least by Biggs himself, that it was he who was responsible for first alerting the East India Company to the potential benefits of photography.

Biggs was duly released from his regimental duties and appointed official government photographer to the Bombay presidency in February 1855. In the course of the year, with an entourage of twelve camels to transport his supplies and photographic equipment, he produced a series of views on large paper negatives of buildings first at Bijapur and then further south in Dharwar and Mysore. His work was cut short, however, by demands for his return to regimental duties. In November 1855 he was replaced by William Pigou of the Bombay medical service, an officer recommended by Biggs himself as possessing "a good knowledge of chemistry" and "the advantage of several years of experience of photography in this country."[6] Pigou set out in early 1856, making an extensive tour of Dharwar and Mysore and photographing temples and inscriptions. With the official confirmation of his post in August 1856, he made a second tour of the area that resulted in some seventy-five negatives before he, too, was ordered to return to his regular duties in March 1857. Although Pigou appears to have retained the title of "government photographer," there is no indication that he produced any further work from that time until his death in Poona in September 1858 at the young age of forty-one.

During their short period of active photography, Biggs and Pigou had produced some remarkable and pioneering work in documenting the temple architecture of western India (nos. 22–25), but with Biggs's recall and Pigou's death the initiative lapsed. Only a decade later was scholarly use made of this material, with the 1866 publication of their photographs in two volumes under the auspices of the Committee of Architectural Antiquities in Western India. Entitled *Architecture of Dharwar and Mysore* and *Architecture at Beejapor,* edited by author and administrator Colonel Philip Meadows Taylor and James Fergusson, these heavily subsidized books were issued in massive folio volumes illustrated with original albumen prints. Even so the English public expressed little interest in India's architecture, leading a disconsolate James Fergusson to report that despite the give-away price of twenty-seven guineas, "or less than two shillings a plate . . . the public . . . said they were too dear, and would not buy. I think we sold two copies of one, and three of the other volume."[7]

While the work of Biggs and Pigou was conceived with the goal of producing an objective documentary record of architectural remains, it was inevitably biased because of their positions as representatives of a foreign ruling class whose Judeo-Christian values were inherently antagonistic to the subject of much of their work. Biggs, in particular, considered that the "indecent" Hindu sculptures he encountered in the Badami district only proved "the early date at which the morals of India assumed such a headlong and downward tendency, and anyone who has the opportunity of comparing the ancient and modern sculptures cannot fail to see the gradual but remarkable flight of steps down from artistic beauty and chaste tendency to the greatest deformity and disgusting immorality which the sculptures betray."[8]

These were arguments that strengthened British claims over a land that apparently had little respect for its historical buildings and whose monuments bore such graphic evidence of moral decay. Indeed, the cause of architectural preservation was reversed when Biggs wrote a letter seeking permission to destroy any of the "truly disgusting" modern sculpted images that he might encounter in the course of his travels (though he did not, in fact, destroy anything).[9]

In February 1855 the East India Company broadened the scope of its initial instruction to use photography in western India and directed the "Government of Bombay to discontinue the employment of draftsmen in the delineation of antiquities of Western India, and to employ photographers instead, and it is our desire that this method be generally substituted throughout India, in cases where it may be considered desirable by the Government to obtain representations of objects of interest."[10]

Further support for photography was offered in the same year by the introduction of classes in photography at various educational establishments, of which the Elphinstone Institution in Bombay was probably the most successful. Following this renewed encouragement of photography, and a request in March 1856 "for an officer who could be deputed to various parts of the South of India for the purpose of taking photographic representations of the many interesting objects there, edifices, sculptures and inscriptions of much beauty or interest both historical and artistic,"[11] Captain Linnaeus Tripe of the 12th Madras Native Infantry was appointed presidency photographer in Madras. Tripe himself envisaged a wide-ranging program of work that would embrace, in addition to "objects in the Presidency that are interesting to the Antiquary, architect, sculptor, mythologist and historian," ethnographical subjects, topography, geology, and natural history. Finally, "the picturesque may be allowed, perhaps, supplementally."[12]

Tripe was the obvious and undisputed choice for such a task, having the previous year accompanied the diplomatic mission to the Burmese court at Ava as official photographer, a posting from which he returned with some 220 large paper negatives, primarily of architectural subjects. This work was published by the government in an edition of fifty portfolios each containing 120 prints. Although Tripe attached a printed disclaimer apologizing for the quality of the photographs and blaming poor weather, sickness, and the demands of other duties, his modest assessment was countered by widespread praise for the views at the 1857 exhibition of the Bengal Photographic Society.[13] Indeed, this first official commission reveals Tripe to be an assured and skillful photographer whose softly toned studies of Burmese architecture are clearly the result of considerable experience in the medium.

For his work in southern India, Tripe gained permission to be based at Bangalore, which had a more favorable climate for photographic operations, as long as he came to Madras for two months each year to teach photography at the School of Industrial Arts. Due to various delays, particularly in finding suitable Indian assistants, it was not until December 1857 that he set out from Bangalore on his first photographic expedition. Traveling via the Salem district to Srirangam, Tiruchirapalli, Madurai, and

Tanjavur, he reached Madras with his entourage of four bullock-drawn carts in April 1858. He had produced 275 large paper negatives, sixteen large glass negatives, and 160 stereographs on glass. The ensuing months were spent printing up this work (nos. 26, 27). Before he could set out on another tour, he, too, fell victim to official retrenchment. The governor of Madras was of the opinion that the maintenance of a photographer was a luxury that "might be justifiable with a fuller exchequer [but] not in the present state of finances." He felt additionally that the existence of such a formally sanctioned post discouraged amateurs from sending in photographs that could be obtained at no cost to government.[14] Nevertheless Tripe's period as presidency photographer did result in a series of handsome volumes published by the Madras government in 1858 and illustrated with original photographs, covering the architecture of Madurai, Tiruchirapalli, Srirangam, Ryakotta, Pudukottai, Tanjavur, and Tiruvadi.

The all-inclusive nature of Tripe's original photographic plans, designed to delineate all aspects of Indian life, was no doubt overambitious. His actual output was limited almost entirely to architectural subjects. Yet the comprehensive nature of the original scheme illustrates how among colonial rulers photography was gaining implicit acknowledgment as another tool for accumulating knowledge that would reinforce ideas of imperial legitimacy. While it is possible to view Tripe's published images as politically neutral interpretations of architecture and topography, their accompanying text anchors them firmly within a defining imperial view of India. Thus J. A. C. Boswell of the Madras civil service, in the text accompanying Tripe's *Views of Ryakotta and Other Places, in the Salem District* (Madras, 1858), enlisted the images to support a message of material progress following the upheavals of the 1857 mutiny in northern India. For example, in relation to the image of the irrigated, cultivated country surrounding Rayakottai Hill, Boswell wrote, "[E]verything speaks in language that cannot be mistaken, that a brighter day has already dawned in India." Similarly, the ruins of the fort at Palakoddu were a solemn and picturesque reminder of "the anarchy which generally prevailed" in earlier periods of Indian history, in contradistinction to "Christian European Civilisation," which would make the "influences of her Government manifest in their social, moral, and political advancement."[15]

The photographers who worked for the government in the 1850s produced an impressive body of work—using mostly paper negative processes—in a consciously artistic period of early photography when the expressive qualities of the medium were as assiduously exploited as its documentary exactitude. Most of these early projects, however, were not followed through in terms of an organized schedule of work covering the country as a whole. The abolition of Tripe's post was succeeded, on an official level at least, by a period of inertia, compounded if not caused by the more pressing administrative and political priorities that followed the Indian Mutiny of 1857.

Although official sponsorship of the medium waned in the late 1850s, many amateur photographers continued to use the medium for their own architectural and antiquarian pursuits. The most distinguished of these was Dr. John Murray of the Bengal medical service, who came to India in 1833. His first experiments in photography appear to have started around the time he moved to Agra as civil surgeon in 1848. He and his family remained in Agra until his retirement in 1870, as this location was ideally suited for both his architectural and photographic interests. During the 1850s and into the 1860s Murray was to produce a comprehensive series of views of the Mughal monuments of Agra, Delhi, Fatehpur Sikri, and other sites. By the mid-1850s he had become a master of the calotype process, working with large paper negatives (up to 37 x 47 centimeters) to produce prints that exploit to the full the glowing expressiveness of the salt print (nos. 16–20). Returning repeatedly to the same subjects—particularly the Taj Mahal—Murray used the medium to examine the building in minute detail, photographing it from slightly shifting viewpoints. The cumulative effect of his technique not only illustrates each aspect of the building but also captures his own fascination with photography's potential to investigate the effects of light and shade on architectural subjects. These repeated experiments were likely part of a purely technical investigation. Murray certainly was acquainted with such talented amateurs as John Nicholas Tressider, Robert Tytler, Clarence Comyn Taylor, and Reverend William Simpson. There is evidence that these men formed a small photographic circle in the city, producing prints that they distributed and criticized among themselves. While on leave in England in 1857, Murray also achieved European recognition for his work when publisher John Hogarth issued thirty of his most impressive images under the title, *Photographic Views of Agra and Its Vicinity.* On his return to India in late 1857, Murray's expertise was also acknowledged by Governor-General Lord Canning, who instructed him to photograph Benares (Varanasi), Kanpur, and Delhi, sites associated with the 1857 mutiny. A second volume published by

Hogarth in 1859—*Picturesque Views of the North Western Province of India*—presented twenty-six of Murray's architectural views with text by Major General J. T. Boileau.

Murray appears to have abandoned photography in 1865, by which time commercial photography had secured a permanent foothold in the subcontinent. The paper negative processes had been largely replaced by the wet-collodion technique. At the 1857 exhibition of the Bengal Photographic Society , the daguerreotype, calotype, and collodion processes were all well represented. But only five years later, while highly praised as "very superior examples of the art," Murray's calotype method was considered inferior and old-fashioned when compared to the "more recent discoveries in clearness, sharpness, and artistic effect" of the glass negative.[16]

Much of the architectural photography of the 1860s was produced by commercial photographers who sold to visitors and residents. The quantity of such material making its way back to Europe may have had a stimulating effect, for by the second half of the decade, interest in the study and preservation of Indian architecture was once again beginning to grow. It is more likely, however, that this renewed interest can be credited to James Fergusson, who in December 1866 gave a lecture on the study of Indian architecture to the Society of Arts in London. The published version of this talk included fifteen photographs illustrating the styles of some of the most important building types in the subcontinent. Most of the images were the work of Samuel Bourne.[17] Fergusson's introductory comments stress the importance of photography in the study of Indian architecture, the medium having brought the discipline within the reach of every researcher, whether or not he had the opportunity to visit the actual sites. The proliferation of such material could be expected to increase knowledge of and interest in the subject. Until recently, he noted, published works on the subject, had been "both cumbrous and expensive" (here no doubt referring to the recently published *Architecture of Dharwar and Mysore and Architecture at Beejapoor*), but photography was now in a position to transform this situation considerably. In his own case, he was able to assert that "I have learnt as much, if not more, of Indian architecture [from photographs] during the last two or three years, than I did during my residence in India, and I now see that the whole subject may be made intelligible, and I see how it can be done."[18]

In the discussion that followed Fergusson's lecture, Sir Henry Cole echoed his plea for the cre ation of a systematic collection of architectural photographs and stated that at the forthcoming international exhibition in Paris, architecture would be represented in the Indian court by photographs, plans, sections, and casts.[19]

For the Paris Exhibition of 1867, it was natural that Fergusson should be invited to organize the photographic display, which consisted of "about 500 representations of Indian buildings, which were selected out of a collection exceeding 1,000 in number, which I either possessed or had at my command."[20] This important display had its practical results, one of which was the publication of a convention signed by most European countries "for promoting universally works of art for the benefit of museums of all countries."[21] This in turn spurred the Indian government once more to assume responsibility in the matter. In August 1867 instructions were issued by the governor-general regarding the "desirability of conserving ancient architectural structures, or their remains, and other works of art in India, and of organizing a system for photographing them."[22] Mindful of the costs of past projects, the government was of the opinion that "competent amateurs," who might in some circumstances be reimbursed for basic expenses, would be sufficient to carry through such a plan. This approach was not without its dangers, relying as it did on the response of officials and other residents whose photographic skills did not always match their enthusiasm. (In Jessore, for example, Dr. Kenneth McLeod offered his services, but with the commissioner's unpromising codicil that "he is not a very experienced or successful artist."[23]).

By the early 1870s the influx of uneven amateur material led Major General Alexander Cunningham (overall head of the Archaeological Survey) to assert that in the long run hiring professional photographers might be a more economical way of compiling such records. But even before this decision had been made, several professionals had been employed in the late 1860s as a result of the renewed importance accorded to photographic documentation. This new burst of activity is probably best represented in the work of Edmund David Lyon, a former British Army officer, who had set up as a professional photographer in Ootacamund in the mid-1860s. In November 1867 he was appointed government photographer in an arrangement that required the Madras administration to pay his traveling expenses and to purchase ten copies of the photographs deemed essential. Traveling with his wife (who acted as his assistant), Lyon undertook a grueling seven-month tour of which he wrote, "I traversed the whole of the southern part of the Peninsular, the whole of Mysore, Bellary, the ruined city of Vizianuggur, and Tarputry, a distance little short of 2,000 miles."[24] With justifiable pride, he went on to state that "I secured two hundred and seventy nine negatives in Madras alone, which have been universally allowed to be the best ever taken in the east, and quite equal to any taken in Europe by the very best photographers."[25] Preparing to return to Europe at the end of 1868, Lyon received a similar commission from the Bombay government and subsequently took photographs at Bijapur, Ahmadabad, Karli (no. 28), Ambernath, Surat, and Palitana. While Lyon's work contains a good deal of duplication of sites covered by earlier workers (a fact noted by Fergusson, who also complained of their expense), their outstanding technical and artistic qualities make his photographs among the finest produced in the 1860s.

Lyon's officially commissioned work was among the last to be ordered from independent photographers. With the formal establishment of the Archaeological Survey of India in 1871, photography became an accepted part of the duties of its officers. Men like James Burgess, Joseph Beglar, Henry Bailey Wade Garrick, Henry Cousens, and others combined fieldwork with the production of their own photographs. While these prints were in many cases of a high standard and possessed the further advantage of being taken by archaeological specialists, the absorption of photographic work by the archaeologists themselves effectively brought to a close the first chapter in a documentary project that—contrary to the optimism of early researchers—was destined to continue not for a few years, but up to the present day.

In his 1866 lecture Fergusson had argued that the study of Indian architecture was of an importance extending beyond the examination of the country's purely artistic heritage and that it should be seen, in the absence of extensive written records, as one of the most valuable ways of approaching a general history of the subcontinent: "In fact, the architecture of the country may be considered as a great stone book, in which every tribe and race has written its annals and recorded its faith, and that in a manner so clear that those who run may read."[26] Such research had, in turn, its pragmatic aspect to the rulers of India, as a means not only "of elucidating the manners and customs of the country, but of checking their fables . . . [it] is frequently the only means that remains to us; and, if this be so, is it possible to over-estimate its value to those who wish to know who and what the people are or were, whom we have undertaken to guide and govern."[27]

Linnaeus Tripe had originally viewed his photographic commission from the Madras government as a wide-ranging project to produce a visual record delineating the material culture of the country within the context of its topography, commercial productions, and ethnographic makeup. While such a synthesis was never achieved in Tripe's own work, by the time of Fergusson's lecture photography was in the process of documenting the people of India in terms of the rising science of anthropology. This was accomplished by means and organization analogous to the methods of architectural documentation, and in many instances by the same photographers.

The invention and spread of photography coincided with an era of aggressive European colonial expansion. Photography was soon seen as a potentially important scientific tool for the anthropologist. Studies of newly encountered peoples had been taken since the 1840s, if in a somewhat haphazard way. The series of anthropological portraits by Louis Rousseau shown at the Paris Exhibition of 1855 had inspired Ernest Lacan to recommend its use as "an indispensable means of comparative physical and cultural analysis."[28] In India, while interest in such matters was steadily growing, the creation of a photographic archive of such material was yet in its infancy. Papers from European ethnological societies offering guidance in anthropological matters to travelers had been published by the Asiatic Society of Bengal in the early 1840s. This literature stressed the necessity of collecting material illustrative of racial types, including portraits in full face and profile, and the collection of skulls and casts. The Schlagintweit brothers, commissioned by the East India Company in 1853 to explore and survey in the Himalayas, made a large collection of plaster casts of Indian heads. While they also took a number of photographs, Emil Schlagintweit believed that casts "offer a wider field of enquiry than mere photographs."[29] The scientific writer Robert Hunt disagreed, pointing out the problems involved in both taking and transporting casts. He also noted that by using the camera, the brothers "would have equally served the science of ethnology, by obtaining and preserving photographic portraits of the peoples amongst whom they had travelled."[30] Despite this activity, of the 460 photographs amassed for the 1857 exhibition of the Bengal Photographic Society, only a few examples were shown of the races of India, leading the organizers to note that "the castes and costumes of the natives of the country have not yet received that attention which they deserve, and which they will no doubt in time obtain."[31]

In Bombay efforts were being made to remedy this situation. Two founding members of the Bombay Photographic Society, William Johnson and William Henderson, contributed a number of portraits of Indian races, castes, and occupations to *The Indian Amateurs Photographic Album,* a monthly that ran from 1856 to 1859, issued under the society's auspices and containing three original prints with each number. A few years later Johnson published *The Oriental Races and Tribes, Residents and Visitors of Bombay* (2 vols., London, 1863–66) and declared that "photographic representations of the numerous peoples and tribes frequenting . . . Bombay . . . have long been desiderata both among students of geography and ethnography." This was the earliest ethnological work published on India to make direct use of photography. A significant number of such photographs found their way back to London, among them a series of very fine portraits of East Bengal types, which arrived in 1863, the work of an anonymous photographer whose sympathetic and compelling studies are of an exceptional quality for the period (nos. 30–35).

It is against this background of an increasing use and acceptance of photography as a tool of ethnological investigation that the most far-reaching official attempt to construct a comprehensive atlas of Indian types was made. Edited by John Forbes Watson and John William Kaye, *The People of India* was published by the India Museum in London in eight volumes between 1868 and 1875. Containing nearly five hundred photographs with accompanying text, the volumes represent a significant landmark in the use of the medium as an anthropological tool. Although imbued throughout with resonances of the mutiny of the previous decade, they also served to reinforce notions of dominance and control, both in the selection of their subjects and in the descriptive text. In the latter, the classification of types is often explicitly concerned with matters of political reliability and loyalty, criminal tendencies, and amenability to progress and education. And while designed to illustrate the ethnological characteristics of the whole subcontinent, the editors were limited to the use of material on hand in London, resulting in a wildly unbalanced coverage, which relegated the whole of southern India to one volume.

The preface to the work paints a somewhat oversimplified and distorted account of its genesis, portraying it as a simple development of Lord and Lady Canning's photographic interests and their desire to "carry home with them, at the end of their sojourn in India, a collection, obtained by private means, which might recall to their memories the peculiarities of Indian life."[32] To this end, "officers of the Indian services, who had made themselves acquainted with the principles and practice of photography, encouraged and patronised by the Governor-General, went forth and traversed the land in search of interesting subjects."[33] With the growth of this collection, its scientific value was considered to merit official sanction and ultimately publication.

Contemporary documentation fails to support this version of events; rather it appears that the large-scale collection of photographs of ethnographical subjects did not begin until after an official circular had been sent out to provincial administrations in July 1861. It included a list of "the more remarkable tribes to be found in India" and requested that photographs be made "of a few characteristic specimens of such of them as exist within your jurisdiction."[34] Although any precise purpose for the order is omitted from the document, and it was certainly endorsed by Lord Canning, it was clearly promulgated as more than a request for contributions to the governor-general's private collection. It does state, however, that the order originated from "Her Majesty's Government" rather than from the Indian authorities. It seems likely that the photographs were from the start intended for display at the forthcoming London International Exhibition of 1862. Whatever their precept, within a few months, this became the generally accepted destination for the material, even if, through lack of time and organization, most of the material arrived too late for inclusion in the exhibition. Only the work of Dr. (later Sir) Benjamin Simpson was significantly represented, with a collection of some eighty portraits collected in northeastern India (no. 37). Those whose work arrived too late for display, but would appear in the published volumes, included Henry Charles Baskerville Tanner (no. 40a–d), William Robert Houghton (who worked with Tanner in Sindh), James Waterhouse, and John Nicholas Tressider.

A later account of the publishing history of *The People of India,* contained in a series of memoranda by John Forbes Watson and John William Kaye, stated that the original impetus for publication sprang from the receipt of the East Bengal portraits in 1863 and that the discovery of further material in the India Office finally grew into a published work.[35] Neither Watson nor Kaye mentions A. M. Dowleans, who while in London as the Indian government's agent for the 1862 exhibition, appears to have been the first to raise the possibility of publishing the photographs in some form.[36] Although this issue is unlikely ever to be finally resolved, the work remains among the most important nineteenth-century attempts to harness photography in the service of ethnographic documentation.

The portraits that illustrated *The People of India* had been compiled along similar lines to the architectural photographs commissioned and collected in the 1850s and 1860s, relying largely on the enthusiasm of government officers in the civil and military services, with occasional recourse to professional photographers. This similarity of scope and method was pointed out by John Forbes Watson in a paper advocating the initiation of a systematic program for the gathering of information about India, both for commercial advantage and for obtaining a "moral hold" on its population. Arguing for the institution of an ethnological survey of the subcontinent, he asserted that it should "resemble the Archaeological, in so far as its prime object will be a scientific one." He noted that previous work, including his own *People of India,* had been more "popular and picturesque" than rigorously scientific.[37] With the publication of the final volume of that work in 1875 (and the largely uninterested public response to the project), this scheme also fell largely into abeyance. In the following decades the majority of the material of this type produced in the subcontinent was the work of professional photographers catering for the commercial market. But in the closing years of the century, one notable attempt was made to use the camera to produce a comprehensive cultural and anthropological record of a society according to Watson's mandate for a "scientific" basis.

The Andaman Islands stretching southwards across the Bay of Bengal between Burma and Sumatra had first been taken into British possession in 1789 for use as a penal colony. This function was resuscitated after the 1857 mutiny, when the islands became the principal destination for sentenced rebels. Peopled by shy and hostile Negrito aborigines isolated from and largely untainted by European contact, the Andamans were considered a rich and virgin ethnological laboratory. Specimens of the tribe were first photographed by Oscar Mallitte in 1857. From that time on the aborigines were periodically brought across to Calcutta, where they were exhibited, photographed, and examined by the amateur anthropologists of the capital. Other commercial photographers visited the islands, such as Samuel Bourne and Charles Shepherd in the 1880s, but the major interest in the islanders focused on their unique anthropological characteristics, first recorded in a systematic and scientific photographic method by the administrator Edward Horace Man.

In November 1889 Maurice Vidal Portman, an assistant superintendent at Port Blair in the Andaman Islands, wrote to Sir Wollaston Franks of the British Museum offering to make "a series of photographs of the Andamanese aborigines, in their different modes and occupations of life."[38] This series, which was to include physical studies, body markings, and skills such as adz (cutting tool) and bow making and hut building, was intended to produce "a complete record in imperishable platinotype" of the "Andaman Islander in every action of his life, showing how the tribes differ among themselves, as well as their general peculiarities, and my object, in the photographic part, is to show every step in the making of a weapon, etc., so clearly, that, with the assistance of the finished articles now in the British Museum, it would be possible for a European workman to imitate the mode of work"[39] (nos. 41–44). Portman's grandiose scheme ultimately envisaged the production of multiple sets of thousands of prints, which, together with anthropometrical measurements and data, would take some eight years to complete. Difficulties of transportation around the island, sickness, and finally disagreements about the cost of the work led to the curtailment of this plan, and the final breakdown of Portman's own health. His forced retirement in 1899 meant that only a portion of the project was completed. The many hundreds of prints that were made, however, supply fascinating evidence of a photographic approach that mirrors the shifting course of anthropological studies in the nineteenth century from Watson's "picturesque" portraits towards a rigid examination of physical characteristics. Much of Portman's work shows a disturbing quality found among much late-nineteenth-century photography of racial types, in particular in those studies in which his subjects are clamped in photographic stands to prevent movement and posed against the uniform grid of two-inch squares, whose use had been first advocated by J. H. Lamprey in 1868 for comparative studies of different races.[40] Produced in the awareness that European contact and rule had "admitted the air of the outside world"[41] with potentially fatal consequences to the Andamanese, the photographs are at once a record and an epitaph of a unique culture. They are an impressive, if sometimes chilling, ending to nineteenth-century photographic investigations of racial distinctions in the subcontinent.

NOTES

1. James Fergusson, introduction to *History of Indian and Eastern Architecture* (London: John Murray, 1876).

2. Rev. Joseph Mullins, "On the Applications of Photography in India," *Journal of the Photographic Society of Bengal,* no. 2 (January 1857): 33–38.

3. Governor-General of India in Council, Public Department, 27 January 1847, in India Office Board's Collections, India Office Records F/4/2503, collection 142.127.

4. Bombay Public Despatches, 14 June 1854, India Office Records E/4/1100, 1420.

5. Bombay Public Despatches, 29 December 1854, India Office Records, E/4/1101, 1449–51.

6. Thomas Biggs to W. Hart, Secretary to Government, Bombay, dated Belgium, 4 January 1856, in Board's Collections, India Office Records, F/4/2665, collection 177.202.

7. James Fergusson to Dr. Alexander Hunter, Madras Public Proceedings, 23 January 1869, India Office Records P/439/8, 55.

8. Thomas Biggs to W. Hart, Secretary to Government, Bombay, dated Belgium, 4 January 1856, in Board's Collections, India Office Records, F/4/2665, collection 177.202.

9. Ibid.

10. India Despatches, Public Department, no. 22 of 7 February 1855, India Office Records E/4/829, 624–5.

11. T. Pycroft, Chief Secretary to the Government of Madras, to the Secretary of the Government of India, dated Fort St. George, 11 March 1856, in Board's Collections, India Office Records F/4/2725, collection 198.064.

12. Captain Linnaeus Tripe to F. A. Murray, Private Secretary to the Governor of Madras, dated Bangalore 22 July 1856, Fort St. George Public Consultations, 26 August 1856, no. 31, India Office Records P/249/57, 4483.

13. Report of monthly meeting of 15 April 1857, *Journal of the Photographic Society of Bengal,* no. 3 (20 May 1857): 67.

14. Minutes by the President of the Madras Council, dated 26 November 1859, Madras Public Proceedings, 21–30 November 1859, no. 85, India Office Records P/249/70, 294.

15. Linnaeus Tripe, *Views of Ryakotta and Other Places, in the Salem District* (Madras, 1858), 2. [No publisher given in source.]

16. Report of the Judges of the 1862 Exhibition of the Bengal Photographic Society, *Journal of the Bengal Photographic Society,* no. 1 (May 1862): 40.

17. James Fergusson, *Illustrations of Various Styles of Indian Architecture* (London: South Kensington Museum, 1869).

18. Ibid., 6.

19. Ibid., 28.

20. Dr. John Forbes Watson, *Report on the Illustration of the Archaic Architecture of India, &c.* (London: India Museum, 1869), appendix A [by James Fergusson]: 7.

21. The document is reproduced in H. H. Cole, *First Report of the Curator of Ancient Monuments in India for the Year 1881–82* (Simla: Government Central Branch Press, 1882), appendix C: iv-v.

22. Secretary to the Government of India to Secretary of Government, Madras, 29 August 1867, Madras Public Proceedings, 29 October 1867, India Office Records P/439/5, 1773.

23. R. B. Chapman to Secretary to the Government of Bengal, dated Kishnaghur, 13 February 1868, Bengal Public Proceedings, no. 117, June 1868, India Office Records P/432/4, 66.

24. E. D. Lyon to the Secretary of State for India, dated Geneva, 9 May 1870, Madras Public Proceedings, August 1870, India Office Records, P/439/10, 956.

25. Ibid.

26. Fergusson, *Illustrations of Various Styles of Indian Architecture,* 10.

27. Ibid.

28. Ernest Lacan, *Esquisses photographiques à propos de l'Exhibition Universelle et de la guerre de l'orient* (Paris, 1856), 38.

29. Emil Schlagintweit, "Notes in Reference to the Question of the Aboriginal Tribes of India," *Proceedings of the Asiatic Society of Bengal* (August 1867): 127–32.

30. Robert Hunt, "Photography Considered In Relation to Its Educational and Practical Value," *Photographic News* 2, no. 47 (29 July 1859): 242–44.

31. Report of monthly meeting of 15 April 1857, *Journal of the Photographic Society of Bengal,* no. 3 (20 May 1857): 68.

32. John Forbes Watson and John William Kaye, preface to *The People of India* (London: India Museum, 1868), 1, [unpaginated]

33. Ibid.

34. E. C. Bayley to the Secretary to the Government of Bengal, dated 17 June 1861, Bengal Public Proceedings, no. 13 of July 1861, India Office of Records P/15/21, 5.

35. John Forbes Watson to Sir Louis Mallet, 31 December 1879, India Office Statistics and Commerce Branch, India Office Records L/E/6/37, collection 9.

36. A. M. Dowleans to H. Merivale, 30 June 1862, India Office Public and Judicial Department Letters, L/P & J/2/158 no. 165.

37. John Forbes Watson, *On the Measures Required for the Efficient Working of the Indian Museum and Library, with Suggestions for the Foundation, in Connection with Them, of an Indian Institute of Enquiry, Lecture and Teaching* (London: India Museum, 1874), 26.

38. Report on the Administration of the Andaman and Nicobar Islands and the Penal Settlements of Port Blair and the Nicobars for 1893–94 (Calcutta, 1894) 115.

39. Ibid., 116.

40. J. H. Lamprey, "On a Method of Measuring the Human Form, for the Use of Students in Ethnology," *Journal of the Ethnological Society of London,* new series, vol. 1 (1868–69): 84–85.

41. M. V. Portman, *A History of Our Relations with the Andamanese,* 2 vols. (Calcutta: Superintendent of Government Printing, 1899), 2: 875.

A PASSION FOR DOCUMENTATION: ARCHITECTURE

15 *The Taj Mahal from the East, Agra*

John Murray

early 1860s, waxed paper negative, 37.8 x 46.5
The British Library, Oriental & India Office Collection photo 35 (13)

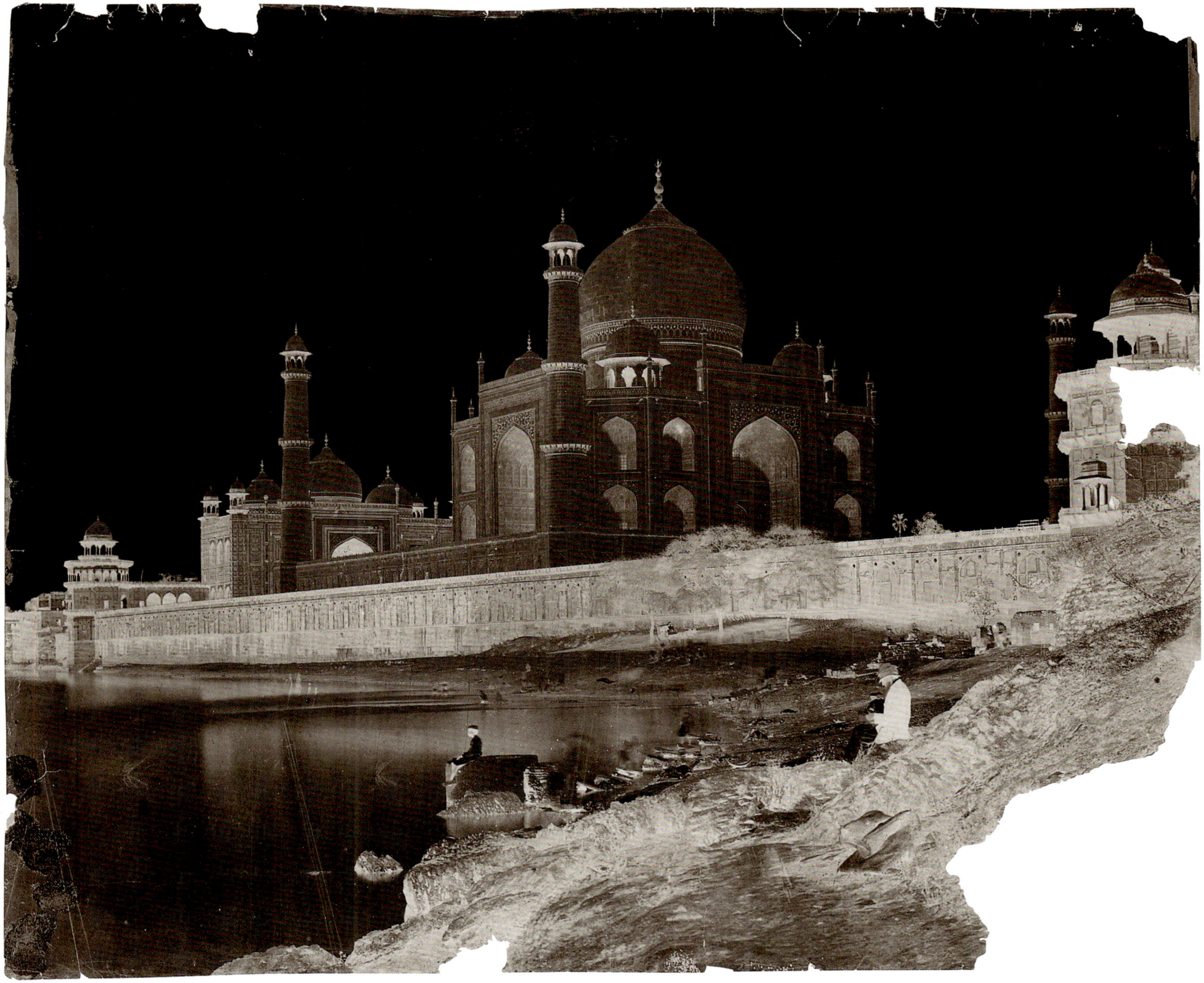

16 *Detail of Outer Tower of the Jamat Khana at the Taj Mahal Enclosure, Agra*

John Murray

6 February 1862, waxed paper negative

37.5 x 46.5

The British Library, Oriental & India Office Collection photo 35 (15)

17 *View of a Chhatri on the Roof of the Taj Mahal, Agra*

John Murray

early 1860s, waxed paper negative, 37.8 x 47

The British Library, Oriental & India Office Collection photo 35 (17)

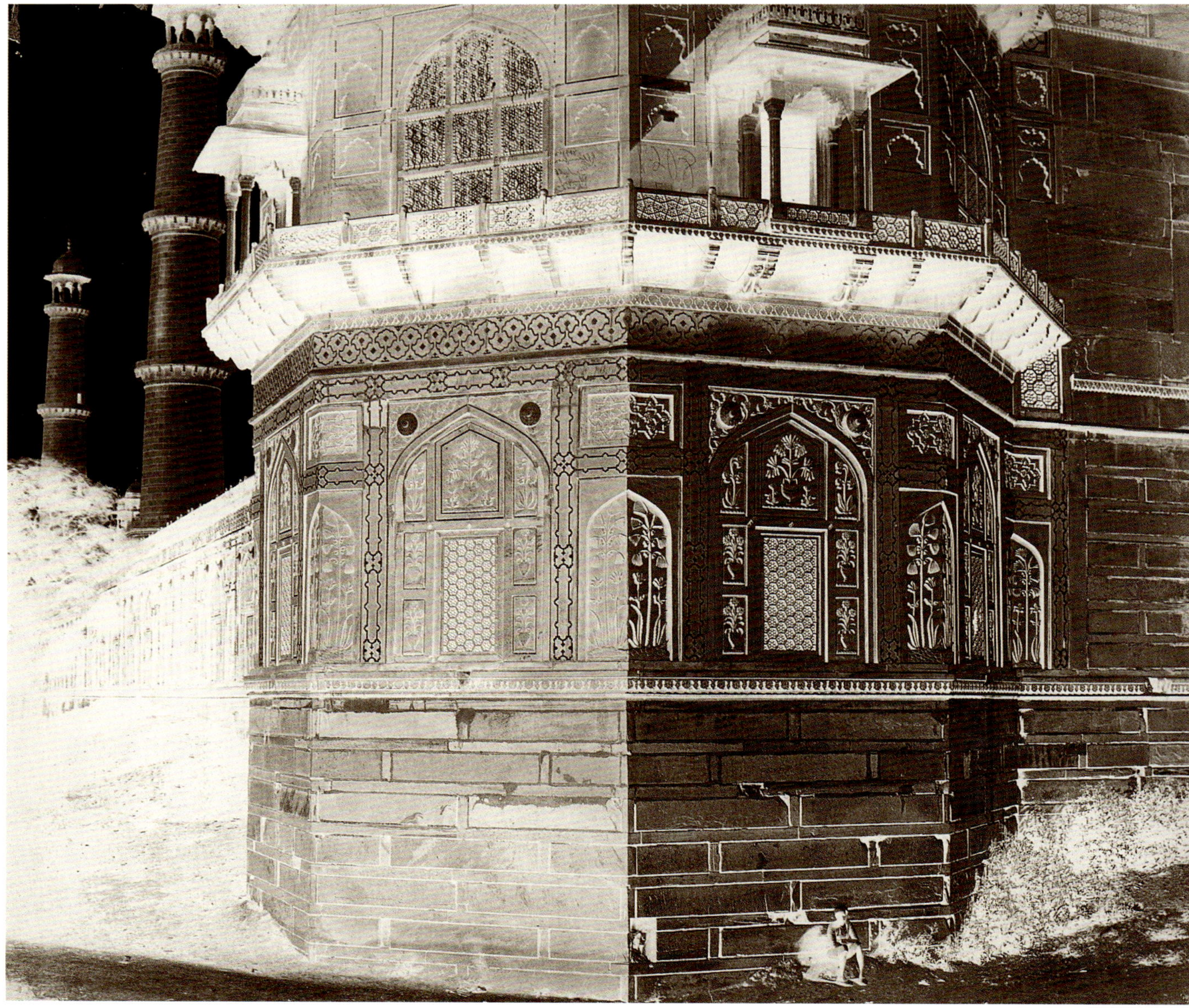

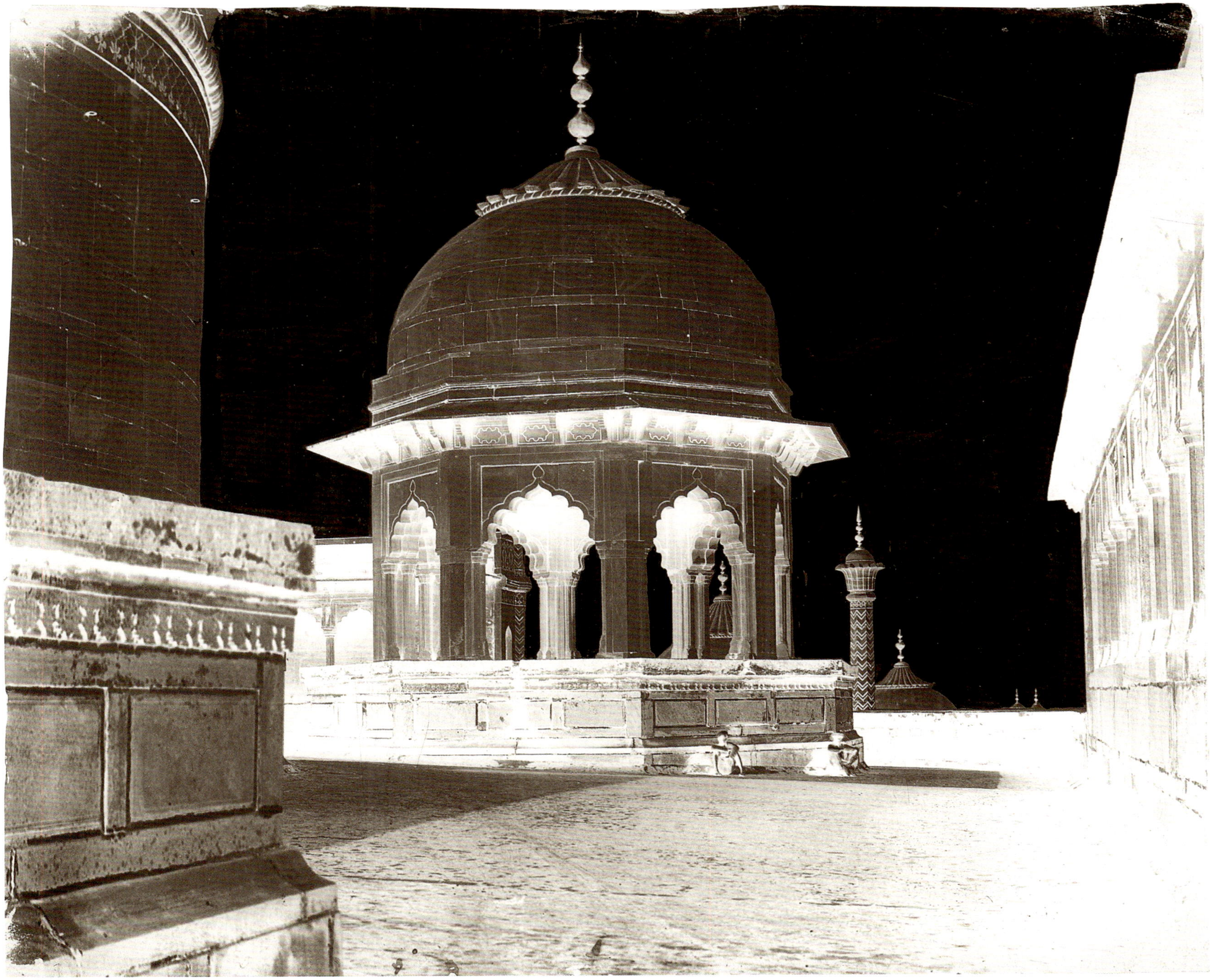

18 *A Street at Muttra, with the Jami Masjid in the Background*

John Murray

mid-1850s, salt print, 45.3 x 36.7
The British Library, Oriental & India Office Collection photo 101 (26)

19 *The Jami Masjid, Agra*

John Murray

mid-1850s, salt print, 35.4 x 45.8
The British Library, Oriental & India Office Collection photo 101 (12)

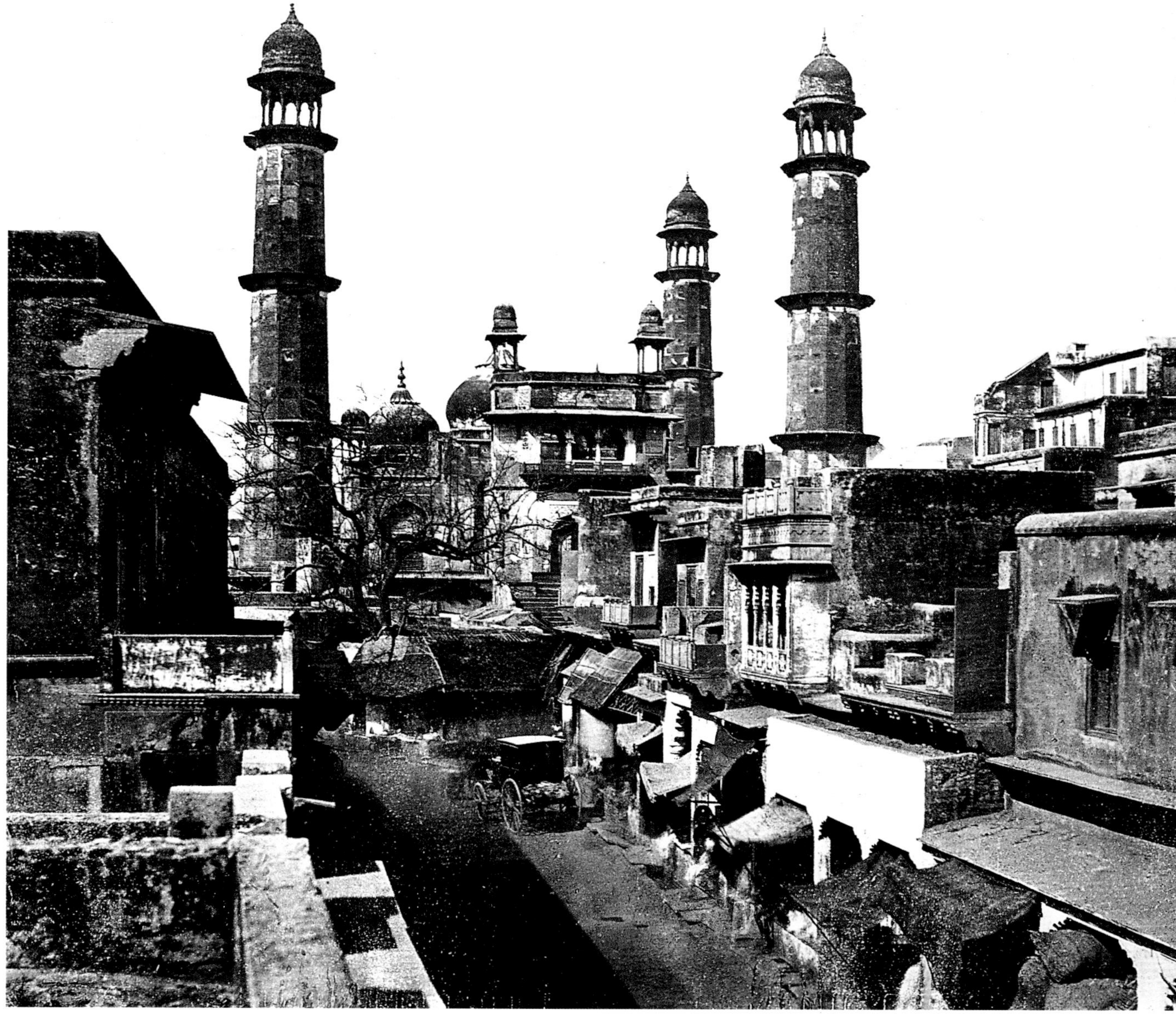

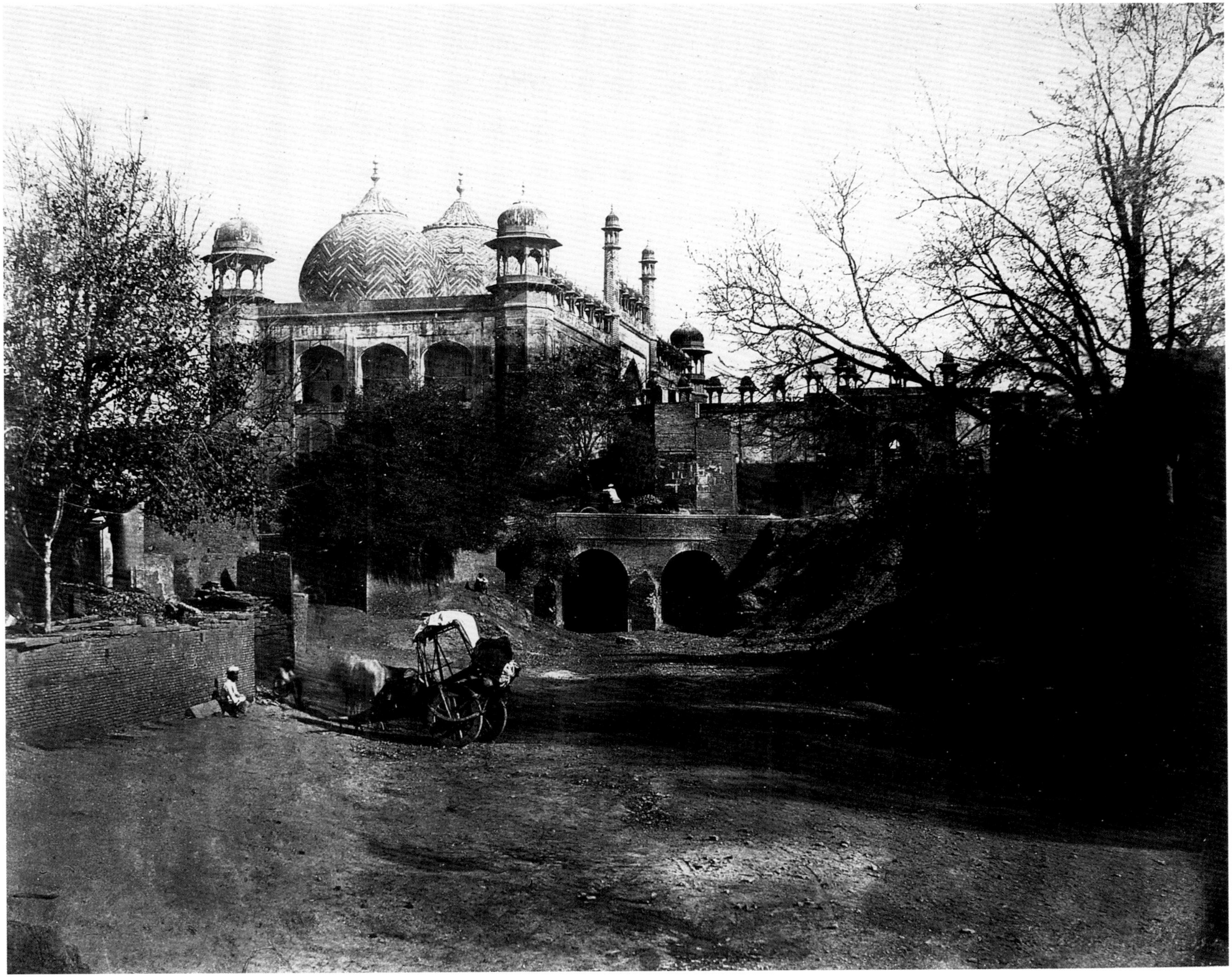

20 *The Tomb of Etmad-ood-Dowlah*

John Murray

mid-1850s, salt print, 36 x 44.7
The British Library, Oriental & India Office Collection photo 101 (14)

21 *The Taj Mahal from the East with Ruins in the Foreground, Agra*

John Murray

ca. 1858, albumen print, 40.1 x 45.4
Howard and Jane Ricketts Collection

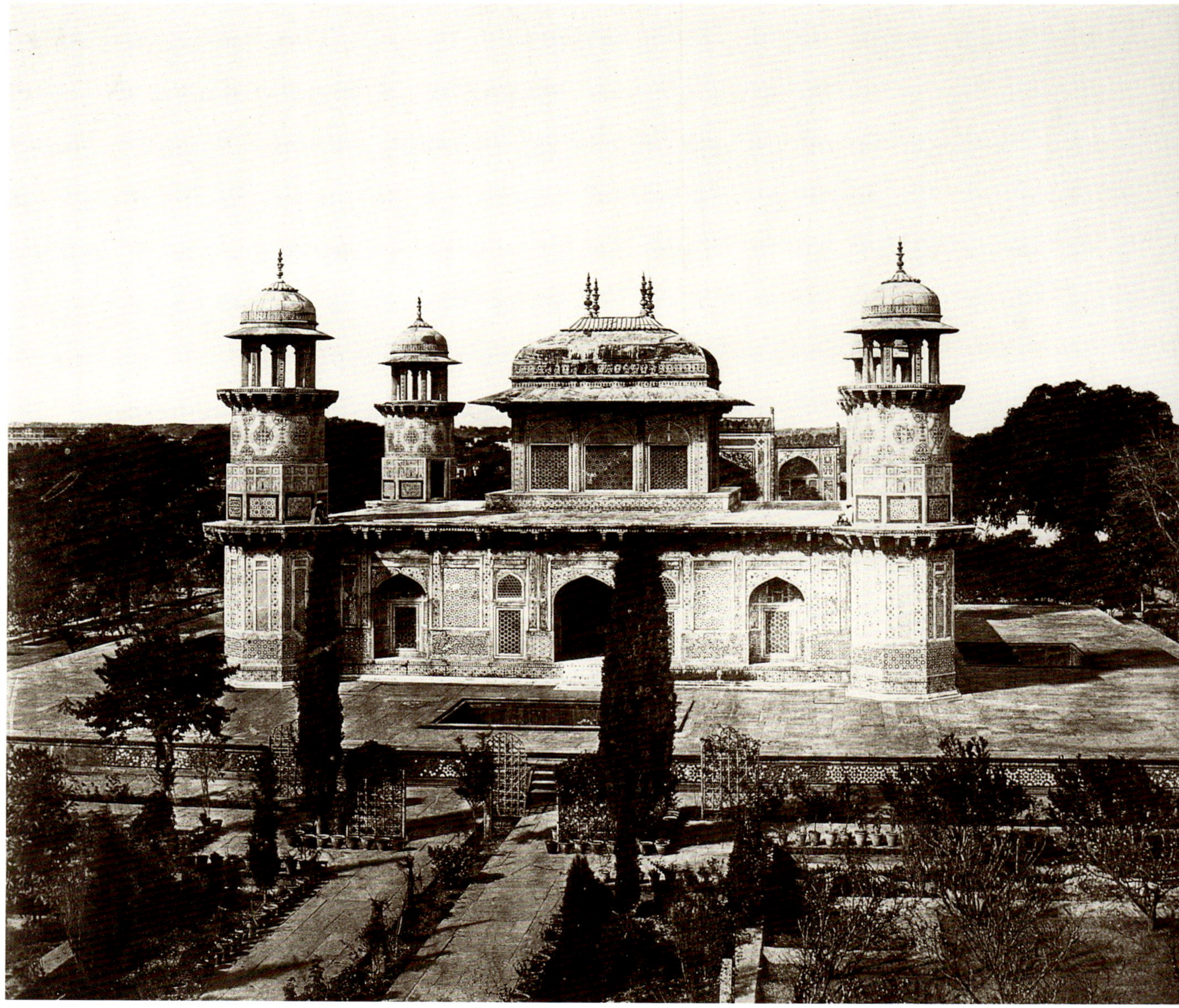

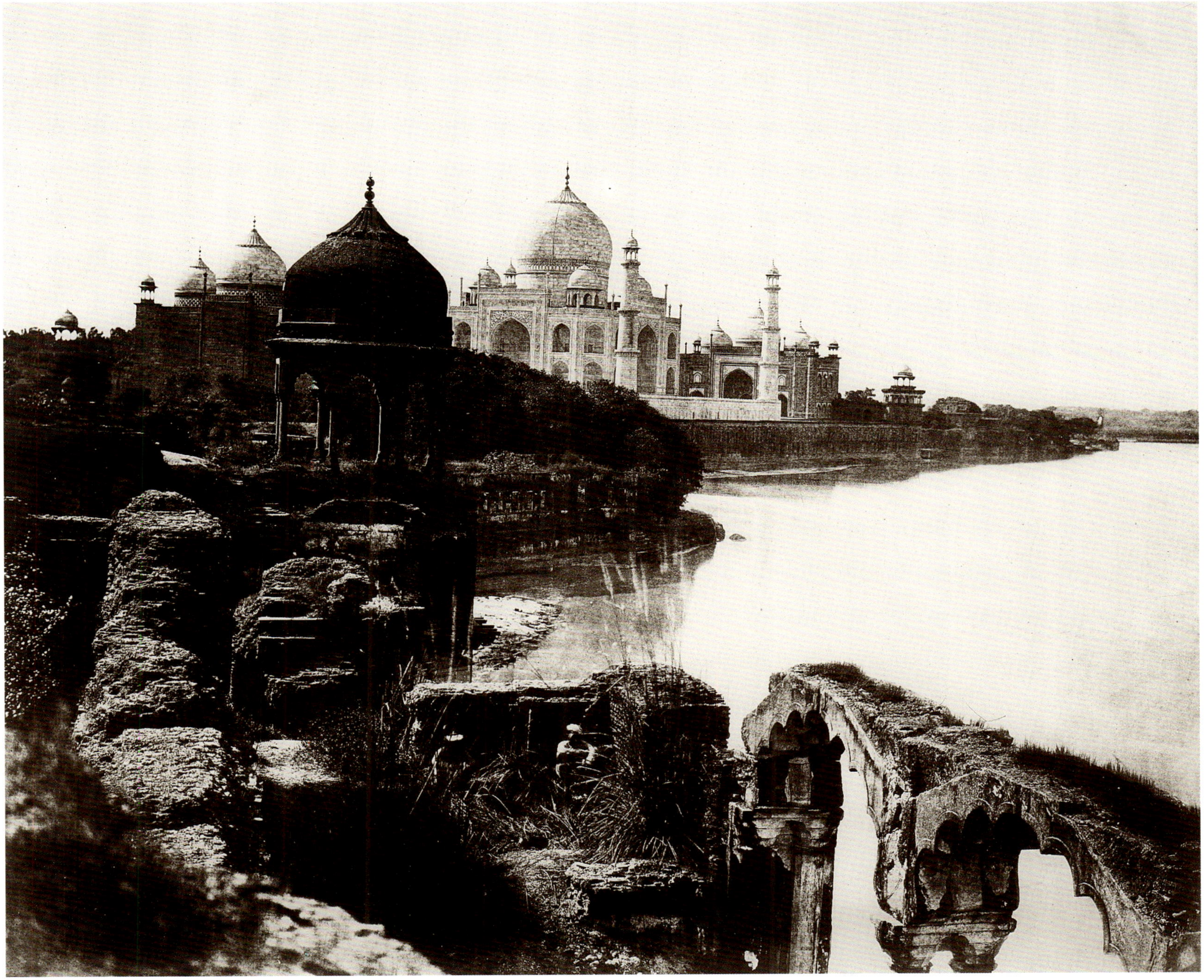

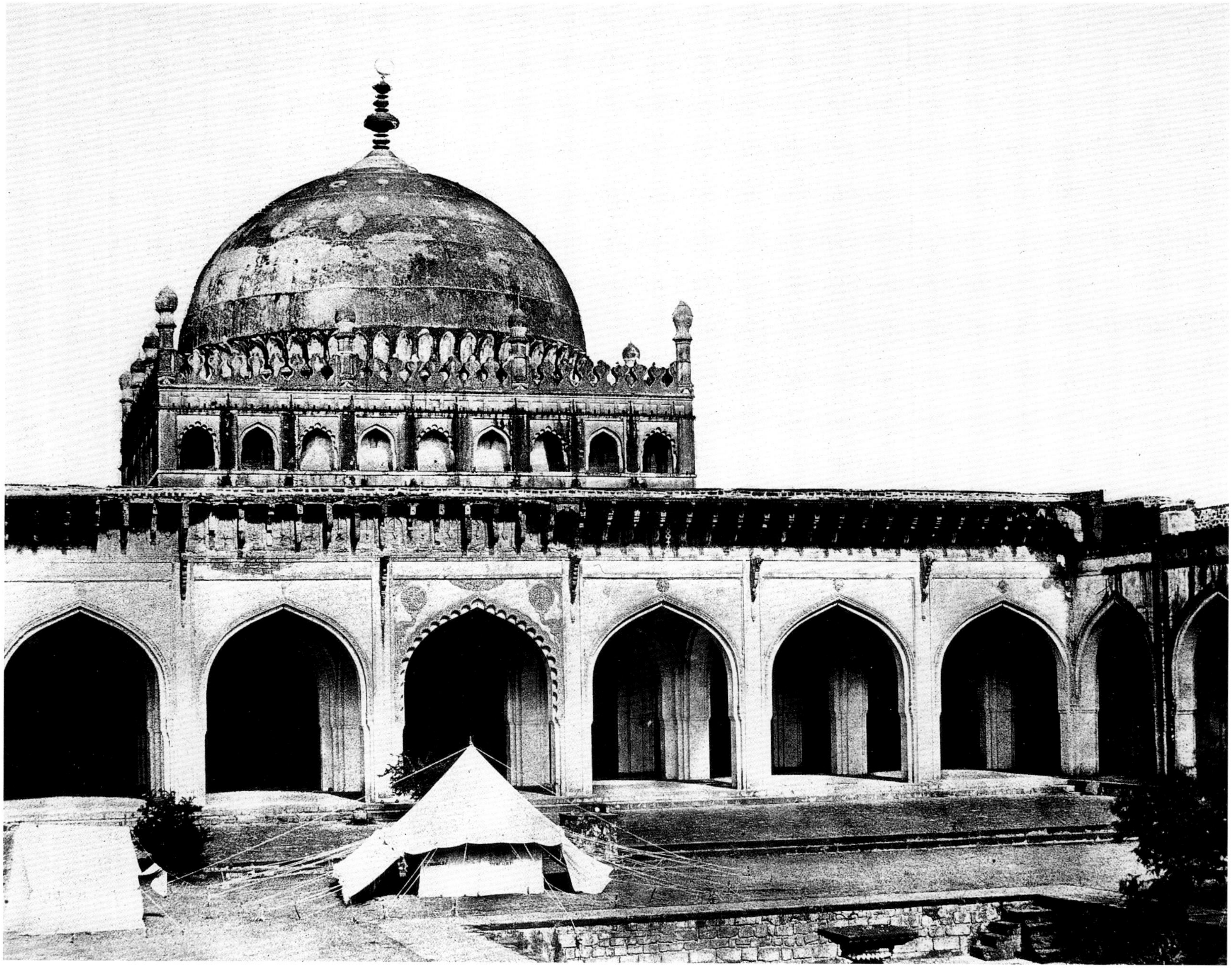

22 *View of Jami Masjid from within the Courtyard, Bijapur, Karnataka*

Major Thomas Biggs

1856, albumen print, 20.9 x 26.8
Canadian Centre for Architecture

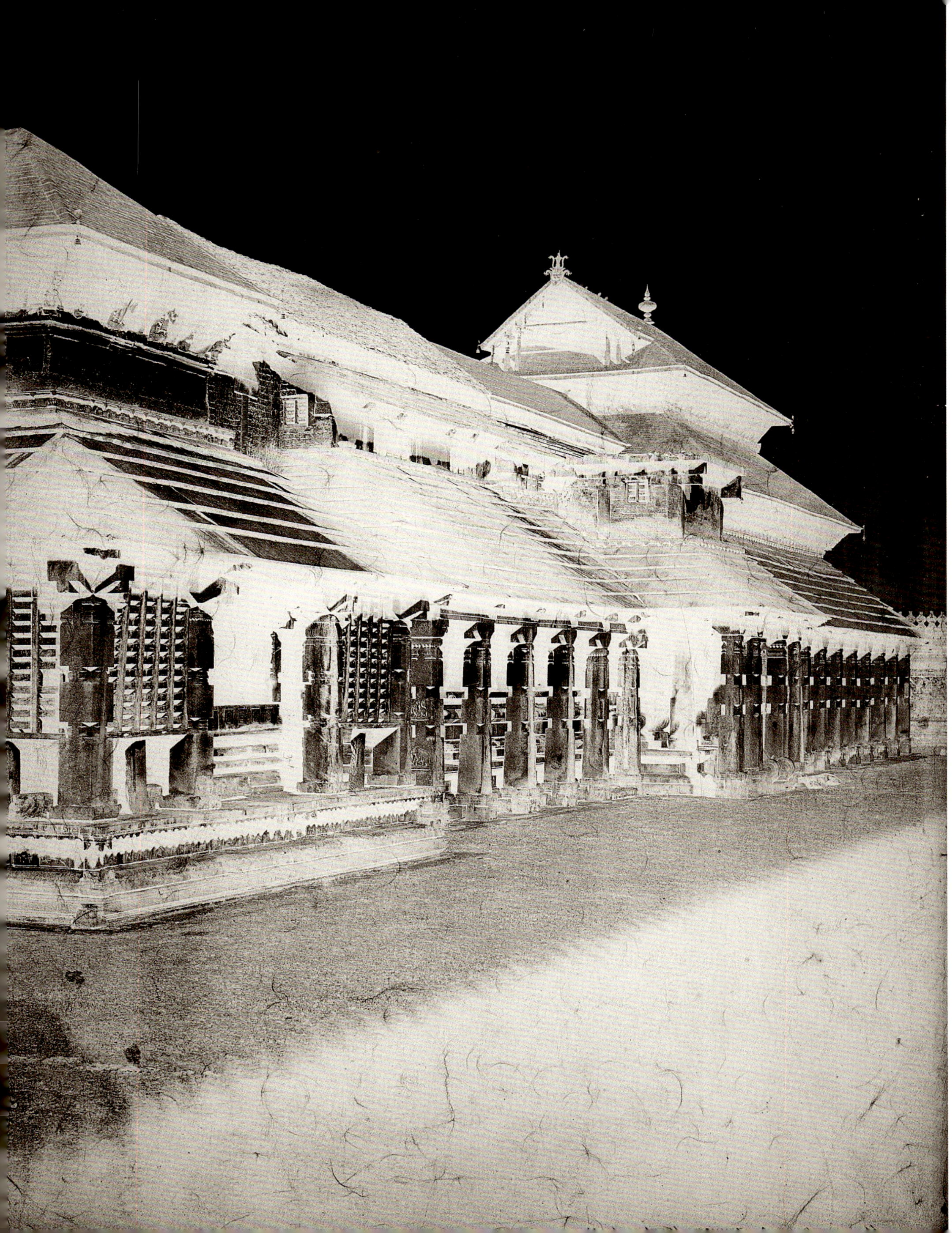

23 *Chandranatha Basti, Mudabidri*

William Henry Pigou

ca. 1857, waxed paper negative, 38.7 x 30.4
The British Library, Oriental & India Office Collection photo 1000 (1045)

24 *Chandranatha Basti, Mudabidri*

William Henry Pigou

ca. 1857, albumen print, 38 x 28
Courtesy of Ken and Jenny Jacobson

25 *Temple of Chamoondee, Chittuldroog, Karnataka*

William Henry Pigou

ca. 1857, albumen print, 27.9 x 39.4
Canadian Centre for Architecture

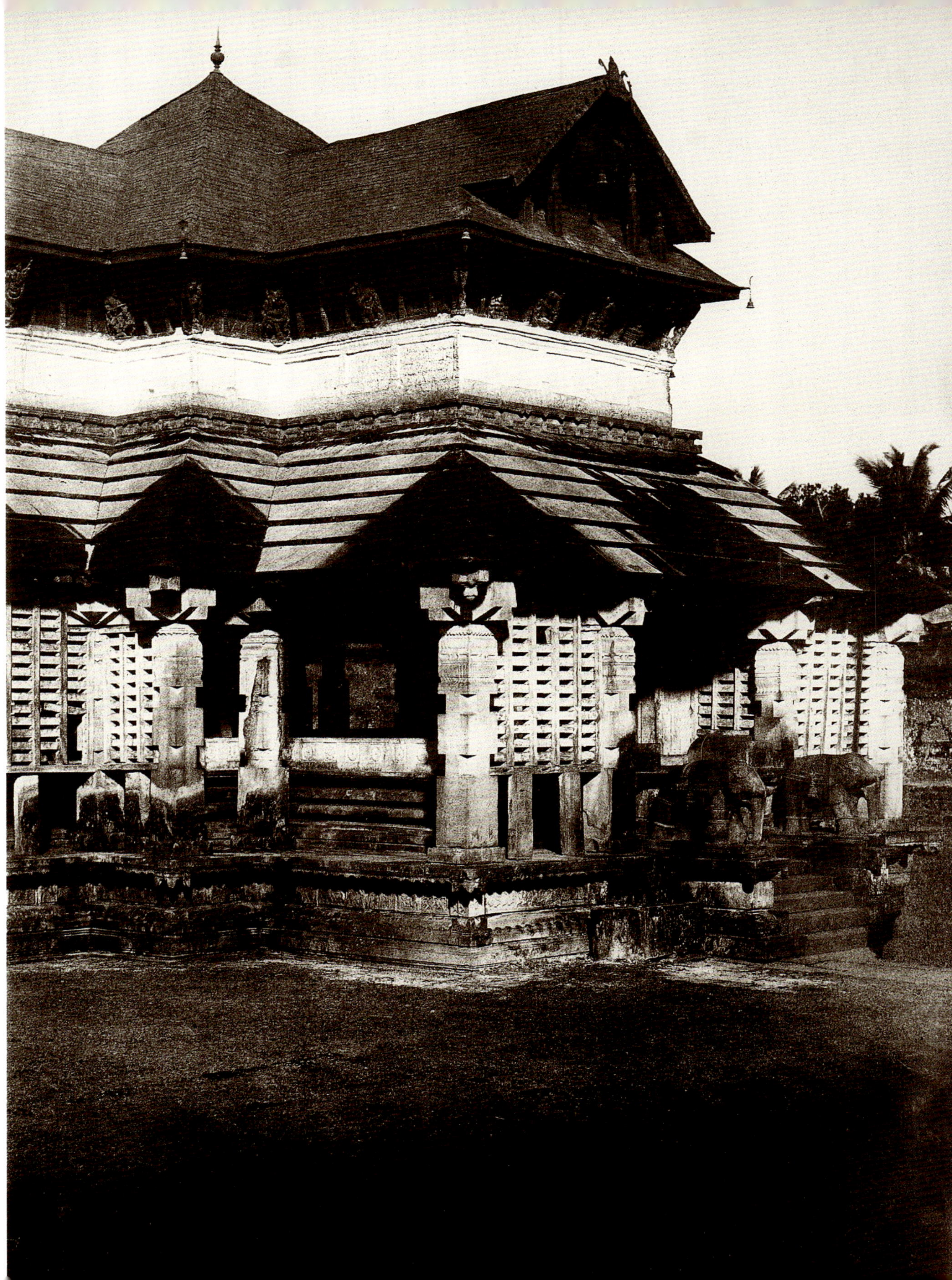

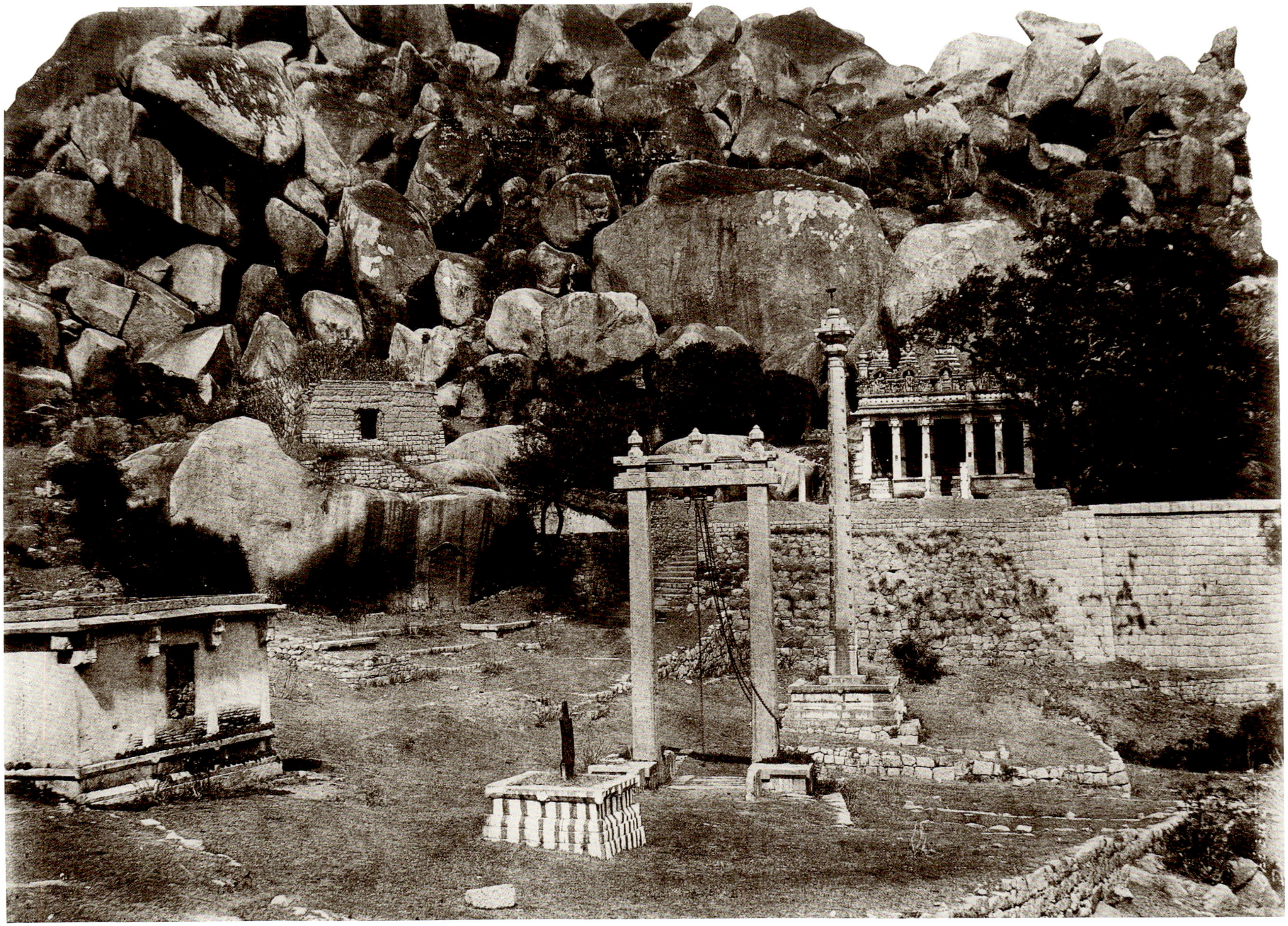

26 *South Façade of Subrahmanya Swami's Temple, Tanjore*

Linnaeus Tripe

1858, albumen print, 28.9 x 36.6

Canadian Centre for Architecture

27 *Façade of the West Side of the Nayaka Durbar Hall, Tanjore*

Linnaeus Tripe

1858, albumen print, 27 x 36

Canadian Centre for Architecture

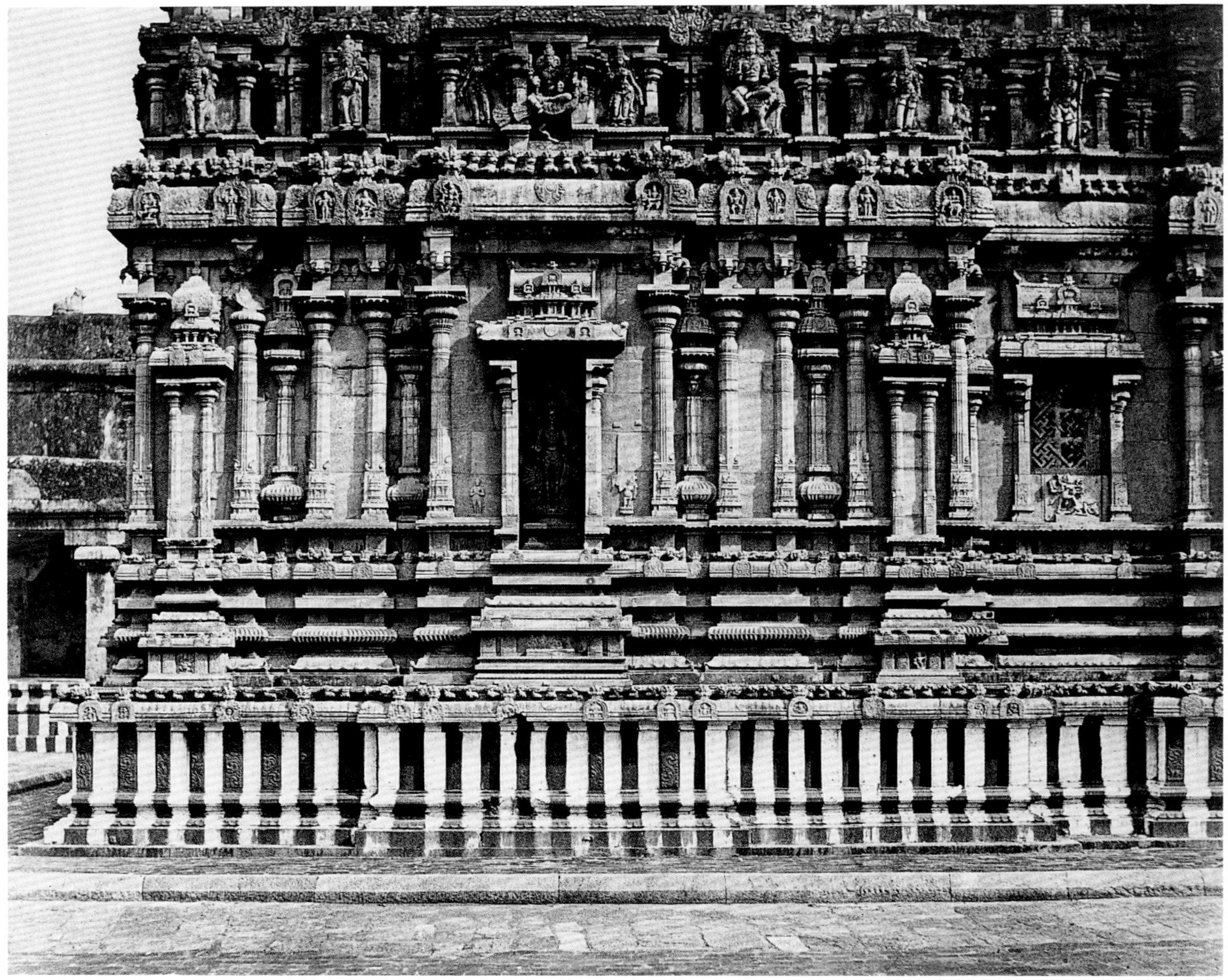

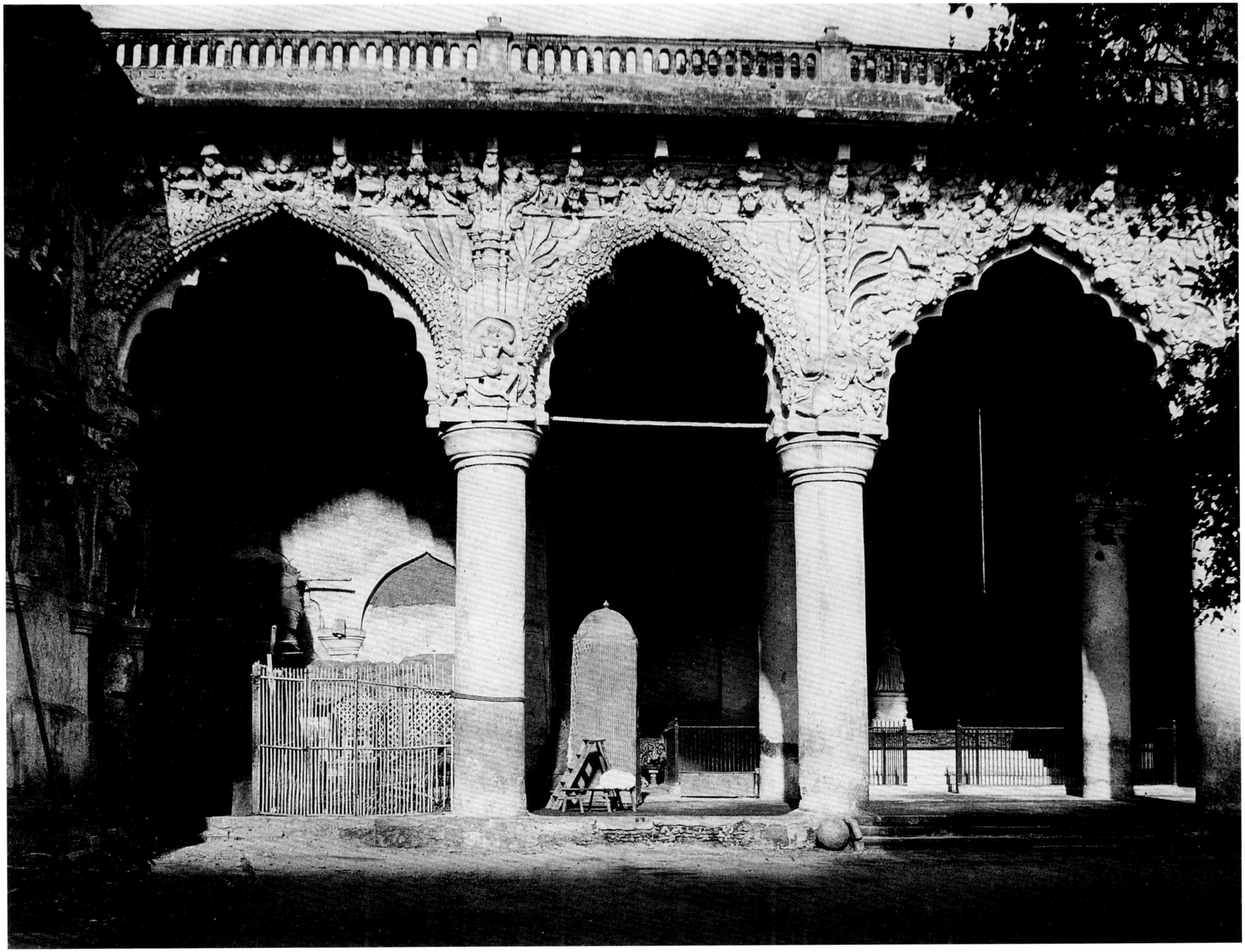

28 *Right End of Chaitya Porch, Karlee*

Captain Edmund David Lyon

1869, albumen print, 25.1 x 30.8

Canadian Centre for Architecture

29 *Dutch Tombs at Surat*

Attributed to Donald Horne Macfarlane

ca. 1860, albumen print, 23 x 29.8

Howard and Jane Ricketts Collection

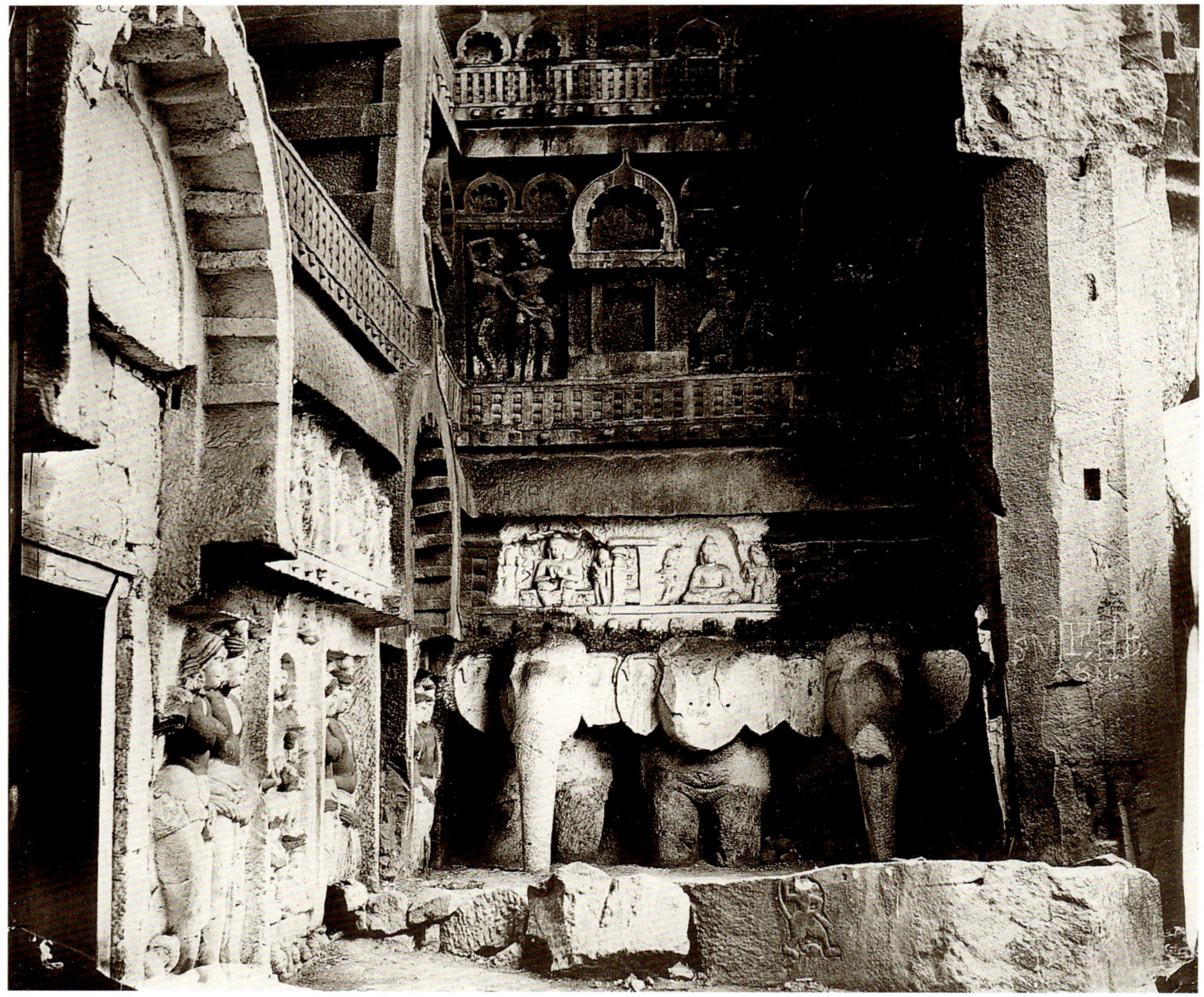

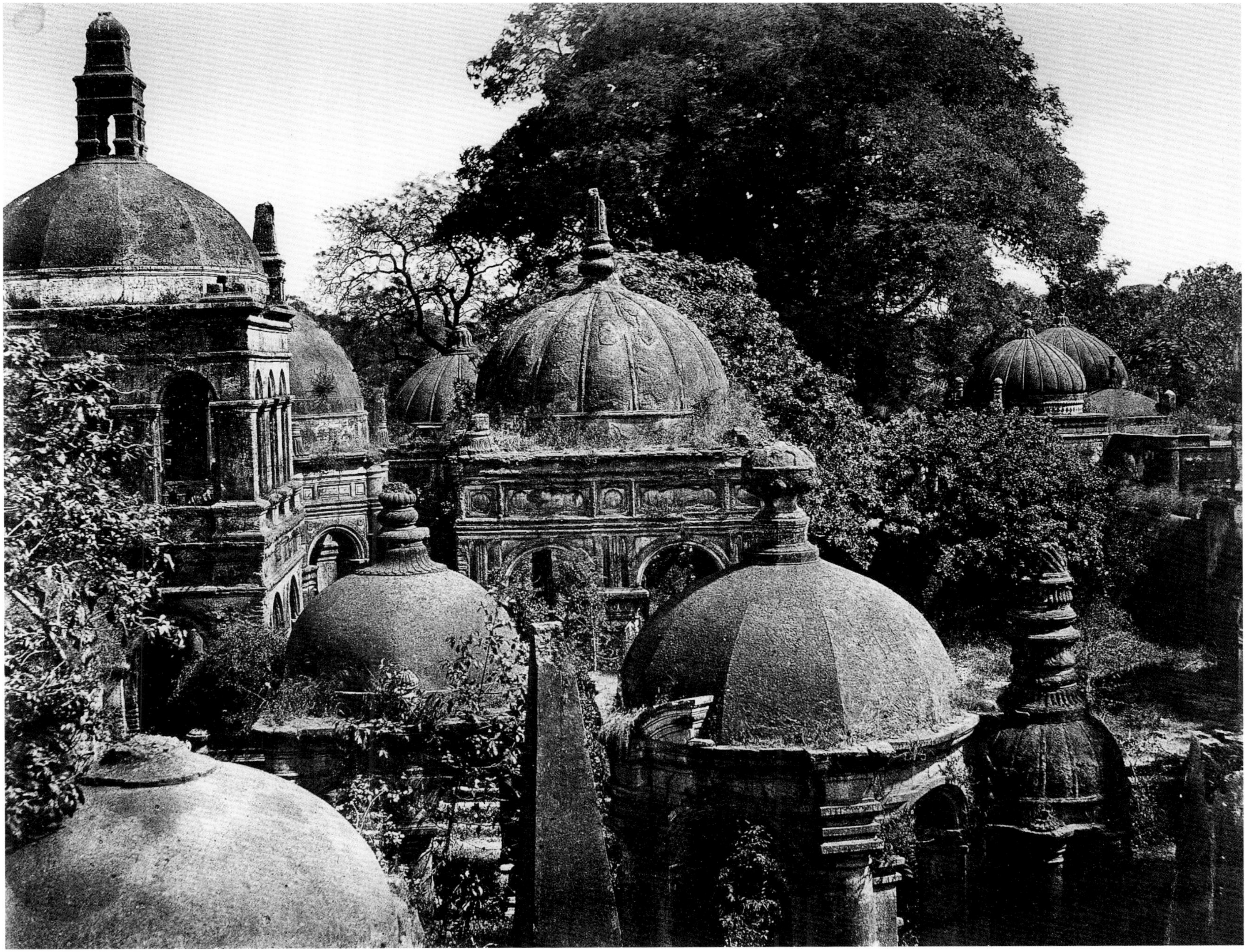

A PASSION FOR DOCUMENTATION: ETHNOGRAPHY

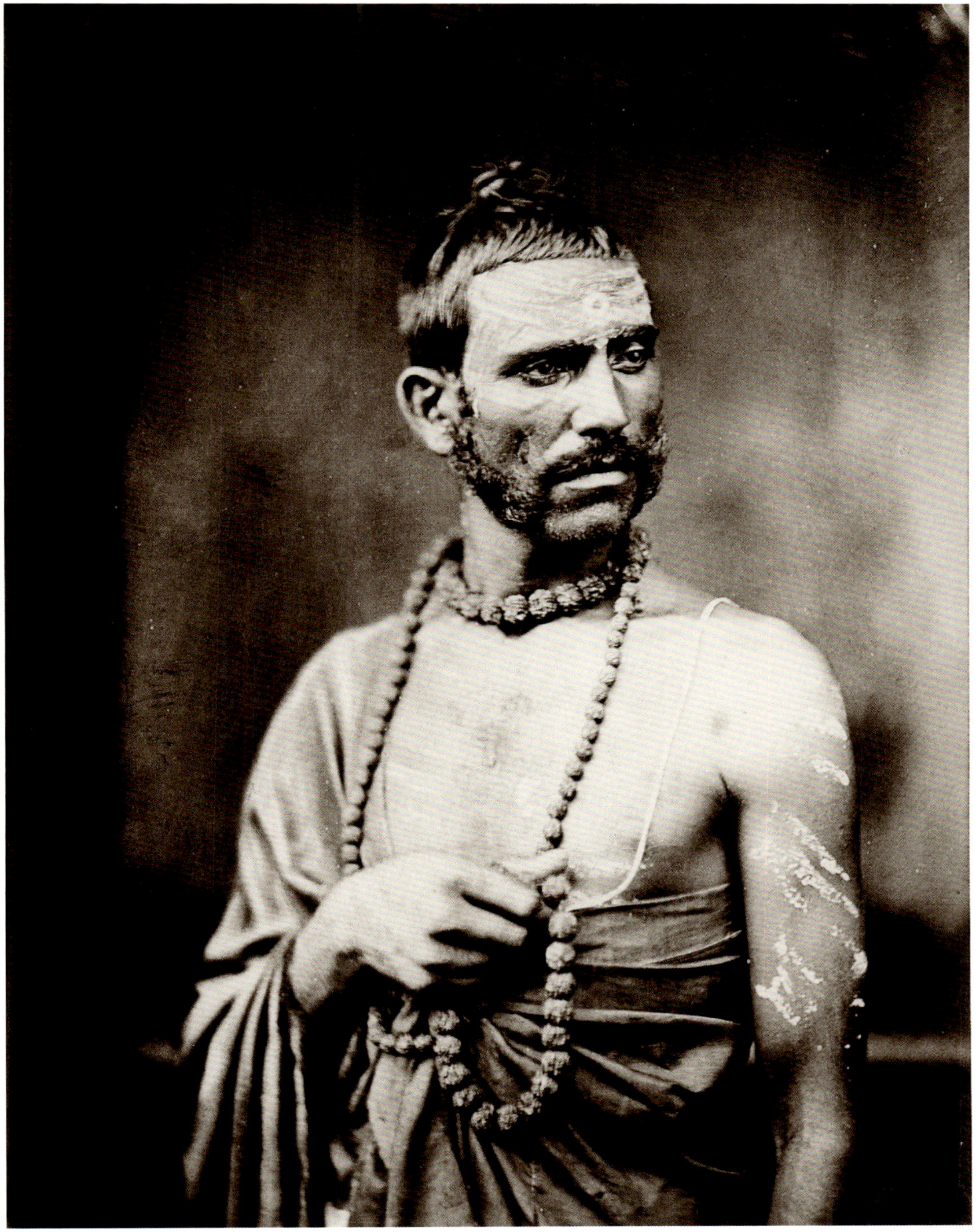

30 *Kanaujiya Brahmin, Eastern Bengal*

Unknown photographer

1860s, albumen print, 23.5 x 18.5

The British Library, Oriental & India Office Collection photo 124 (18)

31 *Manipuri Polo Player, Eastern Bengal*

Unknown photographer

1860s, albumen print, 23.5 x 18.5
The British Library, Oriental & India Office Collection photo 124 (5)

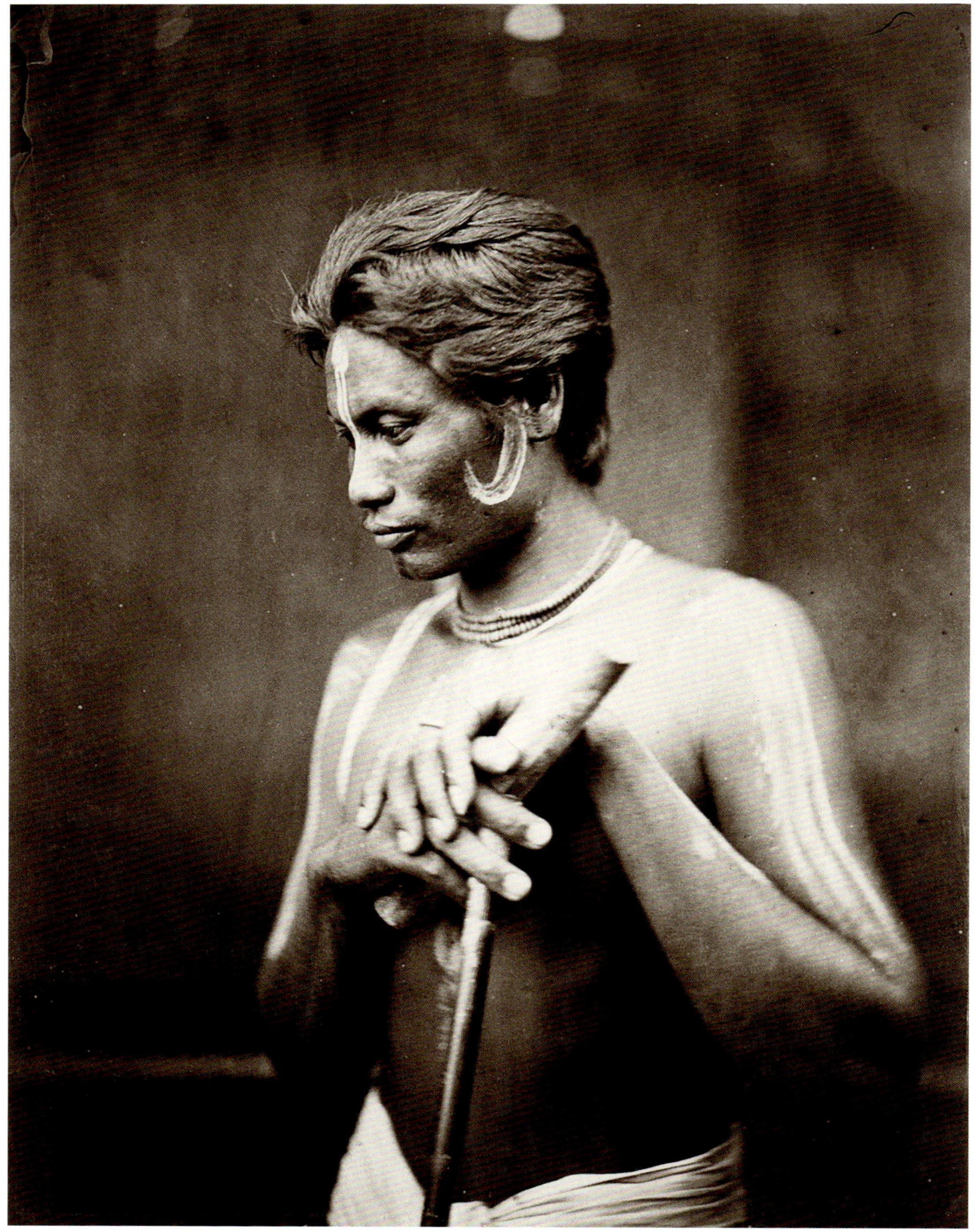

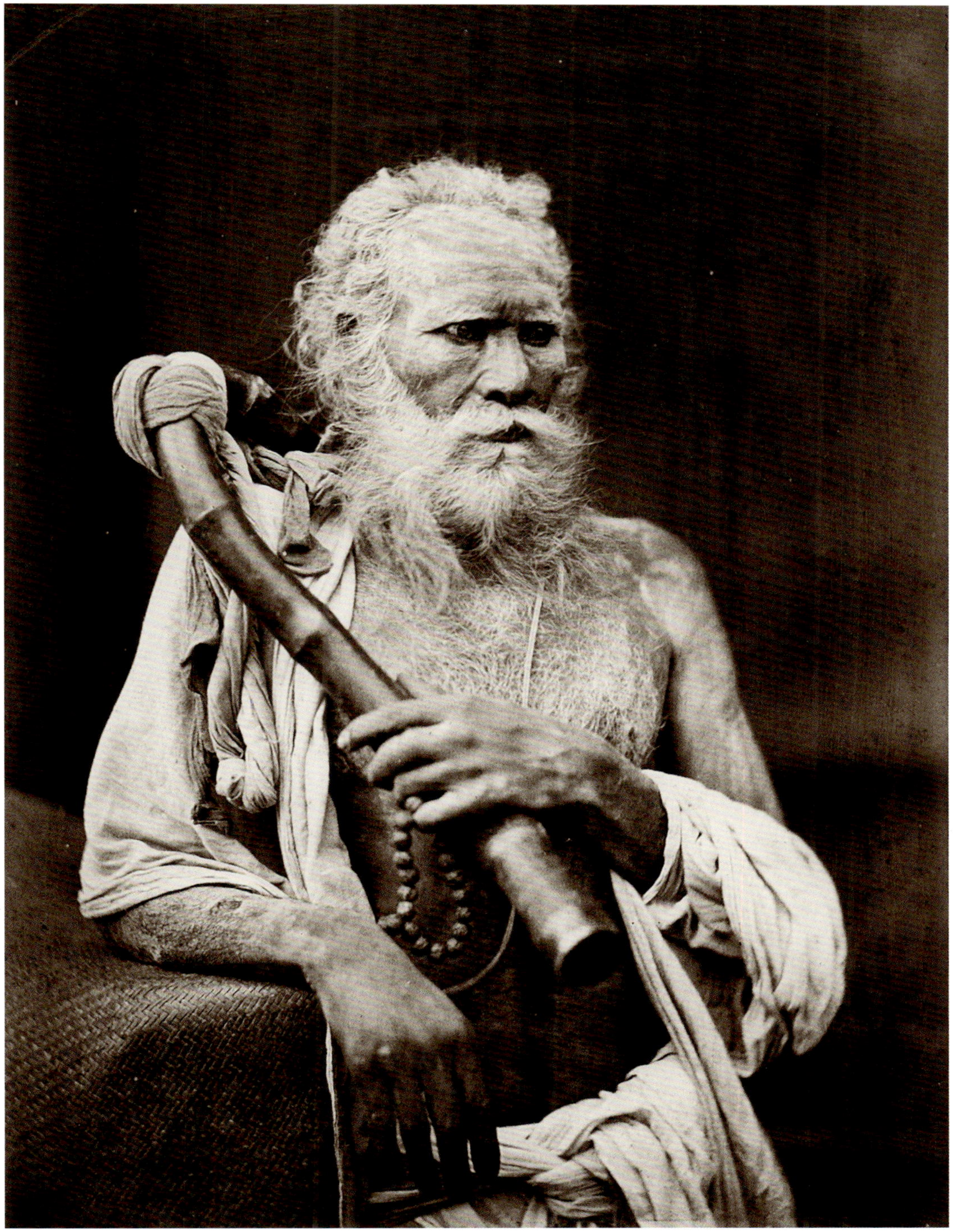

32 *Sadhu Faqir, Eastern Bengal*

Unknown photographer

1860s, albumen print, 22.5 x 17.2
The British Library, Oriental & India Office Collection photo 124 (2)

33 *Portrait of a Young Woman, Eastern Bengal*

Unknown photographer

1860s, albumen print, 22.4 x 18.5
The British Library, Oriental & India Office Collection photo 124 (33)

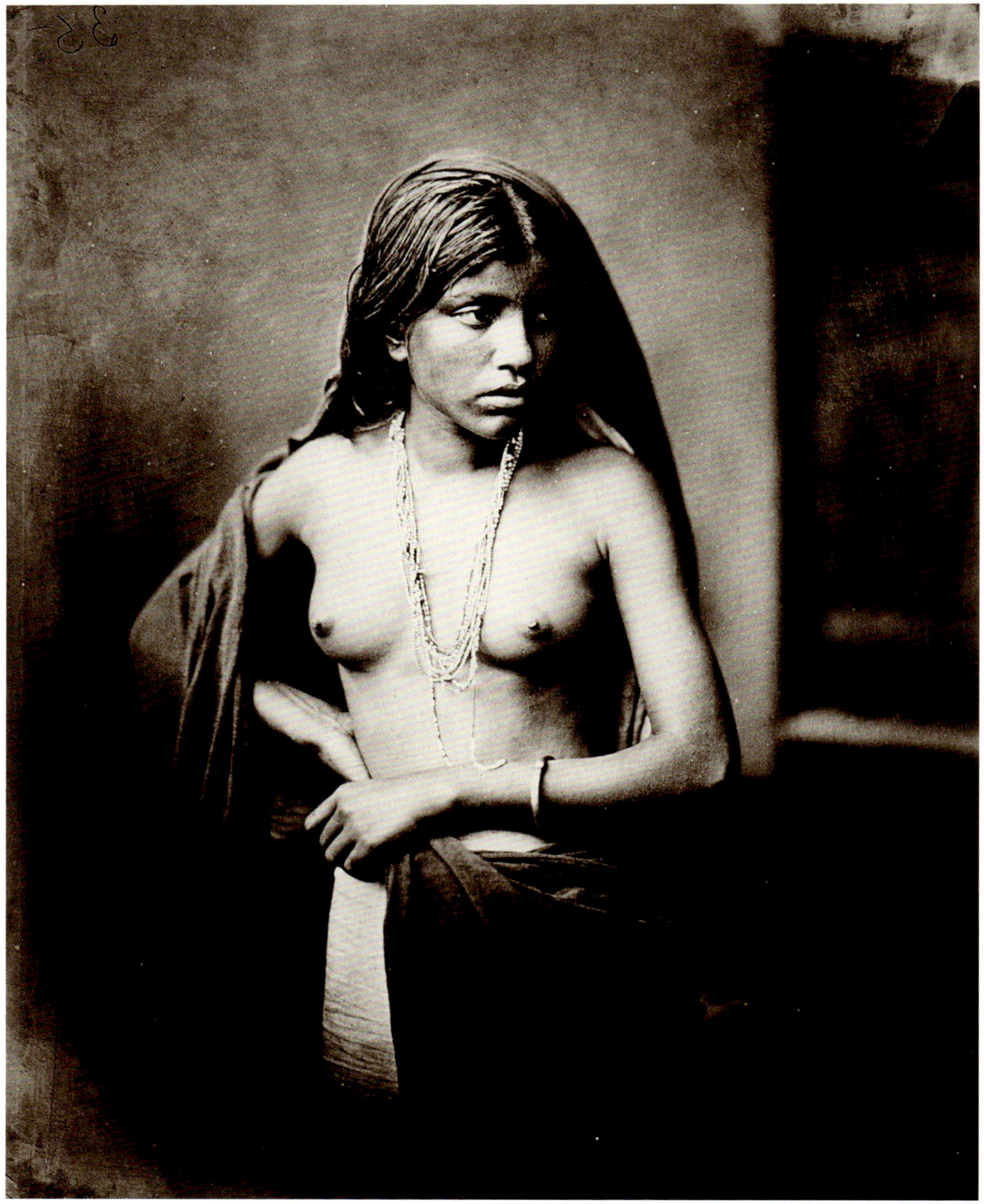

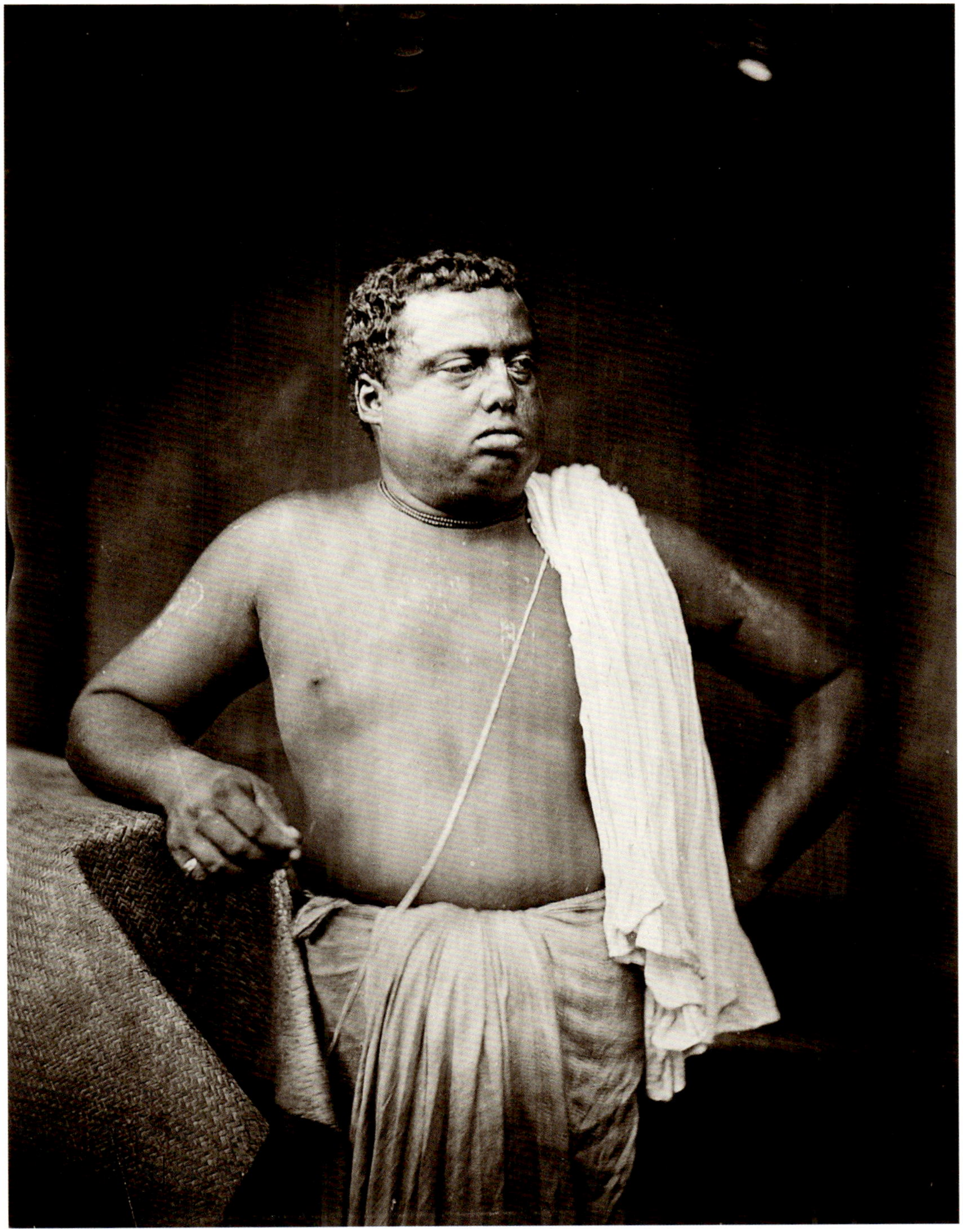

34 *Portrait of a Man, Eastern Bengal*

Unknown photographer

1860s, albumen print, 24.2 x 19

The British Library, Oriental & India Office Collection photo 124 (15)

35 *Bajunia Dom, Eastern Bengal*

Unknown photographer

1860s, albumen print, 23.8 x 18.6
The British Library, Oriental & India Office
Collection photo 124 (23)

36 *Members of the Naga Tribe*

Unknown photographer

1860s, albumen print, 20.6 x 26.7
Howard and Jane Ricketts Collection

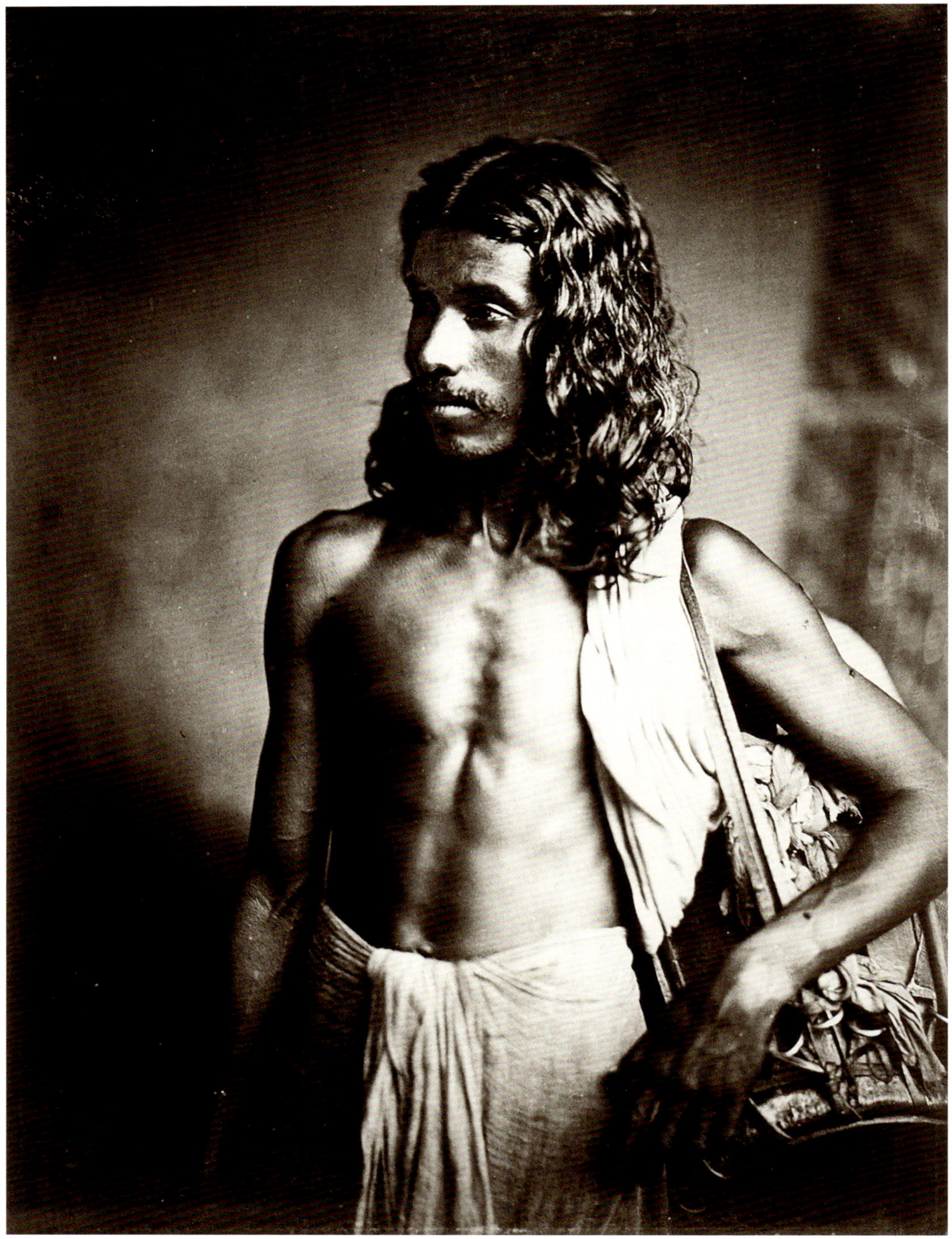

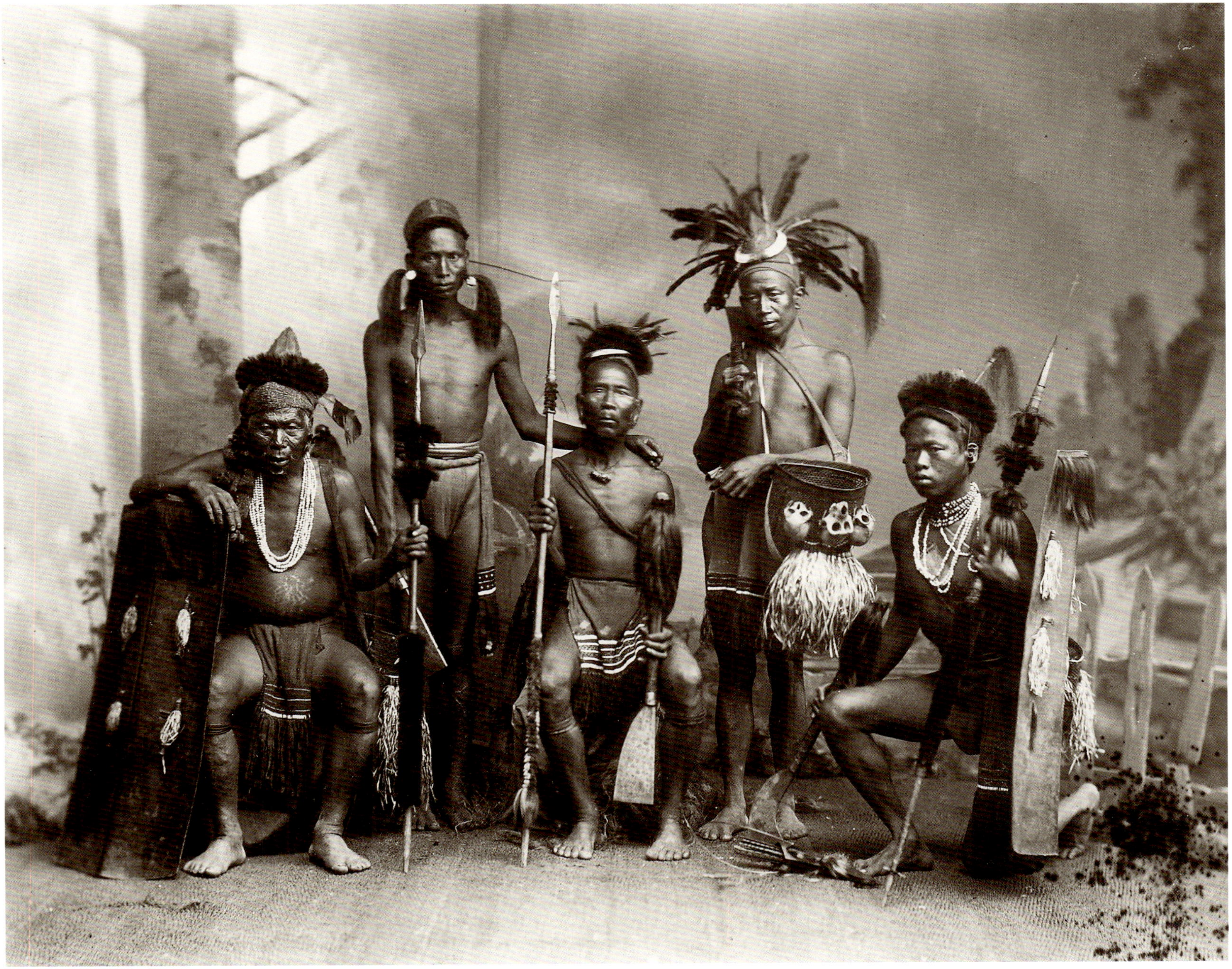

37 *Lepcha Woman*

Benjamin Simpson

ca. 1862, albumen print, 19.1 x 13.9
Howard and Jane Ricketts Collection

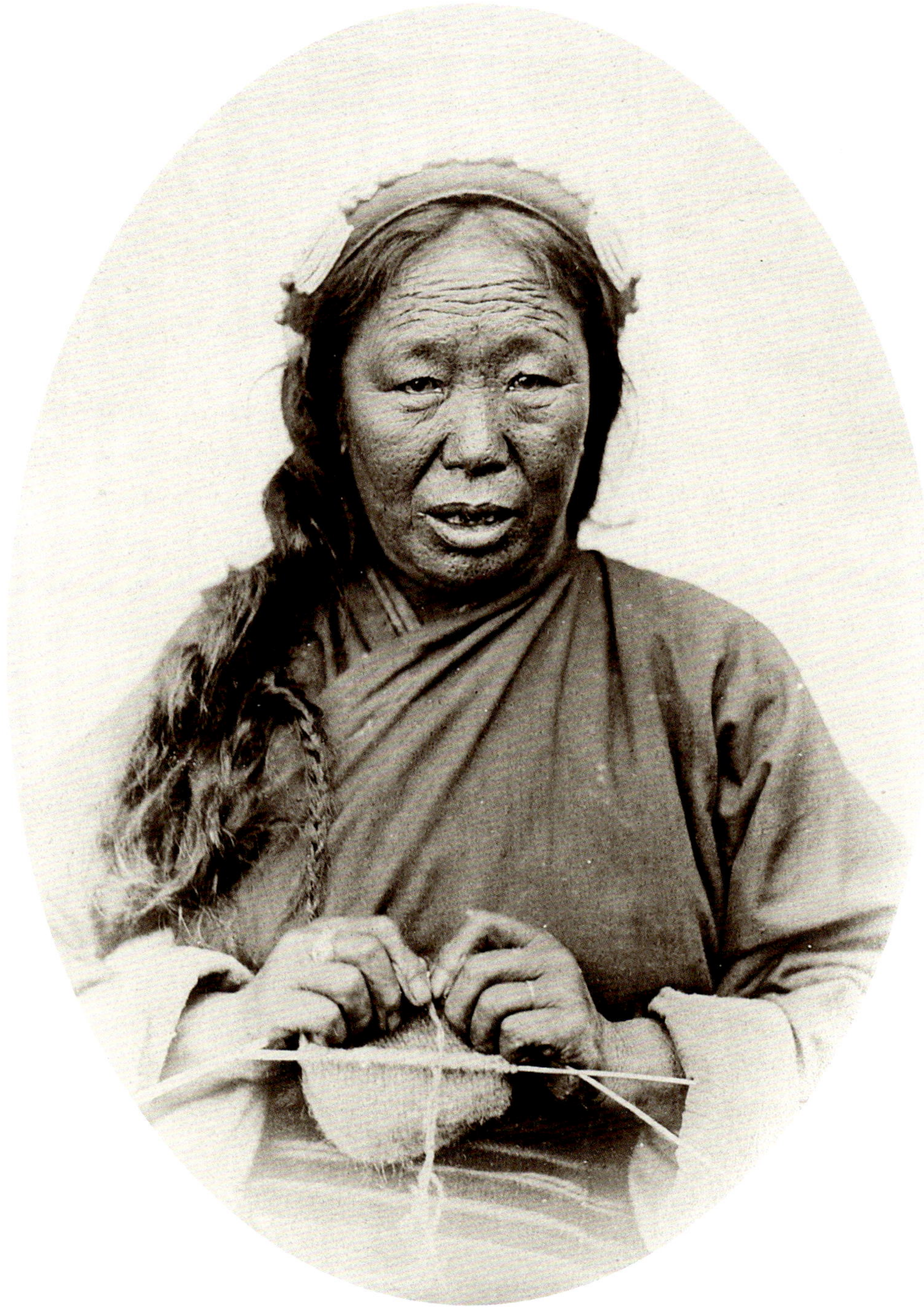

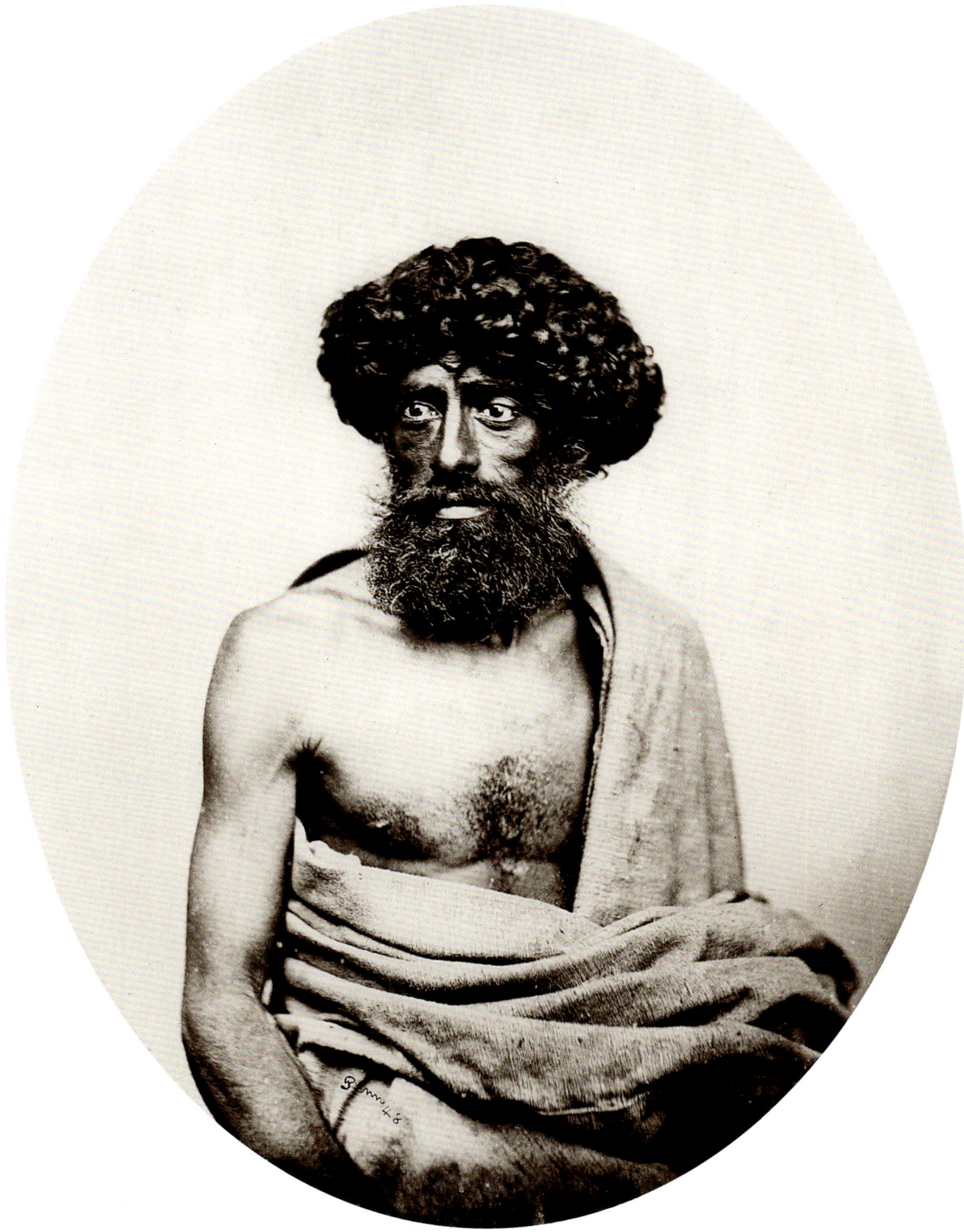

38 *Toda Male*

Albert Thomas Watson Penn

late 1870s, albumen print, 25.5 x 20.3
Howard and Jane Ricketts Collection

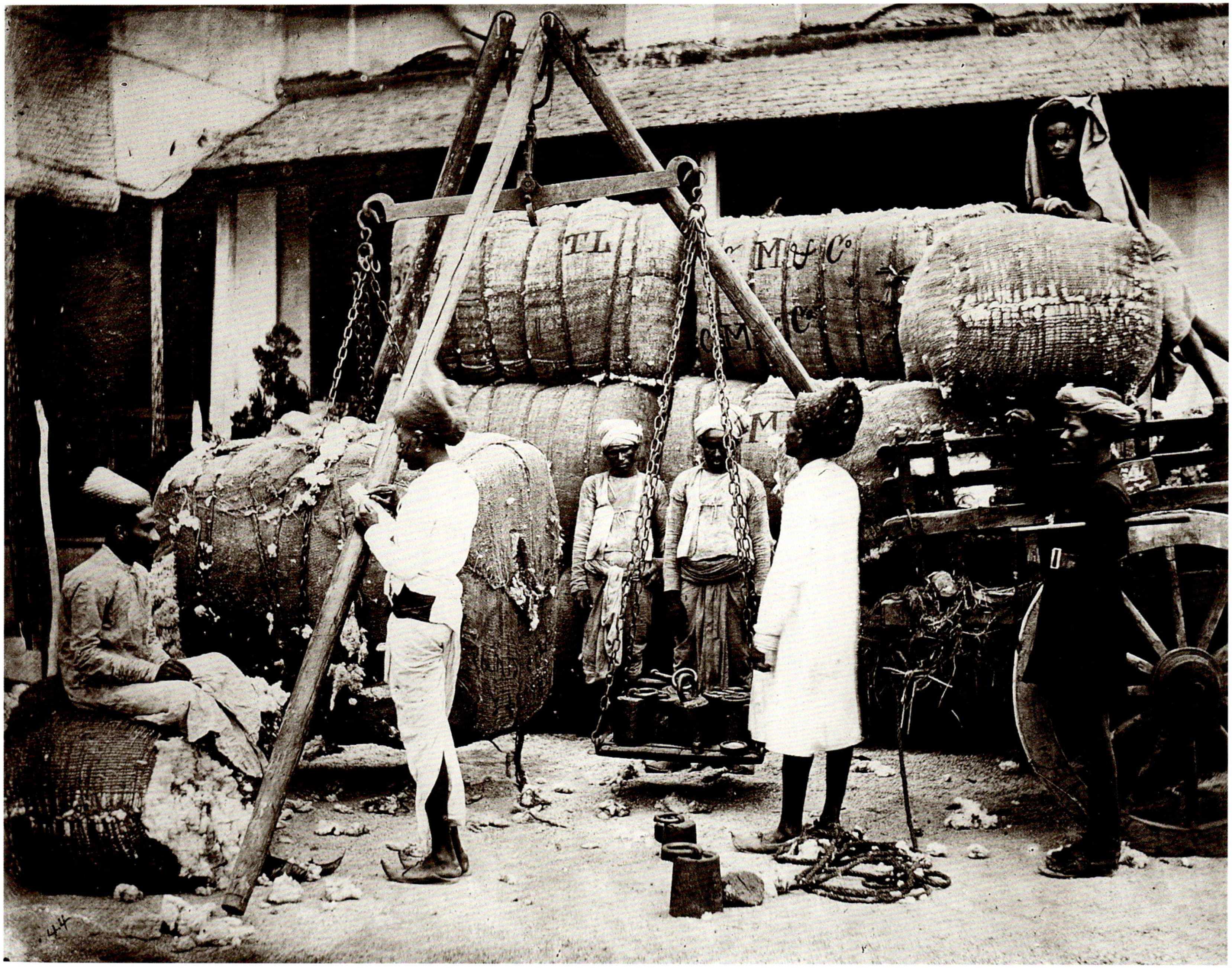
TL
M&Co

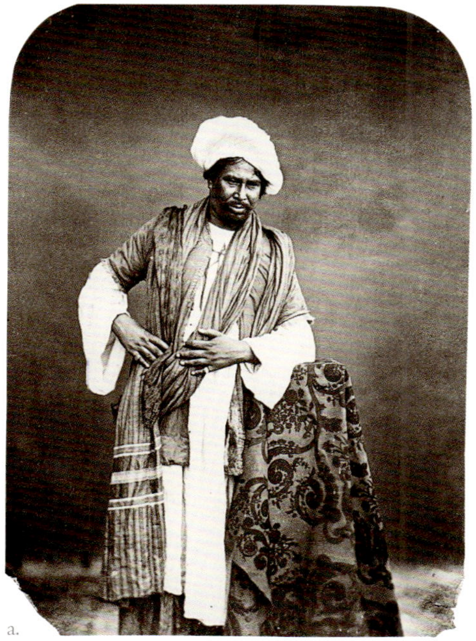

a.

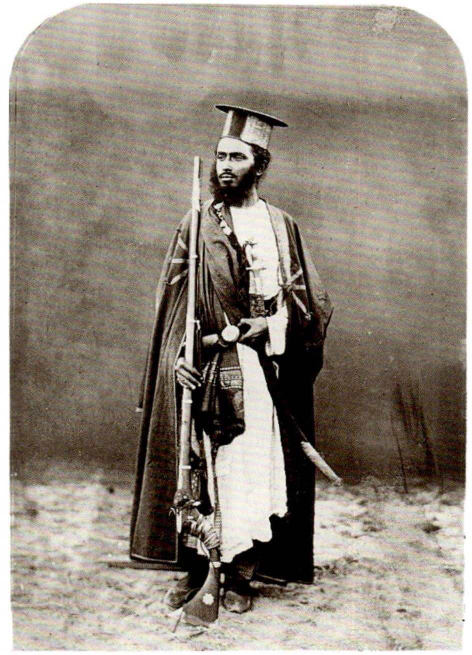

b.

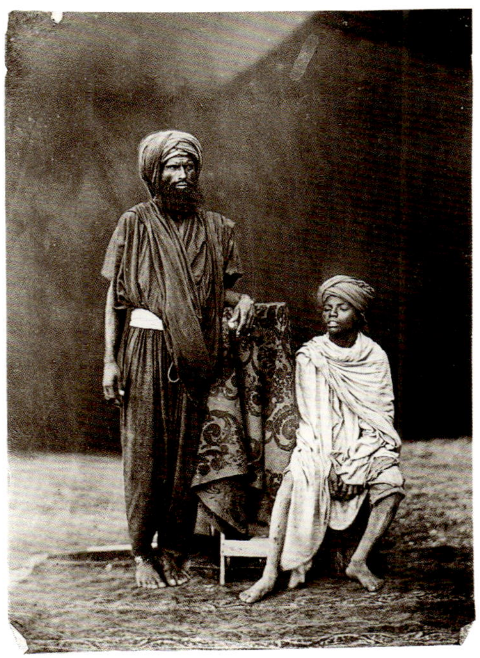

c.

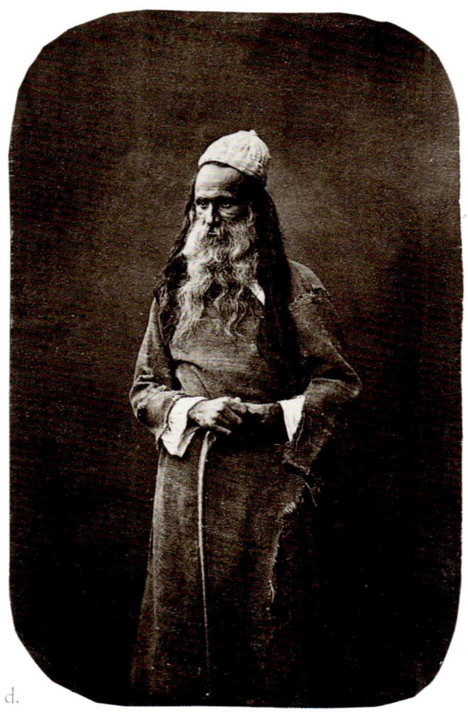

d.

39 *Weighing Cotton*

Johnson & Henderson

ca. 1860, albumen print, 19.8 x 25.1

Howard and Jane Ricketts Collection

40 *People from Sindh*

Henry Charles Baskerville Tanner

1861–62

a. Portrait of a Sindhi Man

albumen print, 18.2 x 13.3

The British Library, Oriental & India Office Collection photo 143 (3)

b. Portrait of Sirdar Khan, Chief of the Numrias, Sindh

albumen print, 19.2 x 13.5

The British Library, Oriental & India Office Collection photo 143 (4)

c. Portrait of a Sindhi Man and Boy

albumen print, 18.2 x 13.5

The British Library, Oriental & India Office Collection photo 143 (8)

d. Portrait of a Chandia from Baluchistan

albumen print, 16.5 x 11

The British Library, Oriental & India Office Collection photo 143 (2)

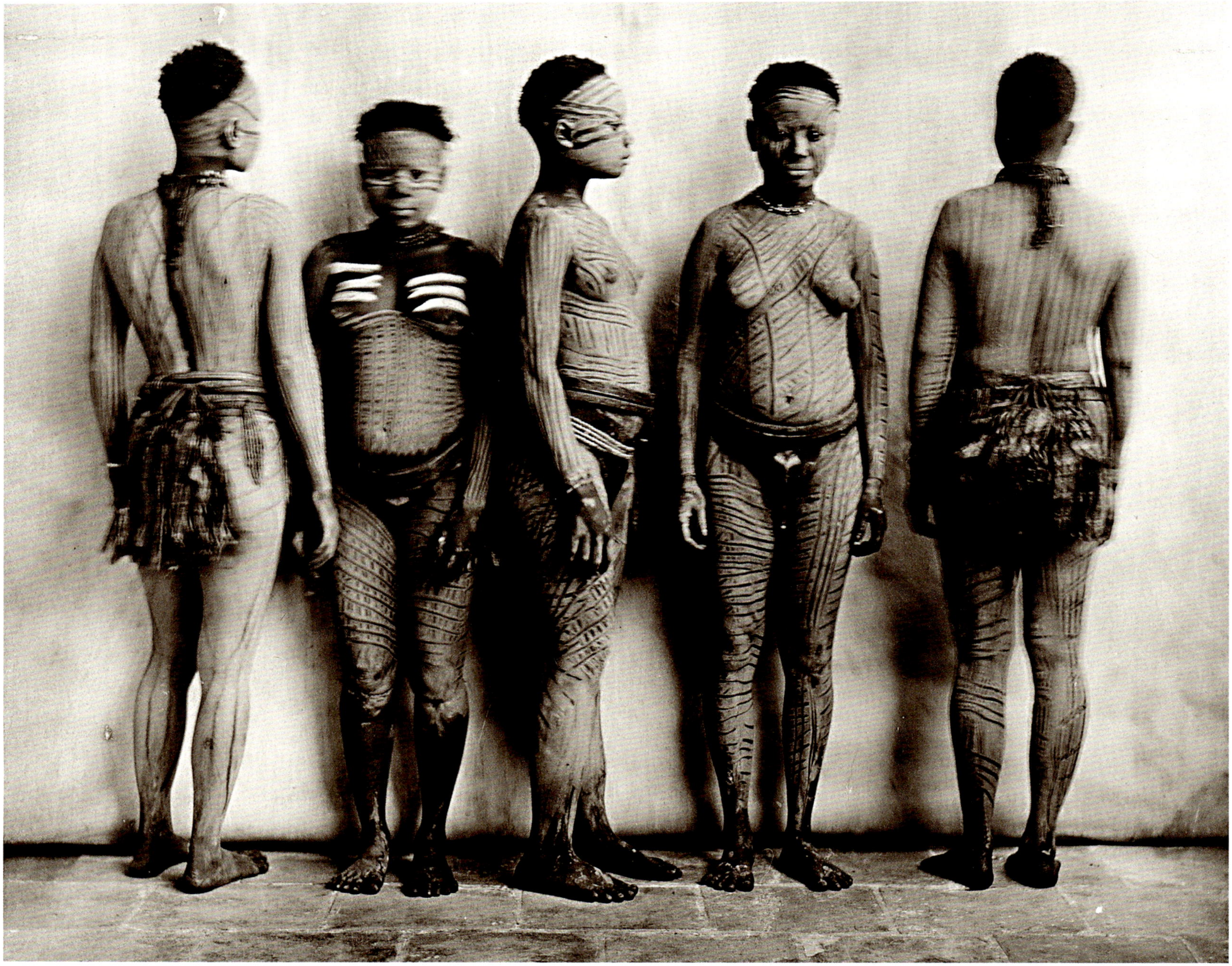

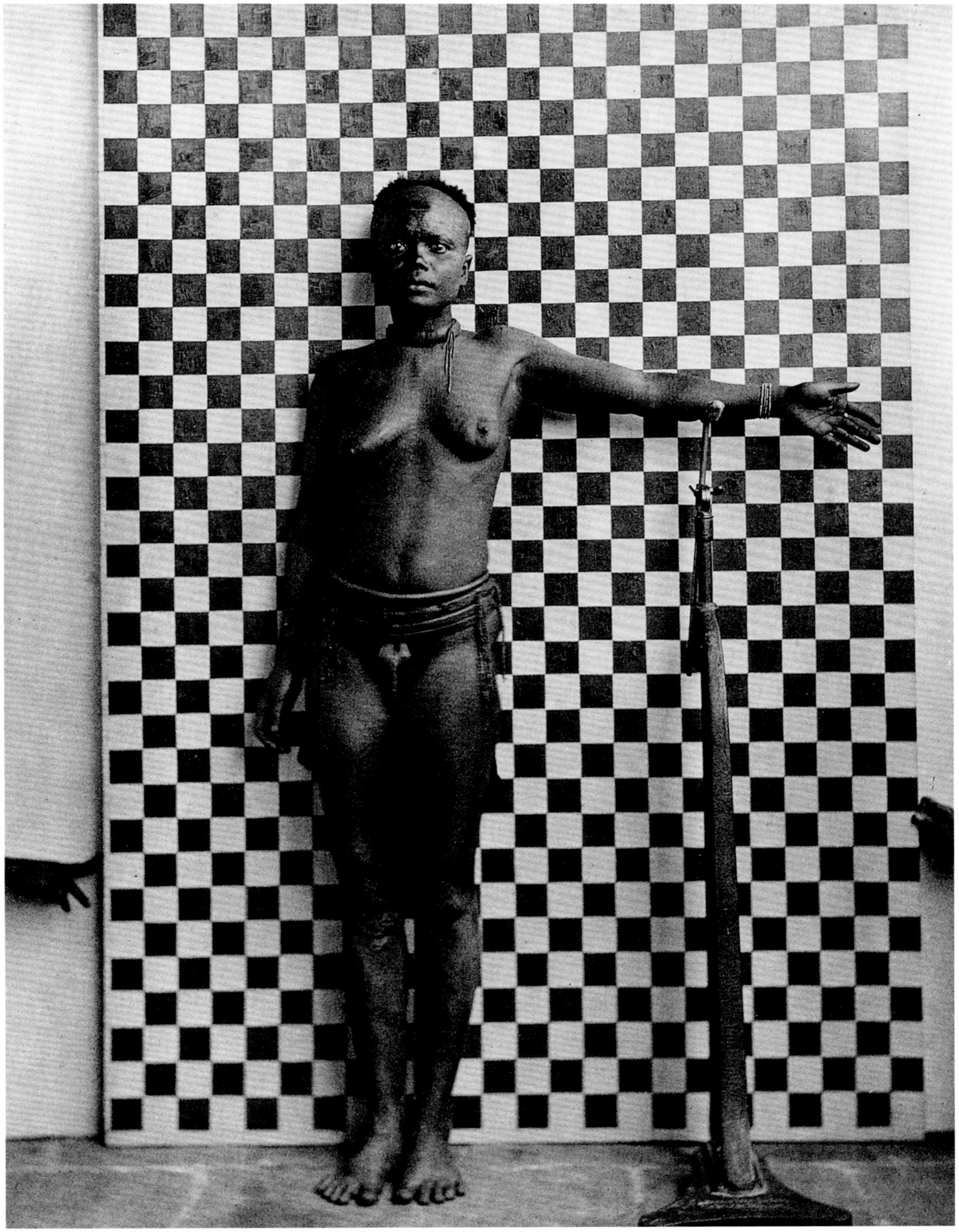

41 *A Group of Andamanese Women Painted with Og*

Maurice Vidal Portman

ca. 1893, platinum print, 28.4 x 35.2
The British Library, Oriental & India Office Collection photo 188/7 (31)

42 *Keliwa Woman of Ta-Keda Tribe, Age about 45 Years*

Maurice Vidal Portman

ca. 1893, platinum print, 34.4 x 26.8
The British Library, Oriental & India Office Collection photo 188/11 (20)

43 *Making the Pig Arrow, Andaman Islands*

Maurice Vidal Portman

ca. 1893, platinum print, 34.1 x 27
The British Library, Oriental & India Office Collection photo 188/7 (32)

44 *A Group of Andamanese Men Painted with Og and Tala-og*

Maurice Vidal Portman

ca. 1893, platinum print, 28.4 x 35.3
The British Library, Oriental & India Office Collection photo 188/7 (30)

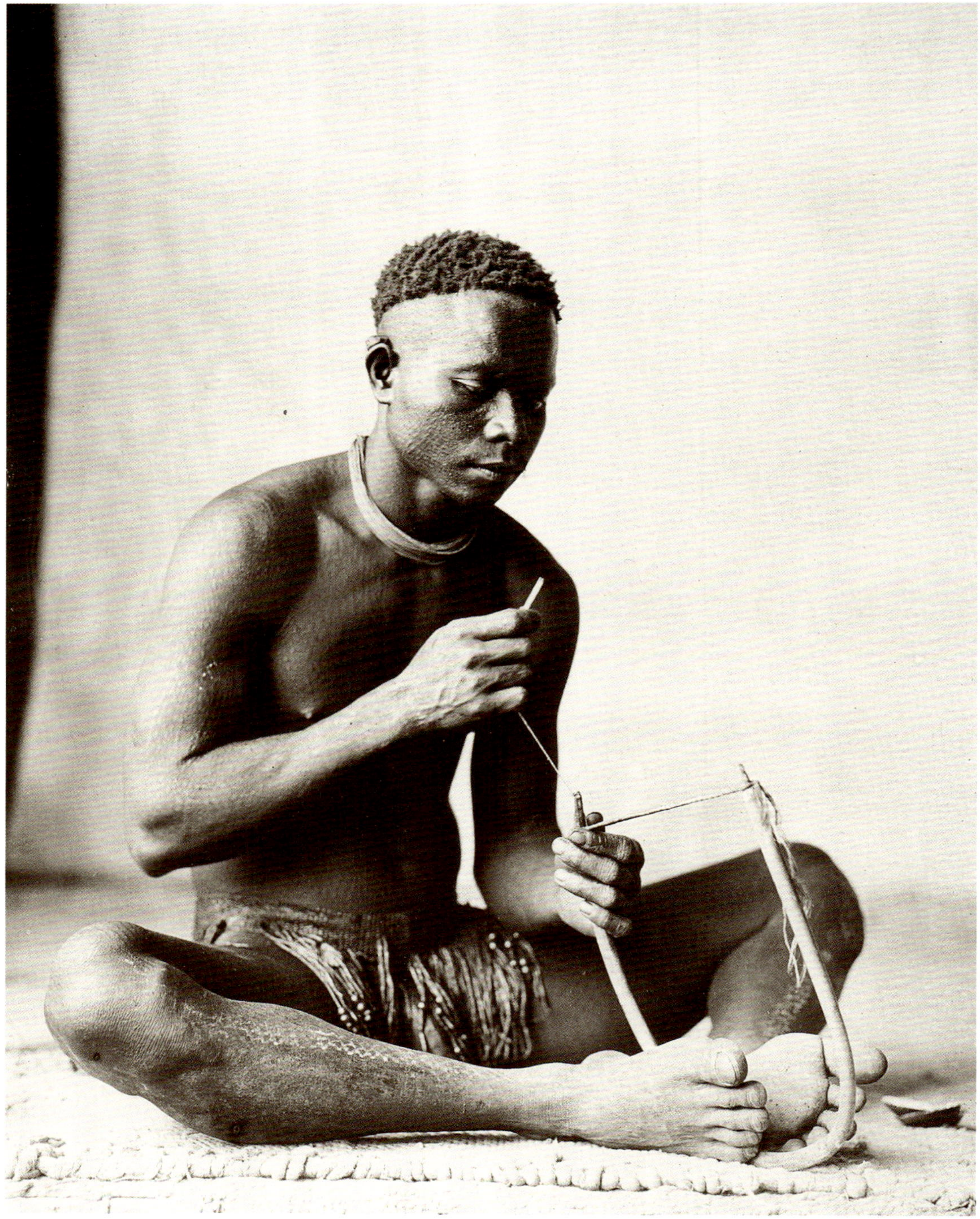

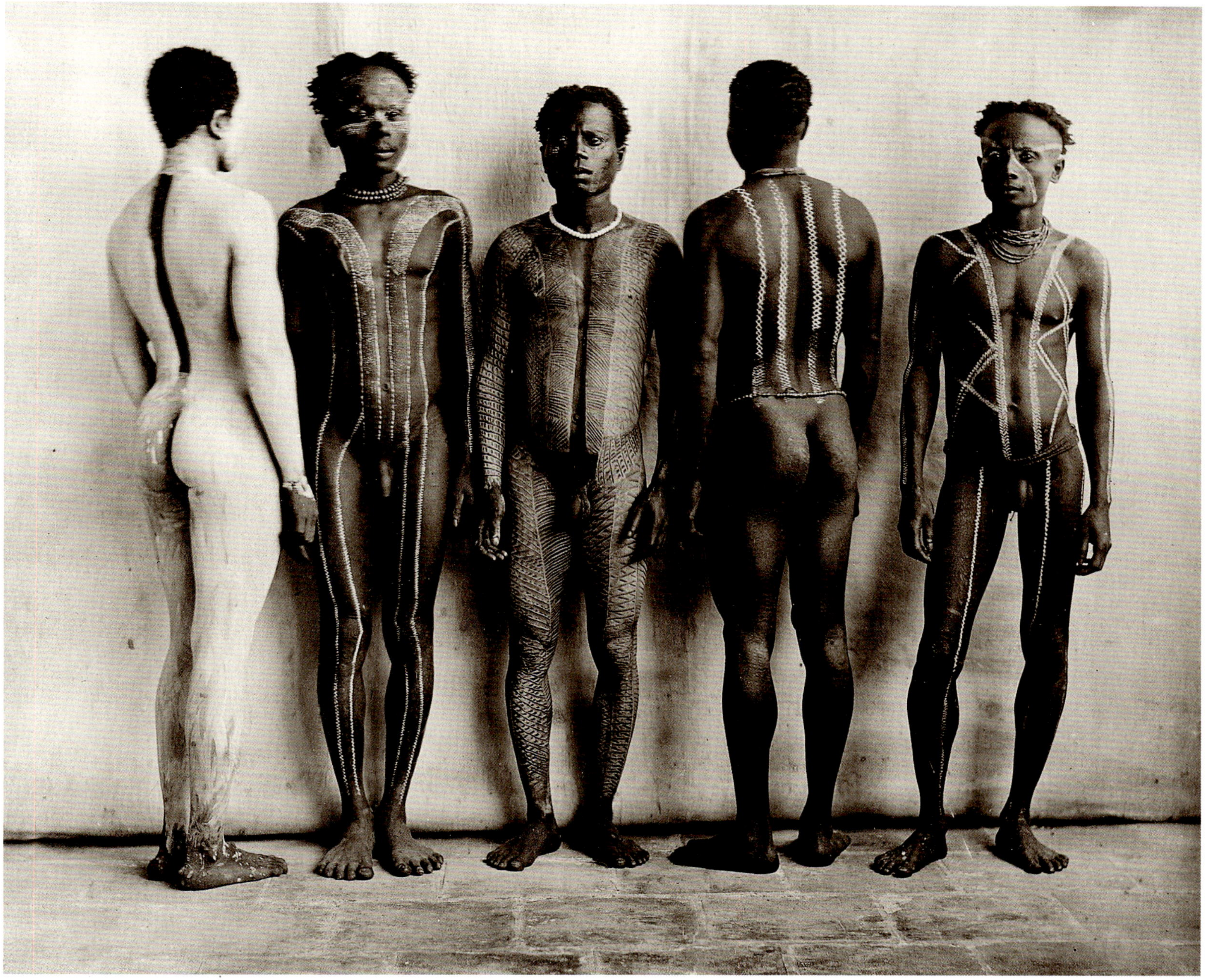

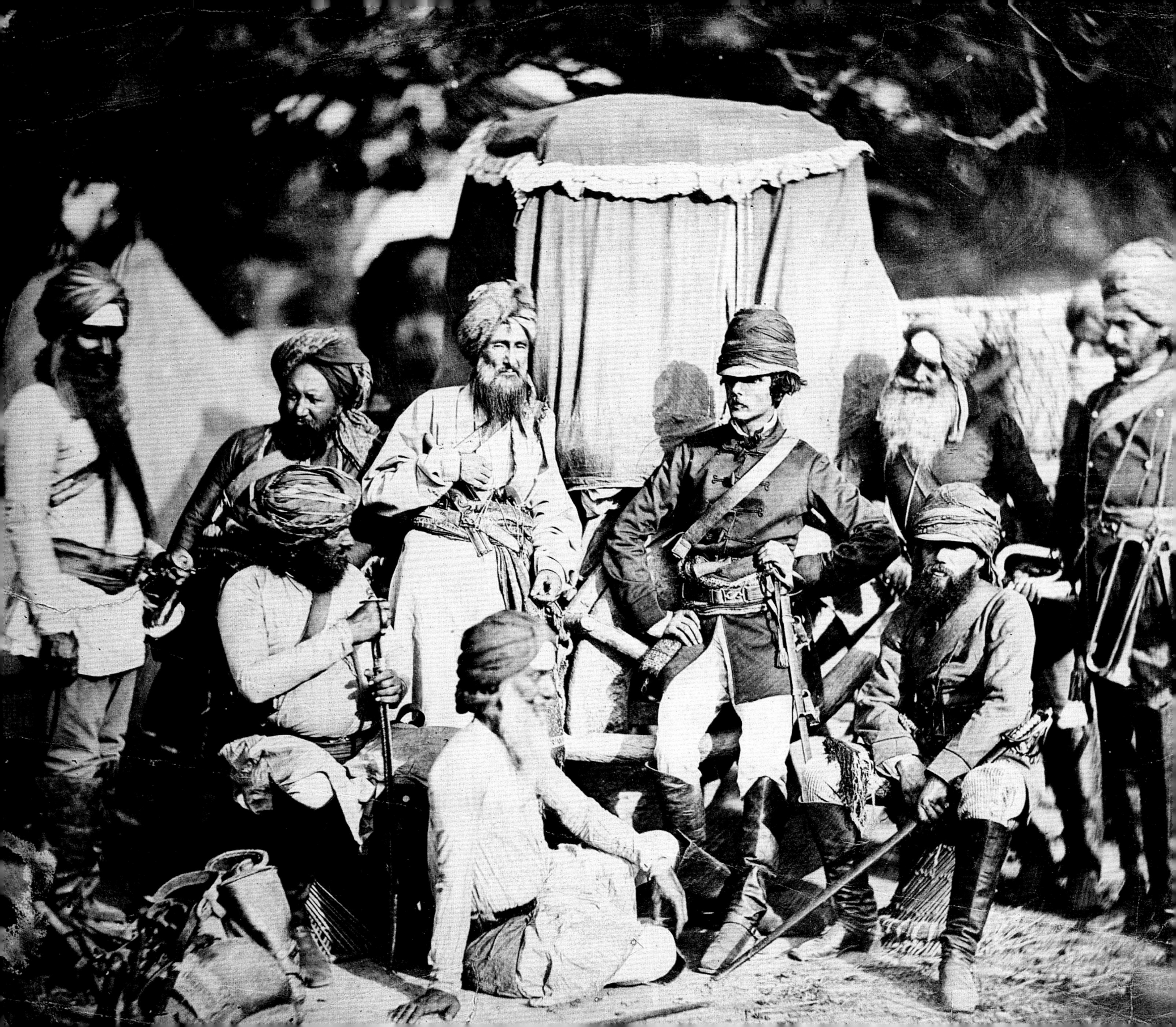

David Harris

Topography and Memory: Felice Beato's Photographs of India, 1858–1859

In the 1858 annual exhibition of the Photographic Society of London, twenty-six of Felice Beato's photographs of the city of Lucknow were exhibited anonymously.[1] A reviewer in the *Journal of the Photographic Society of London* provided the context for his brief listing of the views with the following remarks:

> Besides portraits of a phalanx of Indian heroes, Lord Clyde [Sir Colin Campbell], [Robert] Napier, [Colonel F. M.] Birch, [William Wilberforce Harris] Greathed, and many others known to fame, the views of public buildings and localities in the city connected for ever with the chivalry of [Sir Henry] Havelock, and the successes of [Sir James] Outram and Clyde, are most striking and memorable. . . . These admirable views give us, in fact, the pictorial romance of this terrible war. They are necessary, as our contemporaries say, to an understanding of the war now, and will be indispensable to its future historians.[2]

The reviewer's use of "chivalry" to typify the behavior of one of the participants and his coupling of "romance" and "war" to describe the struggle then unfolding two continents away in northern India may now strike readers as surprising, but such language reveals the depth and tone of contemporaneous feeling. From an impassioned British perspective, this conflict, which the English variously characterized as a "mutiny," a "revolt," or a "rebellion," could be imagined as a medieval "romance" of epic proportions, where geographical, rather than temporal, distance lent an exoticism to the events. The 16 July 1857 massacre of two hundred European and Anglo-Indian women and children after their surrender following the siege of Kanpur seemed an event of startling betrayal and cruelty. The tenacious survival of the British held captive within the narrow confines of the Residency compound in Lucknow (a complex of buildings comprising the official home of the resident, the British representative to the local court, as well as a number of domestic, civil, and religious structures) through eighty-seven days was marked by heroic and stoic endurance, and their eventual liberation by Sir Colin Campbell in late November 1857 became one of dramatic and inspiring military daring. Not only were such events of consuming interest in themselves, but they were animated by equally vivid personalities and marked by grand gestures—the unflinching resolve of the Scotsman, Campbell, or the brutal and misguided sense of justice of William Hodson, who murdered the two sons of Bahadur Shah II, the king of Delhi, following their surrender to him.[3]

From early July 1857, when initial reports of the May 10 insurrection of native soldiers in Meerut first reached England, the British public was kept abreast of the events through continuing coverage in daily newspapers and in weekly and monthly periodicals such as the *The Times* (London), *The Illustrated London News, Blackwood's Magazine,* and beginning in 1857, by illustrated memoirs and histories written by participants in the recent events.[4] With such national interest and concern over the outcome of "this terrible war," it is hardly surprising that Beato's 1858 photographs of the participants and of Lucknow itself, where many of the most celebrated events had occurred, would find an immediate and receptive audience.[5] Here were seemingly objective views, without any of the fictional embellishment or the unavoidable inaccuracies of engravings (derived from drawings) that frequently accompanied the reports and memoirs.

The impact of these photographs as authoritative forms of reportage rich in topographical information would have initially overwhelmed and obscured other, less immediately evident, purposes that the images were created to serve. It is only in hindsight, in light of later interpretations of this conflict and of subsequent political uses of war photography, that we are able to acknowledge and understand the extent to which Beato's photographs formed an integral component of nineteenth-century British colonial ideology. The historical meaning of Beato's images now lies in reconciling these two alternative readings—between seeing his photographs as suppliers of factual information and accepting them as forms of thinly veiled propaganda.

Page 118: Detail, no. 59. *Hodson's Horse,* Felice Beato

Surprisingly little is still known about Beato (1820s?–1907?) beyond what can be inferred from his surviving photographs and gleaned from occasional references in the memoirs of his contemporaries.[6] Even the date and place of his birth and death remain unknown. He is thought to have been born either in Venice or within the Venetian territory, possibly on the island of Corfu, in the 1820s or 1830s. Together with his brother Antonio (1820s?–1905),[7] he acquired his knowledge of the practice of photography in the 1850s from their brother-in-law, the Scotland-born photographer James Robertson (ca. 1813–1888).[8] Robertson specialized in topographical photography of Constantinople and Greece, and with Beato's help, photographed the Crimean War from June 1855 through June 1856. Beato initially served as Robertson's assistant until early in 1857, when they formed a brief commercial partnership, evidenced by their joint credits on negatives. This partnership appears to have dissolved early in 1858, when Beato departed for India.

Beato's formative years with Robertson allowed him an opportunity to perfect his photographic technique—both his preference for using albumen (rather than the commonly used collodion) in making negatives and his photographing of his finished prints to make additional negatives for printing purposes can be traced to Robertson's own practice.[9] Over this period, he absorbed Robertson's skill in producing topographical photographs and constructing multipart panoramas. Beato's experiences in the Crimea had a decisive influence on his subsequent career. He developed a taste and talent for war photography, learning how to work under the extreme and unpredictable conditions encountered during campaigns and understanding the particular requirements of the British military. He first met a number of British officers in the Crimea, such as Garnet J. Wolseley and Henry Hope Crealock among others, whose careers also took them to India in 1857–59, and on to China in 1860.[10]

Beato arrived in Calcutta on 13 February 1858 and remained in India for slightly more than two years. Based upon scattered references in local newspapers and later published diaries and memoirs, his movements can still only be imperfectly traced.[11] Soon after his arrival, he attended the meeting of the Bengal Photographic Society on 17 February 1858, at which he described his use of the "dry albumen process" for making negatives.[12] In early March, he was in Kanpur, where he photographed the ruins of the barracks of Wheeler's Entrenchment[13] (no. 45), and in late March and early April he is documented as having been in Lucknow.[14] This evidence suggests that, at this time, he was following in the wake of the British forces under Campbell, and it seems probable that Beato made most, if not all, of the more than sixty photographs of Lucknow shortly after March 21 when the city was once again secured by the British (nos. 49–58). His brother Antonio arrived in Calcutta on June 30, and operated a studio at 37 Cossitollah until his return to Luxor, Egypt, where he remained until his death, in 1905. On 27 August 1858, Felice Beato advertised his photographs of Lucknow at the Calcutta studio. In October he was once again in Kanpur. In early February 1859, his travels took him to Meerut and back to Calcutta in late March, where he attended another meeting of the photographic society. He subsequently traveled to Agra in mid-April, Simla in early May, and Lahore in October. In late February 1860, he sailed for Hong Kong, where he joined the British contingent of the Anglo-French North China expedition.[15]

As a commercial photographer, Beato was entirely dependent upon the marketability of his images and clearly photographed what he felt to be topical and salable. The British military constituted his principal market, with their interests and needs largely determining his choice and treatment of subjects. In 1858–59, Beato made more than 130 topographical and architectural photographs and concentrated upon the three sites where British military and the public's interest were most sharply focused. He took approximately sixty photographs in Delhi, four at Kanpur, and another sixty photographs in Lucknow. Beato also photographed three additional sites of less military importance but nevertheless of considerable architectural and archaeological value. He photographed the bathing ghats in Benares (now Varanasi) and the Dhamekh Stupa at Sarnath (approximately ten views); the Taj Mahal and the Fort at Agra, as well as Akbar's Tomb at Sikandra (twenty-four views); and the Golden Temple (Hari Mandir) in Amritsar in the plains of the Punjab (seventeen photographs).[16]

Beato worked in the aftermath of sieges and campaigns, long after the 1857 siege and assault upon Delhi and the siege and massacres at Kanpur, but immediately after the final reoccupation of Lucknow in March 1858. As a result, he was able to plan and organize his coverage in advance and produce coherent, related groups of topographical views for his prospective customers. In effect, Beato could tailor his interpretation to the concerns of the British and mirror their perspective as victors. Given the circumstances, it seems likely that he would have not only sought the advice of British officers, who were familiar with the specific topography and the campaigns, but would also have carried out his work with their participation. Judging from the state of the vegetation and the condition of the architecture, Beato appears to have completed his coverage of most of the sites at one time.[17]

Of the sixty photographs that Beato made in Delhi, thirty-nine, including two multipart panoramas, were concerned with the siege and the September 1857 assault on the city;[18] while the remaining images were devoted to the archaeological remains at Qutb, south of the city. In assembling photographs to represent the three-month siege of Delhi (8 June to 13 September, 1857), Beato concentrated upon the British position along the ridge to the northwest of the city, of which he made twelve views. In addition, he produced a three-part panorama from "Hindoo Rao's house," the key British battery, which overlooked and surveyed the city.

The British assault of Delhi was directed at the water bastion and the Kashmir Gate, two places along the city's northern sixteen-foot-high masonry wall. In advance of the assault, they relentlessly shelled these portions of the wall over several days, as well as the adjacent Mori bastion, whose guns protected this section of the wall. On the morning of 14 September they breached the walls and entered the city. In order to provide a framework for describing the assault in detail, Beato made clusters of images of these areas along the wall—two of the water bastion, four, including a two-part panorama, of the Kashmir gate (no. 46), and two-part panorama of the Mori bastion (no. 47). He also photographed Ludlow castle, the Custom House battery (no. 48), and the ruins of a former summer palace, Qudsia, where the British troops were massed immediately before the assault. In order to follow events over the subsequent six days (14–20 September), until the city was finally secured, Beato included views both within Delhi, such as the Lahore gate and the Chandni Chowk, and in the city's vicinity, notably, two views of the tomb of Emperor Humayun (reigned 1530–40; 1555–56), where William Hodson had captured the fleeing king and his two sons.

Beato sold his photographs as unmounted prints.[19] By assembling a selection of images, the purchaser could construct a personal visual record that would reflect his professional interests and mirror his experiences. Each photograph contributed precise information concerning the circumstances of the lengthy siege and carefully planned assault. The characteristics of the surrounding topography were delineated; those places where pivotal events occurred were described; and information of particular concern to the British officers and engineers, such as the composition of the city's massive walls, was included. When ordered and sequenced in albums, these photographs provided the framework around which a narrative of the events could be developed. In Beato's photographs lay the potential for distilling memories for the participants of the conflict and for evoking the places and events for their families as well as satisfying the interests and imagination of the British public.

The more than sixty photographs exclusively devoted to the military campaigns at Lucknow form the most extensive and intricate group of images that Beato made to commemorate the events of 1857–58. Three separate factors contributed to this unusually large number. Firstly, the city itself was physically larger than any of the other centers of conflict, encompassing many palaces, gardens, bazaars, and Muslim mosques along the Gumti River and having a population of about 500,000 in 1857. Secondly, a succession of events had dramatically and continuously unfolded over almost a year.[20] The mutiny of the 7th Light Cavalry on 30 May 1857, and the subsequent humiliating defeat of the British forces at Chanhat on June 30, a few miles north of the city, led to the occupation of Lucknow and the siege of the Residency compound, whither fifteen hundred British and loyal Indians had retreated for their safety. An initial but unsuccessful attempt by the British forces, under General Havelock and Sir James Outram, to relieve the beleaguered British garrison on September 25, ended with their own captivity within the compound. A second and much larger relief force, under Sir Colin Campbell, reached the Residency compound on November 17, and over the next few days successfully evacuated it, but left the city in rebel hands. In March of the following year, Campbell returned with an enormous army of 25,000 soldiers and finally subdued and reoccupied the Lucknow (March 14–21). Thirdly, as the reviewer of Beato photographs in the *Journal of the Photographic Society* intimated, the fate of Lucknow had assumed a far greater importance for the British public than its military and strategic significance alone warranted. Any attempt by Beato to describe the city and the related dramatic events with any degree of thoroughness required many more photographs than had been needed for either Kanpur or even Delhi.

Beato followed his general procedure, organizing his photographs topographically rather than strictly adhering to the chronological sequence of events. He began with two views of the Alam Bagh, a royal palace located three miles south of the city, and then moved in a northeast curve to include the Dilkusha Palace (which Campbell used as his headquarters during both campaigns) and the Martiniere School (still functioning as La Martinière Boys' School) (no. 49) immediately to the east of the city. From this point, Beato's photographs sweep in a northwest direction through Lucknow, and include such royal palaces as the Kaiser Bagh (the headquarters of the rebels) (nos. 50–52) and the Chutter Manzil (no. 53), the Residency compound (nos. 54, 55), and Asaf-ud-daula's Imambara (with its mosque, then used, respectively, as the quarters of the 53d Infantry Brigade and a field hospital) (nos. 56, 57). Beato's coverage ends with a final view of another royal place, the Musa Bagh, built four miles northwest of the city, the final stronghold of the rebels. In addition to describing the city's topography and its prominent structures, this organization also corresponds to the routes taken by each of the three successive relief forces.[21] Within this general framework, Beato was able to document each phase of Campbell's two relief campaigns, [22] a process reinforced by the incorporation of military information into the captions that accompanied each of his photographs. Beato's series of views showed the succession of captured and, in the case of the Kaiser Bagh, savagely plundered palaces, while pausing and lingering over selected sites, such as the Sikandarbagh and the Residency compound, which held particular significance for the British.

Perhaps the most notorious photograph associated with the entire struggle is Beato's image of the interior of the Secunderabad, a relatively small, walled pleasure garden on the eastern outskirts of Lucknow.[23] Beato devoted two photographs to this site, which he conceived as an architecturally and thematically linked pair. Figure 1 shows the exterior wall and formal entrance as seen from the road. Beato carefully positioned figures across the scene to form a frieze, including an Indian who, standing in profile at the right, marked the place where, on 16 November 1857, the British first breached the wall and entered the garden. The second related view (no. 58) shows the pavilion within the garden where, as Beato's own caption dispassionately recalls for the viewer, two thousand Indians were mercilessly slaughtered. It is evident from contemporaneous British military accounts of this incident that the rage that sustained this slaughter sprang from the desire to avenge and seek retribution for the earlier massacre of children and women at Kanpur.[24] In the restaging of the interior view four or five months later, Beato not only posi-

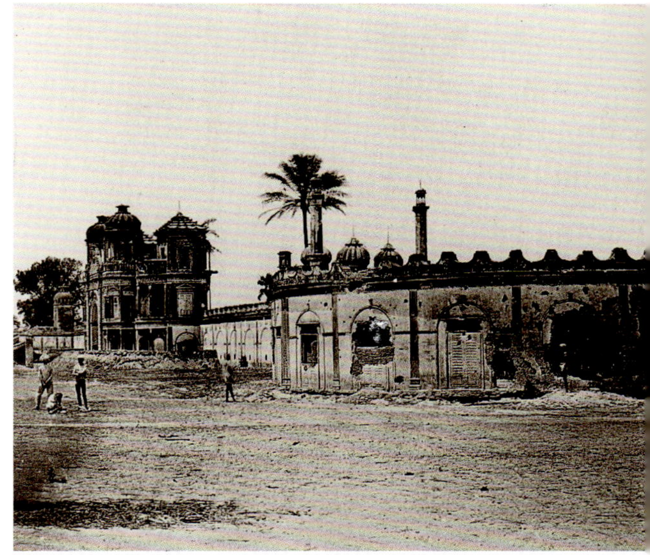

FIGURE 1 Felice Beato (1820s?–1907?), *The Secundra Bagh, Showing the Breach and Gateway. First Attack of Sir Colin Campbell in November, 1857, Lucknow,* March or April 1858 (negative exposed), albumen silver print from albumen on glass plate negative, 23.4 x 29.4. Plate 5 in the album *Lucknow—The Indian Mutiny,* Michael and Jane Wilson Collection

tioned the horse and Indians, but, even more chillingly, arranged for disinterred bones to be scattered in the foreground.

Beato devoted eight photographs, by far the largest concentration, to the Residency compound. Four of his images center upon the shell of the former three-storied Residency building itself, and Beato used one as a memorial to the British commander Sir Henry Lawrence (1806–1857), who had died early in the siege (no. 54). As he had done elsewhere, Beato deliberately positioned an Indian to mark the room in which Lawrence had been mortally wounded by cannon fire. The remaining four photographs focus upon the Baillie guard gate and show it in the context of the surrounding city (no. 55) and the adjacent buildings within the Residency complex. Perhaps because the entire Residency has been preserved in its ruined state as a permanent memorial, these photographs now have a strongly commemorative feeling.

While topographical work absorbed most of Beato's time, he also made portraits of the leading British generals, such as Campbell, Sir James Hope Grant, Outram, as well many of the British officers, including Wolseley and Crealock, and loyal Indian soldiers.[25] In his 1858 portrait of Hodson's Horse (no. 59), for instance, Clifford Henry Mecham standing in the center and Dr. Thomas Anderson seated to his right are shown surrounded by this Sikh cavalry regiment.[26] In addition to satisfying an immediate market for such portraiture among the British soldiers, some of his portraits, particularly of the more prominent participants, were directed at a wider audience. In addition to architecture and portraiture, Beato also produced copy work for the British. For instance, he supplied photographic copies of drawings and sketches, which Crealock had made of the relief of Lucknow and the 1858 campaigns in Rohilkhand, Baiswara, and north of the Ghaghara River.[27]

Later historians would fully concur with the anonymous reviewer in *The Photographic Journal* that Beato's photographs played and continue to play an essential role in our knowledge of this colonial conflict. However, they would also argue that these images have a significance beyond simply supplying topographical information or contributing to the recitation of military adventures. The historical value of such photographs rests upon their ability to reveal aspects of the inner mechanics of imperialism, and particularly in furnishing an apparently objective, but in reality a highly circumscribed and one-sided record of the contemporaneous events.

In the middle of the nineteenth century, photography was still considered a largely mechanical process, which necessarily yielded accurate and impartial *records* rather than, as we have gradually come to accept them, *interpretations,* which are created to validate and support identifiable ideological positions.[28] At the time, Beato's photographs were asked to assume a largely subsidiary and supportive role. They made the places where "significant" events had occurred vividly present to the viewer's imagination. Through a wealth of topographical information, they created a suitable framework within which a single chronological version of events as perceived from the British perspective could be developed and fully articulated. Inherent in the *Journal of the Photographic Society*'s text is the certainty that the events of 1857–59 would always be understood and remembered in the same way, and that Beato's photographs would continue to support that viewpoint and interpretation.

Historians have increasingly moved away from master narratives—those corresponding to a single reading of events—and have sought multiple interpretations, ones that allow for alternative, even contradictory, viewpoints and that more accurately reflect history's inherent complexity. In the case of British colonial history, there has been a widespread scholarly acknowledgment of the symbiotic relationship between economic demands and political priorities in determining policies and shaping attitudes. As part of this process, historians of nineteenth-century photography have become increasingly concerned with examining and clarifying photography's role within the context of colonialism and imperialism.[29] In contemplating how Beato's choice and treatment of his subject were shaped by the circumstances under which he produced and marketed his photographs, and in considering what ideological purposes his images served within the larger demands of British imperialism, his images now invite and elicit further questions. Any interpretation of them is thus an increasingly complex and open-ended process. Rather than appearing as merely documentary records, Beato's photographs reveal as much as they obscure and cloud.

Beato's photograph of the interior of the Secunderabad seems emblematic of the problems now facing viewers as they attempt to confront and contemplate these photographs (no. 58). Undeniably, this is a constructed image of military triumph and celebration. Today, the horror of such an image lies in the strangeness of its composition—in the unsettling juxtaposition of, on the one hand, the battle-scarred European-derived architecture and the picturesquely composed grouping of Indians, and, on the other, of the grisly remains in the foreground. The tranquillity of the background sits uneasily with the implied violence in the foreground, as symbolized by the scattered bones. How does one reconcile the serenity and order of this image with the graphic and repellent descriptions of four hours of continuous slaughter as recorded in British military memoirs? How does the knowledge that Beato deliberately conceived and arranged this scene—that, in an aesthetic sense, he *composed* the view—affect one's understanding of his personal pathology as a photographer of war? What does the existence of such a photograph reveal about contemporaneous public taste, and what was considered suitable as a photographic record of an event? And finally, and most poignantly, what did the Indians, who were posed so picturesquely before the shattered building, understand about the photographic process in which they formed an integral but perhaps unwitting part, and through which they had entered into history?

NOTES

1. I am grateful to Violet Hamilton, curator of the Michael Wilson Collection, and particularly to Janet Dewan for their help in carrying out the research for this essay.

2. *The Journal of the Photographic Society* 5, no. 79 (1859): 185.

3. Hodson's action remains controversial. See the entry, with further bibliographic references, in Sir Leslie Stephen and Sir Sidney Lee, eds., *The Dictionary of National Biography* (Oxford: Oxford University Press, 1965), 2: 969–70.

4. In the bibliography of P. J. O. Taylor, ed., *A Companion to the "Indian Mutiny" of 1857* (Delhi: Oxford University Press, 1996), fifteen memoirs are listed as published in 1857 and fifty-one in 1858. [The immediate trigger for the military insurrection known as the Indian Mutiny of 1857 was a rumor to the effect that the cartridges for the newly issued Enfield rifles were lubricated with beef tallow and pork fat, animal products taboo to devout Hindus and Muslims, respectively. The high-caste sepoys, or soldiers, of the Bengal Army, stationed at Meerut near Delhi, refused to handle them. On 10 May 1857, when sentences of imprisonment with hard labor were imposed on eighty-five sepoys, their fellow soldiers mutinied, murdering their British officers and the British civilians attached to the military garrison, and torching their houses. Freeing the eighty-five prisoners, they marched to Delhi, where the local sepoys joined them in taking their British officers prisoner and killing British civilians. The mutiny spread rapidly across northern India, and the towns of Lucknow and Kanpur were among those hardest hit. In particular, the unfortunate massacre of British women and children at Kanpur was seen as an outrage to Britain's honor, and the British response was to crush the rebellion at any cost. By the time the mutiny was over, thirteen months after the initial insurrection, thousands of Indians had lost their lives to the fury of British forces, supported by loyal native forces. One result of the mutiny was the abolition of the East India Company, which had thus far ruled the country; on 1 November 1858, the British crown assumed direct rule of India.—Ed.]

5. While this essay deals exclusively with Felice Beato, there were other photographers, such as Dr. John Murray, Major Robert C. Tytler (of the 38th Bengal Native Infantry) and his wife, Harriet, and , among others, J. Milliken (of the 23d Company, Royal Engineers) who also made topographical views in 1858–59 of places associated with the mutiny.

6. On Felice Beato, see John Clark, John Fraser, and Colin Osman, "Chronology of Felix (Felice) Beato (1825?–1908?)" in John Clark, *Japanese-British Exchanges in Art, 1850–1930s: Papers and Research Material* (Canberra, Australia: Department of Art History, Australian National University, 1989), 96–118; this chronology now provides the foundation for our present knowledge of Beato's life. Various articles by Colin Osman, including his "The Later Years of Felice Beato," *Photographic Journal* 128, no. 11 (1988): 511–14, have further clarified aspects of Beato's life and career. See also David Harris, *Of Battle and Beauty: Felice Beato's Photographs of China* (Santa Barbara: Santa Barbara Museum of Art, 1999), 19–27.

7. On Antonio Beato, see Colin Osman, "Antonio Beato, Photographer of the Nile," *History of Photography* 14, no. 2 (1990): 101–11.

8. On Robertson, see Bridget A. Henisch and Heinz K. Henisch, "James Robertson of Constantinople: A Chronology," *History of Photography* 14, no. 1 (1990): 23–32; and Bahattin Öztuncay, *James Robertson: Pioneer of Photography in the Ottoman Empire* (Istanbul: Eren, 1992). Robertson married Marie Matilda Beato around 1855 and had three children; see Henisch and Henisch, "Chronology," 30.

9. See Harris, *Of Battle and Beauty*, 21–22 and note 11 below.

10. Ibid., 20, 24, and 133.

11. Information on Beato's movements in India is drawn from Clark, "Chronology," 97–98.

12. There was a very brief reference at the February 17 meeting of the Bengal Photographic Society, and a complete technical description was read at the next meeting of March 17; see the *Bengal Hurkaru* of February 23 and March 23, 1858. I am grateful to John Fraser, who kindly supplied me with these references.

13. For the March 1858 dating, see Pat Hodgson, *Early War Photographs*

(Reading, England: Osprey, 1974), 49. Beato made only four photographs of Kanpur, two of the barracks in Wheeler's Entrenchment, and two of the sites where separate massacres on June 27 and July 16, 1857 had occurred. For an account of these events, see John W. Kaye, *A History of the Sepoy War in India, 1857–1858,* 5th ed., (London: W. H. Allen, 1870), 2: 286–385.

14. John Fraser, "Beato's Photograph of the Interior of the Sikandarbagh at Lucknow," *Journal of the Society of Army Historical Research* 64, no. 237 (1981), 51–55; and *The Journal of the Photographic Society* 5, no. 79 (1859): 185.

15. On Beato's photographs in China, see Isobel Crombie, "China, 1860: A Photographic Album by Felice Beato," *History of Photography* 11, no. 1 (1987): 25–37; and Harris, *Of Battle and Beauty.*

16. The estimate is based upon the evidence of surviving Beato prints and albums and an analysis of Henry Hering's 1862 subscription list, *A Magnificent Collection of Photographic Views and Panoramas Taken by Signor F. Beato During the Indian Mutiny in 1857–58, and the late War in China.* During the winter of 1861–62, Hering purchased and then had duplicated a large number of portraits and "400 views of India and China" (*The Journal of the Photographic Society* 9, no. 136 [1863]: 335), which he then exhibited in his gallery at 137 Regent Street in London, and offered for sale through subscription. Hering's prints are distinguishable from Beato's through their evidence of being copies and from the inscribed reference numbers that appear in white in the lower corners of the prints. This Hering list is reproduced in facsimile in Harris, *Of Battle and Beauty,* 177–80.

17. There are exceptions to this pattern. For instance, in an album (PH1987:1084) in the photographs collection of the Canadian Centre for Architecture, Montreal, formerly from the collection of John Murray, there are variant views of *The Taj [Mahal] from the Fountains, Central View of the Taj [Mahal],* and *Tomb of Etimand-oo-doulah [I'timáduddawla] at Agra* (Beato list nos. 7, 8, and 22, respectively). Each of these pairs was made from virtually the same camera position, but reveals a different arrangement of figures and seasonal transformation of the vegetation.

18. Details of the siege and assault of Delhi are drawn from Kaye, *History of the Sepoy War,* 513–22; and Colonel George B. Malleson, *History of the Indian Mutiny 1857–1858,* 3d ed., (London, New York, and Bombay: Longmans, Green, and Co., 1896), 2: 1–96.

19. Beato's original stock list does not survive, but it can be largely reconstructed through the pencil annotations on the verso of his unmounted Indian photographs and from information contained in Hering's 1862 subscription list; see note 16 above. Beato divided his photographs of India into four series—Lucknow and Kanpur, Delhi, Agra and Benares (Varanasi), and Amritsar—and numbered each series separately, beginning at number one. Normally, he inscribed his title and stock number on the verso of each print that he sold. The Hering list maintains Beato's four divisions and follows his numbering sequence and (with some variants in spelling) his titles.

20. The following highly abbreviated summary of the siege and reliefs of Lucknow is drawn from Martin R. Gubbins, *An Account of the Mutinies in Oudh, and of the Siege of the Lucknow Residency* (London: Richard Bentley, 1858); Lieutenant-General James McLeod Innes, *Lucknow and Oudh in the Mutiny: A Narrative and Study* (London: A. D. Innes and Co., 1895); and Malleson, *History of the Indian Mutiny,* 144–225 and 342–415.

21. A map with all three relief routes indicated is reproduced following the index in Sir Frederic John Goldsmid, *James Outram: A Biography* (London: Smith, Elder & Co., 1880), vol. 2.

22. There are two exceptions to this pattern, which refer to the earlier relief effort of Havelock and Outram, *The Place in Which General Neil was Killed in the Bazaar,* and *The Road by Which General Havelock Entered the Residency* (Beato list nos. 27 and 31 respectively).

23. See Fraser, "Sikandarbagh."

24. See, for instance, Malleson, *History of the Indian Mutiny,* 180–87; and Fraser, "Sikandarbagh."

25. For a partial list of Beato's portraits, see Hering's 1862 subscription list, reproduced in Harris, *Of Battle and Beauty,* 180. Since all of Beato's portraits are unsigned, their attribution is based upon credited reproductions in periodicals and publications. In addition, Beato constructed a makeshift studio, possibly in Lucknow, where

he took a number of these portraits. The same props—notably an elaborately decorated vase and plain cloth backdrop—reappear in many portraits.

26. For the identification of the sitters, see Hodgson, *Early War Photographs,* 55. Mecham also published engravings after his drawings in his and George Couper's *Sketches and Incidents of the Siege of Lucknow* (London: Day and Son, 1858). A copy of this publication, with eight of Beato's Lucknow photographs, was auctioned as lot 54 in the Sotheby's Belgravia sale of July 1, 1977.

27. Six Beato photographs of Crealock's drawings are included in the album cited in note 17 above.

28. On the ideology implicit in war photography, see, for instance, Joel Snyder, "Photographers and Photographs of the Civil War," in *The Documentary Photograph as a Work of Art: American Photographs, 1860–1876,* exh. cat. (Chicago: David and Alfred Smart Gallery, University of Chicago, 1976), 17–22; and Caroline Brothers, *War and Photography: A Cultural History* (London and New York: Routledge, 1997).

29. On aspects of colonialism and photography, see such recent studies as James R. Ryan, *Picturing Empire: Photography and the Visualization of the British Empire* (London: Reaktion Books, 1997); and Richard Ovenden, *John Thomson (1837–1921), Photographer* (Edinburgh: National Library of Scotland, 1997).

TOPOGRAPHY AND MEMORY: FELICE BEATO'S PHOTOGRAPHS OF INDIA

45 *General Wheeler's Entrenchment at Cawnpore*

Felice Beato

March 1858, albumen silver print, 25.5 x 29.9

Michael and Jane Wilson Collection

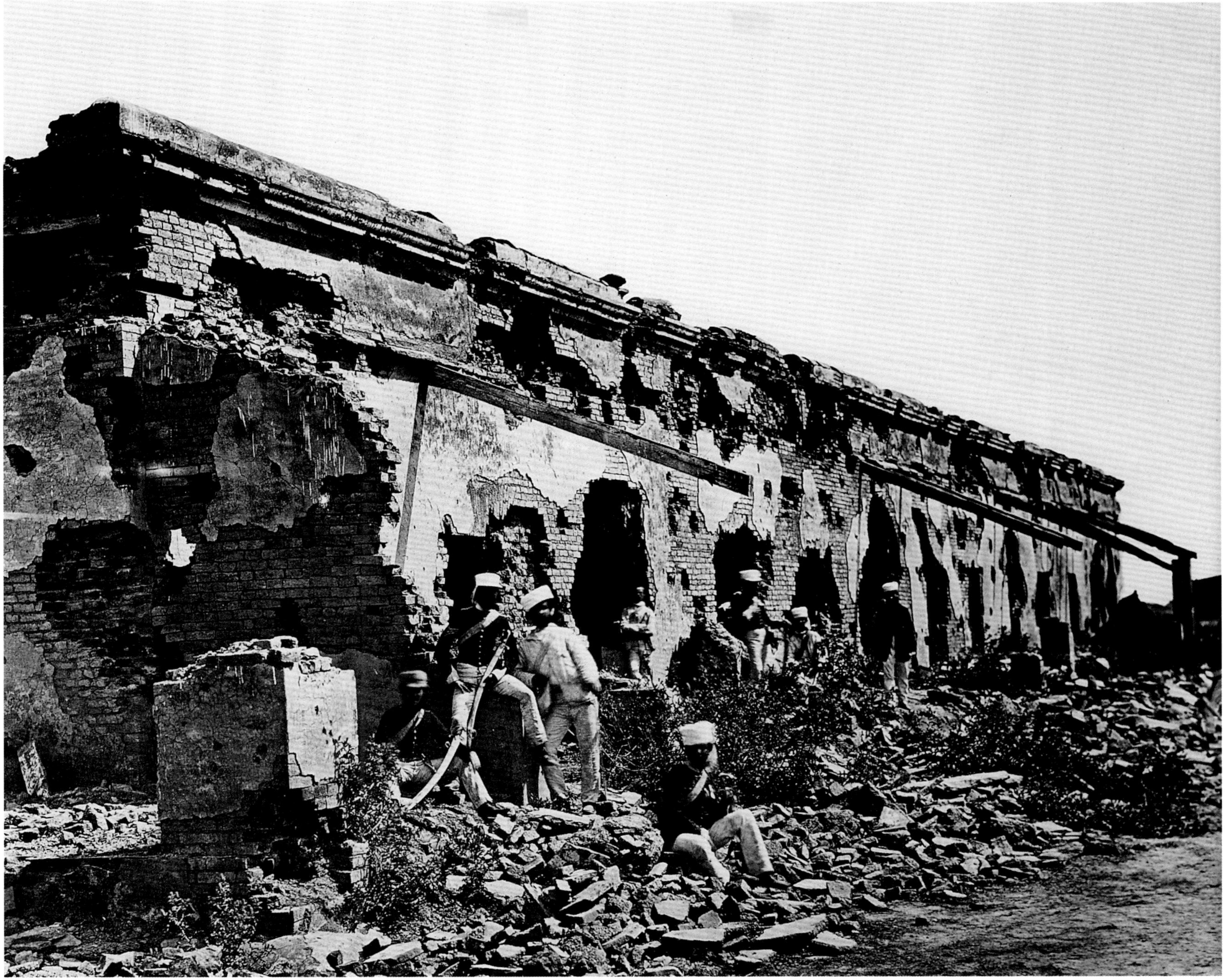

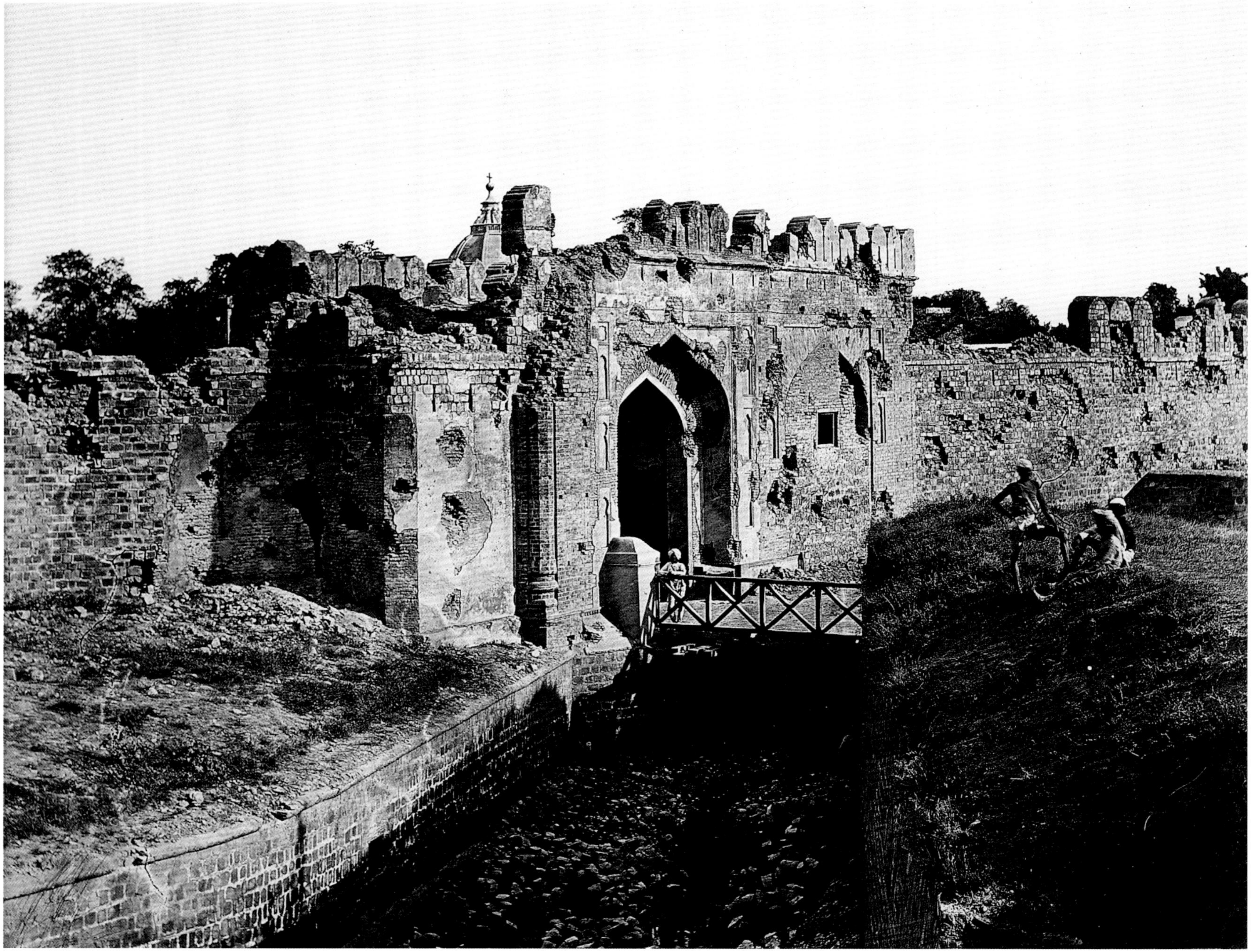

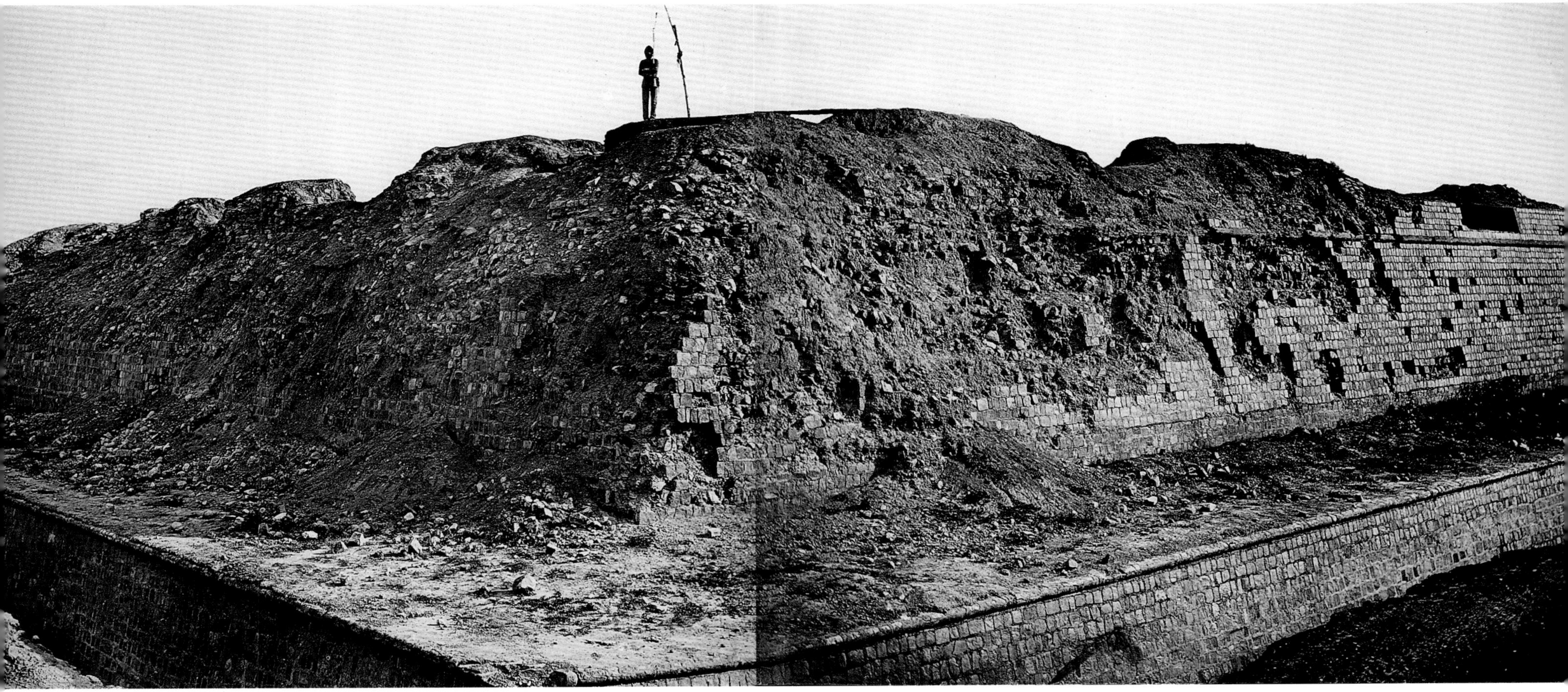

46 *Cashmere Gate, Delhi*

Felice Beato

1858 or 1859, albumen silver print

24 x 30.9

Michael and Jane Wilson Collection

47 *Moree Bastion, Delhi*

Felice Beato

2-part panorama, 1858 or 1859, albumen silver print, 24.6 x 59.7

Michael and Jane Wilson Collection

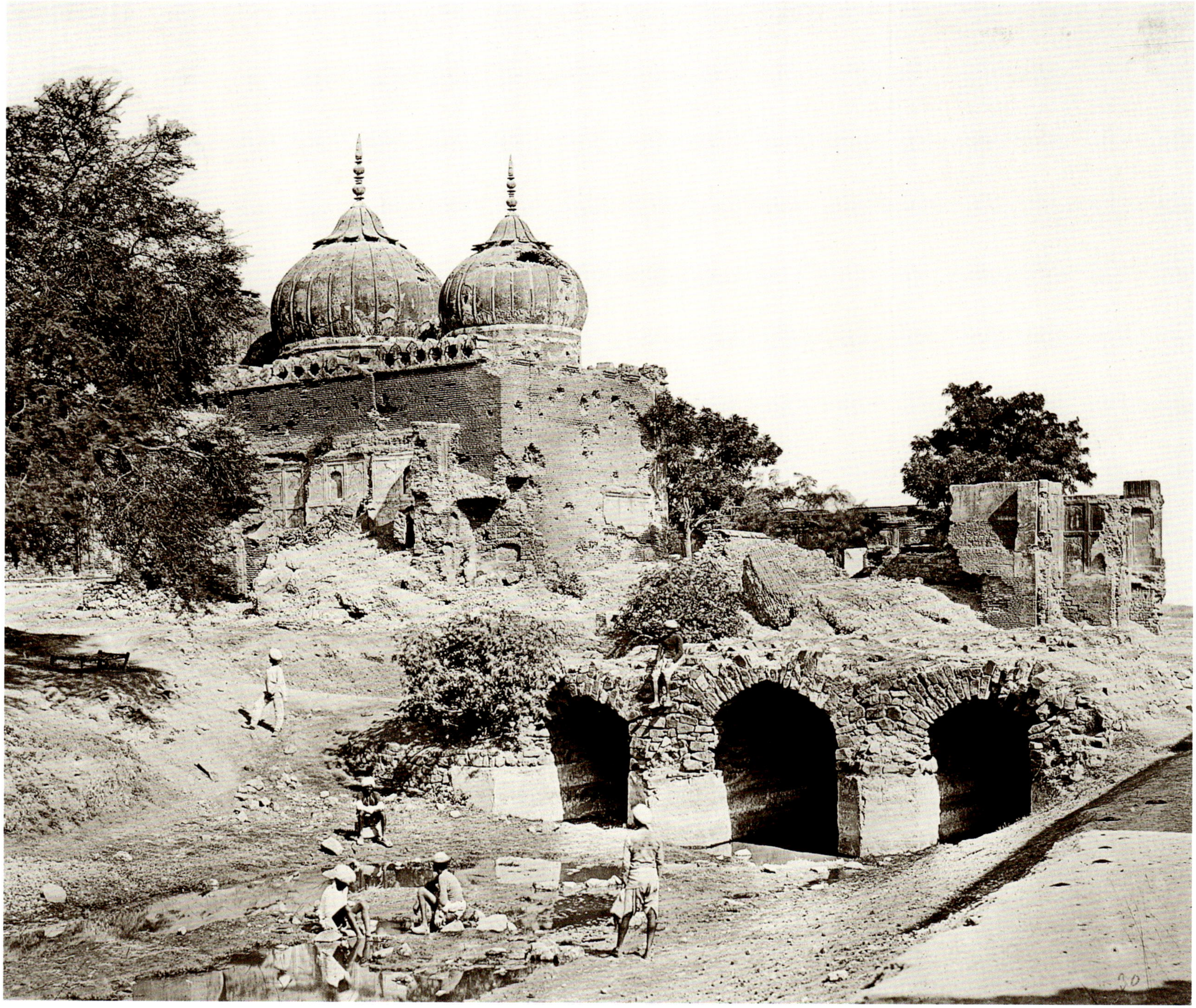

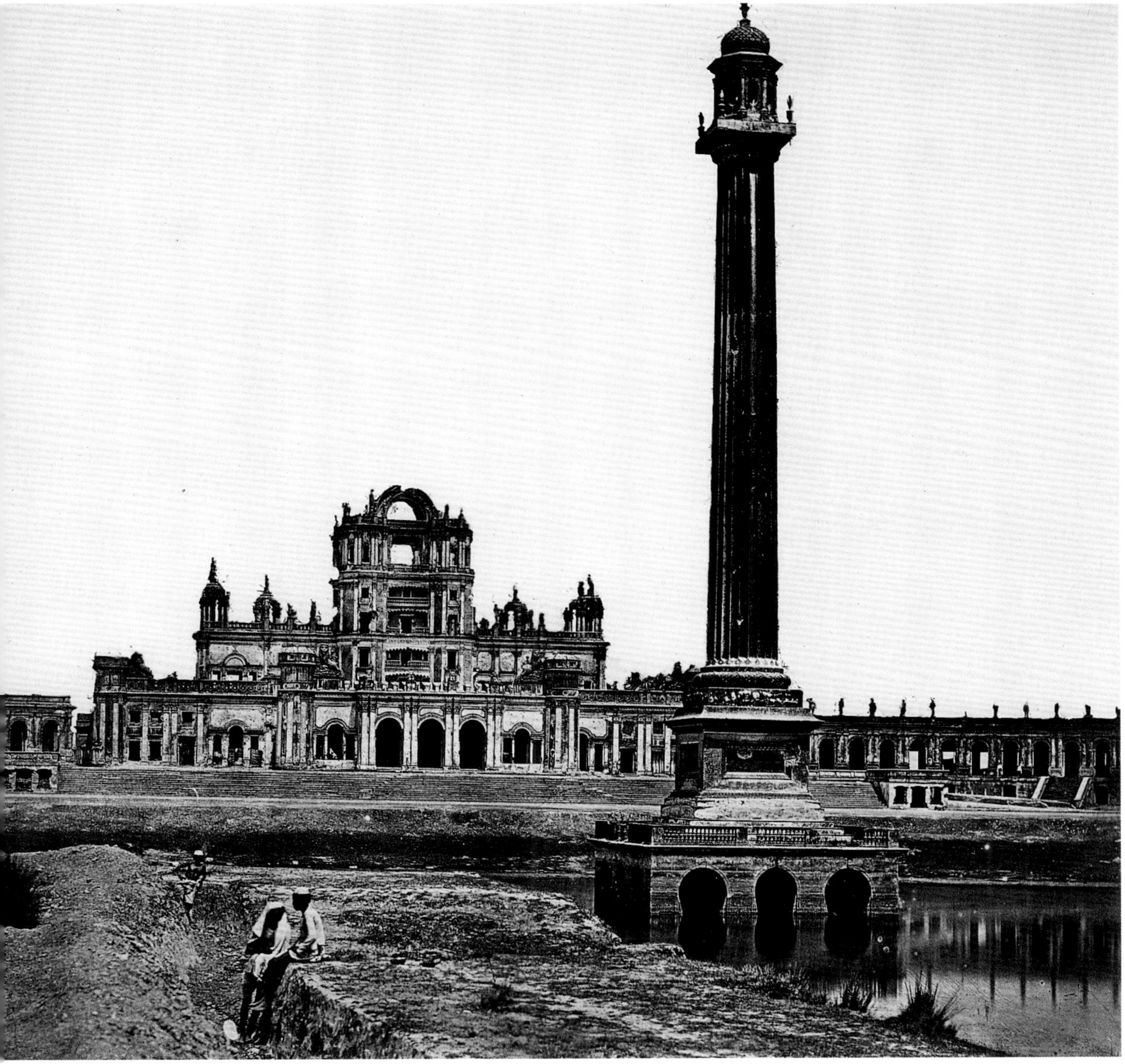

48 *Mosque near the Custom-House Battery, Delhi*

Felice Beato

1858 or 1859, albumen silver print, 25.6 x 30.6

Michael and Jane Wilson Collection

49 *The Martiniere School. First Attack of Sir Colin Campbell in November 1857; Second Attack, 2nd March, Lucknow*

Felice Beato

March or April 1858, albumen silver print

25.4 x 28.3

Michael and Jane Wilson Collection

50 *The Great Gateway of the Kaiserbagh, Lucknow*

Felice Beato

March or April 1858, albumen silver print

25.7 x 30.2

Michael and Jane Wilson Collection

51 *The King's Palace in Kaiserbagh. Second Attack of Sir Colin Campbell in March 1858, Lucknow*

Felice Beato

March or April 1858, albumen silver print

23 x 29.7

Michael and Jane Wilson Collection

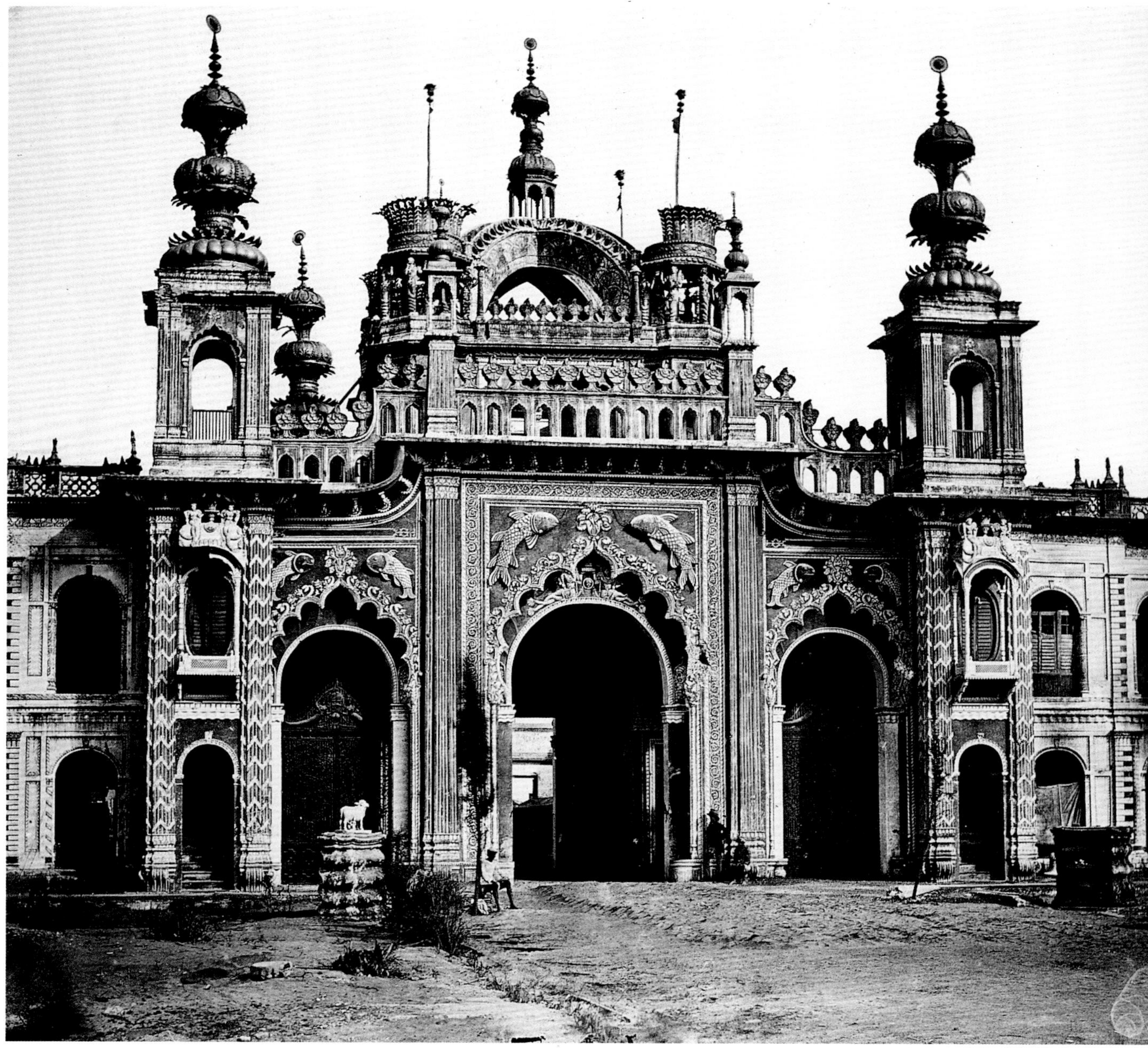

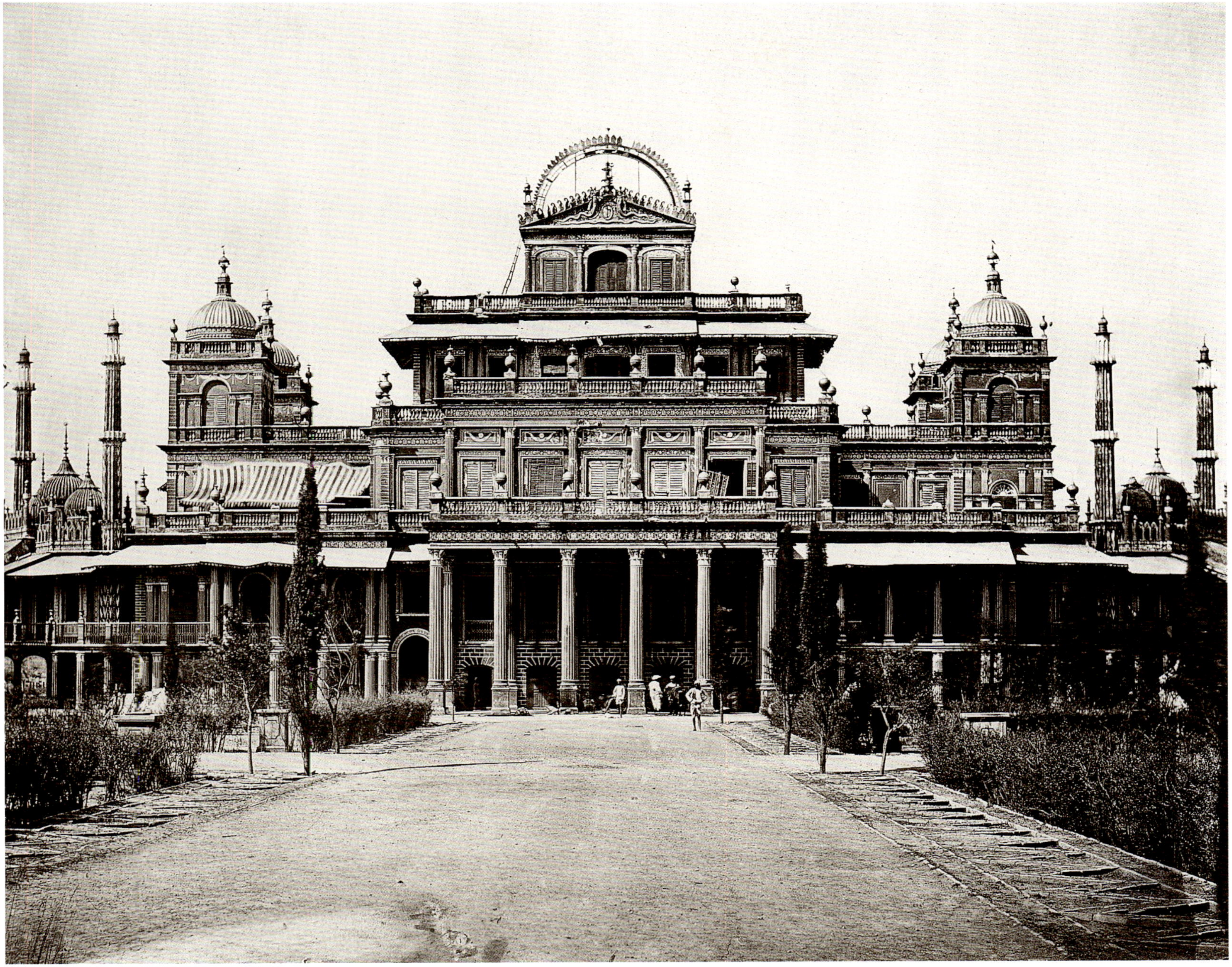

52 *The Tomb of Saadat Ali in the Kaiserbagh Palace. [Second] Attack of Sir Colin Campbell in March 1858, Lucknow*

Felice Beato

March or April 1858, albumen silver print

30.1 x 25

Michael and Jane Wilson Collection

53 *Chutter Manzil Palace, with the King's Boat in the Shape of a Fish. First Attack of Sir Colin Campbell in November 1857, Lucknow*

Felice Beato

March or April 1858, albumen silver print

24.1 x 30

Michael and Jane Wilson Collection

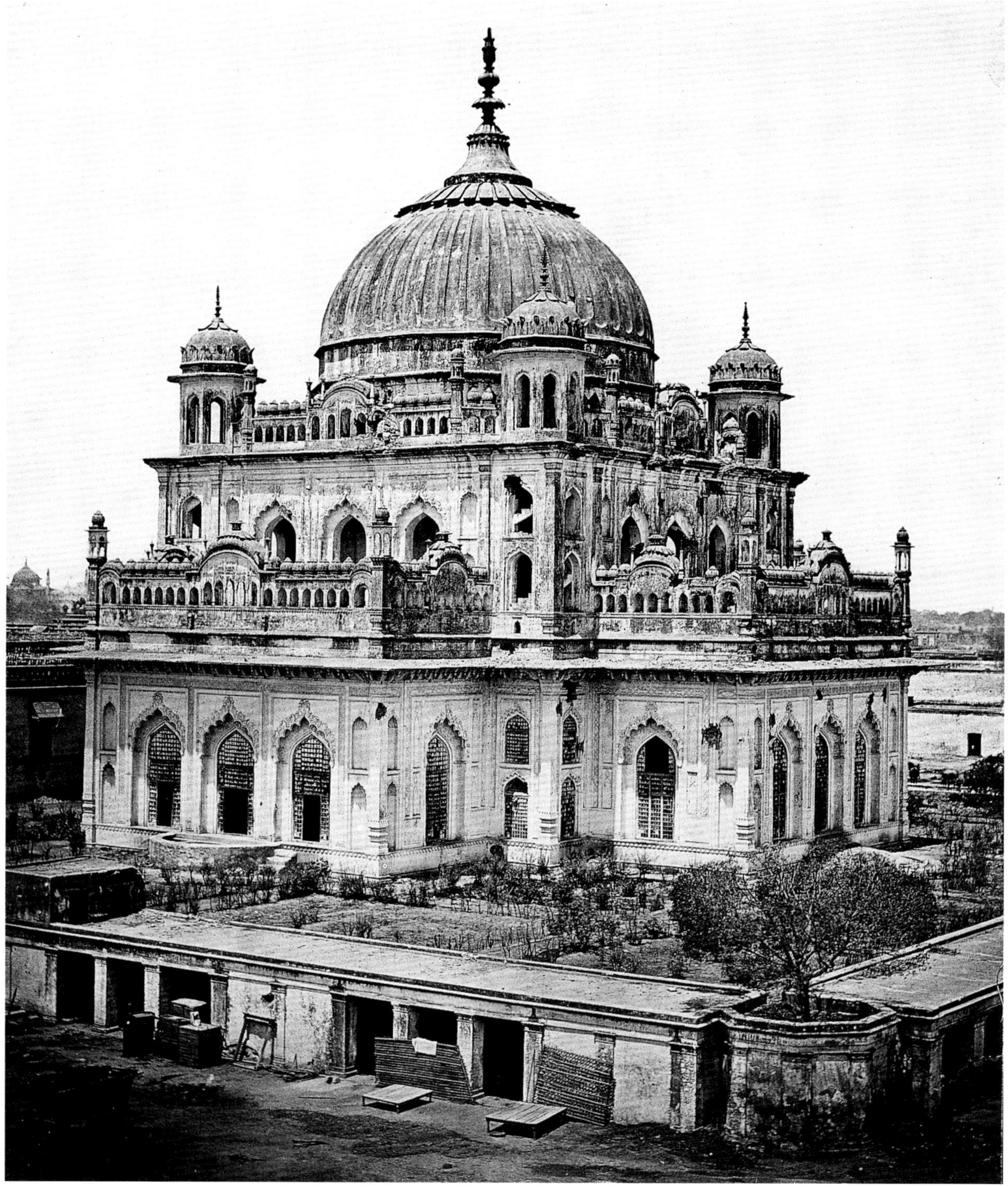

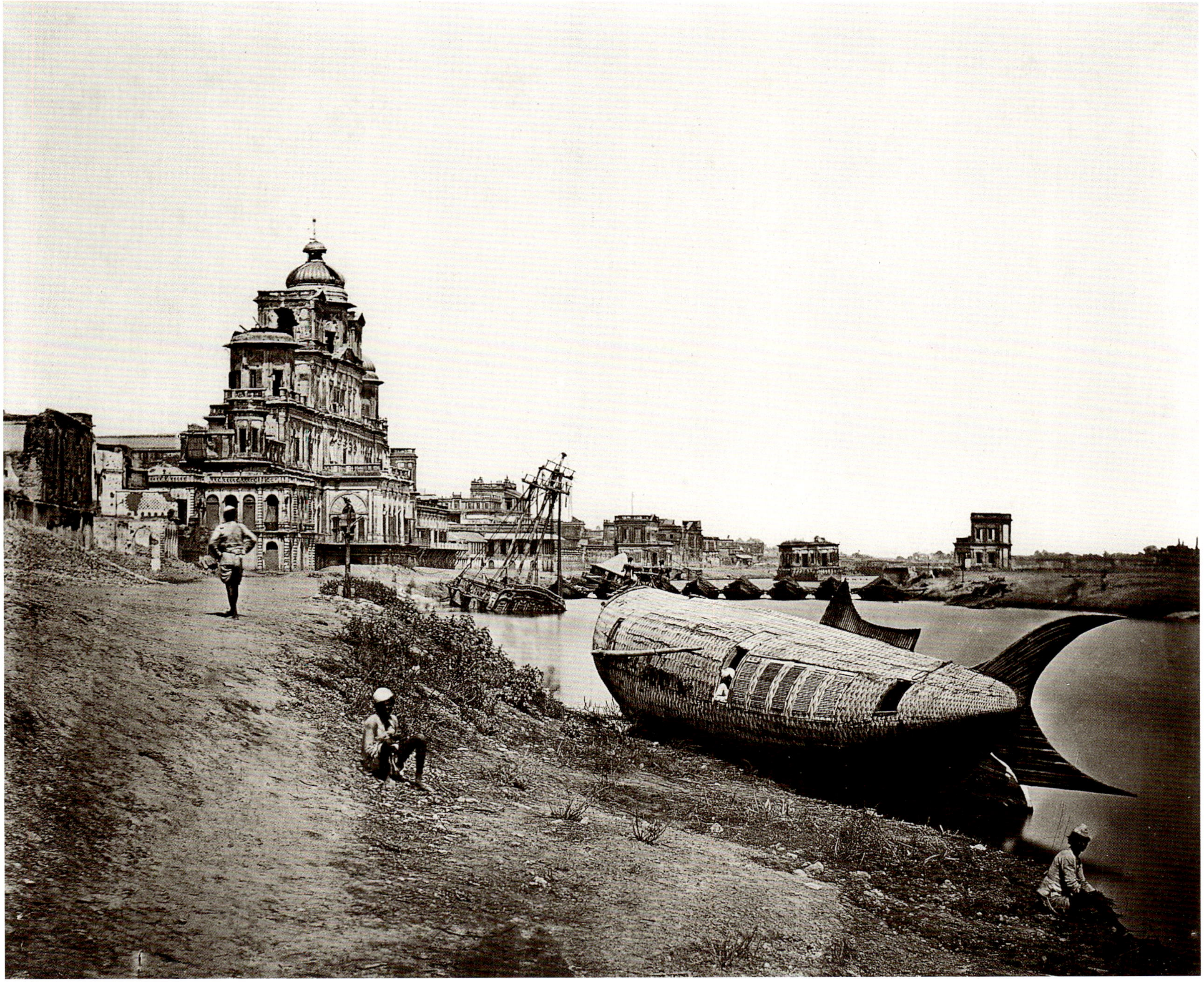

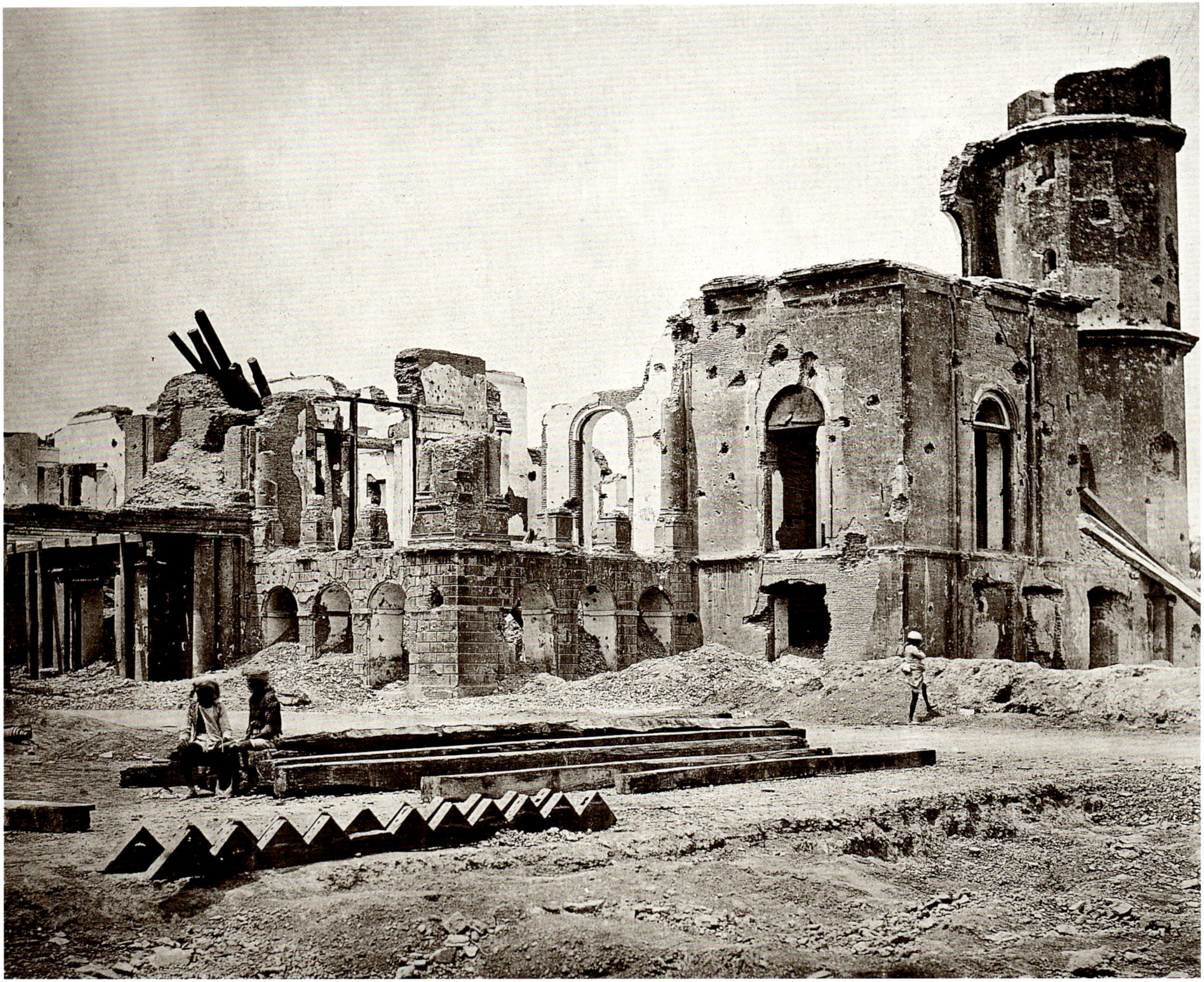

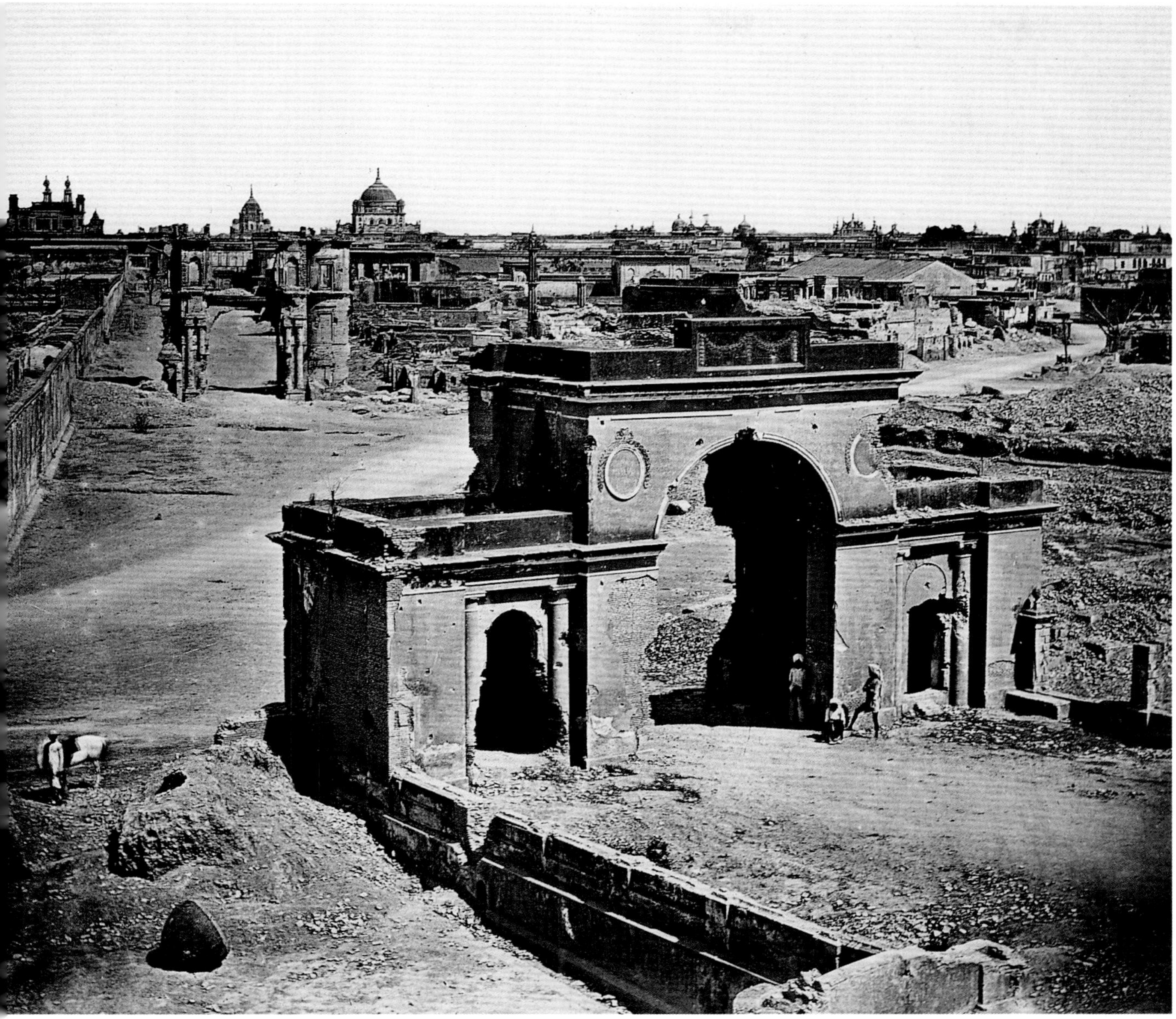

54 *The Residency, Taken in Front, and Showing the Room in Which Sir Henry Lawrence was Killed, Lucknow*

Felice Beato

March or April 1858, albumen silver print

23.6 x 28.7

Michael and Jane Wilson Collection

55 *Bailee Guard Gate, Taken from the Inside, and Showing the Clock Tower, Lucknow*

Felice Beato

March or April 1858, albumen silver print

25.8 x 30.3

Michael and Jane Wilson Collection

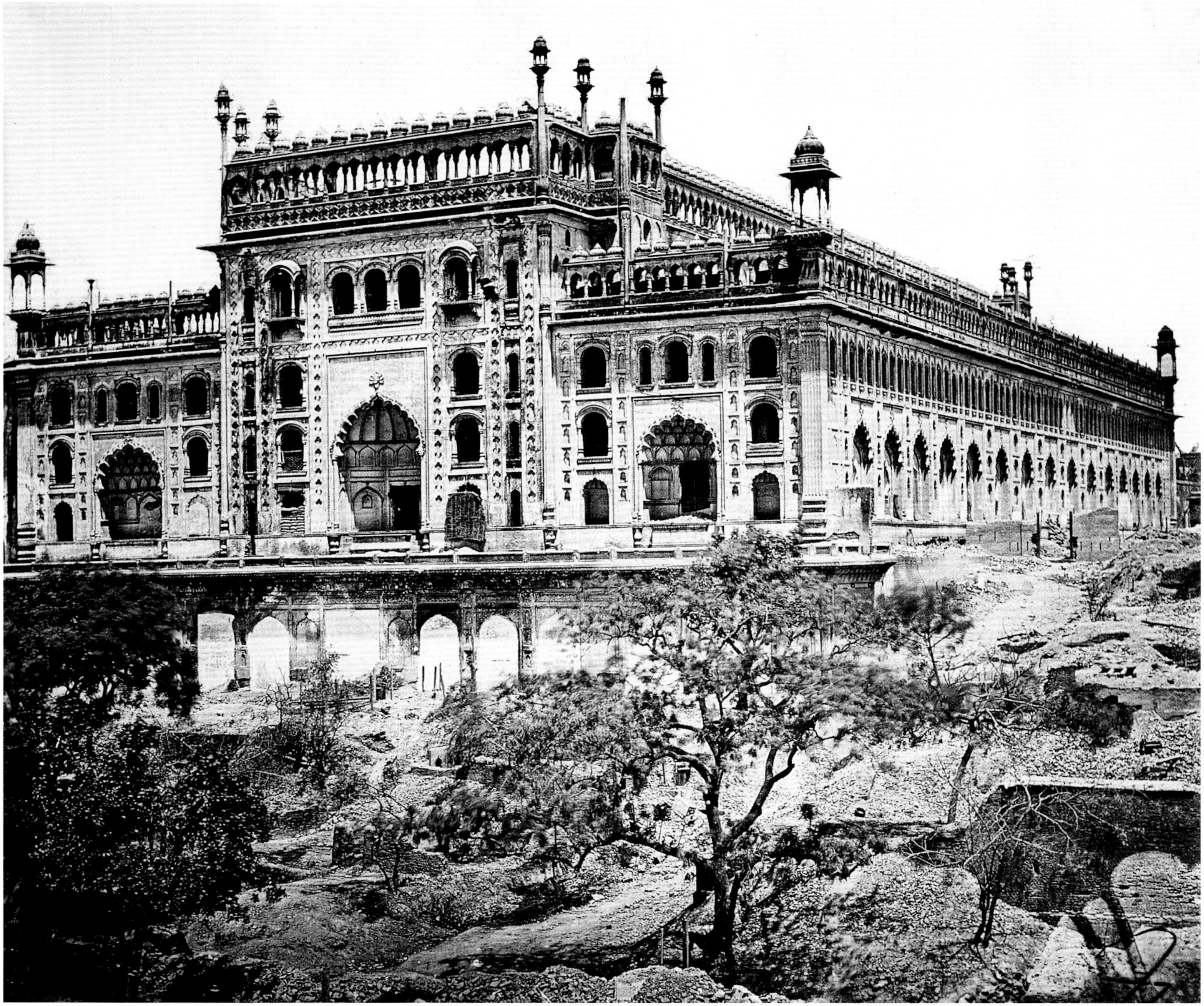

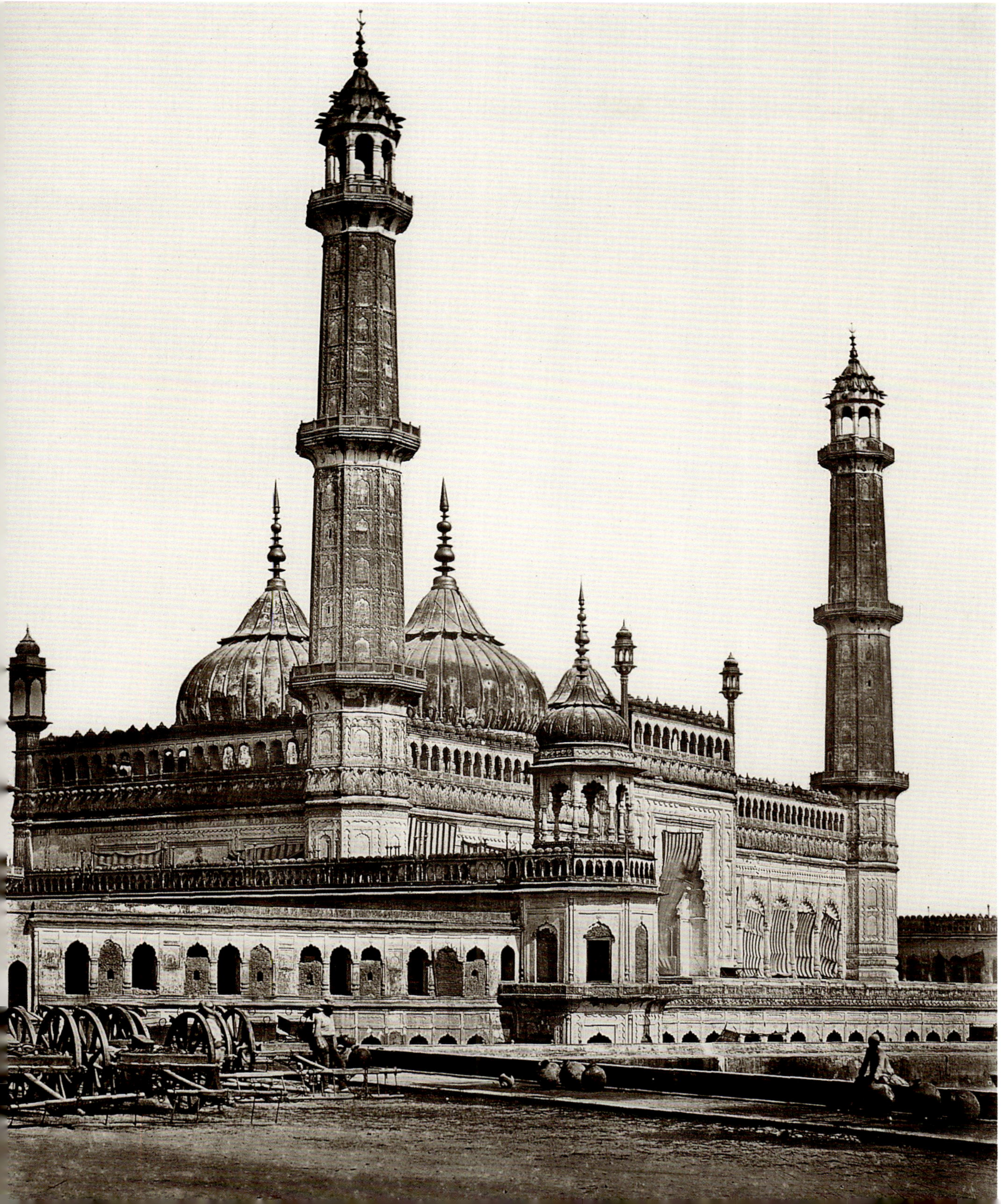

56 *Exterior of Asophoo Dowlah's Emambara or Tomb—Now the Quarters of Her Majesty's 53rd Regiment. The Second Attack of Sir Colin Campbell in March 1858, Lucknow*

Felice Beato

March or April 1858, albumen silver print

24.3 x 29.5

Michael and Jane Wilson Collection

57 *Mosque inside Asophoo Dowlah's Emambara—Now Used as a Hospital, Lucknow*

Felice Beato

March or April 1858, albumen silver print

29.2 x 25.7

Michael and Jane Wilson Collection

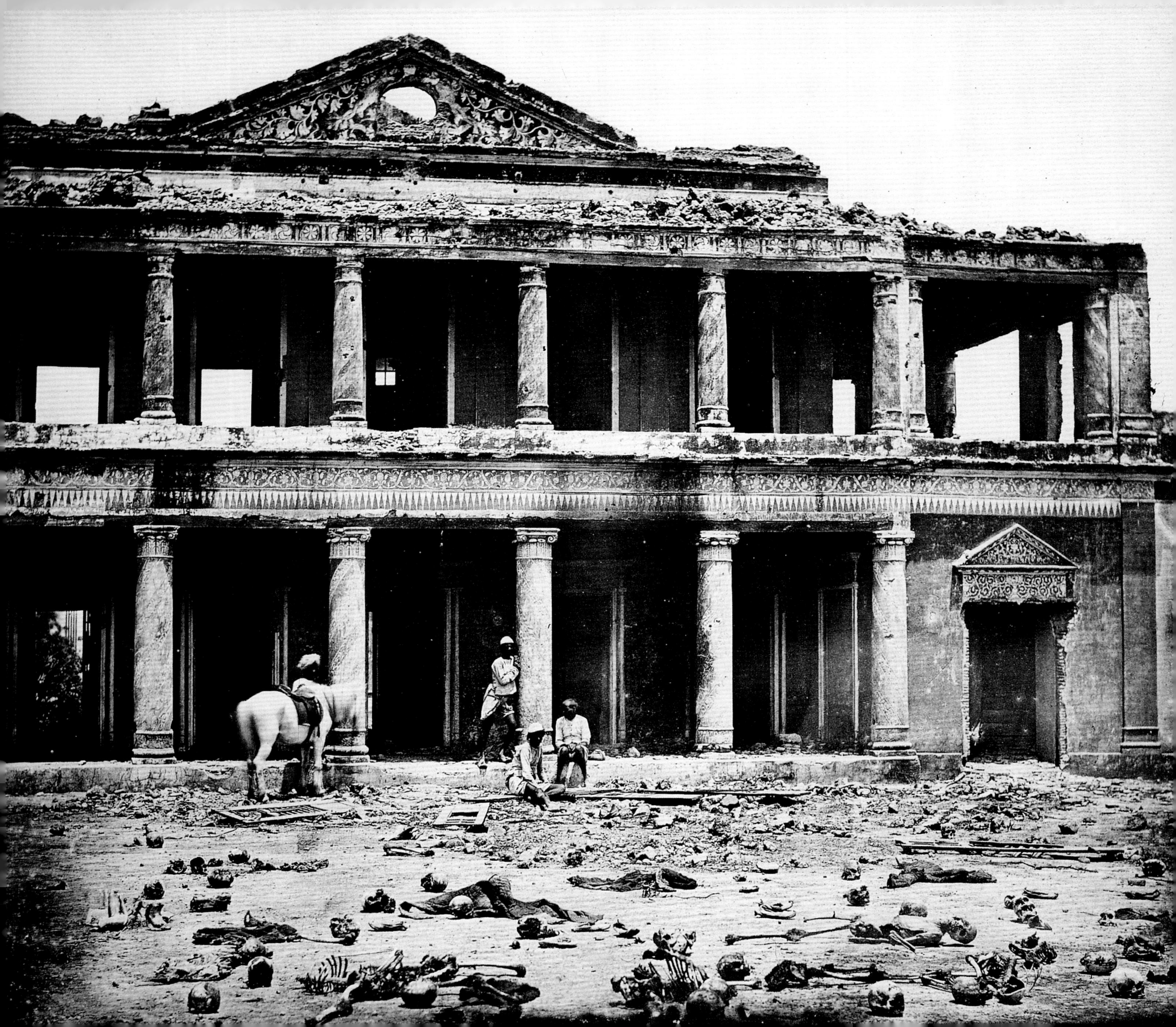

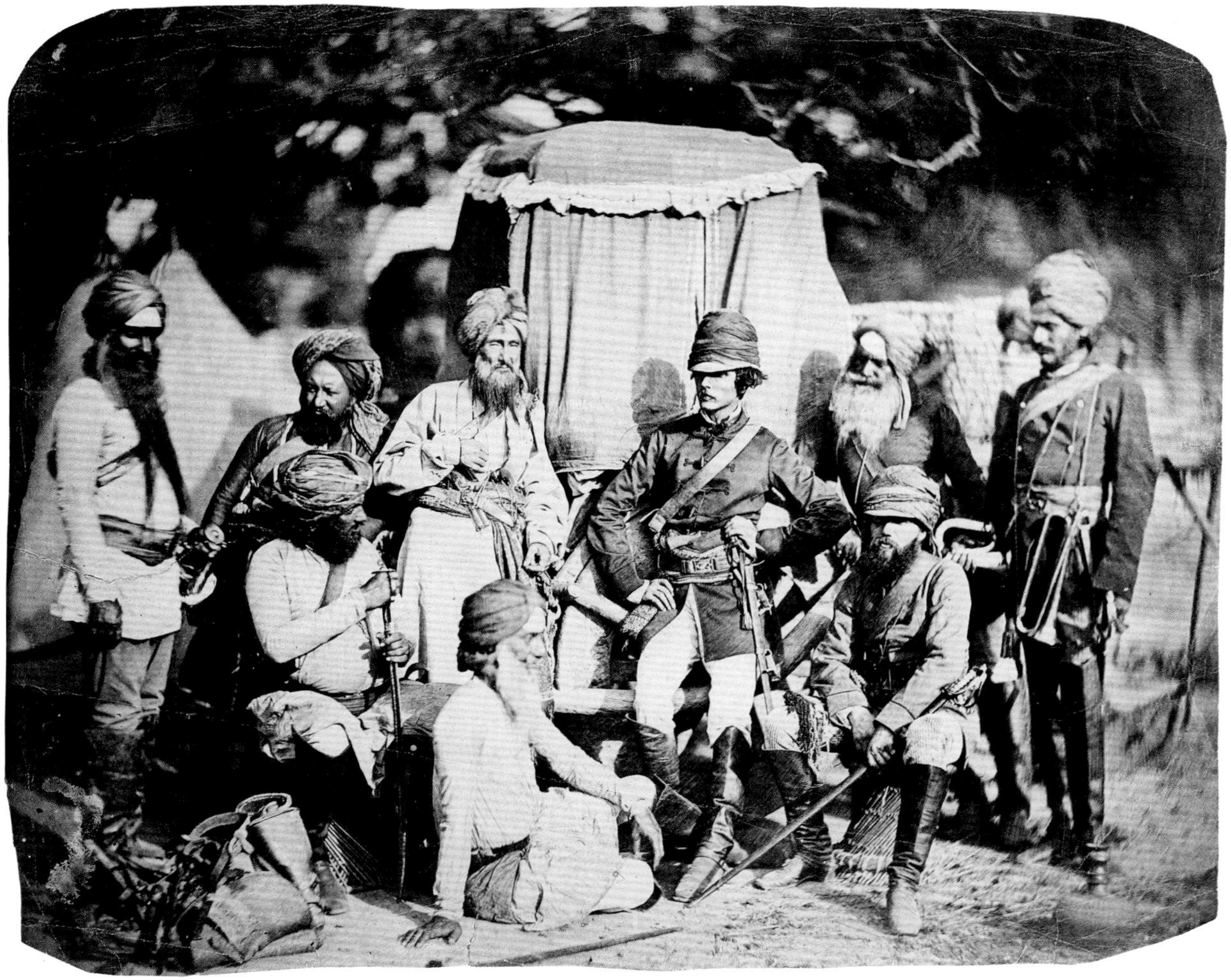

58 *Interior of the Secundra Bagh after the Slaughter of 2,000 Rebels by the 93rd Highlanders and 4th Punjab Regiment. First Attack of Sir Colin Campbell in November 1857, Lucknow*

Felice Beato

March or April 1858, albumen silver print

26.2 x 29.8

Michael and Jane Wilson Collection

59 *Hodson's Horse*

Felice Beato

1858 or 1859, albumen silver print

23.5 x 28.4

Michael and Jane Wilson Collection

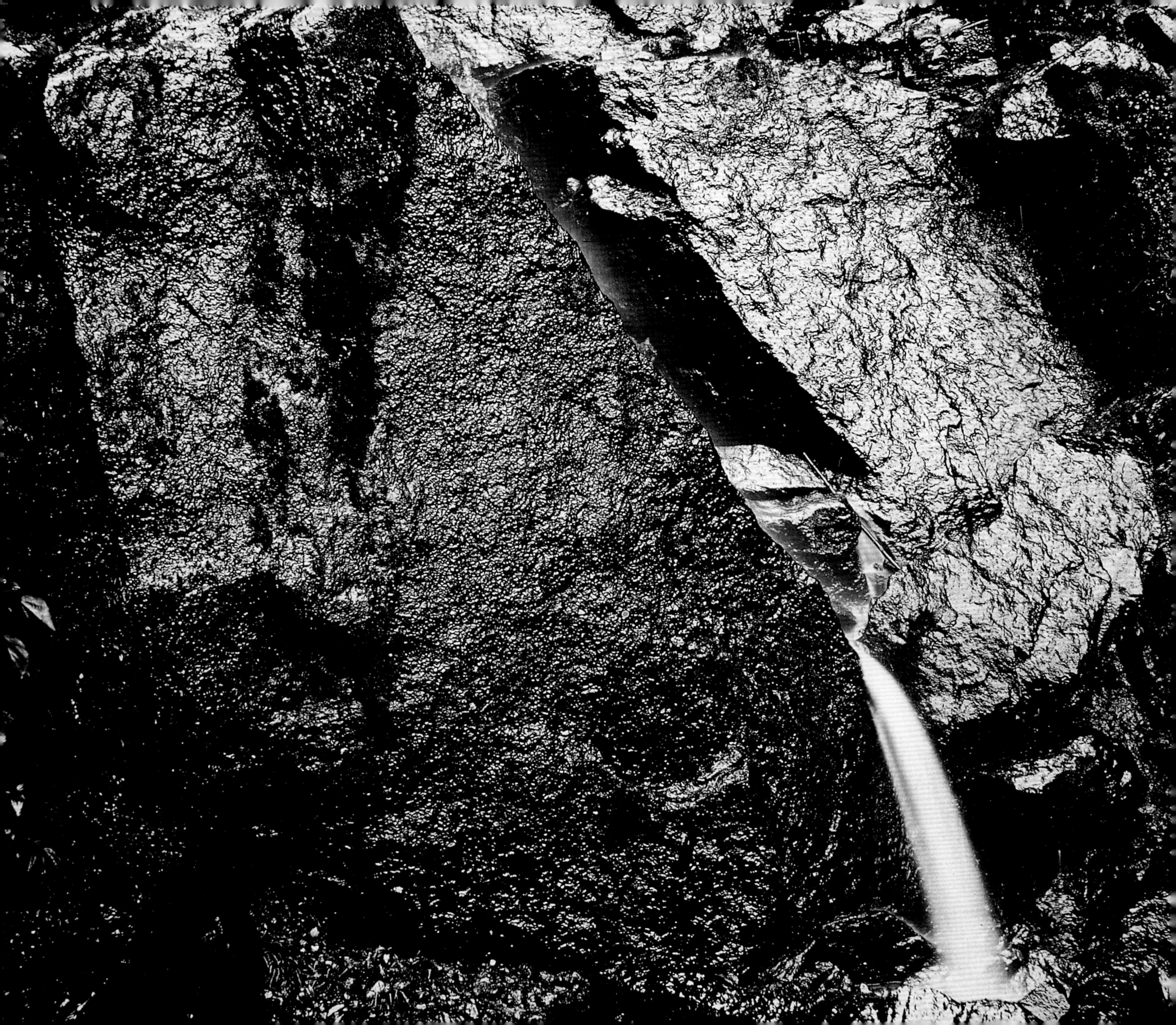

Jane Ricketts

Undiscovered Amateur: Macfarlane and the Picturesque

In the early years of the nineteenth century, it was traveling painters such as Thomas and William Daniell who, with their numerous picturesque views, fed the lively appetite in Britain for depictions of the beauty and exoticism of the architecture and scenery of India. But by the time Donald Macfarlane arrived there in 1859, the camera had not only become the most popular medium through which wealthy travelers and empire-builders could record their experiences of the mysterious East but had also, he felt, "done much to create the public taste" by bringing "beautiful representations of the finest scenery in the world within the reach of millions."[1]

In 1858, Felice Beato had sped from Constantinople to India to record the aftermath of the mutiny of the sepoy troops for the horrified public in Britain, and J. Hogarth of London had issued sets of thirty large prints of Dr. John Murray's views of Agra and its vicinity. Since 1855 the army had increasingly been using the camera for its archaeological surveys and engineering projects in India, and in 1856, the practice of the photographic art by European and Indian amateurs, already popular and fashionable, had been further stimulated by the arrival of Viscount Canning and his wife. The newly appointed governor-general encouraged officers and civilians to assemble collections of photographs of their travels, and Lady Canning, herself an enthusiastic photographer as were many of her circle,[2] became patron of the recently established photographic societies of Bombay, Madras, and Bengal, in which enthusiasts from different walks of life met monthly to discuss methods and display their results.

In 1861, after her death, Charlotte Canning was succeeded as patron of the Bengal Photographic Society by Sir Bartle Frere (fig. 1.), a member of the viceroy's council and his confidential adviser. His

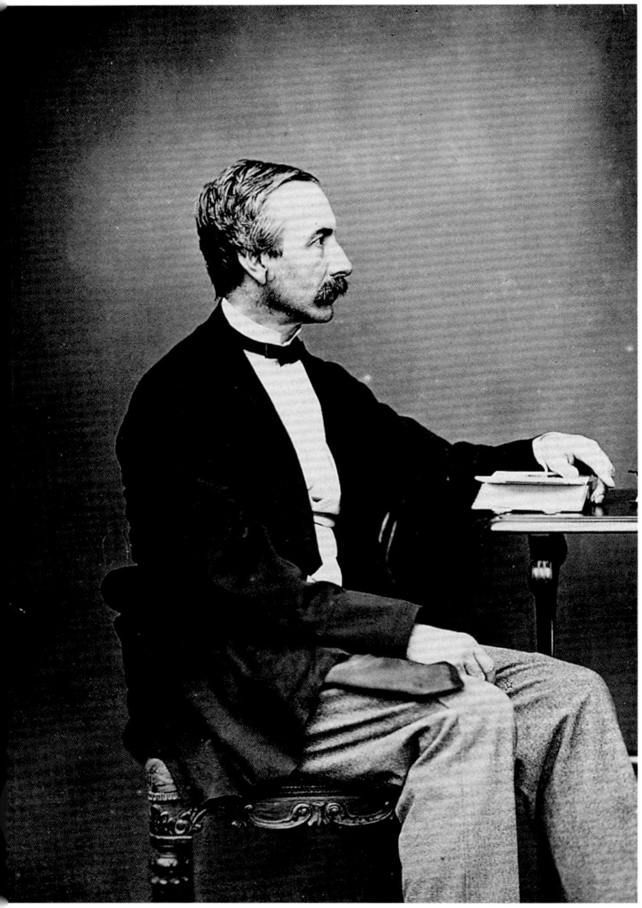

FIGURE 1 Anonymous, initialed Dr. MP (?), *Sir Bartle Frere* (1815–1884), 6 July 1864, albumen print, 14.8 x 10.7. Howard and Jane Ricketts Collection

Page 148: Detail, no. 64. *Rocks, Darjeeling*, Donald Horne MacFarlane

tenure was necessarily brief as in 1862 he was appointed governor of Bombay, where in 1865, in his official capacity, he supervised the publication of a photographic survey by Thomas Biggs and Dr. W. H. Pigou of the monuments of Bijapur and Ahmadabad. But his personal desire to possess a photographic souvenir of his distinguished career in India is demonstrated by the existence of an album containing eighty-one plates and entitled *General Views of India. Sir Bartle Frere's Collection.* Included in this album are a large group of exceptionally fine unsigned images, one captioned "First Prize 1862," (no. 60) which are stylistically unlike the work of any identified photographer active in India at that period.

Although some of these plates were attributed to Howard when exhibited in New York in 1976,[3] another album in which some of the same images were ascribed to "D. McF," combined with research in the Calcutta press and the few extant journals of the Bengal Photographic Society established their true author as Donald Macfarlane (fig. 2).

Donald Horne Macfarlane (1830–1904), the youngest son of a Caithness, Scotland magistrate, seems to have decided, like many of his peers, to seek his fortune in India. A partner in the firm of Begg, Dunlop and Co., agents for tea and coal companies, he was initially based in Kanpur, but seems to have spent much of his time at the head office in Calcutta or traveling in Darjeeling, Madras, and the Nilgiri Hills accompanied by his camera, chemicals, and personally designed collapsible dark tent.[4]

No one knows whether he was already an accomplished photographer before his departure for India or whether he was inspired to learn the art after his arrival. But if the latter was the case he must have been an apt pupil because at his first meeting of the Bengal Photographic Society in November 1860, when he was proposed for membership by Mr. Rowe, he exhibited what was considered to be a "very fine collection of views taken in Lucknow, the North West and in and about Calcutta." Macfarlane was lauded for his "taste and manipulation" and his views lavishly praised for their "delicate half-tone and just distribution of light and shade" said to be comparable to the work of the "most successful European operators."[5]

Macfarlane also took portraits and stereoscopic photographs, but it was the challenge presented by large-scale landscape photography that primarily interested him. His initial series was followed in February 1861 by a further highly acclaimed group of views taken in the vicinity of Calcutta (nos. 62, 63), including studies of trees and Hindu huts on the margin of a lake "in whose water the shadow of the objects described was most faithfully and clearly represented."[6] In July of that year his efforts were crowned with success when, in the society's fourth annual exhibition, he carried off not only the gold medal for the best landscape series but also the silver for the best single photograph, entitled *Creepers,* which is similar in style and subject matter to *Trees and Stream* (no. 61).[7] The critic of the *Bengal Hurkaru,* a Calcutta newspaper that recorded the society's activities at some length, was particularly struck by their "superiority as works of art, the subjects being chosen with the eye of a true artist and not that of a mere mechanical operator."[8]

However, these artistic images were not achieved without much technical experimentation and hard labor as Macfarlane pointed out in 1862 in his paper "Landscape Photography in India," in which he described his preferred materials and methods of developing and printing his plates. Here he maintained that a successful photographer must never become complacent, but that in a continual quest for improvement he must be his own most exacting critic and stated that he, himself, "had never yet taken a picture with which he was satisfied."[9] Like his fellow practitioners in India he had to contend with an intensely hot climate, unstable collodion, and faulty albumenized paper for his prints. Nevertheless, he had striven to achieve results as true to nature as possible, declaring, in the language of the Victorian aesthetic, that "the object should be to choose only what is in itself picturesque and having found it to represent it exactly as it is." However, this he did with an eye that was purely original.

In England a year later, Lieutenant Colonel Stuart-Wortley, an admired and active member of the photographic society of London, also read a paper on landscape photography in which he expressed, though in more florid tones, similar sentiments to Macfarlane's and also stressed the importance of pictorial realism. Landscape photography was, he felt, "immensely uplifting" but "it required a knowledge of high art" and a "feeling for all that is beautiful and glorious in nature." But he, unlike Macfarlane, found the stock ingredients of "rocks, tree-trunks, a man in the foreground" or perhaps "a cow and a waggon team" a virtual "necessity to the composition of a picture."[10]

Likewise Samuel Bourne, who arrived in Calcutta in January 1863 but left almost immediately for the potentially lucrative marketplace of Simla, was educated in the same artistic conventions. Imbued

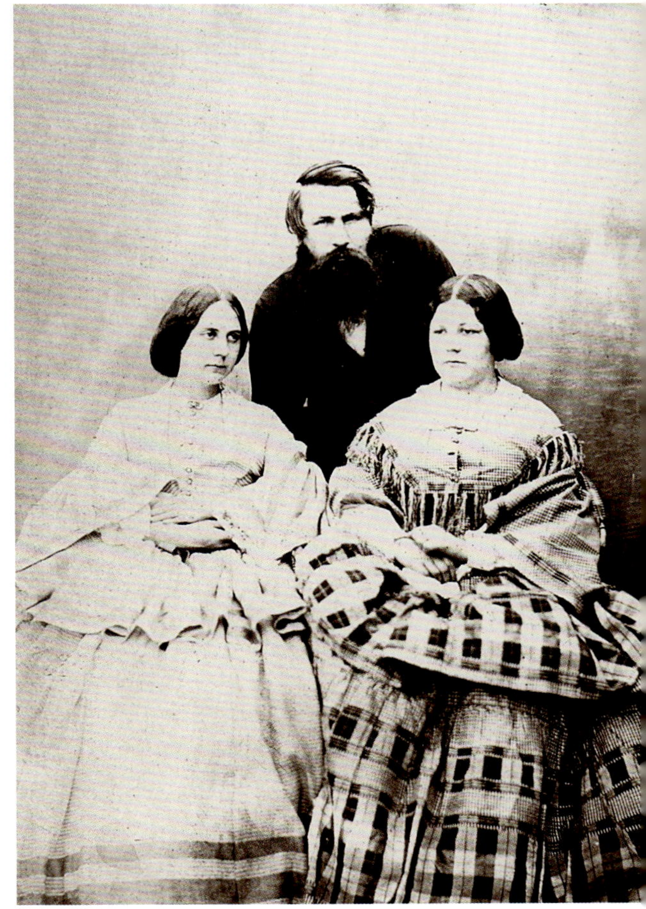

FIGURE 2 Dr. John Tresidder (1819–1889), *Mr. and Mrs. Macfarlane and Miss Bagshawe (sister-in-law),* Kanpur, 1860, albumen print, 19.2 x 15.1. The Alkazi Collection of Photography (97.15.0002/38e)

with many of the common British prejudices and preconceptions he, at least initially, lamented the un-Britishness of the Indian scenery, which lacked "pleasing variety of hill and dale, cornfields and pastures" and many of the other elements such as "lakes, rivers and verdure" that were mandatory to his mind for the production of a "pleasing and enjoyable picture."[11]

Few of these conventionally picturesque ingredients are visible in *Tolly's Nullah* (no. 62). But this sparse view, dominated by the strong diagonal of the river that fades atmospherically into the distance within its oval frame, is nevertheless in Macfarlane's hands transformed into a scene of exceptional calm and restrained beauty.

Unlike Bourne, Macfarlane, working without commercial imperatives, was free to produce a completely personal record of his years in India. From the images so far identified, he seems to have been less interested in documenting its famous monuments or its sublime mountain ranges than in concentrating on discovering his personal vision of the picturesque in the superficially uninteresting surroundings of Calcutta, damned by Bourne as being "totally devoid of architectural beauty or its immediate neighbourhood of pictorial interest."[12]

MacFarlane was based with his wife in Kanpur, the scene of the notorious massacre of women and children only two years before, his series of creepers, photographed in the countryside around Calcutta, perhaps expressed a subconscious desire to regiment, control, and impose a sense of order on the vast and alien postmutiny environment by subjugating it within the artificial confines of his camera lens. But he was also undoubtedly driven by the technical challenge of accurately producing equal definition in all areas of his photographs given the extreme contrasts of light and shade created by the brilliant Indian sun.[13]

In these complex photographs of foliage a deliberate rejection of the artificial constraints of pictorialism can be sensed. Some of the views, unrelieved by sheets of water or architecture, are almost claustrophobic with the dazzle and flicker of their enveloping masses of rampant vegetation reproduced in minute detail. Lacking a gentle introduction into the image, the viewer is projected directly into the dense foliage that occupies the entire picture, an impression emphasized in some cases by the intimate oval format of the image and the minimal area of sky.

However, in *A Landscape, Bengal* the scene is more open and less oppressive and is given some human dimension by the Indians seated on a distant bridge toward which the eye is drawn (no. 60). In general, Macfarlane's village scenes contain few, if any, figures, but with these pictures he also broke new ground in finding, unlike his more conventional fellow photographers, these simple mud huts worthy subjects for his camera, and he photographed them with dignity (no. 63).

But in *Rocks, Darjeeling*, the ultimate test of his scientific and artistic powers, Donald Macfarlane went one step further than he had in his creepers series. Here he demonstrated categorically his ability to transcend the merely picturesque and produced an extraordinarily powerful image that must be seen as one of the most remarkable and innovative photographs of the nineteenth century. Although still working strictly within the aesthetic of "straight-photography," in his quest for realism Macfarlane has moved into the realm of abstraction, a style of vision that was not further developed until the twentieth century (no. 64).

It was not surprising perhaps, that this advance was too radical for numerous members of the Bengal Photographic Society, who complained when *Rocks, Darjeeling* was chosen for distribution with their journal in 1862.[14] Nevertheless the prescient art critic of the *Friend of India* did recognize that Macfarlane's Darjeeling photographs "proved that the Photographer has got an original taste in him, which is developing every year."[15]

By mid-1862, Macfarlane was vice-president of the Bengal society and continuing to win gold and silver medals for his views, which included a prize for the best single photograph taken in India.[16] He went on to become president in 1863, and thus withdrew his series, which included photographs of foliage and Indian peasant life, from the postponed 1863 exhibition. This left the field open for Samuel Bourne, whom he had seconded for membership in January 1863,[17] to win his first medals in India for his landscape photography. In January 1864 Macfarlane resigned, as he was soon returning to England.

On his return to London, Macfarlane immediately joined the photographic society and in its 1865 exhibition was awarded a medal for his Indian views, which were considered exceptional for their "purity and beauty" and superior to any others previously taken there.[18] Finally, proof that the quality of his photographs was also appreciated outside Britain was his inclusion, alongside Bourne and Shepherd as well as Colonel Stuart-Wortley, in the small group of English bronze medal winners in the great Paris International Exhibition of 1867.[19] Sir Donald Macfarlane, knighted in 1894, prospered as an East India merchant, represented Scottish and Irish constituencies as a liberal member of parliament, and apparently remained a keen photographer until his death at the age of seventy-three,[20] although no photographs taken by him in Britain have so far been identified.

It is conceivable that had Macfarlane been active as a photographer during the 1920s rather than the early 1860s his semiabstract work would have been better understood and appreciated, and that in turn he would have had greater impetus to experiment further in this style. His stay in India was short and his body of work comparatively small, but from what we know of it, it seems that Macfarlane was in many ways a man before his time—a nineteenth-century photographer with a twentieth-century eye.

NOTES

1. Donald Horne Macfarlane, "Landscape Photography in India," *Journal of the Bengal Photographic Society* 2, no. 1 (1 September 1862): 30.

2. Charles Allen, *A Glimpse of the Burning Plain* (London: Michael Joseph, 1986), acknowledgments and 138, 139.

3. Thacker's *Bengal Directory* (Calcutta, 1864), lists two separate photographic firms, Shepherd and Robertson and Howard and Bourne as established in Simla. But by 1865 Howard and Bourne had joined with Shepherd to form the firm of Howard, Bourne, and Shepherd. By 1870 Howard had left the partnership. Also see Clark Worswick and Ainslie Embree, *The Last Empire: Photography in British India, 1855–1911* (Millerton, N.Y.: Aperture, 1976), 35, 38.

4. Donald Horne Macfarlane, "New Dark Tent," *Journal of the Bengal Photographic Society* 1, no.3 (30 December 1862), 1: 58–60.

5. Report of the monthly meeting of the Bengal Photographic Society on 27 November 1860, *Bengal Hurkaru*, 6 December 1860.

6. Report of the monthly meeting of the Bengal Photographic Society on 26 February 1861, *Bengal Hurkaru*, 6 March 1861.

7. Jane Ricketts, "Donald Macfarlane: A New Name in Indian Photography," *The Photographic Collector* 3, no. 1 (Spring 1982), pl. 4.

8. Report of the monthly meeting of the Bengal Photographic Society on 30 July 1861, *Bengal Hurkaru*, 5 August 1861.

9. Macfarlane, "Landscape Photography in India," 26–30.

10. Lieutenant Colonel Stuart-Wortley, "On Photography in Connexion with Art," *The Photographic Journal, Being the Journal of the Photographic Society* 138 (15 October 1863), 365–68.

11. Samuel Bourne, "Photography in the East," *The British Journal of Photography*, (1 July 1863), 268–69.

12. Ibid., 269.

13. Macfarlane, "Landscape Photography in India," 28–29.

14. Report of the monthly meeting of the Bengal Photographic Society, 30 December 1862, *Bengal Hurkaru*, 12 January 1863.

15. Exhibition of the Bengal Photographic Society, extract from a report in the Calcutta newspaper the *Friend of India*, reproduced in the *Journal of the Bengal Photographic Society* 1, no. 2 (September 1862): 45–48.

16. Report of the monthly meeting of the Bengal Photographic Society on 9 July 1862, *Bengal Hurkaru*, 7 August 1862.

17. When attending this, his first meeting, Bourne was surprised by the large membership of the society, its high attendance, its healthy financial state, and the number of distinguished members present including Sir Mordant Wells, chief justice of Calcutta. "Photography in the East," 268, *The Photographic Journal* 157 (15 May 1865).

18. Extract from the review of the exhibition in the *Illustrated London News*, *The Photographic Journal* 159, (15 July 1865), 115.

19. *The British Journal of Photography*, (12 July 1867), 327.

20. *The Times, London* (4 June 1904) and *Who Was Who* 1, London (1897–1915).

UNDISCOVERED AMATEUR: MACFARLANE AND THE PICTURESQUE

60 *A Landscape, Bengal*

Donald Horne Macfarlane

1862, albumen print, 26 x 35.9

Sir Bartle Frere Collection Album

Howard and Jane Ricketts Collection

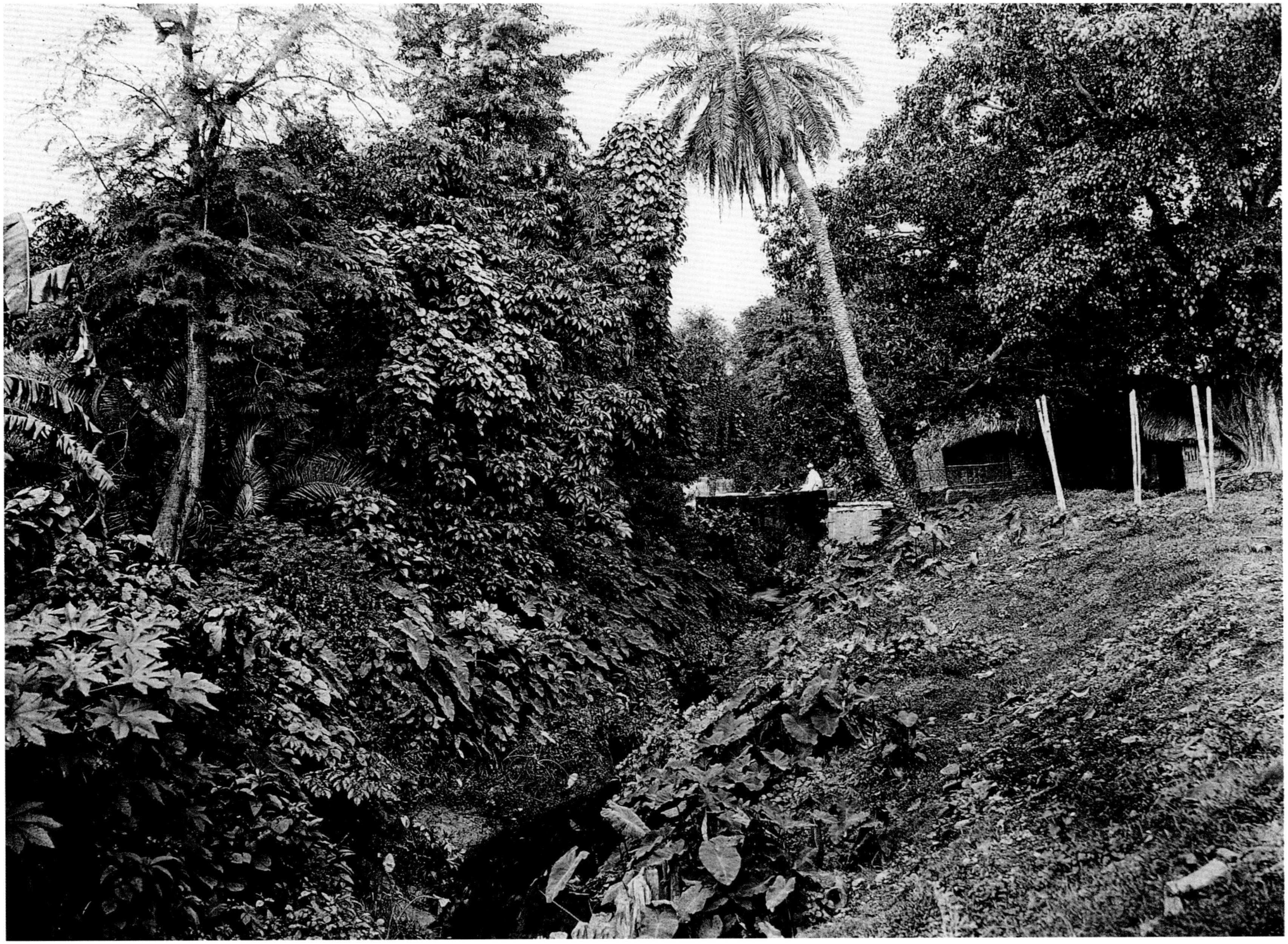

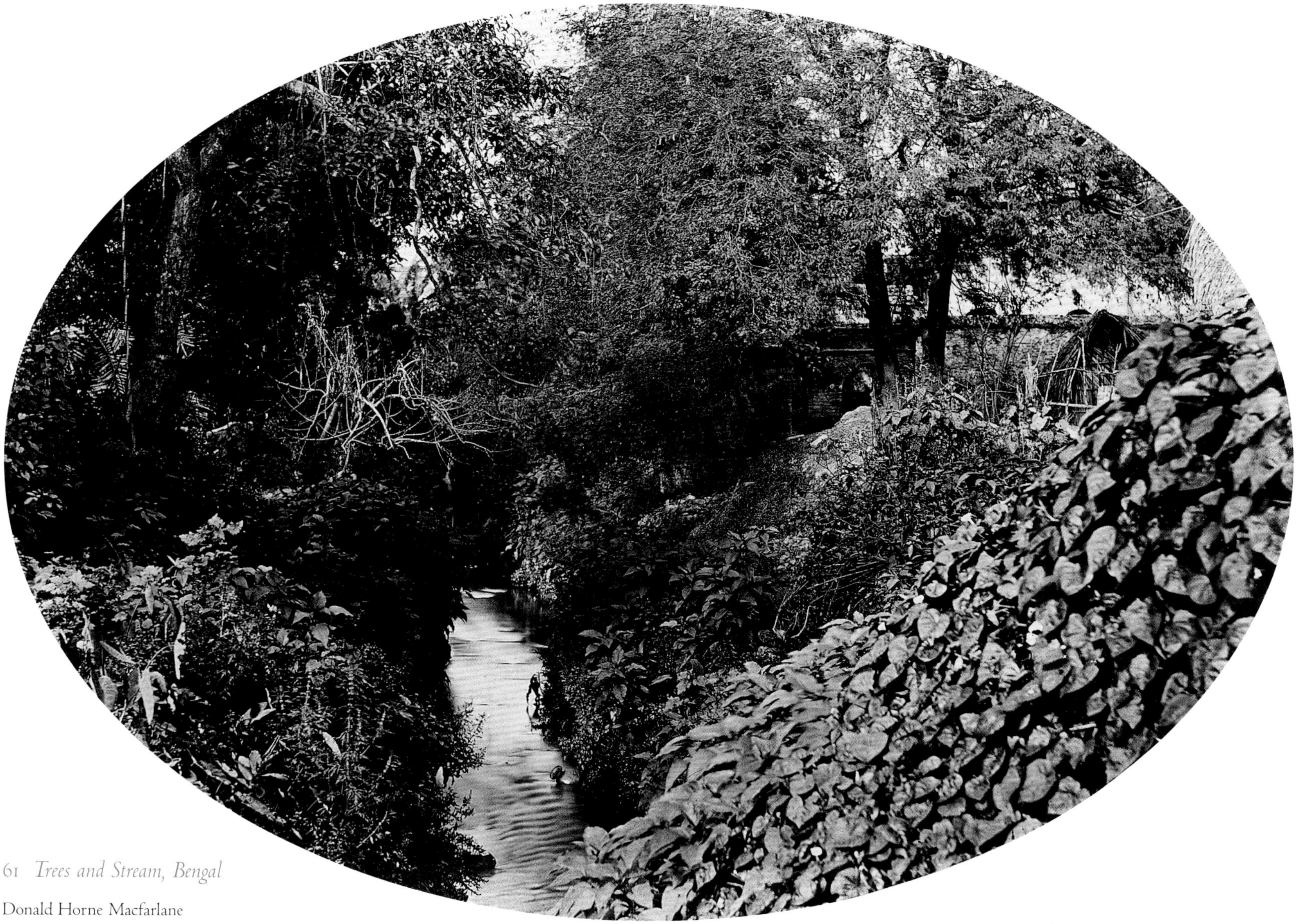

61 *Trees and Stream, Bengal*

Donald Horne Macfarlane

ca. 1861, albumen print, 24 x 34
Sir Bartle Frere Collection Album
Howard and Jane Ricketts Collection

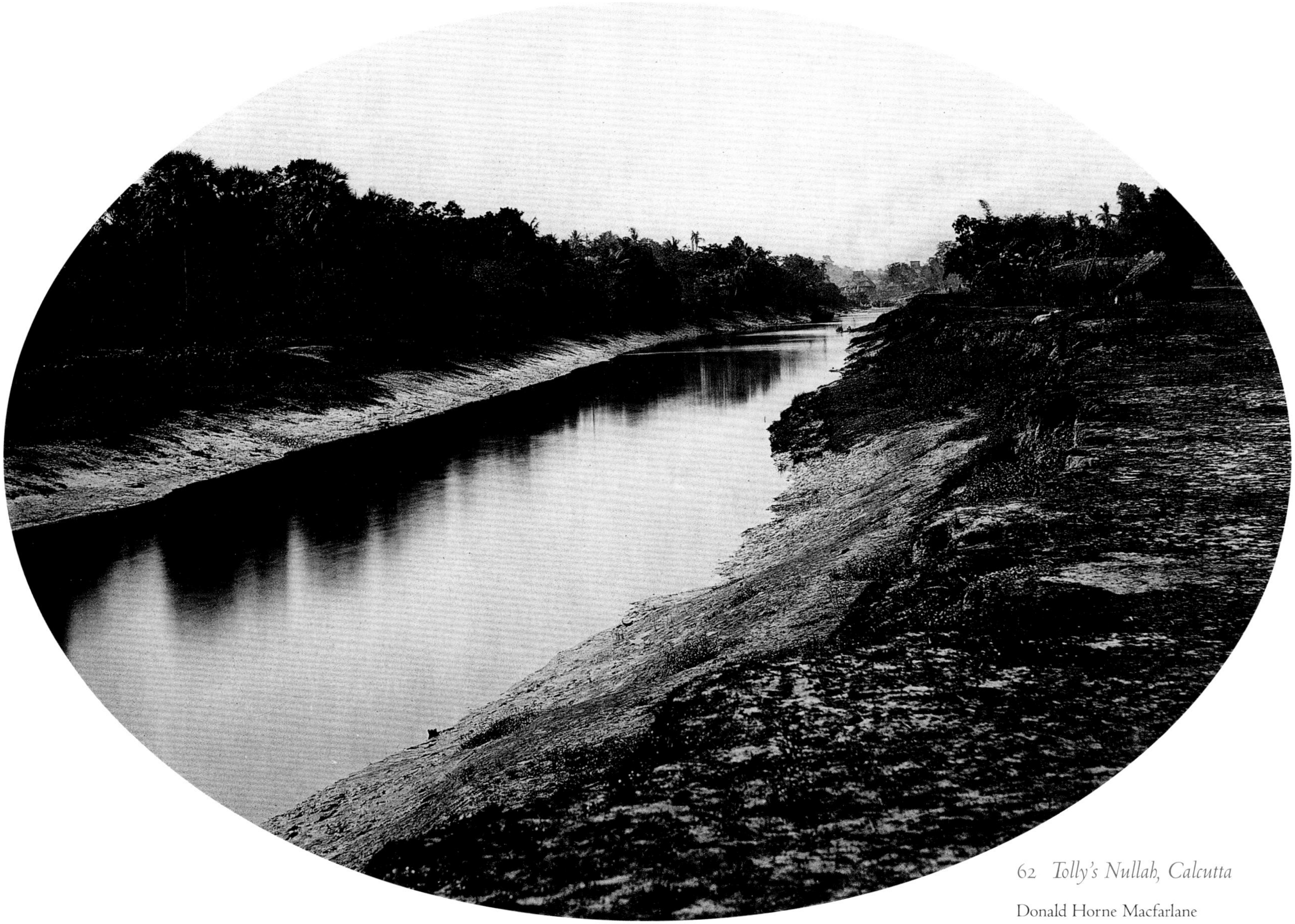

62 *Tolly's Nullah, Calcutta*

Donald Horne Macfarlane

1859–1863, albumen print, 24.5 x 34.2
Sir Bartle Frere Collection Album
Howard and Jane Ricketts Collection

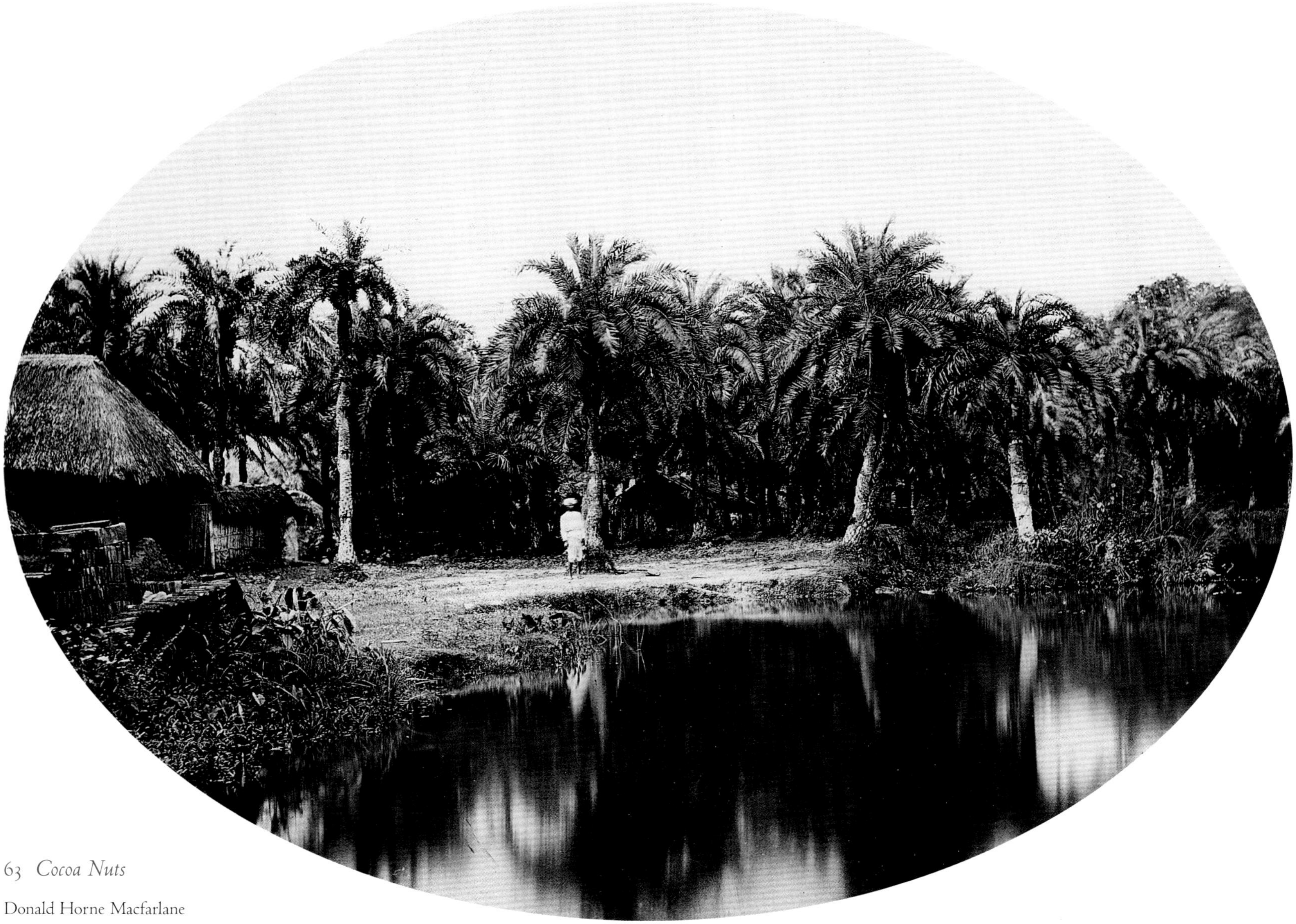

63 *Cocoa Nuts*

Donald Horne Macfarlane

ca. 1862, albumen print, 24.5 x 34.2
Sir Bartle Frere Collection Album
Howard and Jane Ricketts Collection

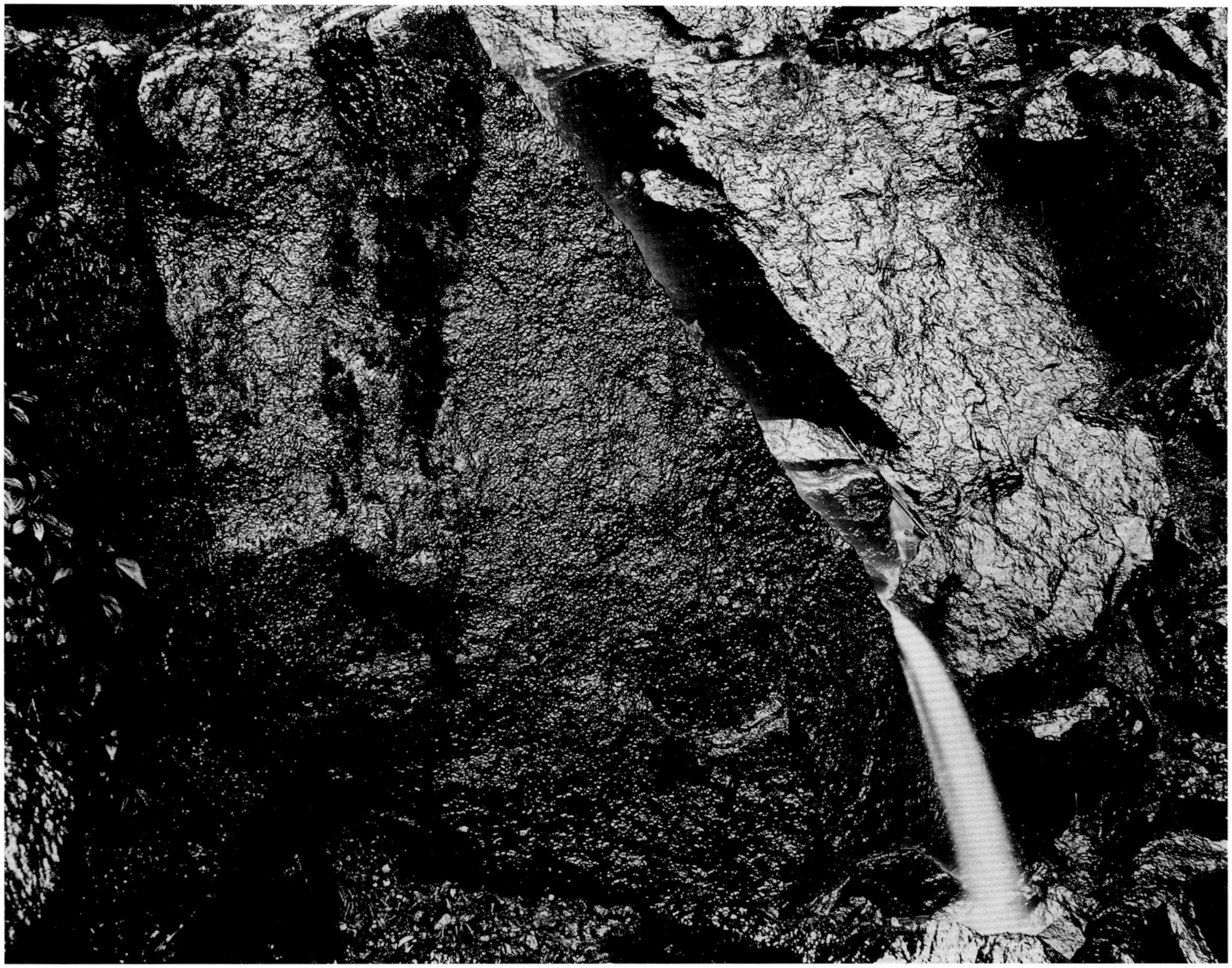

64 *Rocks, Darjeeling*

Donald Horne Macfarlane

1862, albumen print, 22.9 x 29.2
Sir Bartle Frere Collection Album
Howard and Jane Ricketts Collection

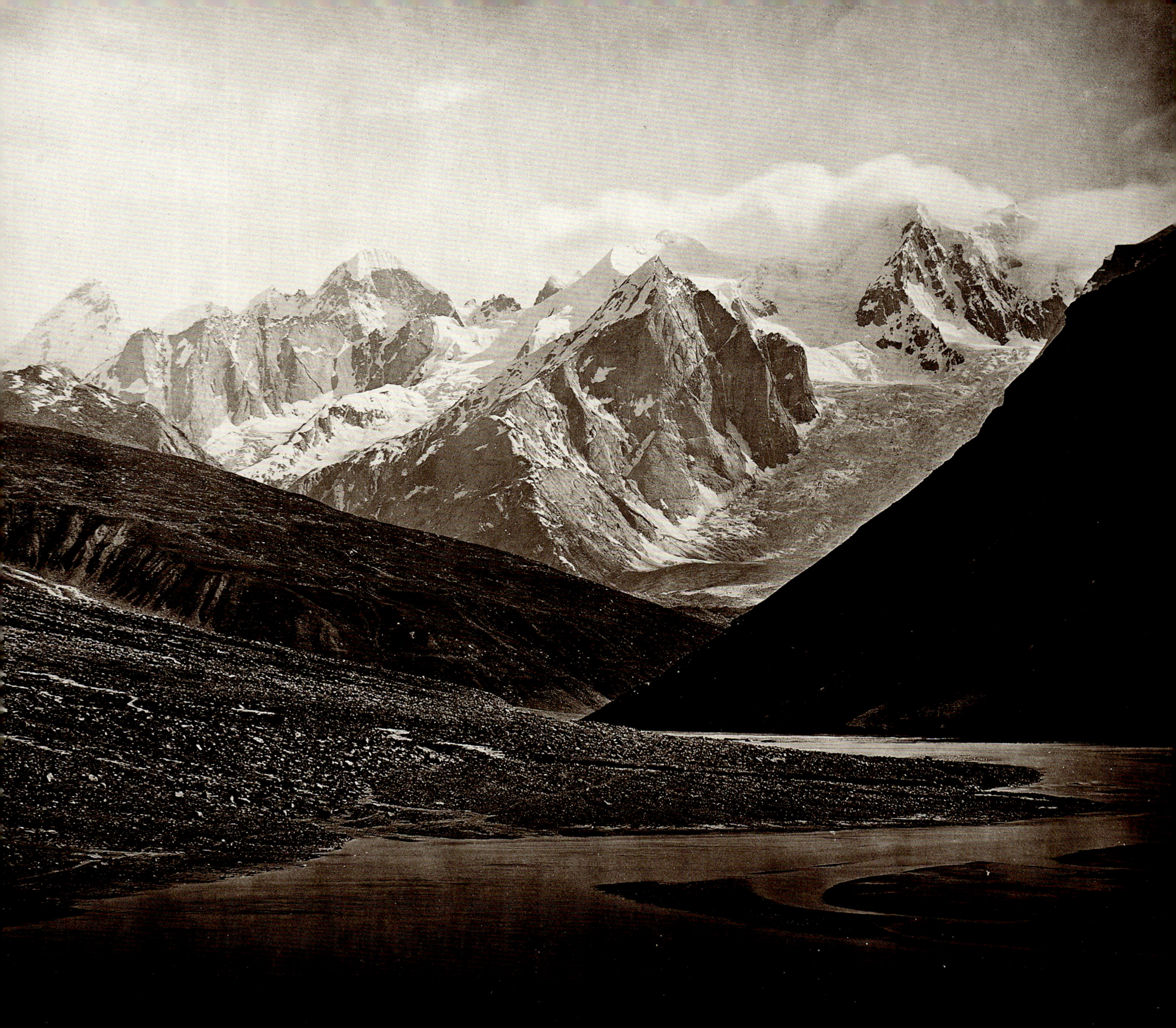

Gary D. Sampson

Photographer of the Picturesque: Samuel Bourne

When the English photographer Samuel Bourne (1834–1912) first ventured into the Himalayas in the summer of 1863, his primary objectives were clear. According to his published narrative of the trip in *The British Journal of Photography*, he had decided "to see what elements of beauty and grandeur lay concealed in some of the higher and little known regions of the Himalayas." This undertaking was soon to be followed by two far more grueling treks, each lasting many months: to Kashmir, "in search of the picturesque," and to the remote source of the Ganges River, "this holy and not altogether unpicturesque object."[1] Bourne's desire to attain such rarefied spectacles and conceive of them as pictorially compelling photographs was partially driven by a spirit of deep religious sentiment with regard to nature. But he was also obsessively determined to secure the best, most interesting, and widely varied pictures as conditions would allow. For similar reasons, not the least of which was entrepreneurial, he extended his photographic activities to the plains of the upper subcontinent and to the hills and temple cities of the south. By the time he left India in 1870, he had established with his partner Charles Shepherd an enduring trade in photographic views at the British hill station of Simla and the imperial cities of Calcutta and Bombay.[2] Bourne's immediate legacy was to make available through the firm's internationally distributed catalogues upwards of two thousand of his own images, the majority of which were marked by a consummate technical facility for the difficult wet-collodion process and by an idealizing vision of India's diverse natural and hand-built environments.

Despite his having obtained an apparently promising position at a Nottingham bank, Bourne's real passion was for photography, which he had begun to practice around 1854. His development as a young amateur culminated in several major excursions to Wales, England's Lake District, and Scotland, whereby he was following a nearly century-old precedent of artists and tourists in search of picturesque scenery. Bourne's artistic ideals, as expressed in a lecture to the Nottingham Photographic Society and later repeatedly voiced in his ebullient Indian narratives,[3] were clearly linked to the late–eighteenth-century imaginative conceits of the beautiful, the sublime, and the picturesque. Although there was originally frequent debate over the distinctive meanings of these terms, the picturesque was quite often freely integrated into discussion to characterize any landscape endowed with scenic charm, whether or not it was beautiful in a dazzling sort of way. What natural and complementary human-made features were considered essential for a truly engaging picture? Rugged peaks, wooded glens, meandering and cascading rivers and streams, rustic cottages, various "singular" phenomena—such irregularly formed or fashioned peculiarities composing a landscape were distinguished as picturesque by travelers of the Romantic period. In landscape parlance, any natural spectacle considered "wild" or "rude" or "terrible" in its overwhelming presence might also be considered sublime; yet these same attributes also came to be indiscriminately associated with the picturesque.[4] In any case, the general notion of what constitutes the picturesque had become so thoroughly ingrained in the cultured Victorian imagination that it was imperative for a successful photographer of "views" to be adept at searching out just the right sort of features, then strategically framing and articulating their physical subtleties through proper exposure of the negative. Bourne's particular artistic concerns, which were conditionally based upon his initial fondness for *English* hills and countryside, would have a profound impact on the way he determined his subjects for the camera in the Himalayas.

By 1863 Bourne had quit the bank and voyaged to India, landing first in Madras, then Calcutta. He apparently had grown tired of urban society and was eager to immerse himself completely in his art in a region as far away as possible from the tourist hordes of Britain and continental Europe. In his own words he had answered "the call of the East," but prudently not before having made arrangements to enter into an already established studio in upper India. Keen to share his new experiences with his peers back home, he immediately set about recording his perceptions of the subcontinent, which would eventually be published in installments in *The British Journal of Photography.* What emerges from his earliest cor-

Page 162: No. 74. *Distant View of the Snowy Summits, South of the Shigri Glacier,* Samuel Bourne

respondence is an attraction to the architecture of India's past, in contrast to a singular lack of interest in the abundance of grand colonialist edifices seen especially in the British capital, Calcutta. Places like Agra's Taj Mahal or the palace and mosque complex at Fatehpur Sikri no doubt fascinated Bourne because of their obvious differences from European building traditions, as exemplified by Calcutta—"a place totally devoid of architectural beauty," according to the artist.[5] Only a few years prior to Bourne's arrival numerous bloody clashes had occurred at Delhi and other locations throughout north central and eastern India between the British and Indian troops in the British army. This uprising of Indian sepoys (soldiers) against their British superiors (and the European presence on the subcontinent in general) came to be known as the Indian Mutiny of 1857, although from an Indian perspective it could be readily interpreted as an early effort to gain freedom from British rule.[6] That the rebellion was still fresh in the minds of the British in the early 1860s is evident in Bourne's account of his first visit to Delhi, "a name sadly famous to every Englishman." "Of course," he continued, "Delhi can't fail to be of interest to the photographer: the 'Cashmere Gate,' the fort, and other noted places must be taken, while its mosques and similar buildings will be photographed for their own merits."[7] Bourne certainly knew that his sentiments would resonate with his fellow Anglo-Indians as well as the English back home. He would thus return to Delhi, Agra, and other localities partly out of personal desire to photograph their architectural splendors, and partly because as a merchant of photographic views, he could ill afford to overlook a patronage desirous of pictures of places associated with the conflict.

Bourne's location of his studio in the foothills of the western Himalayas was clearly calculated to give him the most advantageous situation for launching his photographic campaigns. Simla was at the time the seasonal retreat of the British government and therefore a key location for its social and political connections with the rest of colonized India.[8] It was *the* place to be for many Anglo-Indians while the upper plains were enduring the intense heat of late spring and summer: a bustling extension of urbane society, the scene of romantic and political intrigue alike. Perhaps most significantly from Bourne's personal point of view, Simla was a crucial trailhead for access into the high country; from the hill station, which varied in elevation from seven thousand to eight thousand feet, the photographer would begin each of his three treks. He chose his routes with great care, planning his itineraries based on the latest maps, the locations of renowned geological phenomena—glaciers, high passes, the sources of major rivers, unusual landforms with fossils—and indigenous structures specific to the Himalayas, including villages, temples, bridges, and places of archaeological note. For all his preliminary planning, however, there was much that would be unpredictable along the trail. He was often faced with the severest conditions, taxing both his own physical limits and endurance as well as the willingness of his many "coolies" to stay with an obsessive, hard-driving, and sometimes abusive sahib. His generally large entourage of porters (forty-two at one point) were often assembled from reluctant villagers at different stages en route to his destinations; apart from them he could not possibly have undertaken his expeditions. But as far as Bourne was concerned, any unpleasant business with the "natives" was justified if it helped him to obtain his objectives. One has only to read his words at the end of his first trip to realize the tremendous pride that he took in his accomplishments: "I had been absent ten weeks, and with the exception of a broken ground-glass, returned with all my instruments uninjured, and with a stock of 147 negatives, representing, as I believe they do, scenery which has never been photographed before, and amongst the boldest and most striking on the face of the globe."[9]

Bourne's zealous pursuit of pictorially worthy scenes in the Himalayas was frequently tempered by his frustrations over trying to frame the vast spectacle of terrain within his camera's field of view and still maintain his English sense of balanced composition and containment of suitably picturesque or sublime features. Yet this only challenged him to produce more than one view of a given area, often with the most subtle variations and in two or three different formats (nos. 65, 66, 72, 74), by which he was able to expand the possibilities for comprehending the unwieldy and very often *un*-picturesque topography encountered on his treks. Many of his photographs, however remarkable for their individual pictorial appeal, yield further perceptual revelations of a locale or prominent feature when considered in relationship to the artist's carefully selected alternates. River and glacial chasms gave him particular difficulty because of their immensity, but one finds that he gradually improved his ability to frame and to vary his vantage points to approximate on-the-spot sensations both aesthetic and physical. There was also the question of whether to incorporate a few "pilgrims" into the foreground of an image of towering peaks and plummeting abyss, which would help to establish a fixed position for the outside spectator of the picture. The alternative would be to leave the foreground out of the picture altogether in order to encourage a kind of vicarious thrill of suspension before the precipice. Bourne would indeed do both with increasing sophistication, sometimes experimenting with smaller sized formats (10.8 x 8.9 and 17.8 x 10.7 cm) before exposing one of his precious, preferred larger glass negatives (30.5 x 25.4 and 33 x 20.3 cm).

The sheer delight that Bourne derived from his wilderness encounters of cascades, thickly wooded slopes, and high peaks was matched only by his pleasure when reconnoitering and photographing the Islamic gardens and waterways of Srinagar, the principal town of the "Vale of Kashmir." The written narrative of his lengthy stay in Srinagar provides a colonialist's perspective of the social and political conditions of the region, which was formerly the summer refuge of the Mughal emperors of the late sixteenth through seventeenth centuries. His pictorial representation, however, scarcely reveals anything of the present-day realities of the place, while seeming to revel in the aura of enchantment associated with Srinagar's legendary past. As one would expect, the scenery was compelling because it could be imagined as an exotic counterpart to the English scenery (no. 67). In his pictures, Bourne was able to obtain an exquisite delicacy of detail, tonal nuance, and careful composition, an achievement for which he would receive much acclaim from his fellow members of the Bengal Photographic Society.

By way of contrast, British hill settlements or "stations" were hardly a match for Srinagar, although even at Simla Bourne managed to parlay his skills into coaxing out its more scenic prospects. Still, other sites of British occupation in the mountains he found more photogenic, such as Nynee Tal to the northeast of Delhi (no. 68), Ootacamund in the Nilgiri Hills in south India, and Darjeeling to the north of Calcutta in the Himalayas. Winding roads, lakes and rivers, and the bungalow and chaletlike residences of Anglo-Indians were framed to appear as pictorially attractive as possible—often short perspectives through the trees, which were given titles that included the words "bits," "peeps," and "glimpses." (no. 69) One might well forget that they were actually taken in India, save for an Indian or two placed informally within the composition. If the town contained any indigenous quarter, one would scarcely know it: any architecture of vernacular appearance must conform to a pictorial code of rusticity. Features like the "native bazaar" at Simla, for instance, with its disorderly array of merchant stalls, would only be glimpsed from afar in Bourne's pictures, but the ramshackle wooden structures and Islamic ogee arches of Srinagar would be fair game for the camera. These, after all, were emblems of the exotic East, easily conforming to Western aesthetic requirements. The streets and shops themselves, however, were held in symbolic contrast to the residences of the European population—"abodes of comfort and civilization" as Bourne once characterized them. Schools, churches, cemeteries, club buildings, hotels, general stores, even racetracks and polo fields: these signs of the pervasive spread of Western culture were also directly recorded by the artist, of certain interest for the residents and tourists of the hills who were among Bourne's best patrons (no. 70). But in such pictures the "native" element was either invisible or transmuted into an overall pictorial scheme.

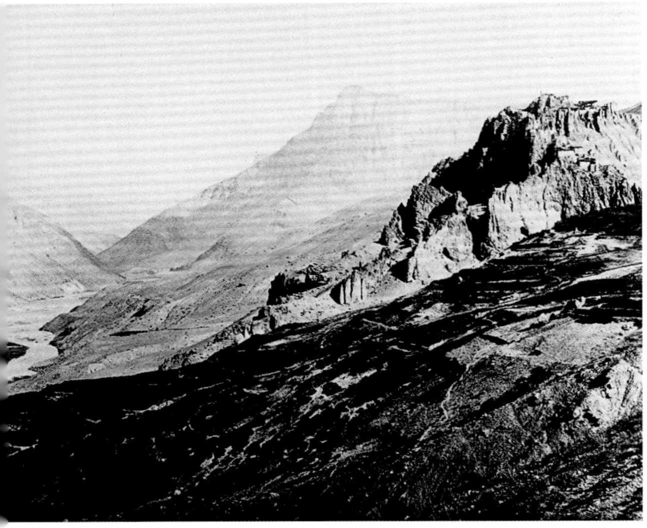

FIGURE 1 Samuel Bourne, *Distant View of Dunkar and the Spiti Valley*, 1866, albumen print from wet-collodion negative, 19 x 32, Bourne and Shepherd catalogue number 1463. Victoria and Albert Museum, London

The same could also be said of Bourne's vision of Himalayan peoples who lived in the remote wilderness. Anything natural or of human design that might pique Western curiosity could be regarded as "singular." Singular objects composed their own subgenre of picturesque subject matter,[10] which varied from crudely fashioned rope or wooden bridges, stone monuments to *sati* (the sacrificial burning of Hindu widows), multistoried temples and storage buildings, to odd or horrific geologic formations. Although the singular abounds in the images produced on all three of his treks, the most pronounced occurrences can be seen in the pictures he secured on his third and final trek, at the climax of which he attained the nearly inaccessible source of the Ganges River. His itinerary along the way led him through the "wild" and "desolate" Spiti Valley region where, for instance, the Tibetan Buddhists of Dunkar had built their mud-brick and stone edifices on the rockiest of mountain escarpments. That he was captivated by the spectacular siting of the Dunkar buildings, which seemed as if they had been geologically extruded from the very earth, is apparent from the several dramatic views he was able to obtain of the fortress and village (see fig. 1 and no. 73).

At Spiti and elsewhere, environmental extremes held a special double intrigue for Bourne. On the one hand, he was awed by the sheer enormity and imposing physical presence of the Himalayas. With characteristic consistency, he was able to record within a single exposure the hard textures of rock surfaces, the variable densities of foliage, and the tonal subtleties of cloud formations. On the other hand, he would find himself transported to alternating states of utter humility and exhilaration by the breathtaking vistas high atop a pass. On a number of occasions, the photographer became the mystic. After a panoramic description of the scene at Meribul Pass on his Kashmir expedition, Bourne digressed:

> What a scene was the whole to look upon! And what a puny thing I felt standing on that crest of snow!—a mere atom, and scarcely that in so stupendous a world! To gaze upon a scene like this till a feeling of awe and insignificance steals over you, and then reflect that in the midst of this vast assemblage of sublime creation *you* are not uncared-for nor forgotten, cannot fail to deepen the veneration of every right-feeling man for that Almighty, but Beneficent Power, who upreared the mountains, and in whose hand is the breath of every living thing.[11]

Such sentiments were the clear expressions of one who felt deeply the intimations of the divine in nature (no small surprise since Bourne was known by his friends to have been a devout Unitarian). His choice of words and the ease with which Bourne was able to step out of the prosaic retelling of his experiences on the trail to ruminate on his place in the universe before the sublime spectacle of mountain wilderness is remarkably akin to the narratives of his explorer predecessors, who liberally applied the language of the sublime and the picturesque whenever so inspired during their ostensibly scientific exploits in the higher Himalayas.[12] The photographer's Himalayan narratives are in fact liberally seasoned with attention to natural curiosities that were ultimately determined by the scientific discussions of his day. This interest was reinforced considerably with the presence of one George Rankin Playfair (1816–1881) on the first half of Bourne's third expedition. Playfair, a surgeon in the Indian medical service, was knowledgeable in natural history. He kept his photographer companion informed with respect to the latest theories of glacial movement and directed his attention to specific demonstrations of such phenomena as at the Great Shigri Glacier,[13] which they encountered on the way to Spiti. On at least one occasion Playfair recruited Bourne to help him dig for fossils in Spiti, which was also particularly noteworthy in its striking eroded landforms and irregular conglomerate pillars of dirt and rock. Bourne recorded these in several photographs with titles like *Contorted Strata at Losar,* and *Curious Formations on the Spiti River at Kioto, Spiti.* Playfair had to eventually abandon the trek, having sustained a serious sprain, but Bourne continued to pick his way over the most difficult of routes: the 18,600-foot-high Manirung Pass, where he captured in three views a sense of the tremendous upheaval of mountain geology.

Bourne's cultivated awareness of the natural and human-built environment through which he traveled is also witnessed in his photographs of Hindu, Buddhist, Jain, and Islamic architecture. They reveal that he had read at least some of the recently published travel guides and scholarly journals to sort out which sites merited photography. A proof of the timeliness and perspicacity of his photographic pursuits in the upper and southern regions of the subcontinent was the purchase of nearly the entire inventory of his large-plate views of India's architectural legacy, in addition to his Himalayan pictures, by London's South Kensington Museum, established in 1856. The South Kensington, which would later become the Victoria and Albert Museum, took an avid interest in the cultural patrimony and works of industry of the growing British Empire, so much so that by the early 1870s it had produced actual plaster casts of major monuments of India. These included one of the thirty-three-foot gateways from the ancient Buddhist Great Stupa at Sanchi and the central pillar from the audience hall (or Diwan-i Khass) of Akbar's palace at Fatehpur Sikri.[14] Bourne photographed Fatehpur Sikri extensively (including the intricately carved pillar, no. 77), along with other wonders such as the Taj Mahal and lesser-known buildings of the Mughal Empire (nos. 75, 76, 78). Their ornate, richly articulated surfaces and bold structural masses held a general fascination for the educated Victorian public. To the category of picturesque remnants of former civilizations or cultures deemed of significance in the grand narrative of history—especially the ancient Roman and European culture of the high Middle Ages—could be added the crumbling Buddhist shrines and Hindu temples of antiquity, as well as "Muhammadan" architectural forms. Although the last Mughal ruler had been only recently deposed following the sepoy rebellion, the climax of the empire was viewed as having passed with the age of Akbar (reigned 1556–1605), Jahangir (reigned 1605–27), and Shah-Jahan (reigned 1628–58), under whose direction the Taj had been built. The British regarded the Mughal dynasty with special veneration because as a colonialist power, it was believed to have made a superior cultural and social impact on indigenous India.[15] Bourne's photographs of the palace precinct of Fatehpur Sikri and other imperial edifices of upper India would therefore have played to the fantasizing of former Mughal splendor against a background of historical destiny.

As might be evident by now, the line separating Bourne's choice of subjects for their promise as artistic expressions and for their larger cultural associations was often very fine indeed. His photographs suggest the uneasy relationship between native India and the Raj (the British rule) that existed in the years following the queen's assumption of power after the sepoy conflict. Bourne pictured the major sites of the "mutiny" that surely lingered in every European resident's mind: Lucknow, Delhi, and Kanpur. Because each had been the scene of siege and massacre of the English, any related photographs would serve to underscore the former treachery of the rebellious Indians and the ensuing violent retribution, which from a British perspective would have seemed mostly, if not entirely, justified. The Residency at Lucknow, in ruins at the time of Bourne's visit, had been made a kind of pilgrimage site for tourists. Its surroundings had been cleaned up, but ivy was left to grow luxuriantly up the fragmented walls so that the buildings presented themselves to the beholder in a eerily picturesque sort of way. Similarly, the Kanpur Well, into which numerous women and children were thought to have been thrown by mutineers, had been memorialized by a full-length seraphim surrounded by a Gothic Revival screen. The cenotaph was erected within the sequestered confines of a memorial garden, which was generally off limits to Indians. Though the memorial well had been planned several years earlier, it was only unveiled in 1865. Soon thereafter Bourne arrived on the spot to photograph it from various angles, fully exploiting the appealing character of the foliage that had been cultivated all around (no. 79). Undoubtedly his photographs contributed to the shrine's rise as a major tourist destination, which for a time was visited more frequently than the Taj Mahal.[16]

Bourne occasionally produced pictures that explicitly evoked the economic foundations of colonialist India, such as the tea and cinchona plantations of the lower Himalayas (the bark of the cinchona tree—native to the Andes and introduced to India in 1859—is used to make quinine). At least one series taken in Darjeeling appears to have been actually commissioned by a plantation owner. Another series depicts the bustling shipping operations along the Hooghly River, the main artery that channeled the goods of empire in and out of Calcutta. In these, there are vessels large and small, whose irregular vertical masts of varying height engage the eye in a manner reminiscent of earlier and contemporary maritime paintings. One particularly engaging example shows Indian stevedores momentarily rendered immobile by the dictates of photographic exposure (no. 80). Both the Darjeeling plantation and the Calcutta shipping photographs—exceptional glimpses of Indian production and labor in support of British enterprise—essentially deny the native worker any real identity. They are present only insofar as they have been assimilated by Bourne into his overall compositions, thus symbolically reiterating their generally anonymous compliance with the demands of the Raj.

The closest Bourne would come to depicting the people as individual subjects rather than picturesque characterizations came at the very end of his time in India, in which the viewer is presented with direct frontal images of specific mountain "tribes" in the vicinity of Darjeeling. Following his trip to the latter region in 1869, he made one final tour in India, of the southern portion of the subcontinent. There he visited the hill country of the Nilgiris, at the heart of which was the popular British station of Ootacamund. The people of these hills, the Todas, were thought by contemporaneous ethnologists to be a primitive yet noble shepherd people. Bourne depicted a group of them in front of a pair of thatched roofed, wooden huts. Despite their having been given a more prominent position as subjects, one becomes aware of the difficulty of trying to distinguish an honest effort to understand the Todas from a sense of rapt fascination with a vanishing breed of preindustrial humanity.[17] No such difficulty is encountered, however, in the majority of Bourne's pictures in which villagers are either nowhere to be seen or are merely available indigenous types who are integral to an exotic genre of representing "native" habitations as part of a larger continuum of nature. This can be witnessed in the pictures of villages in the Spiti region and in a series of jungle views taken near Calcutta, which Bourne revealingly titled as a whole, *Rustic Scenes and Village Life in Bengal* (no. 81).

The jungle can be appreciated as a nineteenth-century metaphor for the unknown, the darkness of ignorance, and for the inhabitants who subsist by instinct and custom in any region characterized by dense growth and tropical climate. In contrast, the park, as evinced by the surroundings of the memorial well at Kanpur, or the cultivated grounds located at Barrackpore near Calcutta, was emblematic of nature civilized, where reminders of the wilderness might flourish in botanical form, but with the careful restraint of refined taste and bridled passions. Barrackpore Park and Government House, which were located a few miles up the Hooghly from Calcutta, had been an unofficial country retreat for the governor-generals of British India since early in the century. The grounds had been planned in accordance with a picturesque garden sensibility to allow for grand prospects, similar to the luxurious country estates of eighteenth-century England. Bourne photographed Barrackpore within the same two-month period as his Bengal and Calcutta series in 1867 (he also opened a new branch of Bourne and Shepherd in Calcutta at this time). The photographer had recently returned from a trip to England, where he had married Mary Tolley (1844–1912). She appears in two of the most extraordinary of her husband's photographs of Barrackpore, which show her as modestly dressed young woman, contemplatively seated amid a variety of indigenous tree and plant specimens. One of these rather amusingly reveals her next to some tree ferns with a vine-covered, sham Gothic ruin behind her; in the other, Mary Bourne appears beneath the canopy of an enormous banyan, whose fantastic array of vertical shoots had made it one of the more exotically intriguing trees known to the Western world (no. 83).[18] The hybrid nature of the park—an English picturesque plan into which had been selectively integrated natural tokens of indigenous India—might well be considered a trope for the ongoing effort on the part of the British to bring order to a vastly complex, at times unfathomable, subcontinent. When one realizes that the adjacent cantonment, or military garrison, had been the locale of the first mutinous assault on the British in 1857, the idea of Bourne's wife at Barrackpore becomes more than simply a personal touch. It must have conveyed to contemporaneous patrons a reassuring sign of momentary stability within the empire, but with a subliminal cautionary note that Britain's political hold on India might eventually give way to internal efforts to loosen it altogether.

Bourne returned to Nottingham with Mary and their first child in 1870 in order to join his brother-in-law in the operation of a cotton yarn factory, but the studios of Bourne and Shepherd would continue to thrive well into the next century. While little is known regarding the photographers who carried on the business, before Bourne left he and Shepherd had taken on the talented photographer Colin Murray, who would soon advance to partnership at the recently established studio in Bombay. Murray has been considered a kind of protégé of Bourne, primarily because he became quite adept at practicing the wet-collodion process in an artistically expressive manner similar to the older photographer (no. 84). As much as one might be fascinated by the aesthetic eloquence and the grand spirit of adventure that lives on in Bourne's pictorial achievement, perhaps most significant are the wider meanings associated with the dissemination of his and his successors' images as revealed in the surviving albums, collections, and illustrated material of empire. Together they evoke a strong symbolic tie with Britain's surveillance of the subcontinent to secure political control over its peoples, lands, and cultural heritage. Bourne himself displayed a colonialist attitude in his journal articles, deliberately included politically charged destinations on his photographic itineraries, and was well aware of important documentary activities in geology, archaeology, and ethnography that had occurred before and during his own operations in India. In this respect the idealism of the picturesque that generally inflected Bourne's vision of India was complicit in the production of a deceptively benign representation of India as a relatively safe and exotically scenic land for favorable cultural and commercial exploit.

NOTES

1. Samuel Bourne, "Ten Weeks with the Camera in the Himalayas," *The British Journal of Photography* [hereafter, *BJP*] (1 February 1864): 50; "Narrative of a Photographic Journey to Kashmir (Cashmere) and Adjacent Districts," *BJP* (4 January 1867): 4; "A Photographic Journey through the Higher Himalayas," *BJP* (18 March 1870): 126.

2. For detailed discussion and references regarding the establishment of Bourne and Shepherd, and Bourne in India in general, see Gary D. Sampson, "The Success of Samuel Bourne in India," *History of Photography* 16, no. 4 (Winter 1992): 336–47.

3. Samuel Bourne, "On Some of the Requisites Necessary for the Production of a Good Photograph," *Nottingham Athenaeum Society Magazine* (August 1860): 5–34; (October 1860): 35–42; (December 1860): 68–73.

4. A good point of departure for understanding the meaning and legacy of the picturesque is Stephen Copely and Peter Garside, eds., *The Politics of the Picturesque: Literature, Landscape and Aesthetics Since 1770* (Cambridge: Cambridge University Press, 1994), 1–12.

5. Bourne, "Photography in the East," *BJP* (1 July 1863):269.

6. The literature on the Indian rebellion is vast; for an introduction within the context of British rule, see P. J. Marshall, "1783–1870: An Expanding Empire," and Tapan Raychaudhuri, "British Rule in India: An Assessment," in *The Cambridge Illustrated History of the British Empire*, ed. P. J. Marshall (Cambridge: Cambridge University Press, 1996), 46–51, 357–61.

7. Bourne, "Photography in the East," *BJP* (1 September 1863): 345.

8. For an introduction to Simla, see Pat Barr and Ray Desmond, *Simla: A Hill Station in British India* (New York: Charles Scribner's Sons, 1978); and for further study of the colonialist hill station, Anthony D. King, "Culture, Social Power and Environment: The Hill Station in Colonial Urban Development," *Social Action* 26 (July–September 1976): 195–213.

9. Bourne, "Ten Weeks with the Camera in the Himalayas," *BJP* (15 February 1864): 70.

10. See Barbara Maria Stafford, "Toward Romantic Landscape Perception: Illustrated Travels and the Rise of 'Singularity' as an Aesthetic Category," *Art Quarterly* 2 (Autumn 1977): 89–122.

11. Bourne, "A Photographic Journey through the Higher Himalayas," *BJP* (7 December 1866): 584.

12. See, e.g., Maj. Sir William Lloyd, *Narrative of a Journey from Caunpoor to the Boorendo Pass in the Himalaya Mountains, via Gwalior, Agra, Delhi, and Sirhind, by Major Sir William Lloyd, and Captain Alexander Gerard's Account of an Attempt to Penetrate by Bekhur to Garoo, and the Lake Manasarowara . . . ,*" ed. George Lloyd, vol. 1 (London: J. Madden and Co., 1840), 248–49.

13. Bourne, "A Photographic Journey through the Higher Himalayas," *BJP* (31 December 1869): 629.

14. On the South Kensington Museum and the noted monuments, see Tim Barringer, "The South Kensington Museum and the Colonialist Project," in *Colonialism and the Object: Empire, Material Culture and the Museum*, ed. Tim Barringer and Tom Flynn (London: Routledge, 1998), 11–27.

15. Thomas R. Metcalf, *Ideologies of the Raj*, part 3, vol. 4, *The New Cambridge History of India* (Cambridge: Cambridge University Press, 1994), 88–89, 154–58.

16. Andrew Ward, *Our Bones Are Scattered: The Cawnpore Massacre and the Indian Mutiny/1857* (New York: Henry Holt, 1996), 550–51.

17. On the Todas' appearance in the literature of empire, including a reproduction of Bourne's photograph, see C. A. Bayly, ed., *The Raj: India and the British, 1600–1947* (London: National Portrait Gallery, 1990), 301–03.

18. The motif of the banyan tree as metaphor for jungle and race is explored in Christopher Pinney, "Under the Banyan Tree: William Crook and Photographic Depictions of Caste," in *Anthropology and Photography, 1860–1920*, ed. Elizabeth Edwards (New Haven: Yale University Press in association with the Royal Anthropological Institute, 1992), 165–73.

PHOTOGRAPHER OF THE PICTURESQUE: SAMUEL BOURNE

65 *View in Wanga Valley* [Simla]

Samuel Bourne

1863, albumen print, 29.3 x 24.5
Bourne and Shepherd catalogue number
261, Howard and Jane Ricketts Collection

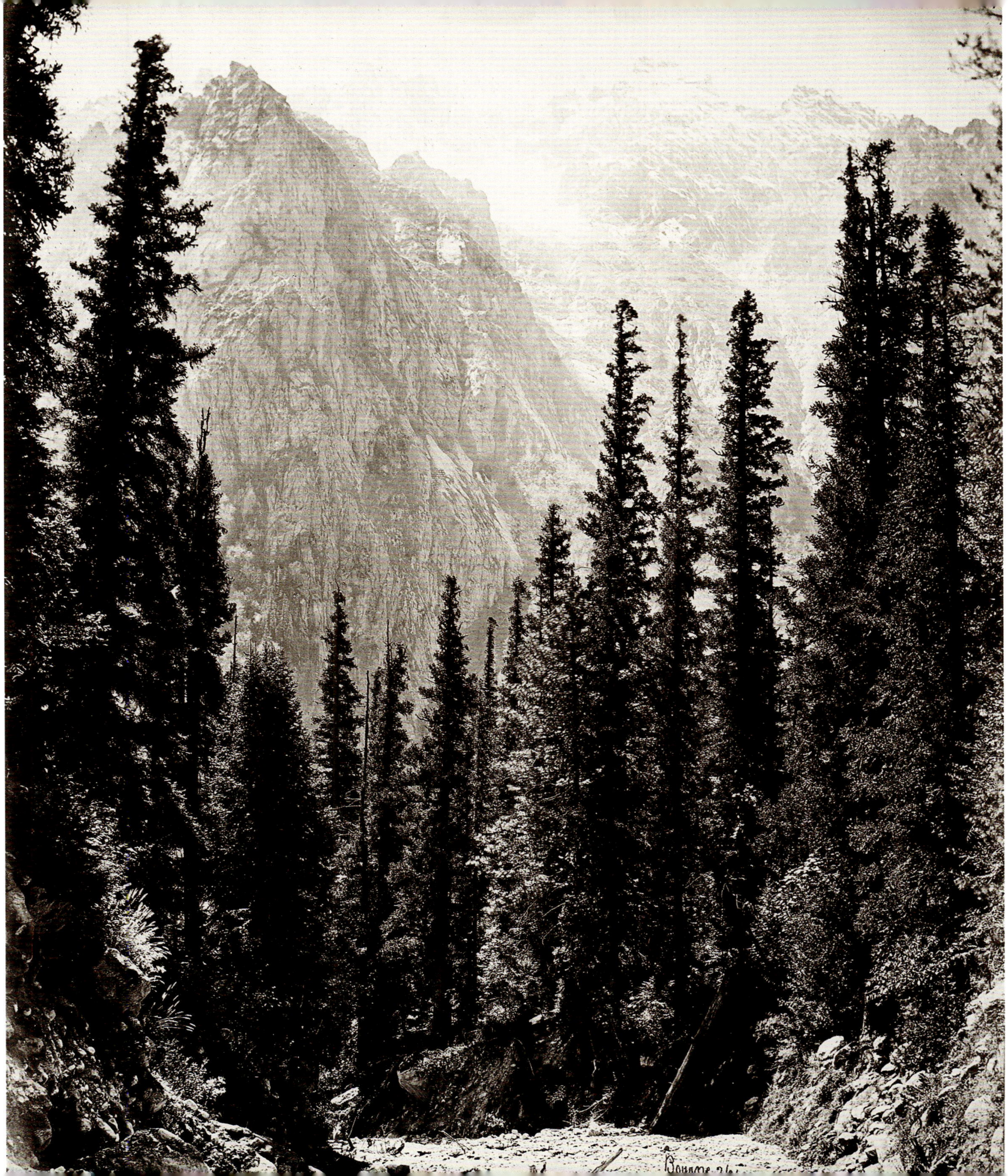
Bourne

66 *View in Zojji-La Pass* [Kashmir]

Samuel Bourne

1864, albumen print, 28.6 x 23.9
Bourne and Shepherd catalogue number
990, Howard and Jane Ricketts Collection

67 *View on the Canal*
[Kashmir. Prize photograph, 1865]

Samuel Bourne

1864, albumen print, 22.4 x 28.3
Bourne and Shepherd catalogue number
825, Smithsonian Institution, Freer Gallery
of Art and Arthur M. Sackler Gallery
Archives

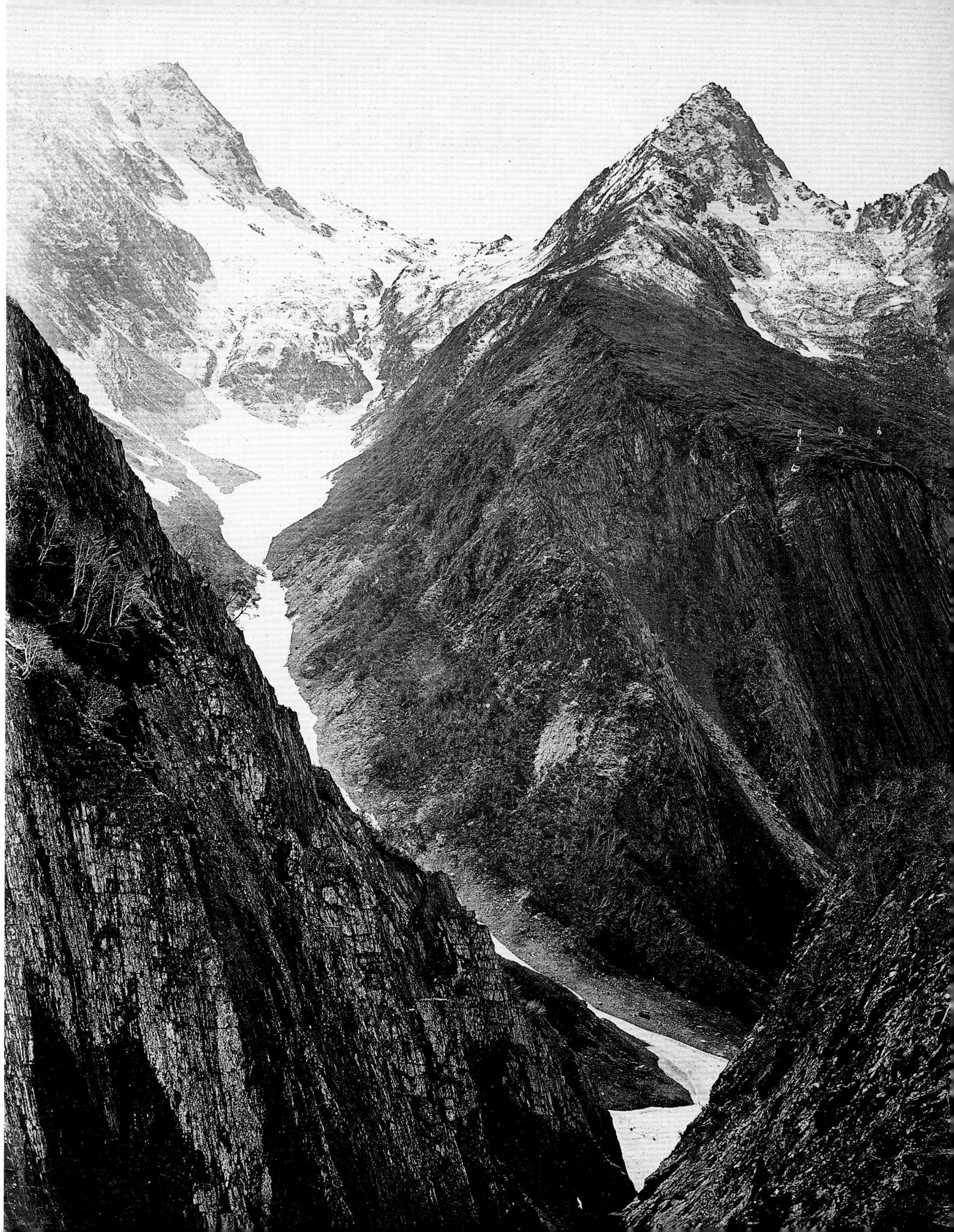

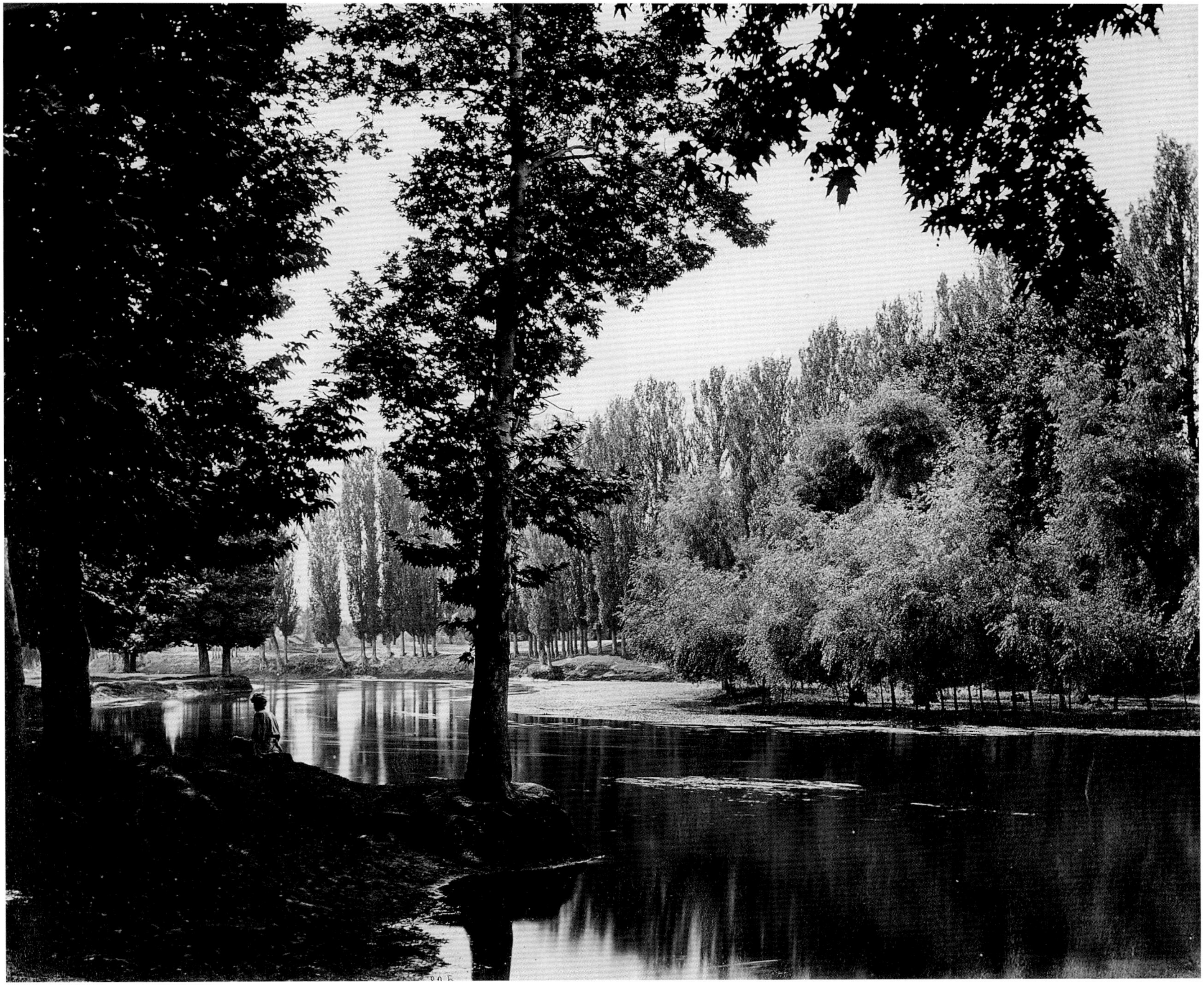

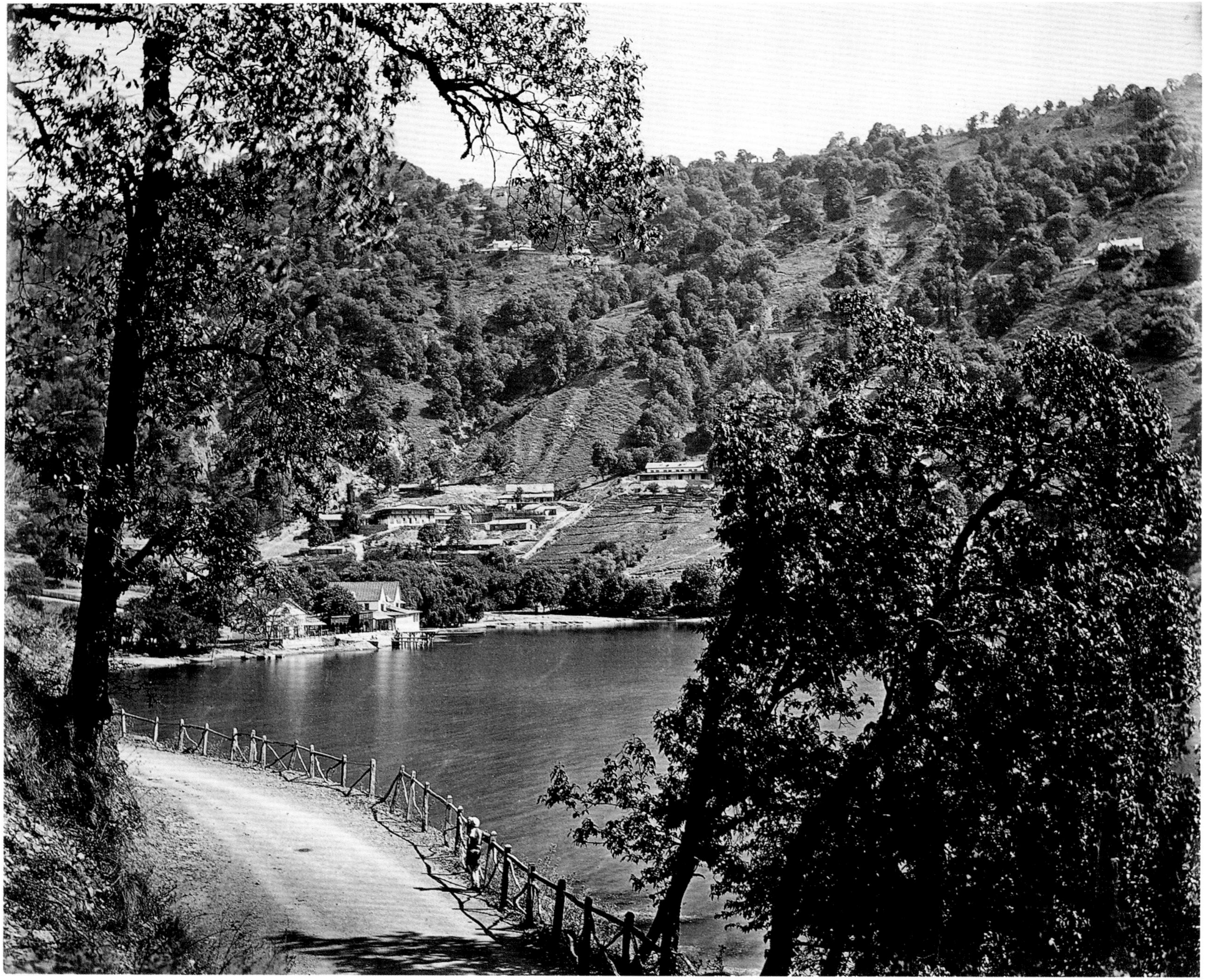

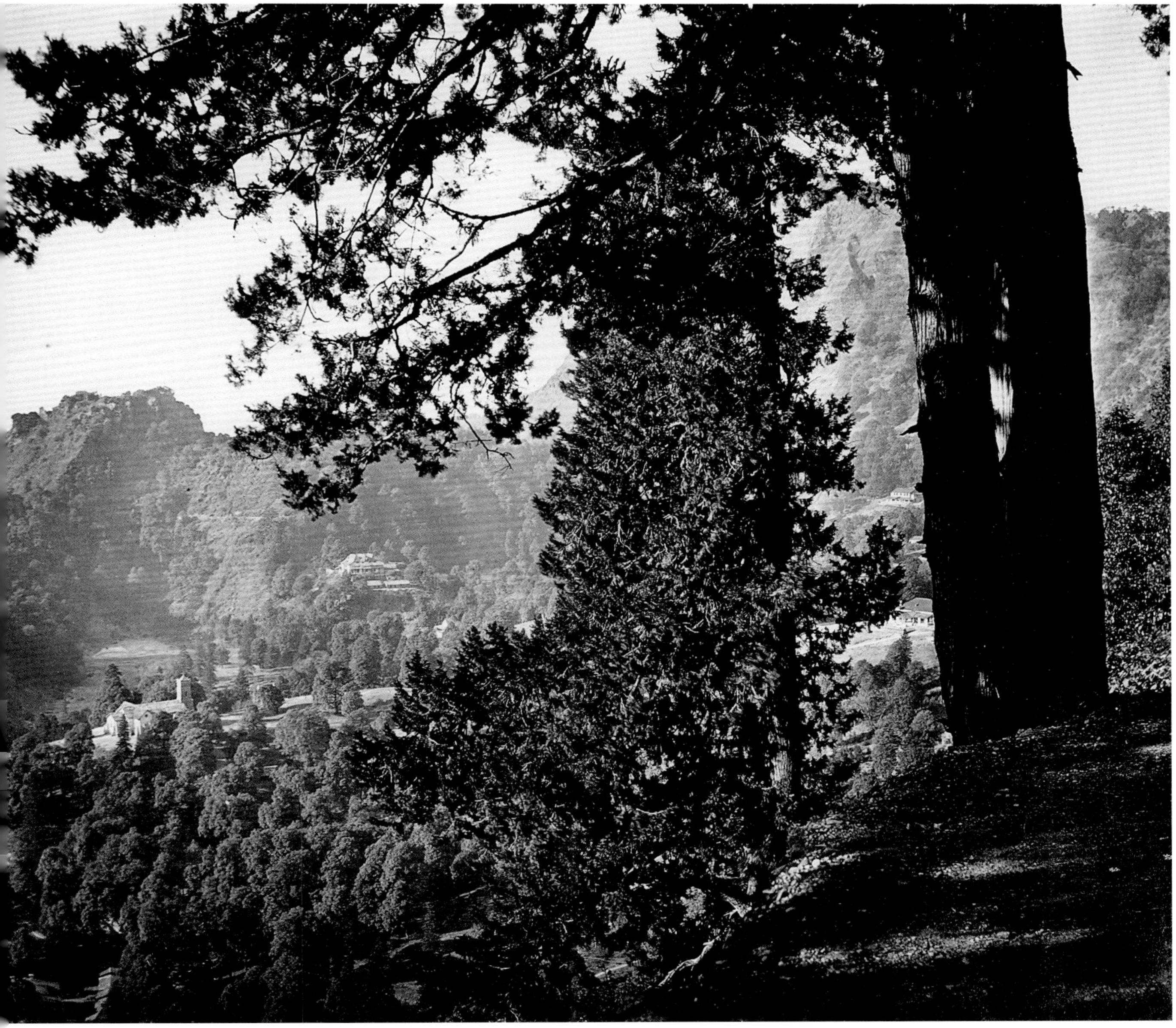

68 *Nynee Tal, North End of Lake, Bazaar, and Surrounding Houses*

Samuel Bourne

1866, albumen print, 23.7 x 29.2
Bourne and Shepherd catalogue number 1630, Smithsonian Institution, Freer Gallery of Art and Arthur M. Sackler Gallery Archives

69 *Nynee Tal, the Church, a Peep from the Upper Mall*

Samuel Bourne

1866, albumen print, 23.2 x 28.3
Bourne and Shepherd catalogue number 1633, Smithsonian Institution, Freer Gallery of Art and Arthur M. Sackler Gallery Archives

70 *Sanawur Church and Girl's School from the Road*

Samuel Bourne

1865–66, albumen print, 22.9 x 27.7
Bourne and Shepherd catalogue number 1135, Smithsonian Institution, Freer Gallery of Art and Arthur M. Sackler Gallery Archives

71 *Temple near Waterfall* [Simla]

Samuel Bourne

1863, albumen print, 23.6 x 28.7
Bourne and Shepherd catalogue number 115, Howard and Jane Ricketts Collection

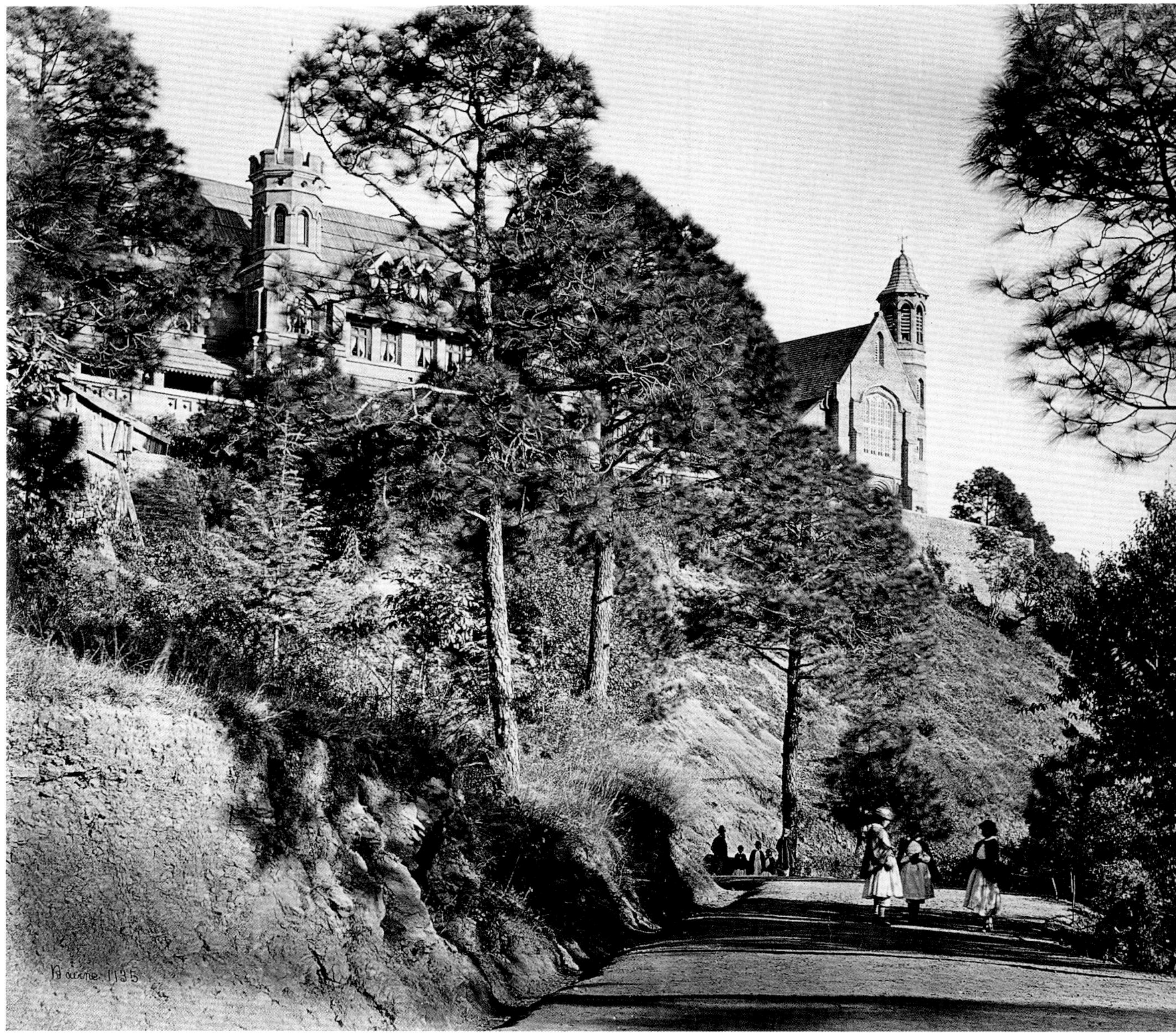

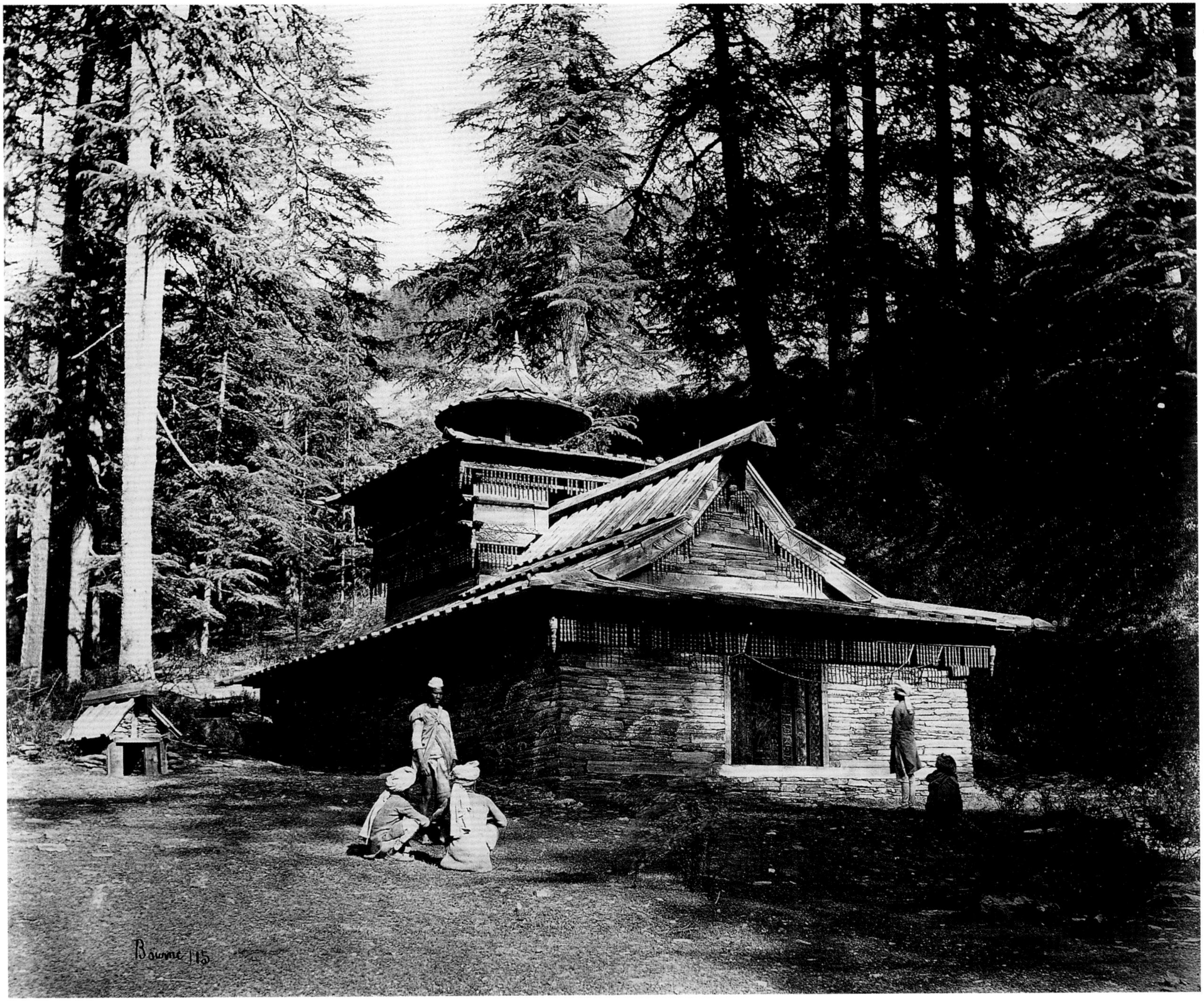
Bourne 115

72 *The Village of Sungnam with the Hungrung Pass Above*

Samuel Bourne

1866, albumen print, 24 x 28.6
Bourne and Shepherd catalogue number
1475, Howard and Jane Ricketts Collection

73 *The Picturesque Village of Dunkar, Spiti*

Samuel Bourne

1866, albumen print, 19.1 x 32
Bourne and Shepherd catalogue number
1461, Howard and Jane Ricketts Collection

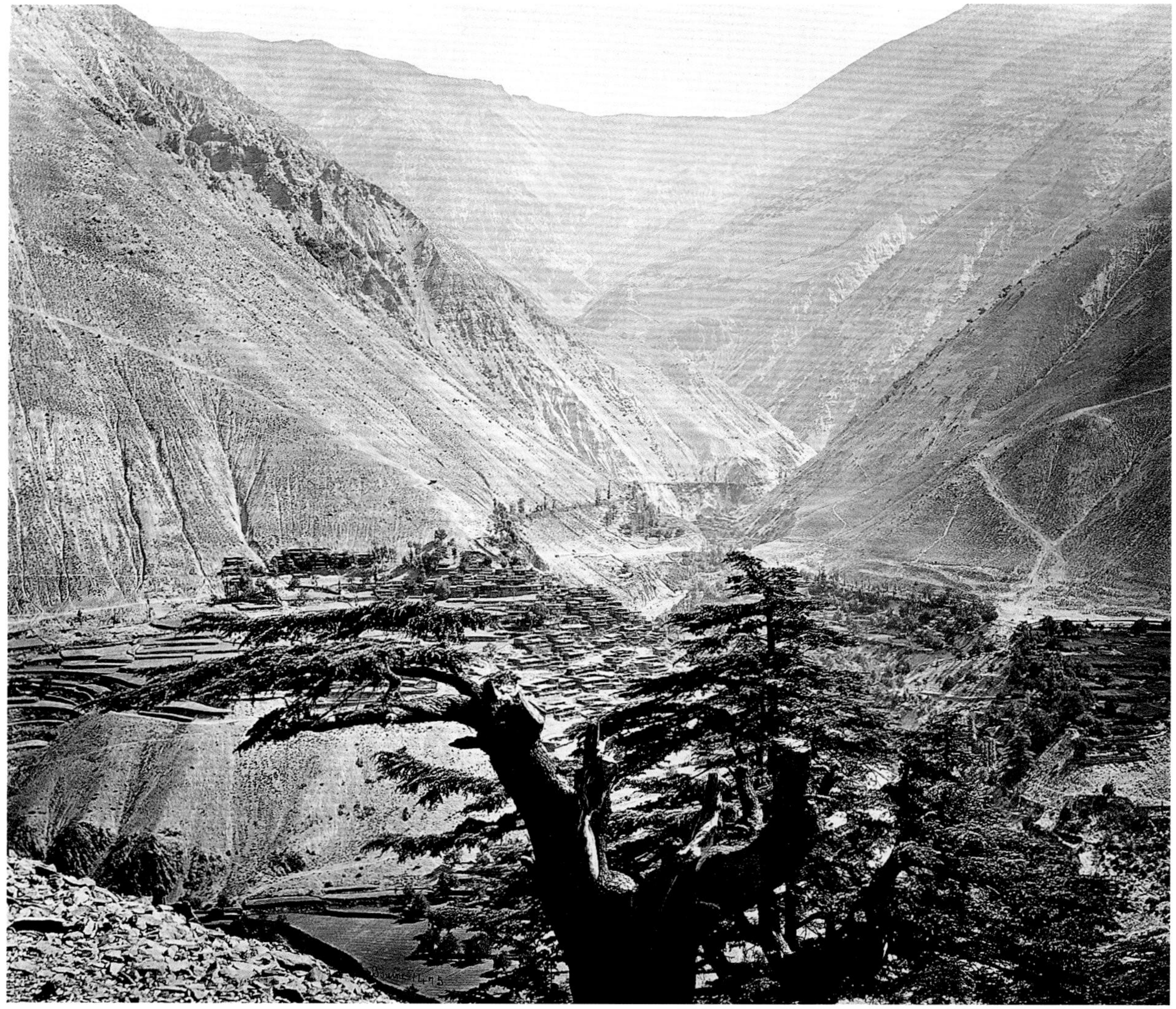

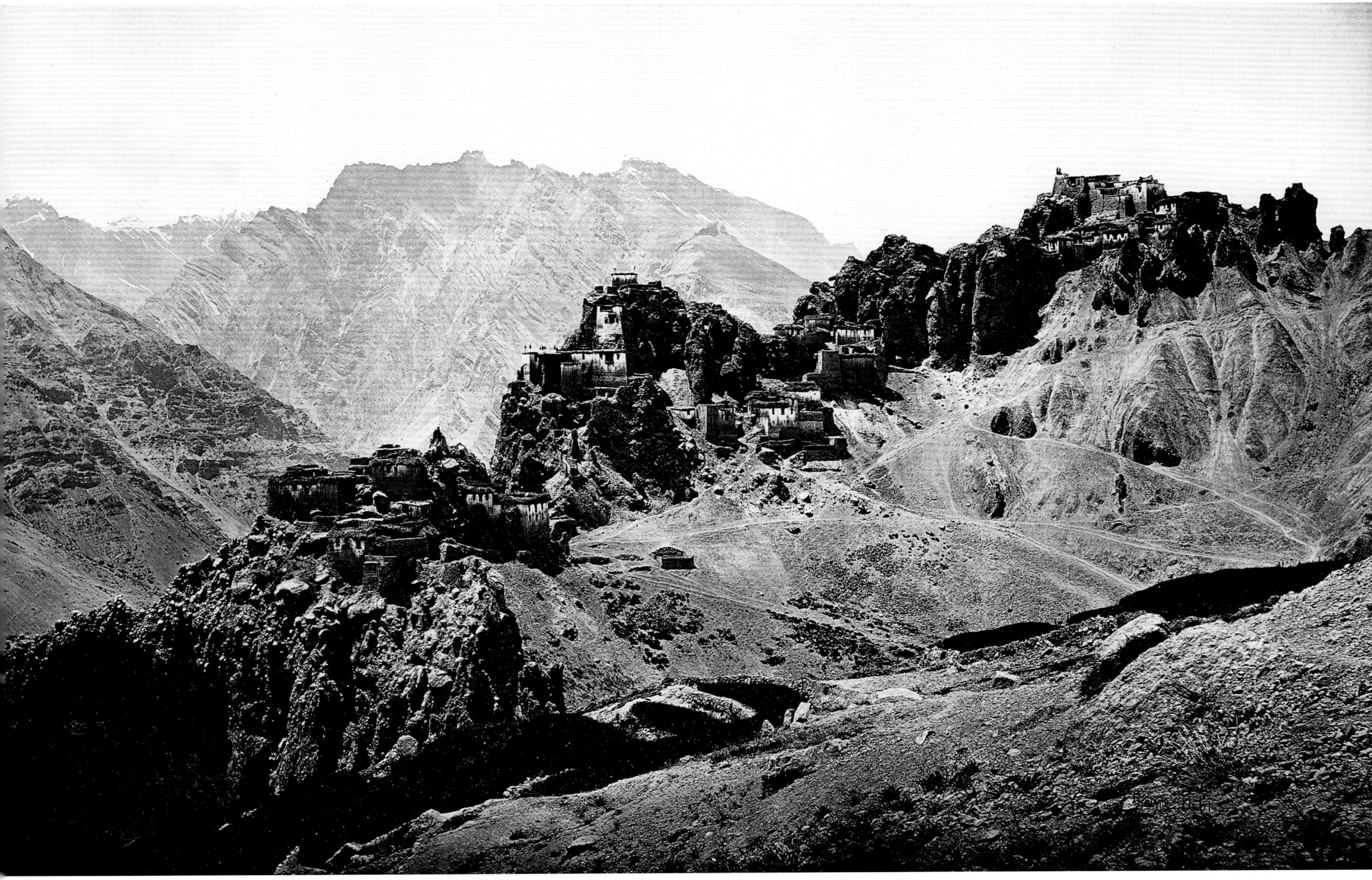

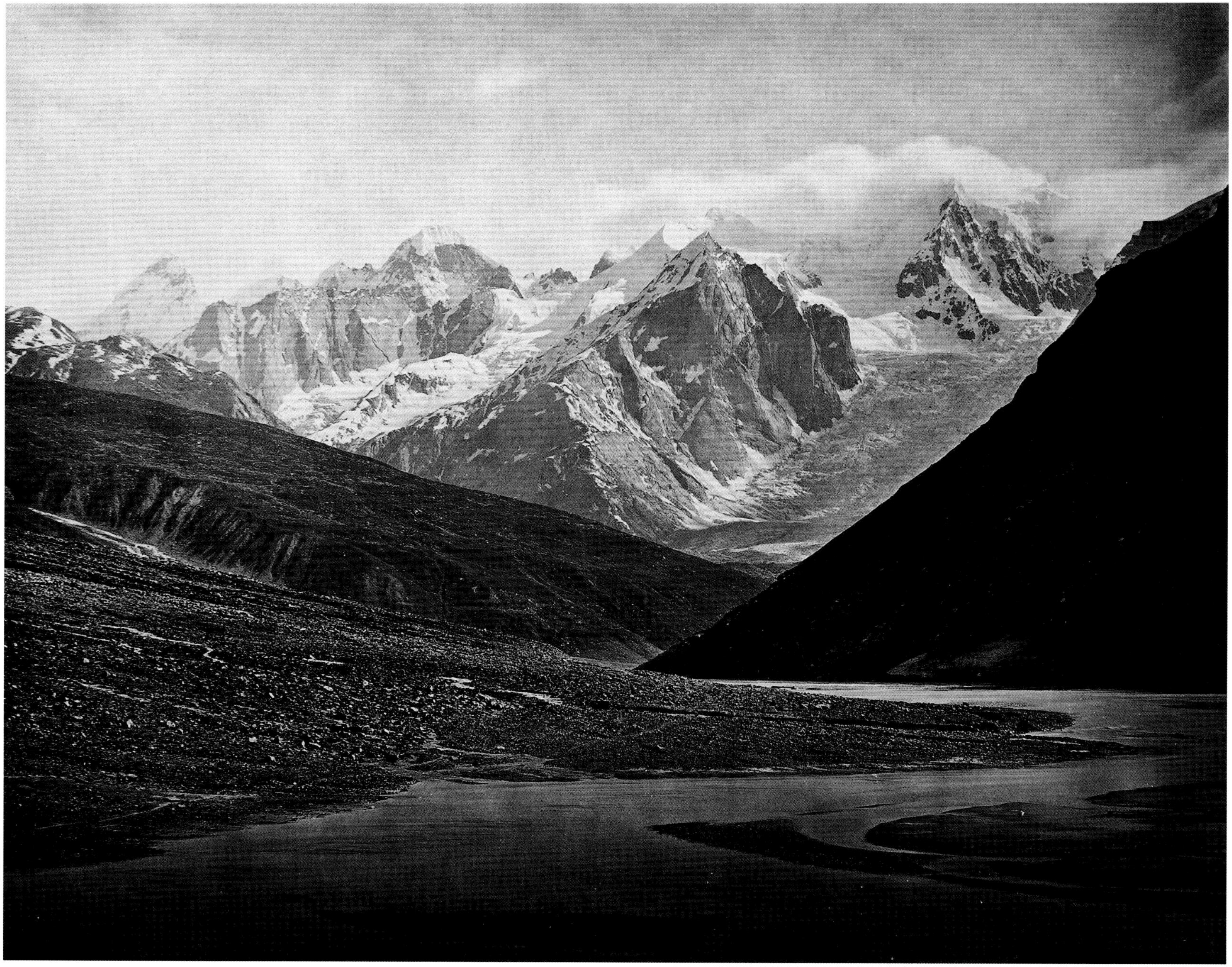

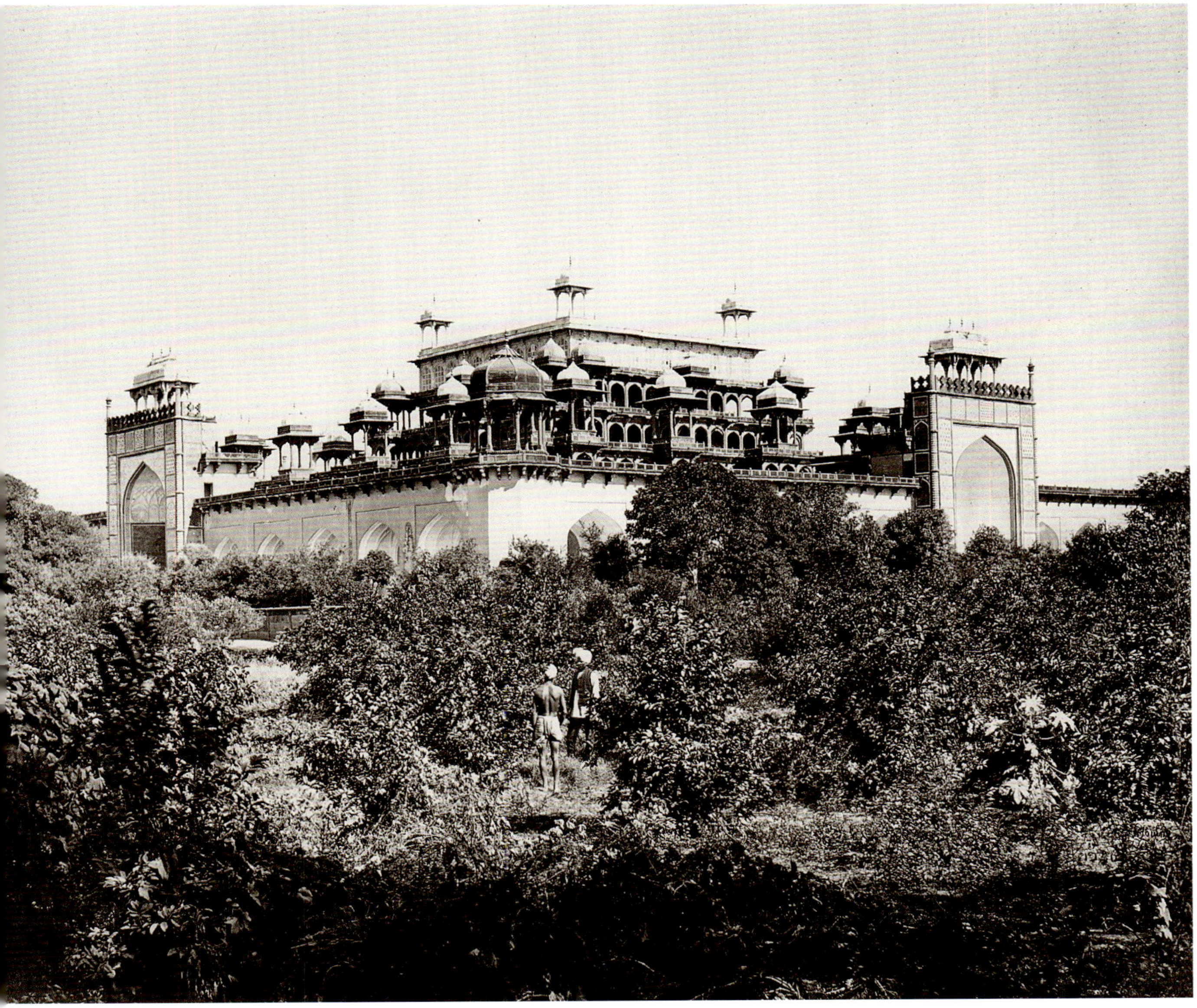

74 *Distant View of the Snowy Summits, South of the Shigri Glacier* [Kulu]

Samuel Bourne

1866, albumen print, 23.6 x 29.5
Bourne and Shepherd catalogue number 1451, Howard and Jane Ricketts Collection

75 *Mausoleum of Akbar* [Sikandra]

Samuel Bourne

1865–66, albumen print, 22.3 x 28.2
Bourne and Shepherd catalogue number 1250, Smithsonian Institution, Freer Gallery of Art and Arthur M. Sackler Gallery Archives

76 *The Fort, Exterior of the Zenana*
[Agra]

Samuel Bourne

1865–66, albumen print, 29.5 x 23.2
Bourne and Shepherd catalogue number
1223, Howard and Jane Ricketts Collection

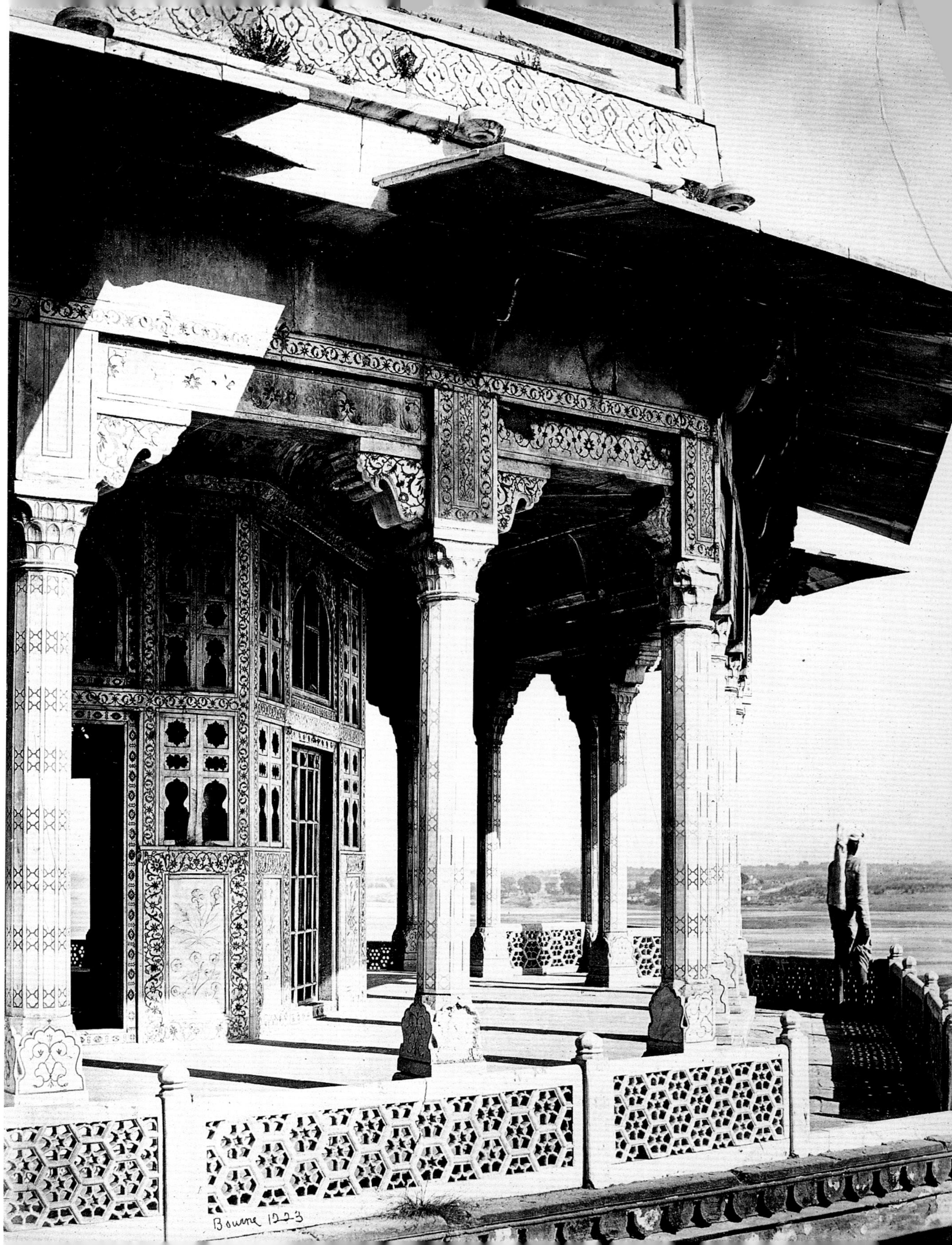

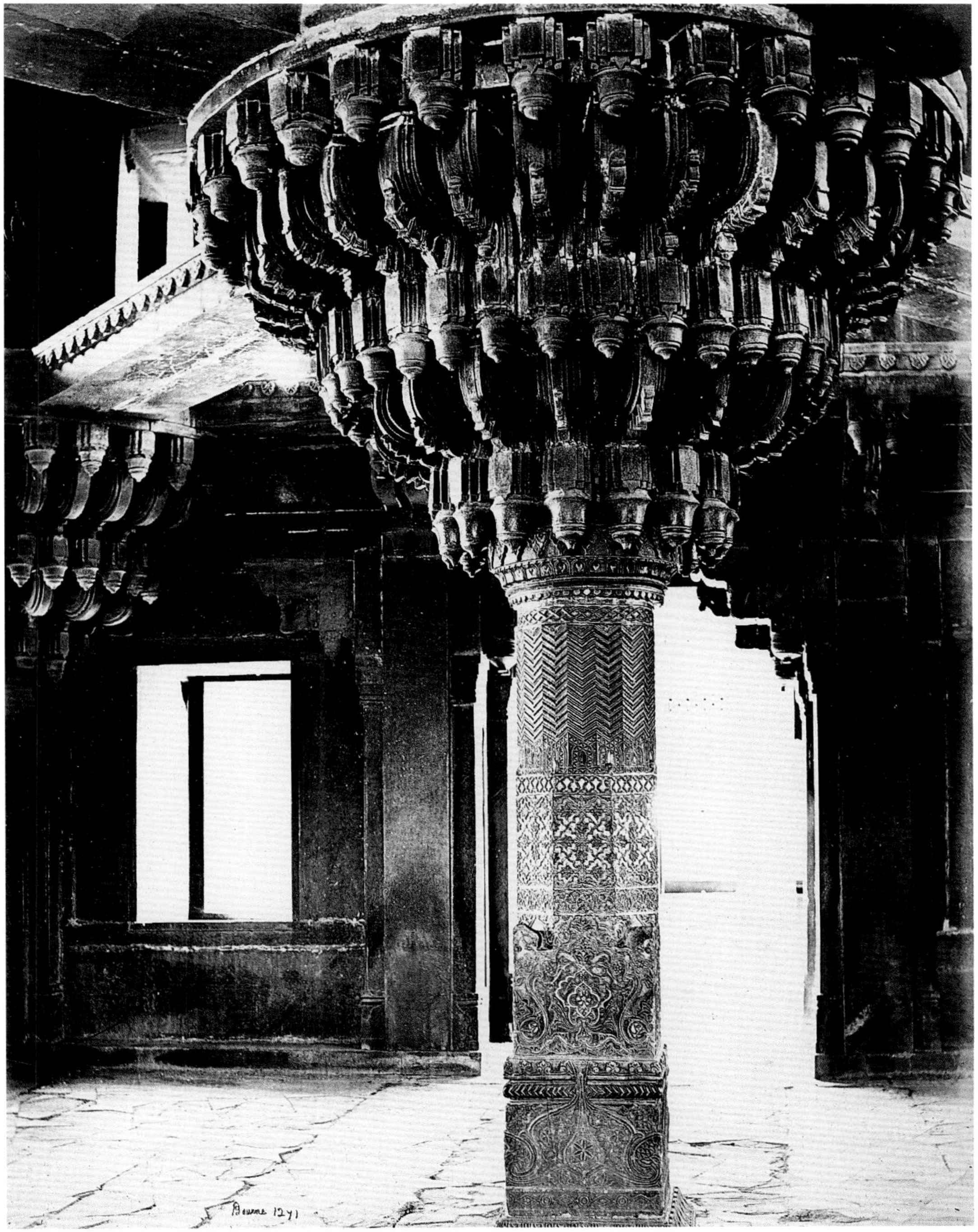

77 *Remarkable Pillar in the Centre of the Dewan-i-Kass, or Hall of Audience* [Fatehpur Sikri]

Samuel Bourne

1865–66, albumen print, 29.2 x 24.1
Bourne and Shepherd catalogue number
1271, Howard and Jane Ricketts Collection

78 *The Great Gate, Distant View from the South East* [Fatehpur Sikri]

Samuel Bourne

1865–66, albumen print, 22.2 x 27.5
Bourne and Shepherd catalogue number 1264, Smithsonian Institution, Freer Gallery of Art and Arthur M. Sackler Gallery Archives

79 *The Memorial Well, Seen through Trees from the South* [Kanpur]

Samuel Bourne

1865–66, albumen print, 22.8 x 28.3
Bourne and Shepherd catalogue number 1205, Smithsonian Institution, Freer Gallery of Art and Arthur M. Sackler Gallery Archives

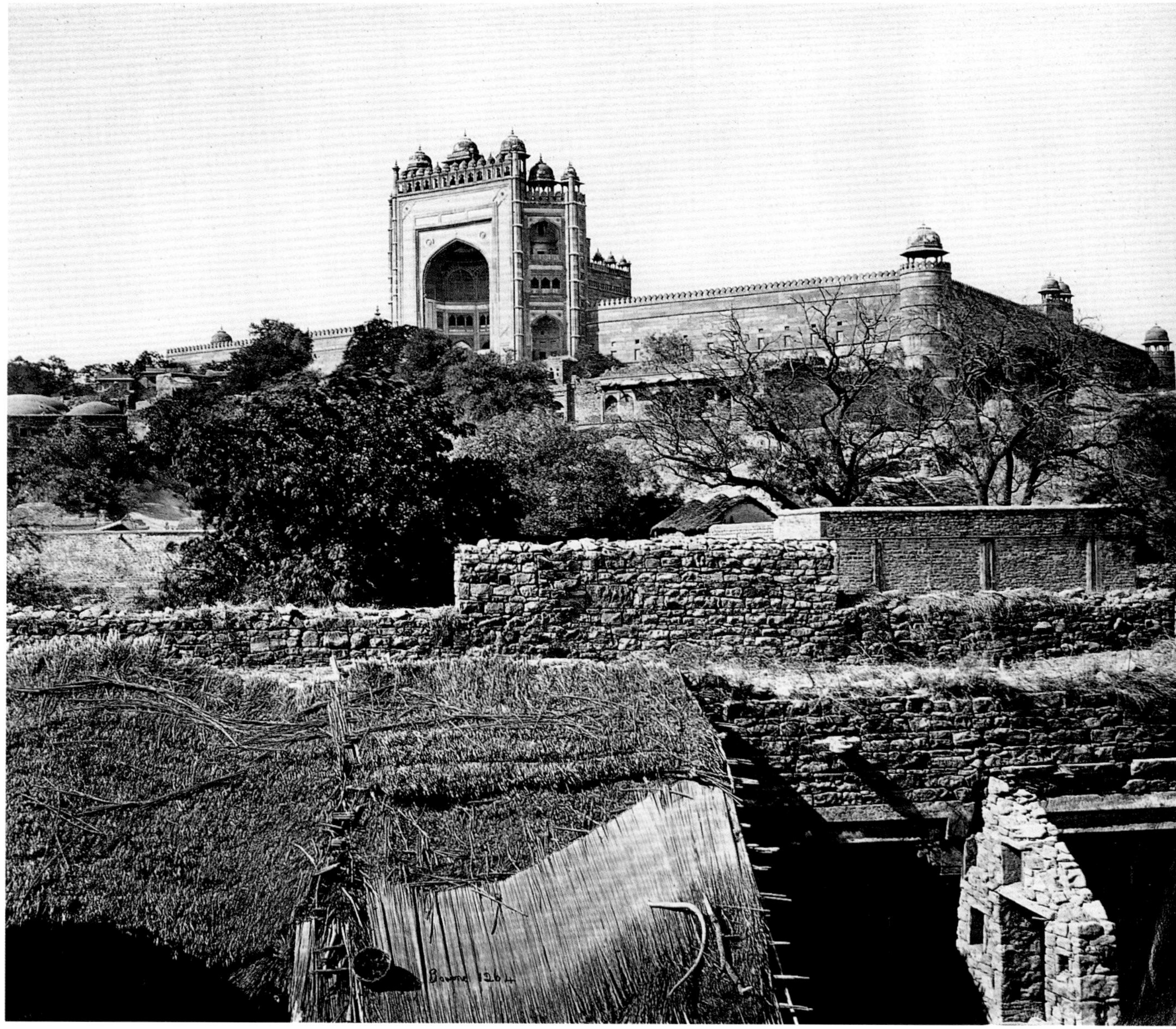

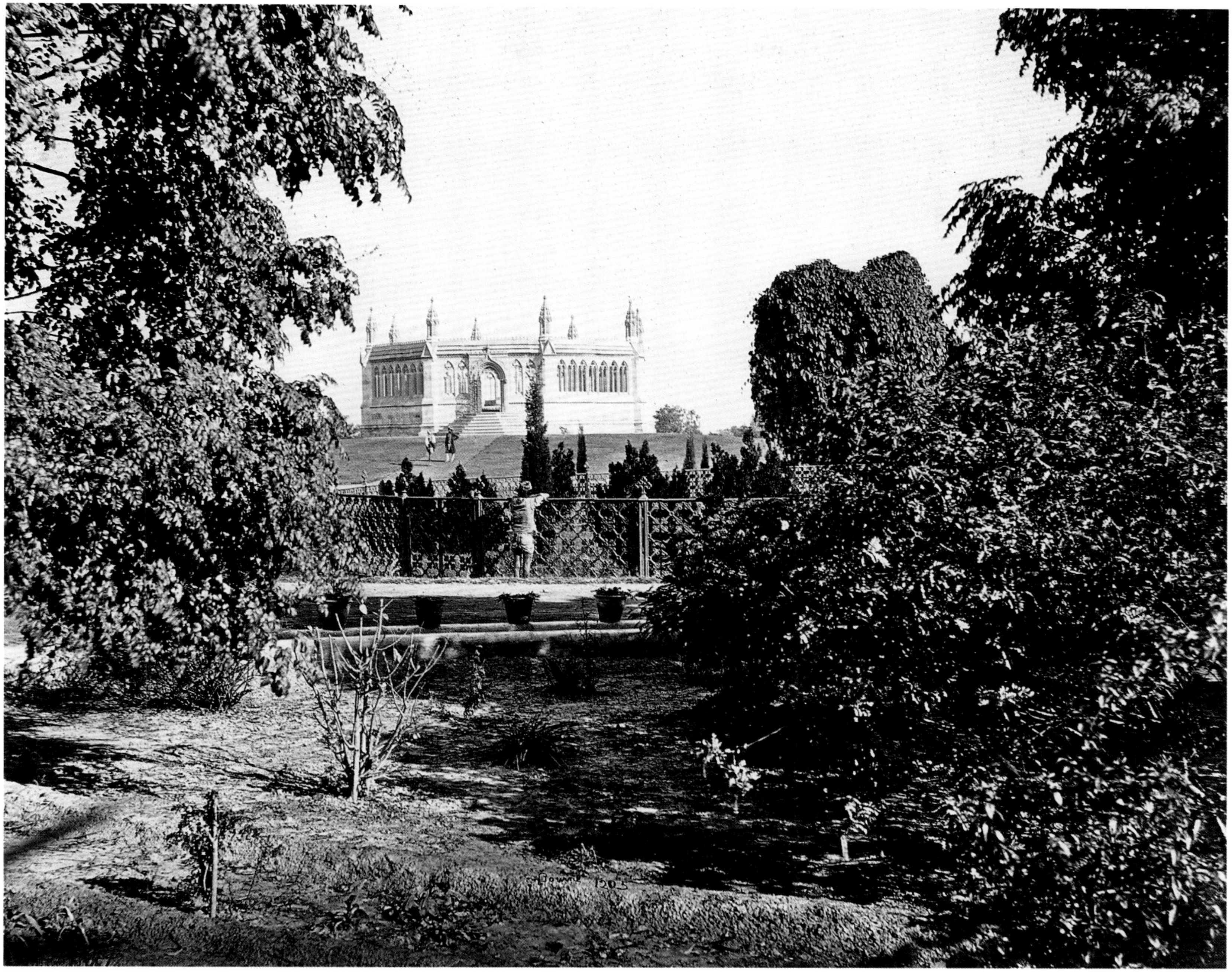

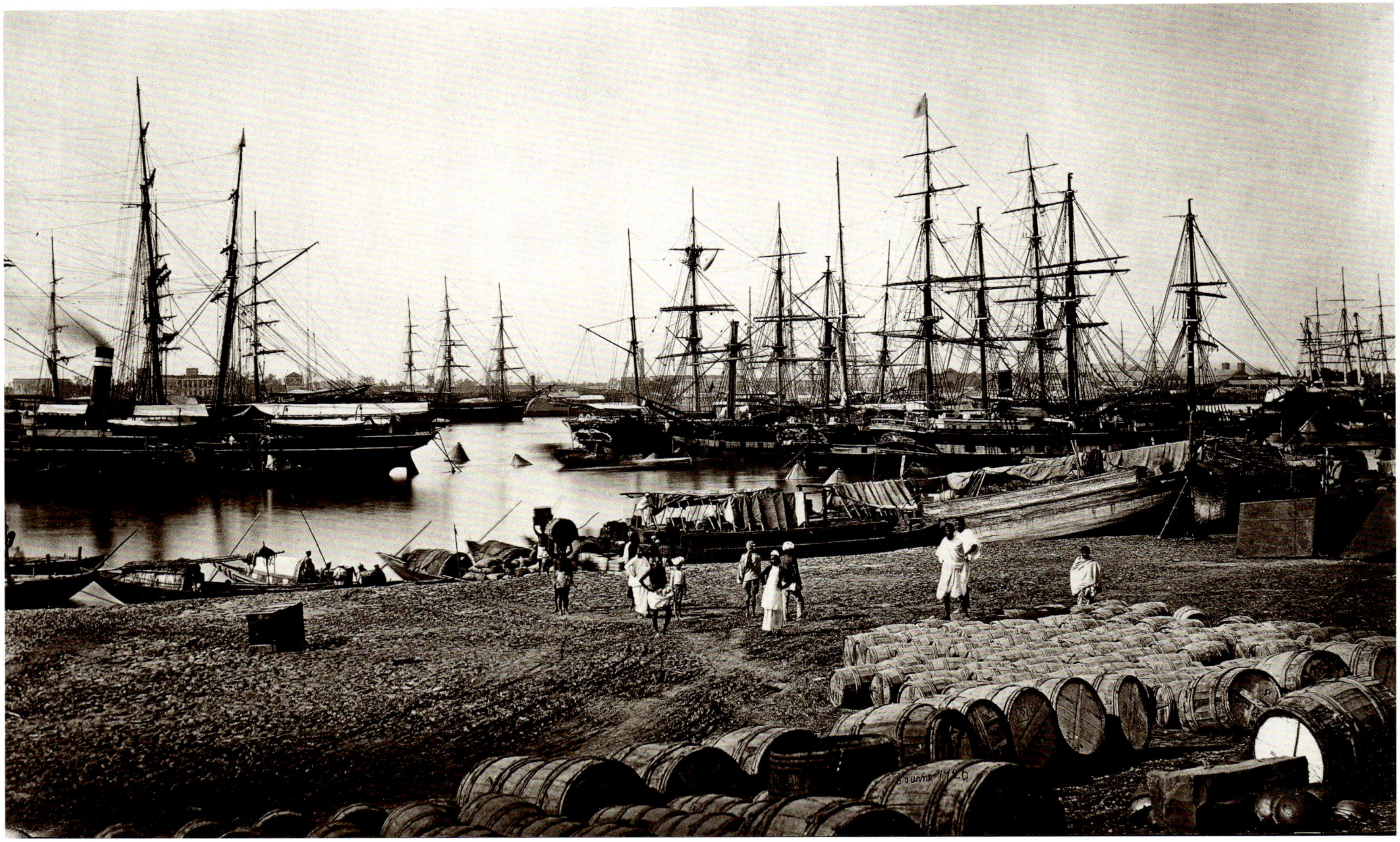

80 *Landing Goods near the Customs House* [Calcutta]

Samuel Bourne

1867, albumen print, 20 x 31.3
Bourne and Shepherd catalogue number 1726, The British Library, Oriental & India Office Collection photo 11 (37)

Detail, no. 80. *Landing Goods near the Customs House*

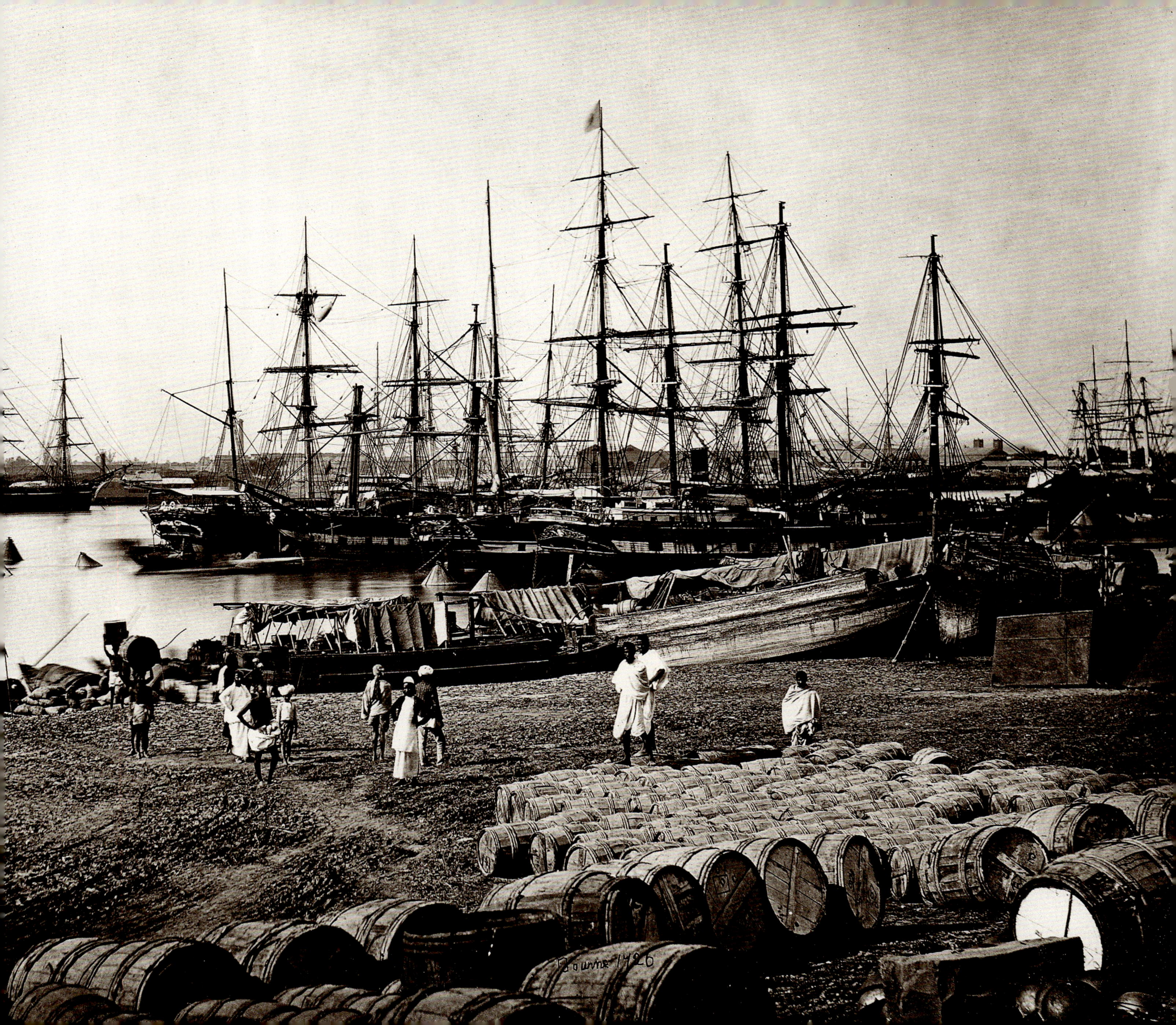
Bourne 1426

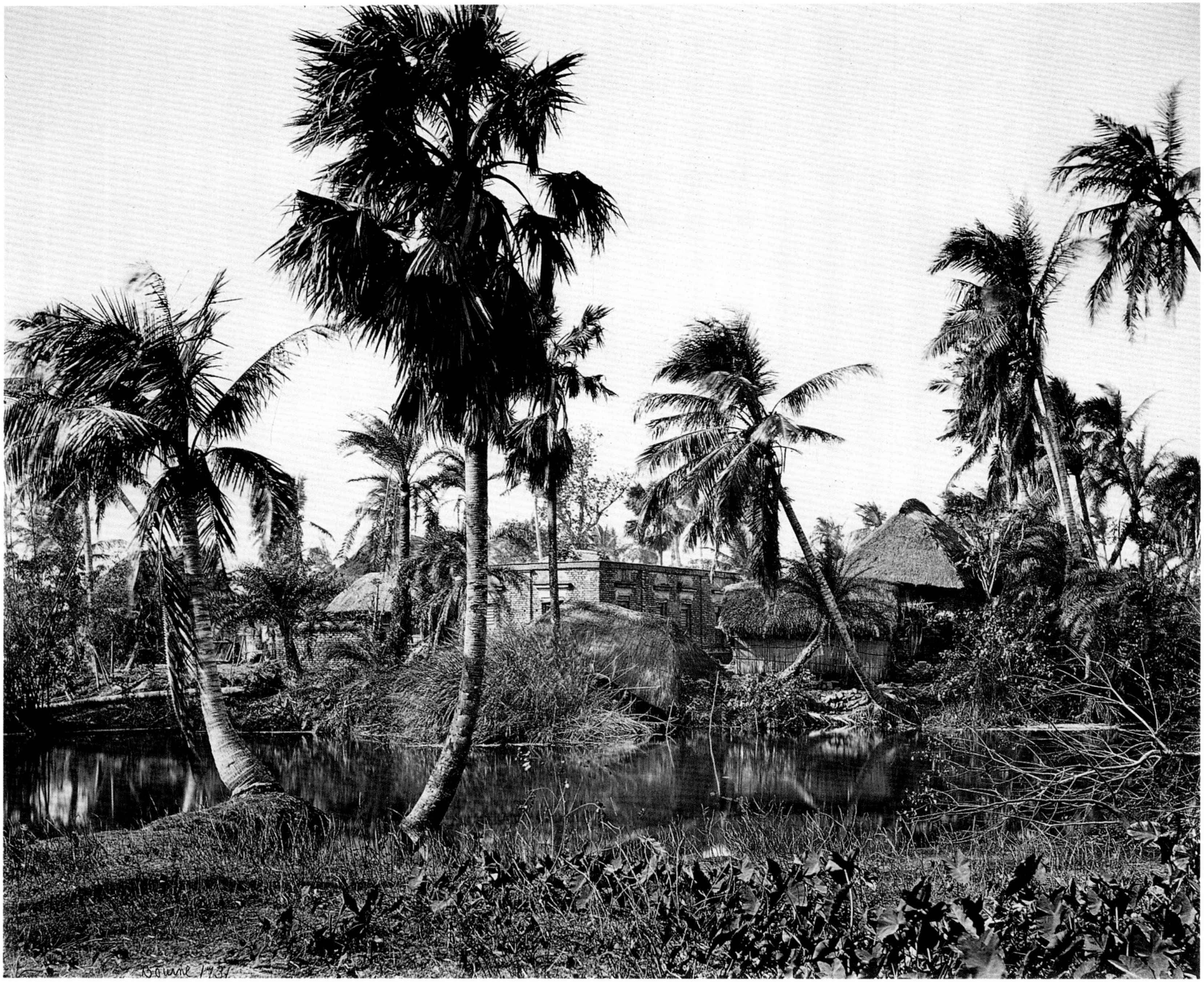
Bourne

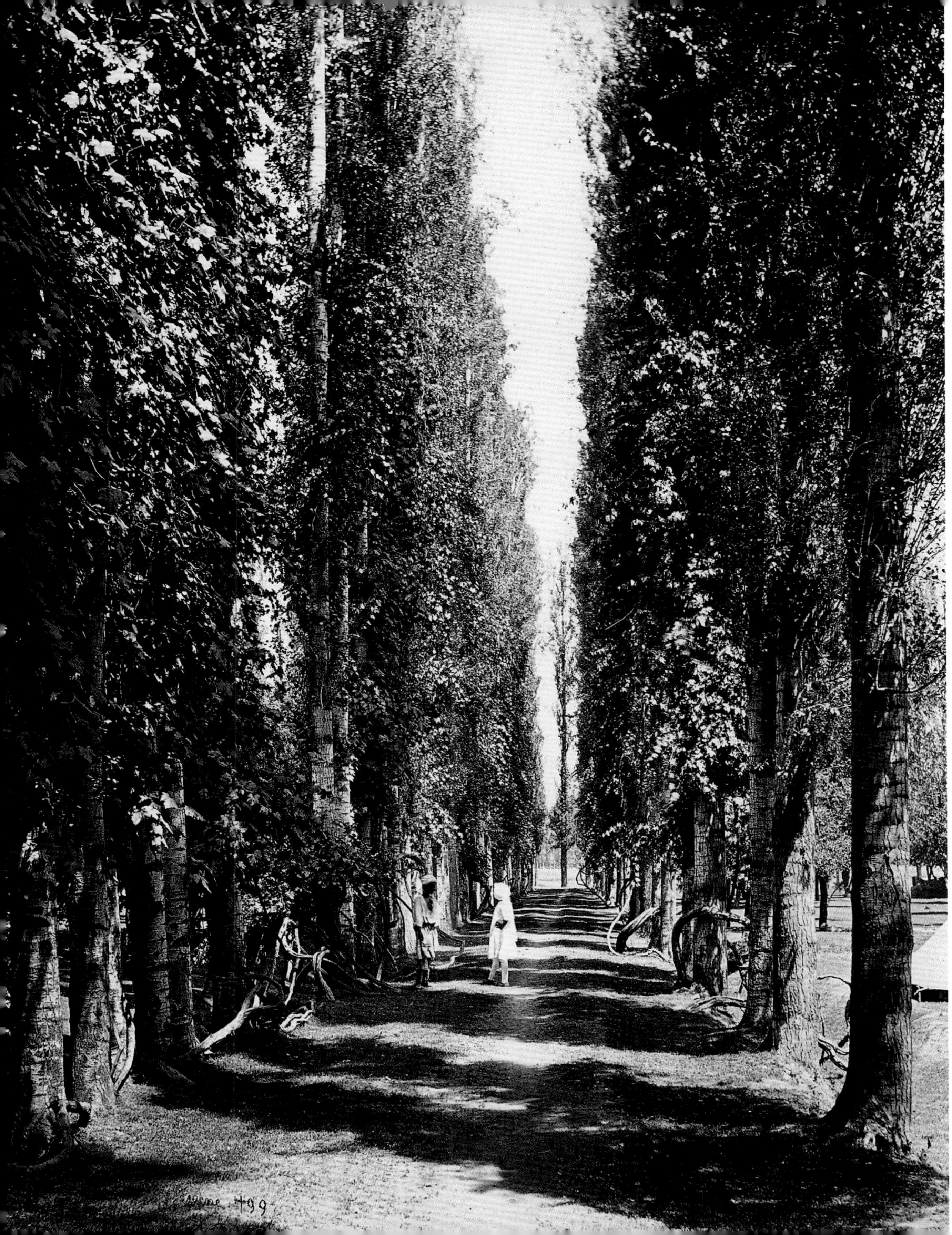

81 Untitled, from *Rustic Scenes and Village Life in Bengal* [Calcutta]

Samuel Bourne

1867, albumen print, 23.2 x 28.7
Bourne and Shepherd catalogue number 1731, Smithsonian Institution, Freer Gallery of Art and Arthur M. Sackler Gallery Archives

82 *Showing How the Vines Grow in Kashmir*

Samuel Bourne

1864, albumen print, 28.9 x 23.6
Bourne and Shepherd catalogue number 799, Howard and Jane Ricketts Collection

83 *Banian Tree in Barrackpore Park, Interior View* [Calcutta]

Samuel Bourne

1867, albumen print, 22.8 x 28.3
Bourne and Shepherd catalogue number 1748, Howard and Jane Ricketts Collection

84 *The Palace in the Lake, Oodeypore*

Colin Murray

ca. 1871–72, albumen print, 17.0 x 30.2
Smithsonian Institution, Freer Gallery of Art and Arthur M. Sackler Gallery Archives

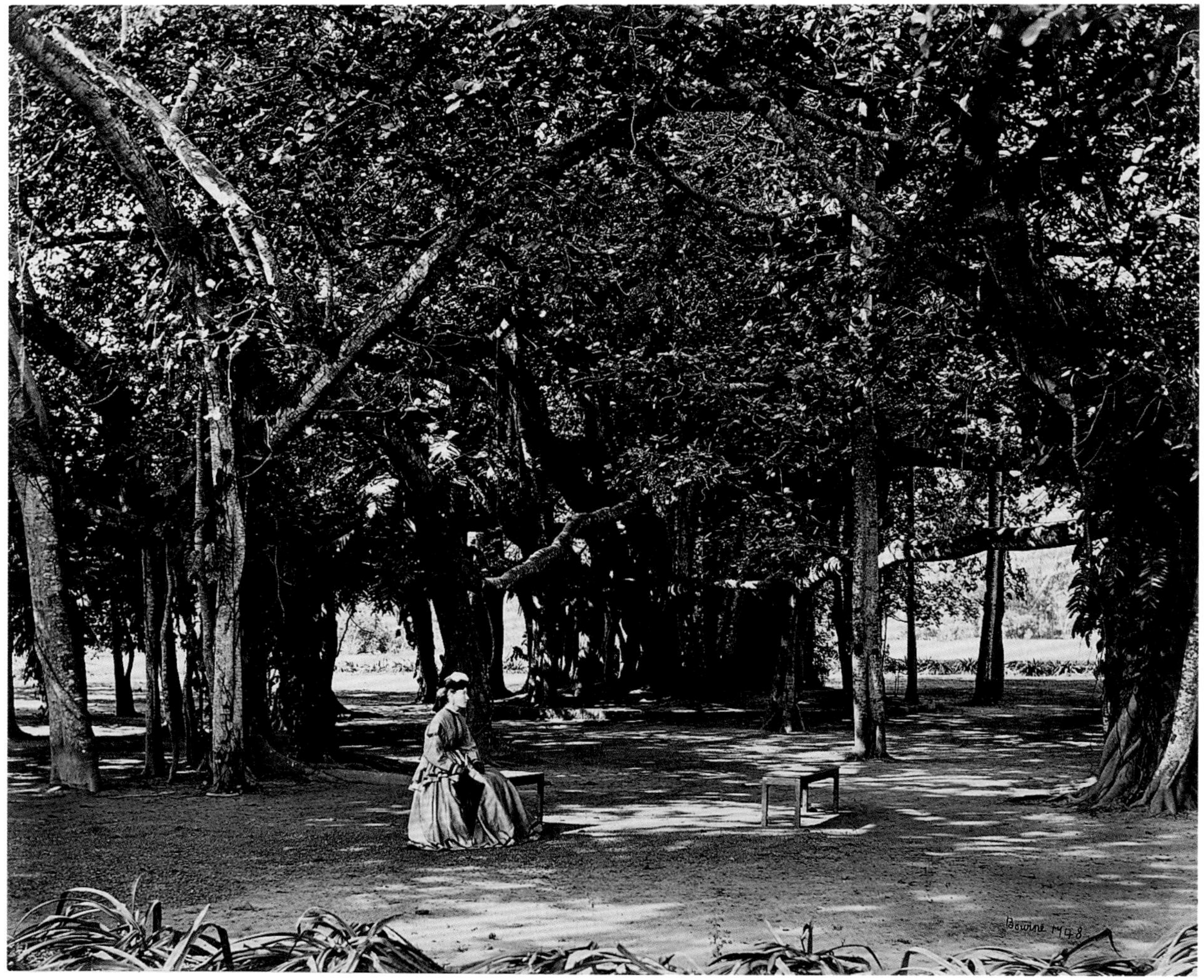

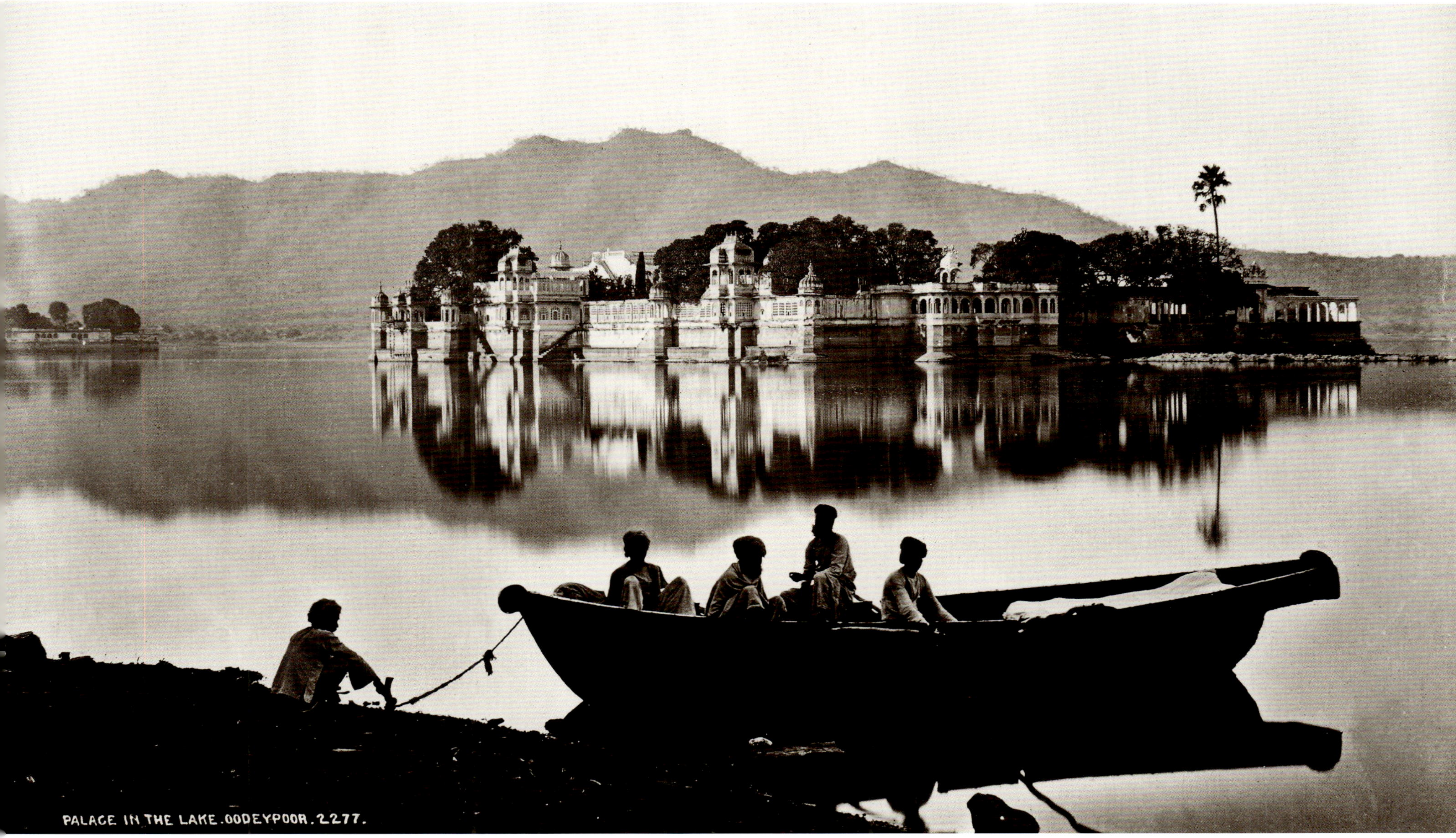
PALACE IN THE LAKE. OODEYPOOR. 2277.

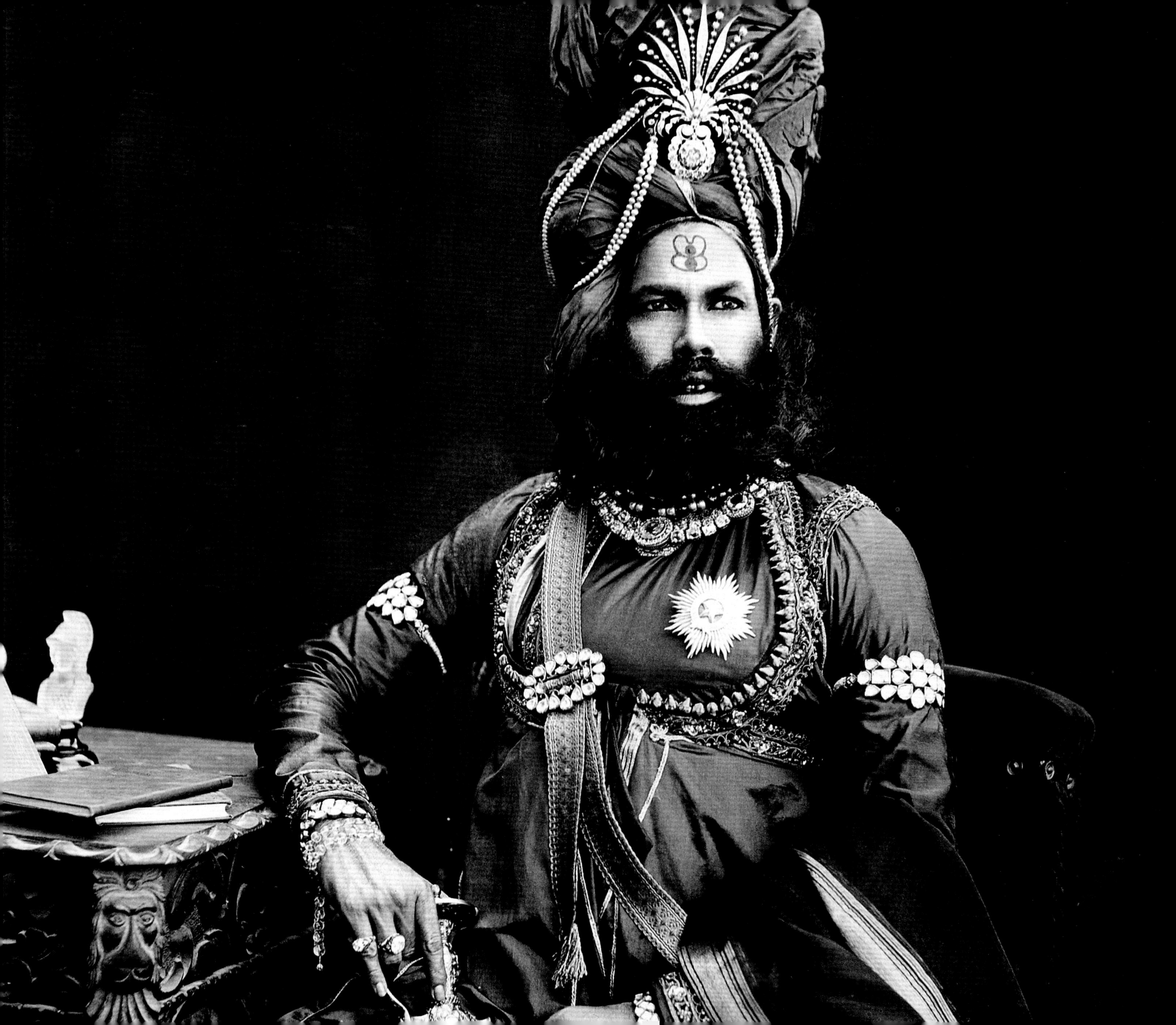

Charles Allen

India of the Princes and Maharajas

EARLY IN JUNE 1947, as British India's last viceroy began the countdown leading to independence for India, officials of the political department in New Delhi set fire to a huge pile of documents. All related to the so-called Indian princes: the *maharajas, maharawals, maharaos, rajas, raos, thakurs, nizams, nawabs, khans, taliqdars* and other local rulers with whom the British crown had entered into political relations. The bonfire—intended to prevent these same documents from falling into the hands of the new government—was highly symbolic: it marked an end to the protection that India's princes had long enjoyed.

A charge frequently leveled by politicians and historians of the Indian subcontinent is that the Indian princes were indeed no more than a protected species, that princely India had somehow been foisted on India by the British. This is to deny the Indian maharajas their place in history. The concept of the raja as "one who rules" can be traced back to the arrival of the Vedic Aryas on the plains of northern India in the second half of the second millennium B.C. In their early texts the raja was selected from the warrior nobility caste and derived his legitimacy from the support of his council, but soon thereafter, the hereditary principle had become firmly established, with the raja assuming authority upon ritual investiture by the priest of the ruler, drawn exclusively from the brahmin priestly caste. This investiture confered elements of divinity but it also brought responsibilities: the raja had a sacred duty to preserve social order and ensure the material well-being of his people as their giver of food, behaving toward them as a father to his children. In return for these services, his people were required to offer the raja their obedience as well as a sixth part of their produce, livestock, and gold—and the fairest of their daughters.

Indian kingship was thus a two-way contract between ruler and ruled, with strict obligations on both sides. The raja was born of a ruling caste but gained divinity only through the complex eight-day rituals of the *rajasuya* or *rajabhishek* (royal purification). He stood before his people as a representative of the gods, and before the gods as a champion of his people.

What is remarkable about this Indian model of kingship is its durability. "All men are my children," proclaims Emperor Ashoka (reigned 272–231 B.C.) on one of his famous rock-and-pillar edicts in about 265 B.C. "I desire that they may be provided by me with complete welfare and happiness in this world and in the other world."[1] Two thousand years later, the same code was still being applied within the scores of kingdoms that had managed to hang on to various degrees of self-government within the nominal boundaries of the crumbling Mughal Empire.

The impact of successive invasions of nomadic tribes of Central Asian origin on northern India, beginning with the Shaka (Scythians) in the first century B.C. and ending with the Huns (White Huns) in the sixth century, might have been expected to weaken the old Vedic traditions. Yet the reverse took place, and what is even more astonishing is that this continuity can be linked to the rise to power of a group of tribes who gave themselves the title of *rajput.* The name Rajput, derived from *rajaputra* (sons of rulers), implies royal ancestry, and to this day the Rajputs still set huge store on their racial purity as true Aryan *kshatriya* (noble warriors). To be a Rajput is to belong to a very exclusive club whose membership is restricted to the tribes known as the *chatis raj-kula* (thirty-six ruling races). Some claim descent from Rama and the sun, others from Krishna and the moon, while four once-powerful tribes claim their ancestors were born out of fire on Mount Abu. In reality, most—if not all—of the chatis raj-kula have their origins in one or another of those same Central Asian invaders who entered northern India from the first century B.C. on. In their search for new homelands, they took on the indigenous tribes of the forests, mountains, and deserts, subjugated them, and then set themselves up as local chieftains.

How these interlopers first established the loose tribal confederacies that hardened into the chatis raj-kula and how they came to be absorbed within the Hindu caste system are a mystery. We can only speculate that to secure their legitimacy as rulers the earliest Rajput chieftans and their kin underwent a dramatic transformation. Within generations rather than centuries they had reshaped themselves

Page 198: Detail, no. 89. *HH the Maharaja of Pannah,* unknown photographer to become paragons of all the warrior caste virtues. A network of intertribal alliances sustained by marriage facilitated the rapid spread of Rajput leadership across northern India and gave rise to a common culture, which has been termed "Rajputization," one that to this day remains the dominant cultural and social force in such regions as Rajasthan.

The Rajput martial ethic was legendary. In his classic history of Rajasthan, James Tod writes: "The Rajput worships his horse, his sword and the sun, and attends more to the Martial Song of the Bard than to the Litany of the Brahmin."[2] However, this fixation on military prowess and Rajput honor proved their undoing, leaving them chronically incapable of uniting against a common enemy. That common enemy was, of course, Islam—in the form of a succession of Muslim invaders from Afghanistan, Turkestan, and Persia, beginning in the year 1000. Two centuries later the raids became conquests and the annexation by stages of large parts of northern India, culminating in the establishment of the Sultanate of Delhi, which survived until the fifteenth century. Many of the Rajput dynasties that had established themselves across northern India were broken up and dispersed, with survivors retreating into the mountains and forests to regroup and, in some cases, to establish new kingdoms.

With the arrival of the Mughals, concerted efforts were made to reintegrate rulers and ruled; the consolidation of Mughal rule under Akbar (reigned 1556–1605) in the last quarter of the sixteenth century laid the foundations for "modern" government across most of India, which later provided the administrative framework both for the British and for their successors in modern India and Pakistan. Equally significant, Akbar won the allegiance of his predominantly Hindu subjects by measures designed to reconcile them to his rule. The rulers of those former sultanates and Hindu kingdoms who offered *nazar* (tribute) to the Great Mughal, in this case, Akbar, as tokens of their submission were permitted to continue as semi-independent feudal states. These included many of the Rajput kingdoms that had opposed the Mughals most fiercely, such as Amber (Jaipur) and Marwar (Jodhpur). Princesses from both these royal houses were given as wives to Akbar and to his son Prince Salim (later Emperor Jahangir, reigned 1605–27), and from that time onward many of the leading Rajput rulers served the Mughal Empire as its most able generals, amassing enormous wealth and war booty in the process. The significant exception were the rulers of Mewar (Udaipur), who suffered accordingly.

Toward the end of the seventeenth century, the Mughal Empire fragmented, weakened within by the rise of the Hindu Marathas and without by new invasions from Afghanistan and Persia. In the south and east former viceroys broke away to form their own Muslim provinces such as Hyderabad and Berar; in the north and west Afghan freebooters moved in to found such Muslim states as Palanpur and Bhawalpur; and in central and western India Maratha generals overran many weakened Rajput kingdoms to found their own, most notably Baroda, Gwalior, and Indore. The ever-expanding British East India Company, founded in 1600 with a monopoly to trade with the so-called "East Indies," also took advantage of the power vacuum, forming alliances with one or another of these new states against others. In their struggles for survival many Indian rulers turned to the East India Company, entering into treaties of "perpetual friendship, alliance and unity of interests"[3] in return for protection. Others, seeing how powerful rulers like the nawabs of Bengal were reduced by the company to the status of mere landowners, did so for fear of following suit. A third category was made up of rulers like the *jat* (low caste) maharaja of Bharatpur, who fought the British and lost but was allowed to retain his powers while acknowledging the suzerainty of the British monarch.

The penultimate phase for the traditional rulers of India began in November 1858 in the wake of the rebellion of 1857–58 known to the British as the Indian Mutiny of 1857. Rule by a commercial trading company now gave way to crown rule and the division of India into "British India" and the "princely states." These last were made up of no less than 565 so-called "native states," all enjoying indirect political relations with the British crown through the viceroy but with their rulers exercising various degrees of independence according to their size and importance. At one end of the scale were the dominions of the nizam of Hyderabad and Berar, occupying 82,700 square miles of the Deccan Plateau; at the other were a score of minute landholdings in western India each taking up less than a square mile. The British dealt with this multiplicity by dividing them into three categories: salute states, numbering 118, whose rulers were accorded the title of maharaja or raja (or their Muslim equivalents, nawab or khan), enjoyed full jurisdiction with their boundaries, and were ranked by the number of gun salutes they merited, descending by odd numbers from 21 to 9 (as compared to the Queen-Empress Victoria's 101-gun salute); 117 nonsalute states, whose rulers enjoyed limited jurisdiction as "chiefs"; and 327 nonjurisdictional estates, whose rulers carried such titles as thakur or taliqdar.

The November 1858 proclamation guaranteed the "rights, dignity, and honour" of the princes and their futures, but in doing so it divested them of their chief duty—to protect their people. It was the moment, according to one of their number, when "we ceased to be kings and became princes."[4] The raja-praja link had been fatally broken: "Whereas the Indian Princes when they were kings were answerable and responsive to local sanctions, as they became responsible to the superior power—here always called the Paramount Power—so they paid less attention to internal sanctions."[5]

Under the eyes of the vicercy and his political agents, the princes continued to rule, some well and some badly, but never as true kings. Indeed, any moves to introduce words associated with sovereignty such as "royal," "crown," "his majesty," or "throne" were vigorously opposed by the British. At the same time the princes were showered with titles, honors, more gun salutes, and all the outward pomp and trappings of rule, and encouraged to anglicize in ways that increasingly isolated them from their subjects. Beginning with the Rajkumar (Princes') College founded in Rajkot in 1870, for example, a number of boarding schools were set up for the sons of the ruling and landowning aristocracy, which were intended to inculcate in them all the virtues of the English public school, including a love of outdoor games such as cricket. Inevitably, the effect was to drive a cultural wedge between rulers and ruled, epitomized by the widespread removal of the former from their ancient forts and palaces sited at the hearts of their capitals to new palaces outside the city built by British architects to European or Indo-Saracenic design. As the British writer Rudyard Kipling put it, the only function left to them was to "offer mankind a spectacle," so it was hardly surprising that a number of rulers did just that: embarking on spending sprees abroad in Europe, building themselves grandiose palaces (including one modeled on Versailles), indulging in sexual excesses, or simply finding solace in drink or opium. Many would no doubt have agreed with the sentiments of the maharaja of Vizagapatam who, on being admonished by the local British resident for his heavy drinking, replied: "I know, sir. I am an idle drunken fellow . . . but what can I do? Your Pax Britannica has robbed me of my hereditary occupation. What is my hereditary occupation? It is fighting."[6] Not surprisingly, it was in those states where the rulers proved most hostile to change and which the British government in India regarded as the most "backward"—most notably in Rajasthan and Hyderabad—that Indian culture and the Indian arts, both Hindu and Muslim, continued to flourish.

Despite the British administration's declared aim of treating the princes "not as relics, but as rulers; not as puppets, but as living factors in the administration,"[7] the princes were effectively barred from entering the mainstream of Indian political life. This was an issue that Lord Curzon made some effort to redress when he came out to India as viceroy in 1899. However, he had first to disabuse Queen Victoria of her romantic notions of the princes and in a series of letters he listed their faults: many, he wrote, were "frivolous and sometimes vicious spendthrifts and idlers"; the maharaja of Patiala was "little better than a jockey"; the rana of Dholpur was "fast sinking into an inebriate and a sot"; the maharaja of Bharatpur had shot his servant; Maharaja Holkar of Indore was half-mad and "addicted to horrible vices." Further enquiries established that this was only the start of it: the Francophile maharaja of Kapurthala was "a third class chief of fifth rate character," only happy when philandering and gambling in Paris; the nizam of Hyderabad was "wrapped up in the sloth of the seraglio"; the nawab of Rampur was "a sensual and extravagant dabauchee"; and a whole number of princes had been found to share that "horrible taint . . . best suggested by the name of Oscar Wilde."[8]

But that was only one side of the coin. A number of rulers were throughly enlightened and patriotic, in the sense of setting up local administrations on the British model, often employing large numbers of British administrators and leaving the running of the state to an enlightened *dewan,* or chief minister. Lord Curzon was particularly impressed by Maharaja Madhavrao Scindia of Gwalior, who provided an excellent model for other rulers to follow. According to his grandson, he was "a down-to-earth, practical type of man, full of common sense. . . . He mixed continually with the public and, unlike some rulers, he only twice went abroad in his life. For six months of the year he used to be under canvas or in small inspection bungalows, where the poorest of the poor could approach him."[9] He also introduced a degree of local government unheard of elsewhere in India: directly elected municipal councils, a five-man council (*panchayat*), a nominated upper chamber, and a partially elected lower chamber. Here was someone who was "the servant as well as the master of his people," Curzon declared in a speech made in Gwalior, and he was proud to claim him "as my colleague and partner."[10] Madhavrao Scindia was also extremely skillful in his relations with the British. The Gwalior tiger-shoots were the best organized in India, with the largest tigers always appearing before the right shooting butt at the right time, so ensuring that the maharaja dealt direct with viceroys rather than the viceroys' political agents. He also ensured that he had the ear of the British monarch, asking the prince and princess of Wales to be godparents to his two children—and naming them George and Mary. He is probably best remembered today as the maharaja who liked to drive his own state railroad engine at enormous speed, while shouting to his alarmed guests, "Never fear! Scindia is driving!" He is also remembered as the one who built a miniature silver train that circulated port, cigars, and sweets round an enormous dining table in his palace.

Two other rulers of this period who were also regarded as progressive were the *begum-sahiba* of Bhopal, Shah-Jahan, and Maharaja Sawai Ram Singh II of Jaipur. Both were equally remarkable in their own ways. The begum was unique in being the only woman ruler in India, although it was a position established by force of personality rather than right by a succession of strong women regents (no. 85). What made the begums of Bhopal all the more remarkable was that they ruled over a Muslim state, where all women remained in *purdah* (literally, behind the curtain) and only appeared in public when covered from head to toe in the loose garment called a *burka.* Begum Shah-Jahan was a widow who became the effective ruler of Bhopal in 1868 at the age forty-three, following the death of her mother. Although there were whispers about the early death of her husband, she ruled extremely effectively, presiding over council meetings from behind a screen and taking a particular interest in women's education.

By Rajput standards Maharaja Sawai Ram Singh II of Jaipur was dangerously progressive (no. 86). He was a reformer who abolished slavery, the infanticide of girls, and the ancient custom of *sati,* in which the wives of Rajputs were expected to immolate themselves on the funeral pyres of their husbands. He was also an enthusiastic amateur photographer who enjoyed taking self-portraits as well as photographing the women of his *zenana* (women's quarters), and he encouraged the photographic recording of the activities of Jaipur state. At the same time, he was a traditionalist in most areas of Rajput custom and religion. His first marriage was to the daughter of the rival state of Marwar (Jodhpur), but to further reinforce this alliance he also married his bride's sister and first cousin.

While Jaipur and Marwar were among the most progressive of the Rajput states at this period, two of the oldest Rajput states, Mewar (Udaipur) and Bundi, remained resolutely old-fashioned. In Bundi the magnificently bewhiskered Maharao Raja Ragubhir Singh lived very much in the past, following the ancient customs of his forefathers and busying himself in his vast and magnificent medieval palace (no. 98). Significantly, both he and his neighbor in Udaipur refused to move out into modern quarters. In Udaipur, Maharana Fateh Singh went to enormous lengths to avoid appearing before the viceroy (no. 90). Forced by Lord Curzon to attend the Delhi durbar of 1903, he arrived by train with a large retinue of retainers but then returned to Udaipur without setting foot in Delhi, officially on the grounds of ill-health. The process was more or less repeated at George V's durbar in 1911, although on this occasion he was received at the railway station by the king-emperor, before again heading back to Udaipur without attending the durbar ceremonies. When the prince of Wales visited Udaipur in 1920 the maharana refused to meet him at the railway station, as demanded by protocol. His explanation—"He [the prince of Wales] is like a son to me. Would you expect a father to receive his own son?"—did not go down well with the British and in the following year Maharana Fateh Singh was formally deposed in favor of his son.

In neighboring Jodhpur, Maharana Fateh Singh's contemporary, Maharaja Jaswant Singh II (no. 87), might also have been deposed had the British known of a youthful indiscretion: as a prince he had been secretly entertaining one of his father's courtesans in his room when his father suddenly arrived at the door demanding entrance. Fearing discovery, Jaswant Singh had grabbed the girl by the hair and hung her out of his window. But then the maharaja had entered and wanted to know why his son was not coming forward to greet him, so Jaswant Singh let go and the girl fell more than two hundred feet to her death. On becoming maharaja in 1873, Jaswant Singh moved out of the ancient Meherangarh fort into a new palace outside the city. Not one to trouble himself with the cares of state, he was wise enough to leave the government of Jodhpur in the hands of his half-brother, Pratap (also Pertab) Singh, an extremely capable administrator who in later years became a great favorite of Queen Victoria, although best remembered today as the inventor of the riding breeches known as jodhpurs.

In 1900 Lord Curzon sent out a circular defining the princes' duties and encouraging them to follow the paths taken by Gwalior and other "model rulers," while also imposing restrictions on their movements when away from their states. Significantly, the one enlightened ruler whom he failed to put forward as an example was Gaekwar Sayaji Rao III, maharaja of Baroda (no. 88). The Gaekwar had been adopted and placed on the royal couch of Baroda in 1877 at age thirteen following the deposition of the previous ruler for gross misrule. Thanks to an enlightened chief minister and tutor, he developed into wise and humane ruler, always eager to seek out and implement the best aspects of the two cultures in which he found himself. This liberalism brought him into contact with Indian nationalism and the Indian National Congress movement, which he discreetly supported and funded while at the same time assuring the viceroy of his loyalty as a subject of the crown. The British remained deeply suspicious of him—suspicions amply confirmed by the Gaekwar's behavior at the 1911 durbar. The princes were all required to advance in turn in strict order of precedence toward the royal dais, bow three times to the seated figure of King-Emperor George V and then to retire by stepping backward. All were dressed in full regalia, richly bedecked with jewels and decorations, except for the Gaekwar, who wore a simple white robe. Instead of bowing deeply three times, he gave no more than a nod before turning about and walking back to his seat. Later, he was unable to give a satisfactory explanation for his discourtesy, but his actions had been recorded by the newsreel camera and to many Indians the message was crystal clear.

When independence came to the subcontinent in 1947, it found the princes unprepared and unable to present a common front to the challenges facing them. The best acted in the greater public interest and, when British paramountcy lapsed, allied themselves with either India or Pakistan. A year later the majority voluntarily surrendered their sovereignty and their states, and in return were granted certain constitutional rights such as the retention of their titles and pensions. Had they then abstained from politics their new status might have remained unaffected, but in India the decision by a number of ex-rulers or members of their families to stand for parliament and their successes at the polls from 1952 onward was seen by the ruling Congress Party as a threat to democratic government. In December 1970 a bill derecognizing the princes and removing their privileges was passed in India's Lower House but voted out in the Upper House. It was then pushed through by presidential order. There was a brief stay of execution when this order was declared unlawful, but a second bill, passed by both houses, saw the princes pass into history.

NOTES

1. E. Hultzsch, *Corpus Inscriptionum Indicum,* vol. 1, *Inscriptions of Asoka* (Oxford: Oxford University Press, 1921).

2. James Tod, *Annals and Antiquities of Rajast-han or the Central and Western States Rajpoot States of India,* vol. 1. (London: Routledge & Keegan Paul, 1914).

3. The first article of the many treaties signed between the East India Company and the rulers of what came to be known as the native or princely states. The standard first article reads in full: "There shall be perpetual friendship, alliance and unity of interests between the two states, from generation to generation, and the friends and enemies of one shall be the friends and enemies of both."

4. Brijraj Singh, current maharaja of Kotah, quoted in Charles Allen and Sharada Dwivedi, *Lives of the Indian Princes* (London: Century, 1984, reprint, rev., Mumbai: Eshwar, 1998), 84.

5. Ibid., 85.

6. William Horne, *Work and Sport in the Old ICS,* 1928, quoted by Lawrence James, *Raj: The Making and Unmaking of British India,* (London: Little Brown, 1999), 325.

7. Lord Minto, viceroy of India, 1905–10, quoted in ibid., 333.

8. Lord Curzon, Curzon Papers 111/35, 111/160–61, Oriental and India Office Collection, British Library.

9. Madhavrao Scindia, current maharaja of Gwalior, quoted in Allen and Dwivedi, *Lives of the Indian Princes,* 102.

10. Lord Curzon, speech published in *Lord Curzon in India,* 1: 237. 1906.

INDIA OF THE PRINCES AND MAHARAJAS

85 *Shah Jehan Begum,
Begum of Bhopal*

Bourne & Shepherd

ca. 1877, albumen print, 30.6 x 26
The British Library, Oriental & India Office
Collection photo 99 (39)

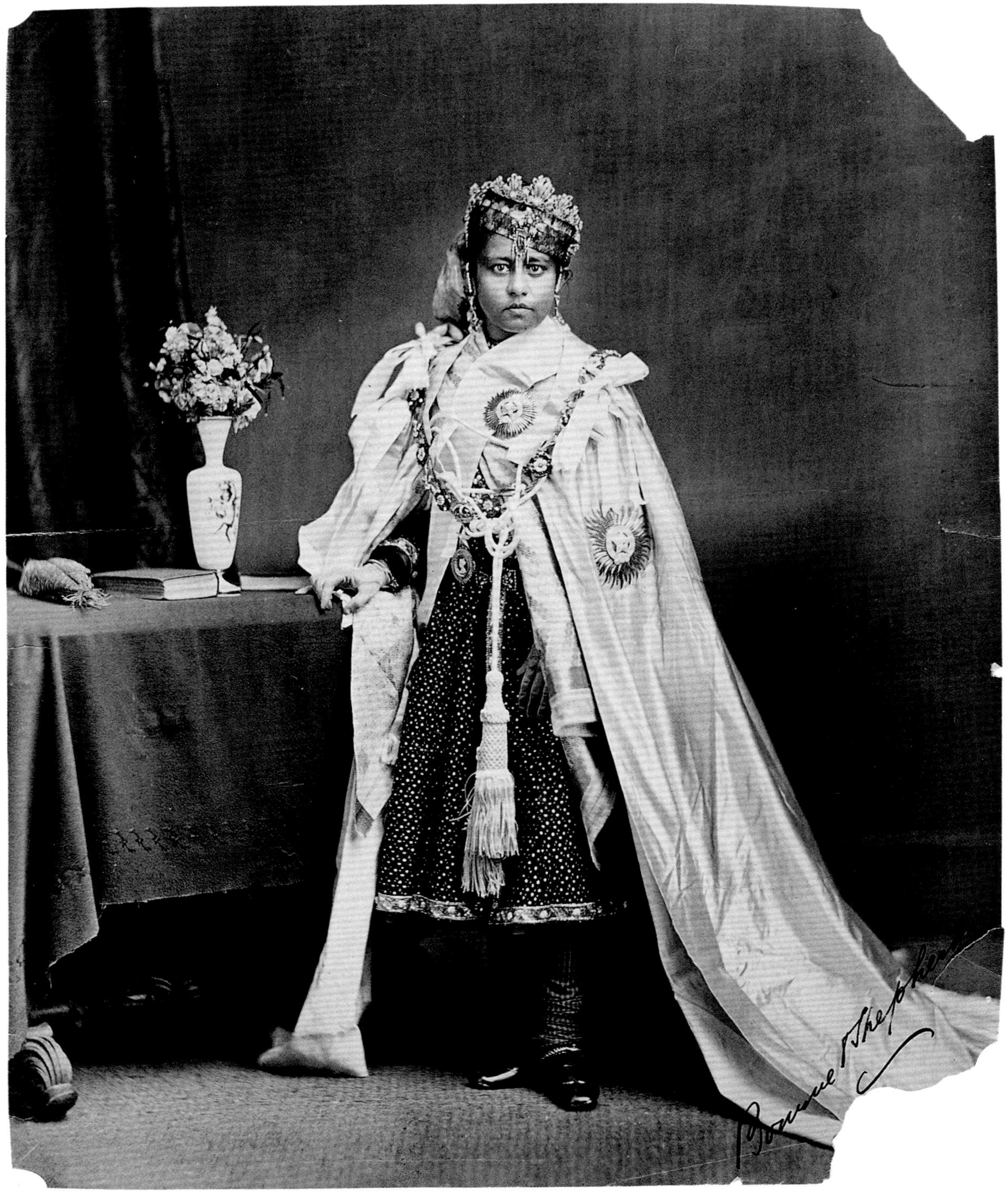

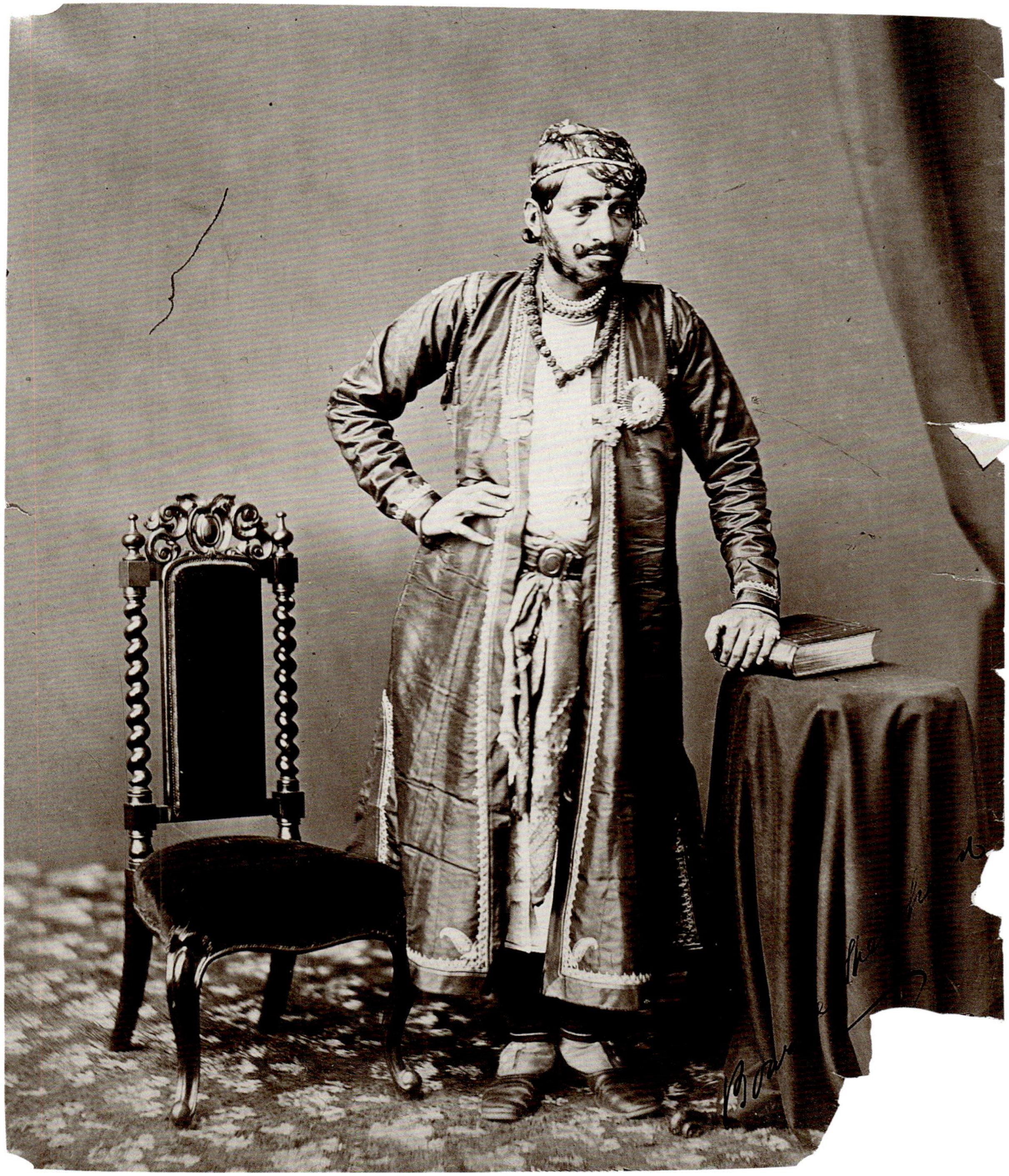

86 *Ram Singh, Maharaja of Jaipur* (d. 1880)

Bourne & Shepherd

ca. 1877, albumen print, 30 x 25.9

The British Library, Oriental & India Office Collection photo 99 (31)

87 *Jaswant Singh, Maharaja of Jodhpur*

Bourne & Shepherd

ca. 1877, albumen print, 24.4 x 27
The British Library, Oriental & India Office Collection photo 99 (35)

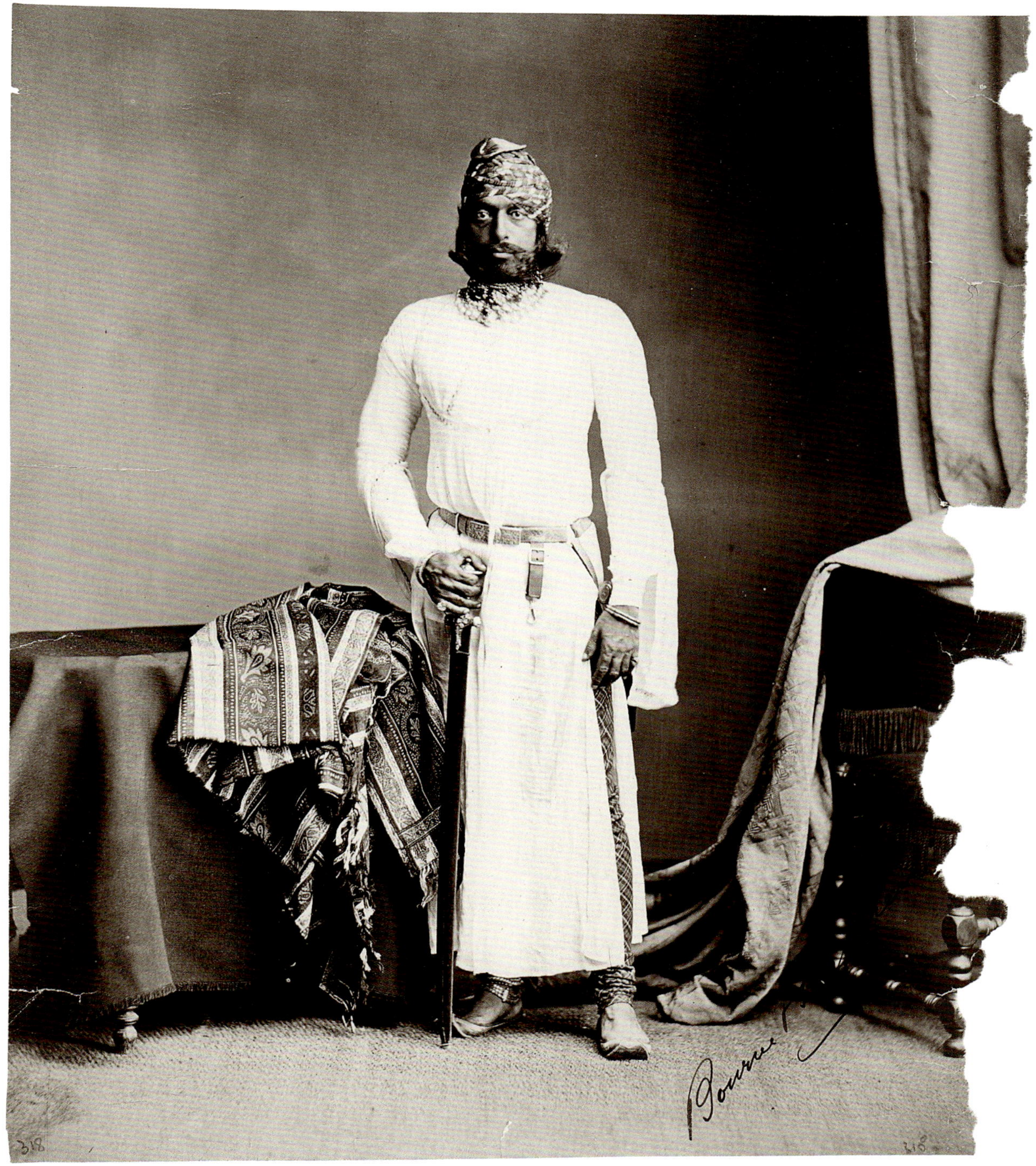

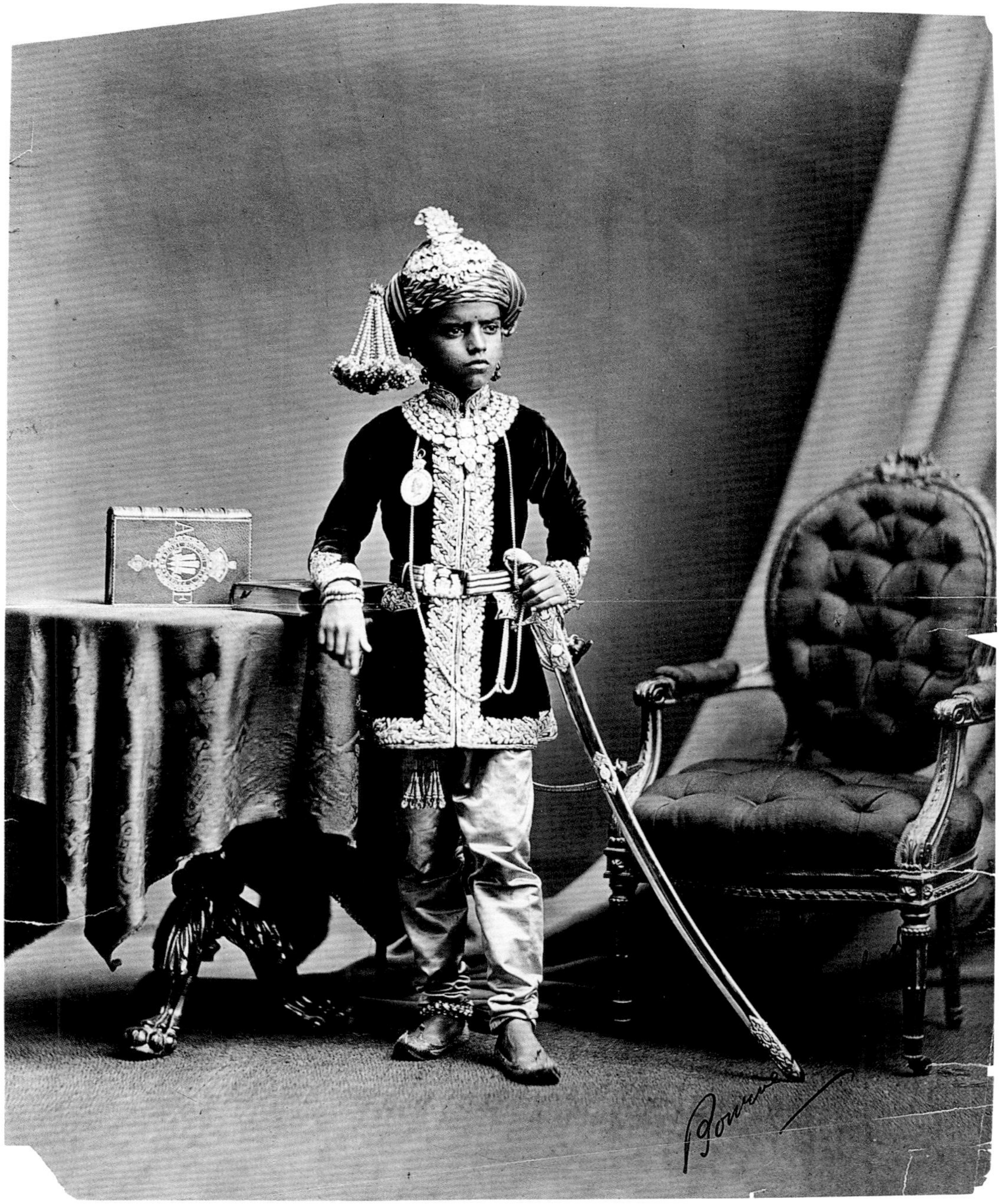

88 *Sir Sayaji Rao, Gaekwar of Baroda* (1863–1939)

Bourne & Shepherd

ca. 1877, albumen print, 31.1 x 25.9
The British Library, Oriental & India Office Collection photo 99 (33)

89 *HH the Maharaja of Pannah*

Unknown photographer

1880s, albumen print, 29.4 x 23.6

The British Library, Oriental & India Office Collection photo 209 (11)

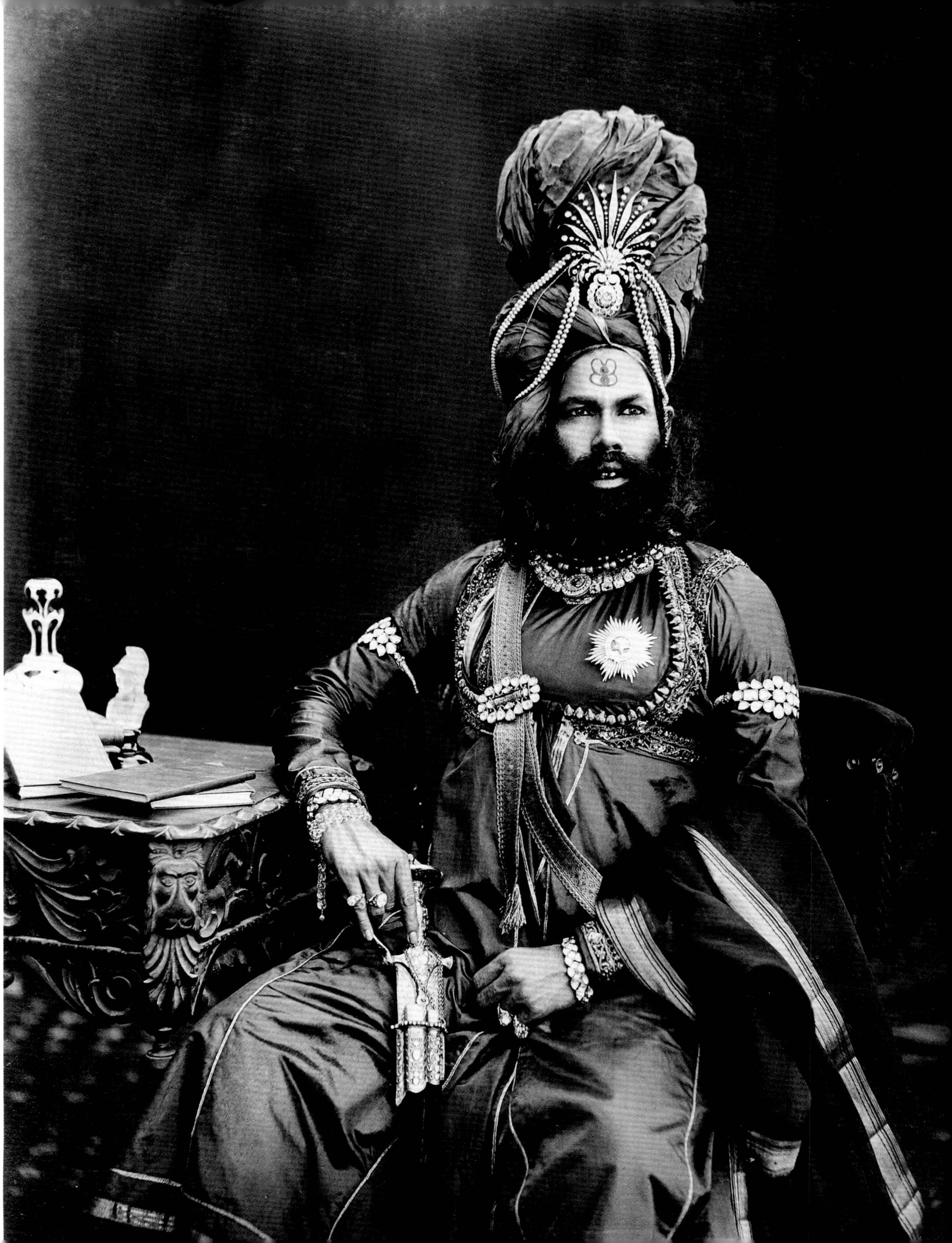

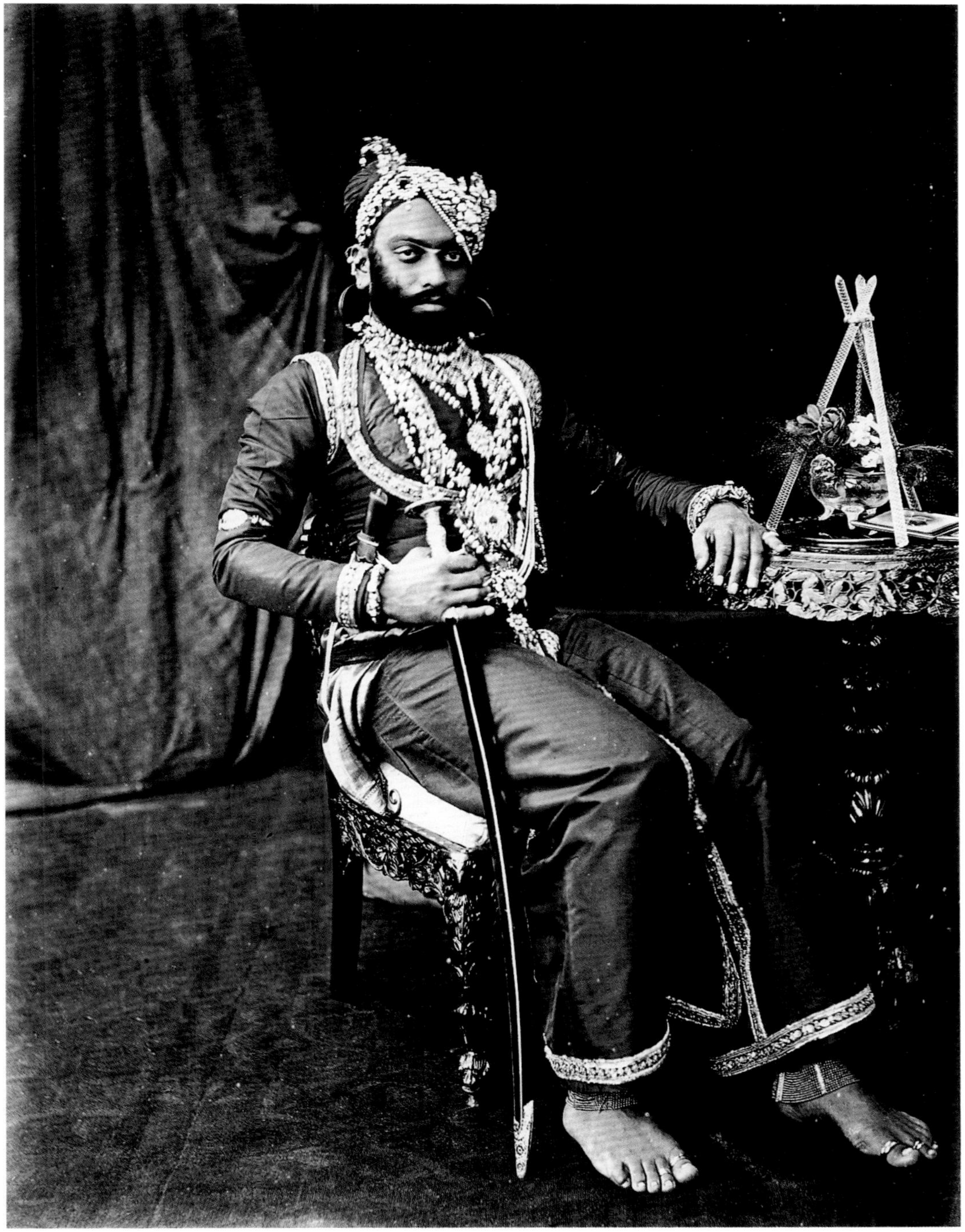

90 *HH the Later Maharana of Oodeypore*

Unknown photographer

1880s, albumen print, 27.5 x 22.8
The British Library, Oriental & India Office Collection photo 209 (9)

91 *HH the Maharaja of Ulwar*

Unknown photographer

1880s, albumen print, 27.1 x 21.2
The British Library, Oriental & India Office Collection photo 209 (10)

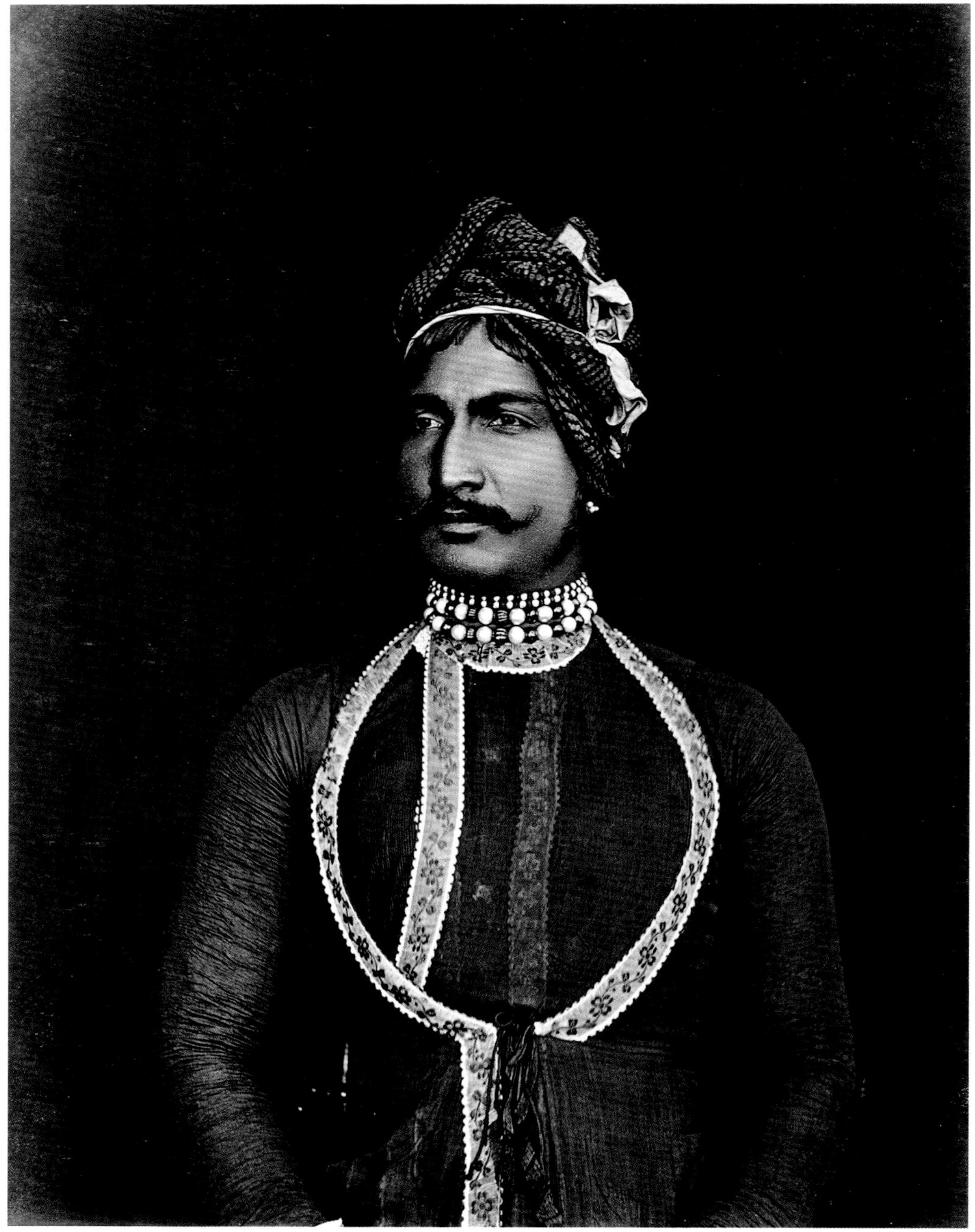

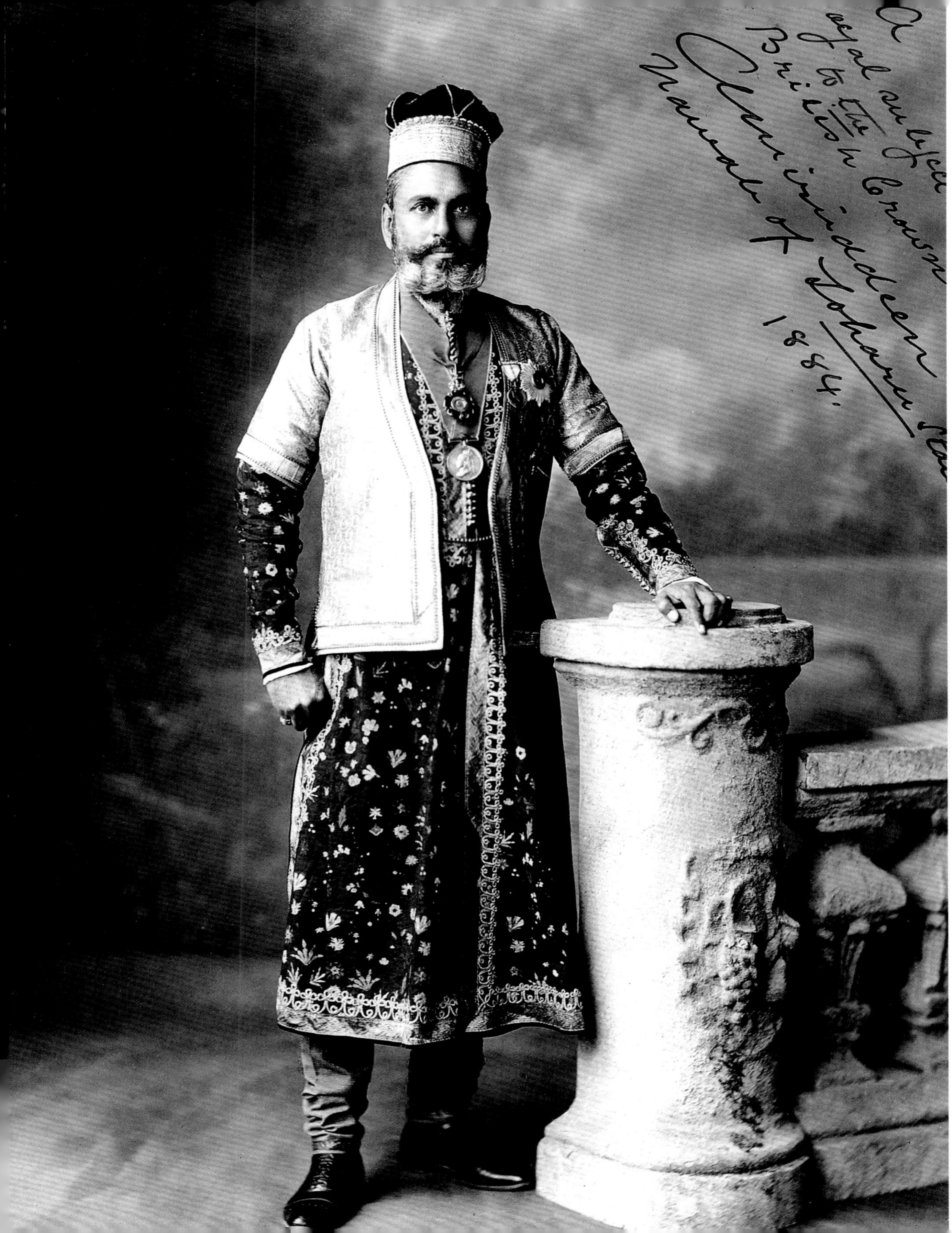

92 *Sir Amir-ud-din Ahmad Khan, Nawab of Loharu* (1859–1937)

G.W. Lawrie & Co.

1884, albumen print, 27.8 x 22.6

The British Library, Oriental & India Office Collection photo 100 (39)

93 *Sir Udaji Rao Ponwar, Maharaja of Dhar* (1886–1926)

Bourne & Shepherd

ca. 1900, albumen print, 27.2 x 23.6
The British Library, Oriental & India Office Collection photo 99 (3)

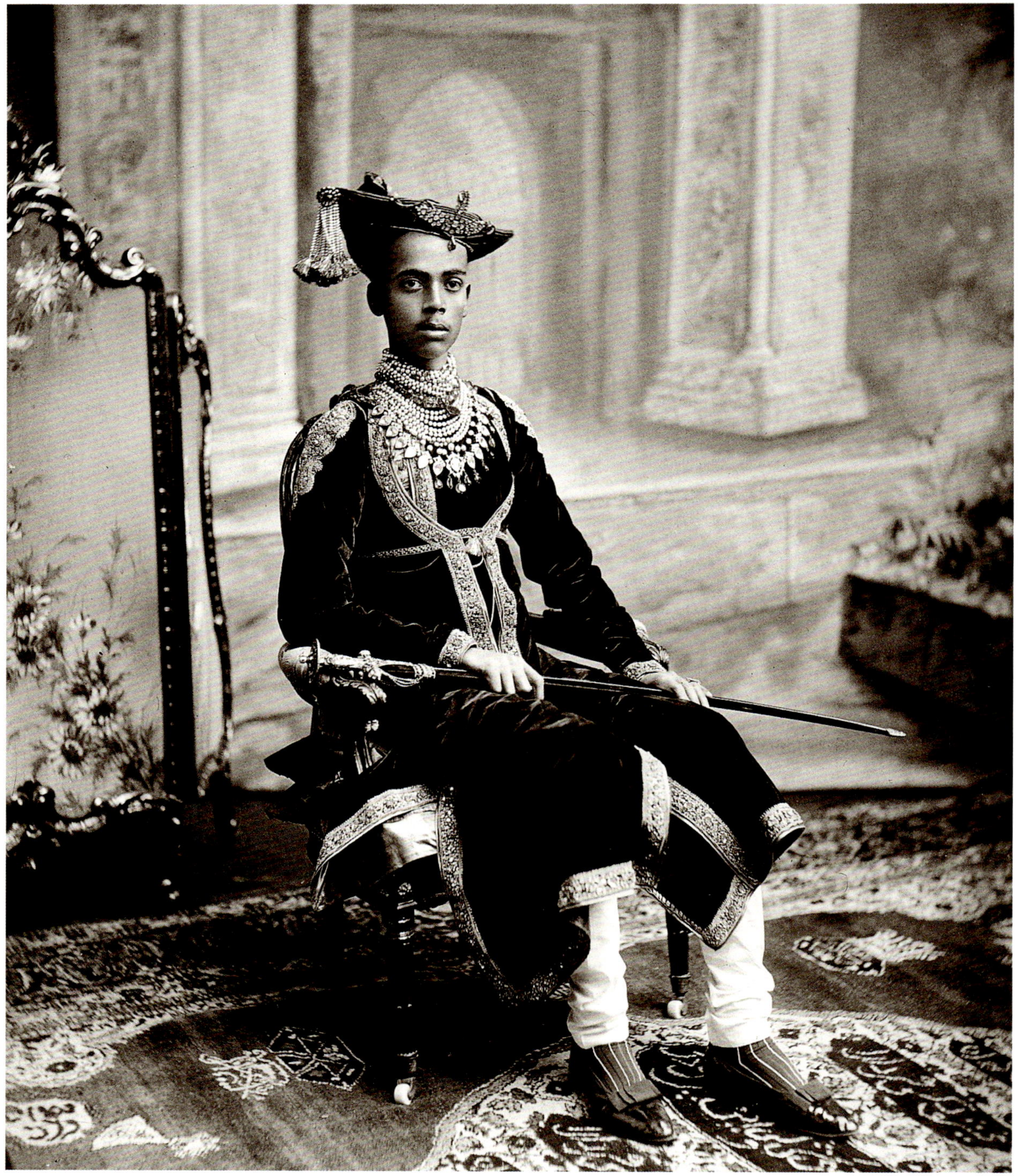

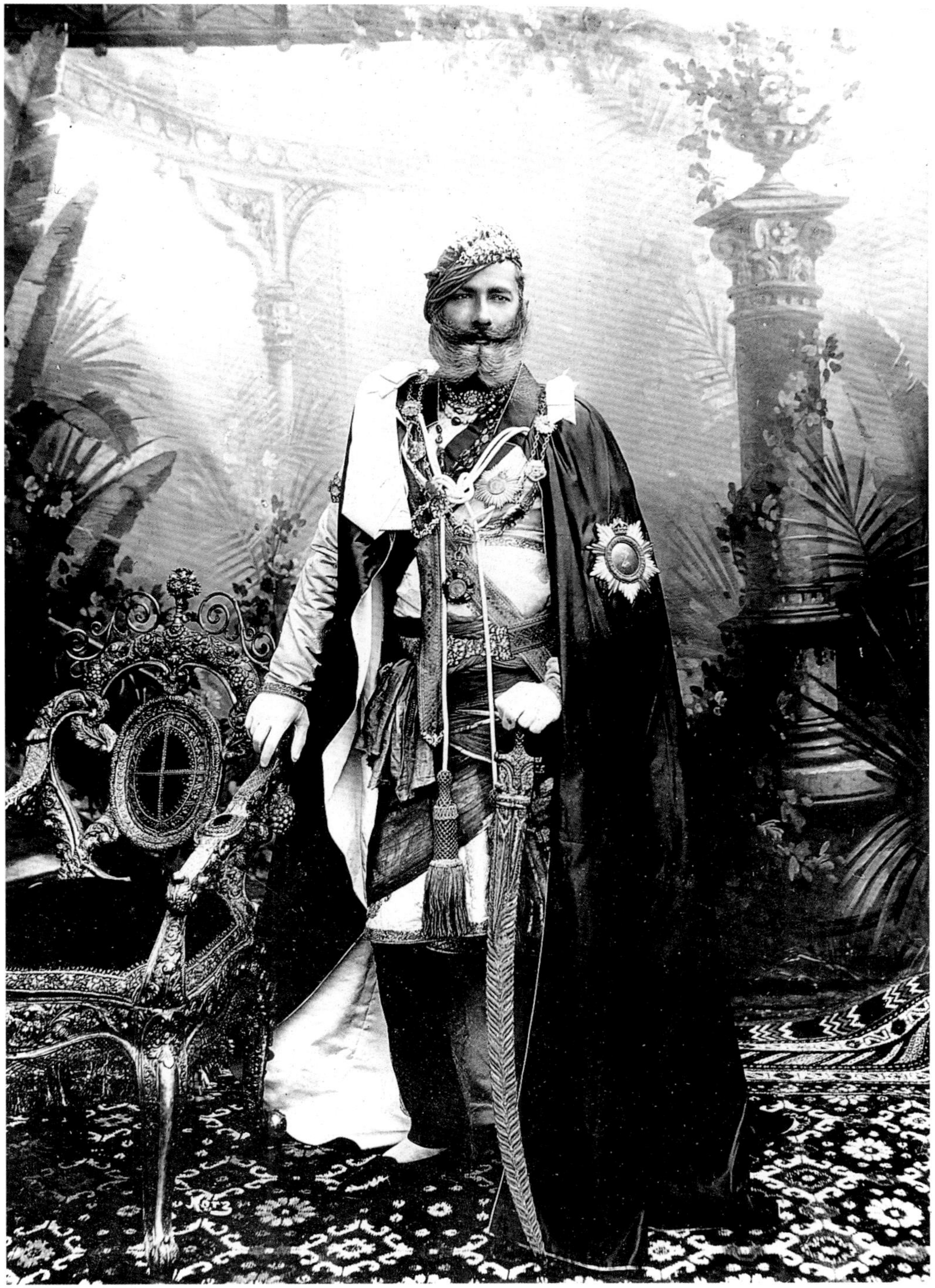

94 *Sir Pratap Singh, Maharaja of Orchha* (1854–1930)

J. Cowell

ca. 1900, albumen print, 29.3 x 21.4
The British Library, Oriental & India Office Collection photo 99 (13)

95 *Sir Jagajit Singh, Maharaja of Kapurthala* (1872–1949)

Bourne & Shepherd

ca. 1903, albumen print, 29.7 x 18.3

The British Library, Oriental & India Office Collection photo 99 (25)

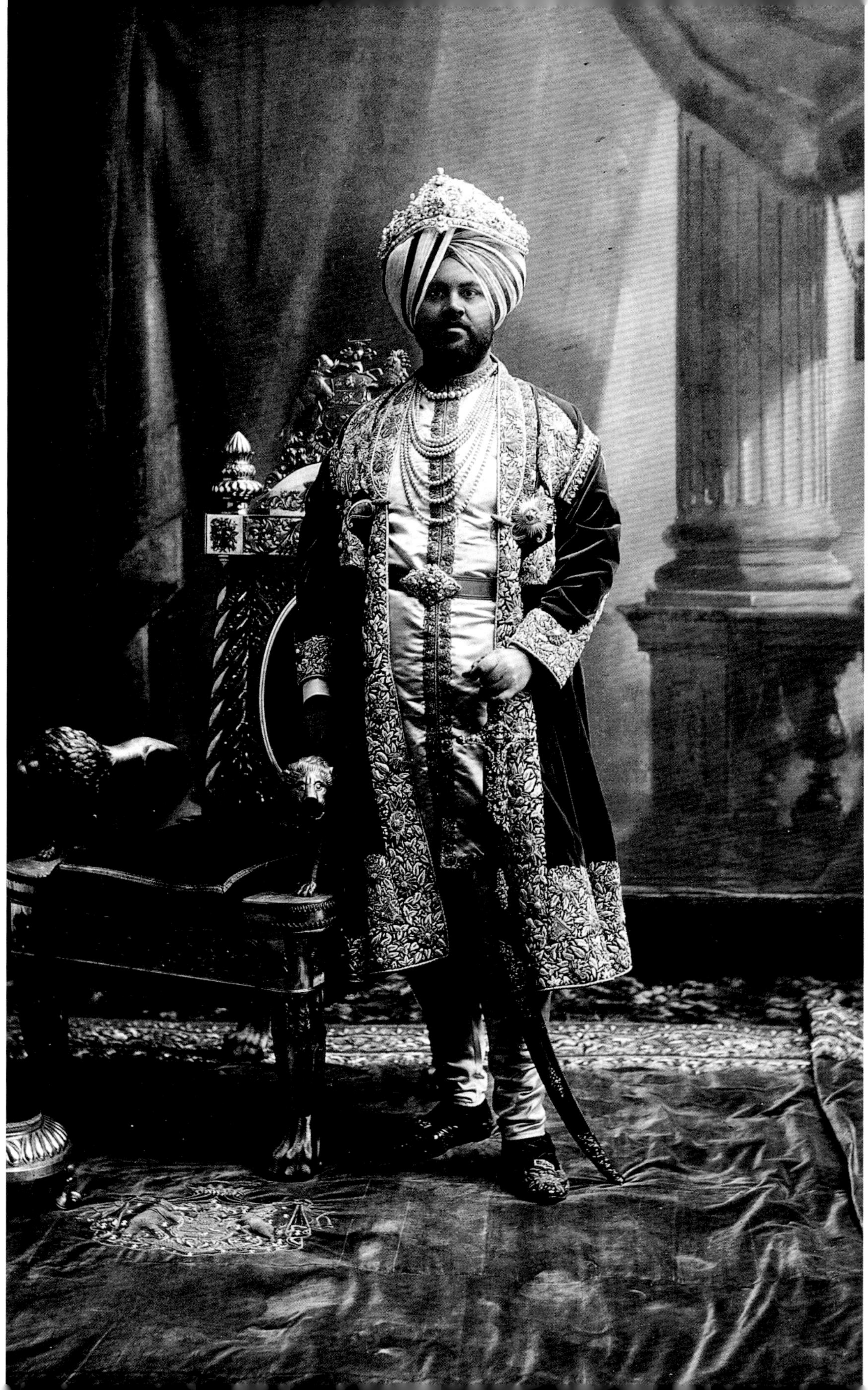

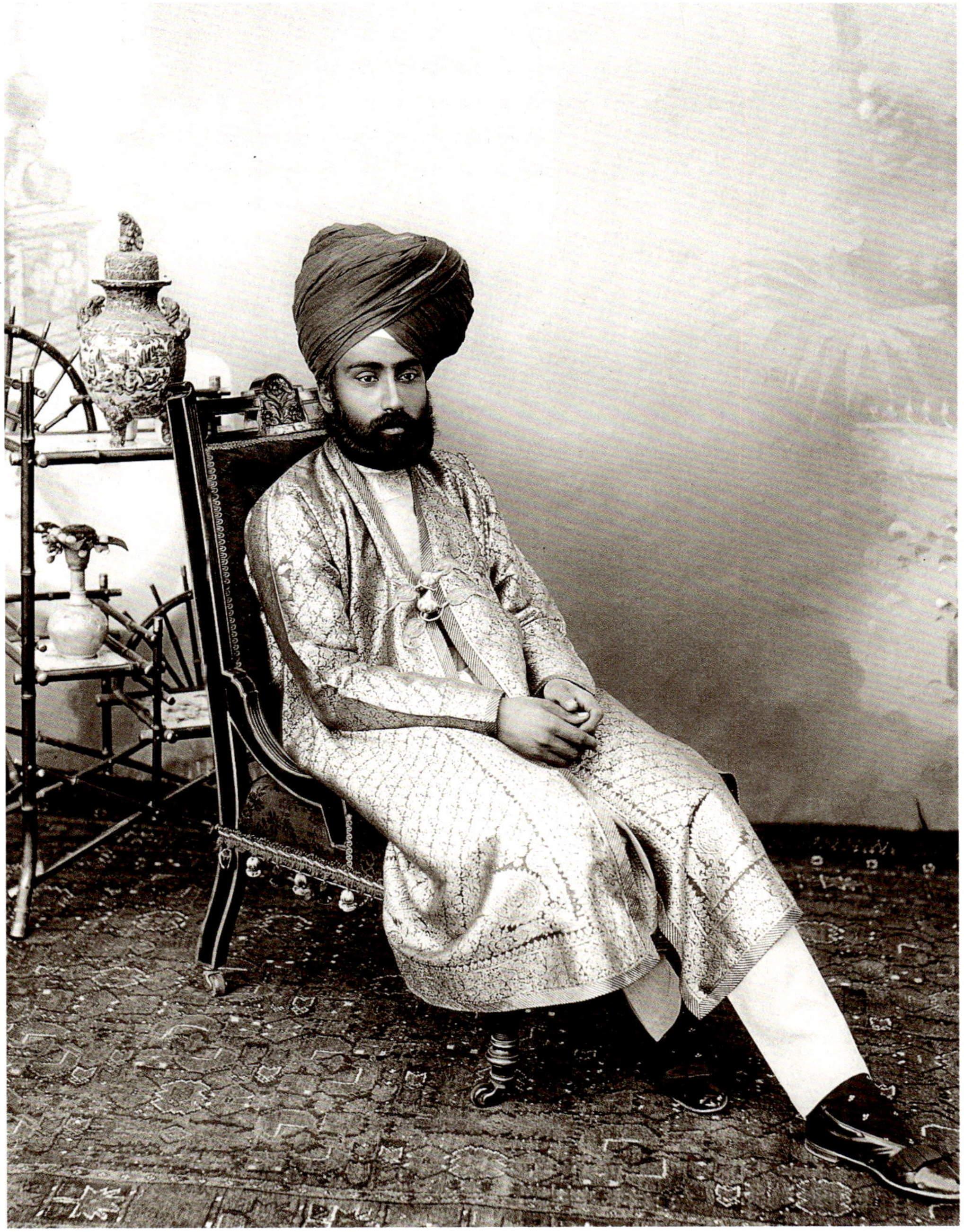

96 *Sir Ranbir Singh, Maharaja of Jind* (1879–1948)

Bourne & Shepherd

ca. 1903, albumen print, 29.3 x 22.9
The British Library, Oriental & India Office Collection photo 99 (24)

97 *Sir Waghji Ravaji, Thakur Sahib of Morvi* (1858–1922)

Walery

ca. 1903, albumen print, 28.8 x 17.7
The British Library, Oriental & India Office Collection photo 99 (23)

98 *Sir Raghubir Singh, Maharao of Bundi* (1869–1927)

Ganpatrao Abajee Kale

ca. 1911, albumen print, 27.4 x 23
The British Library, Oriental & India Office Collection photo 100 (26)

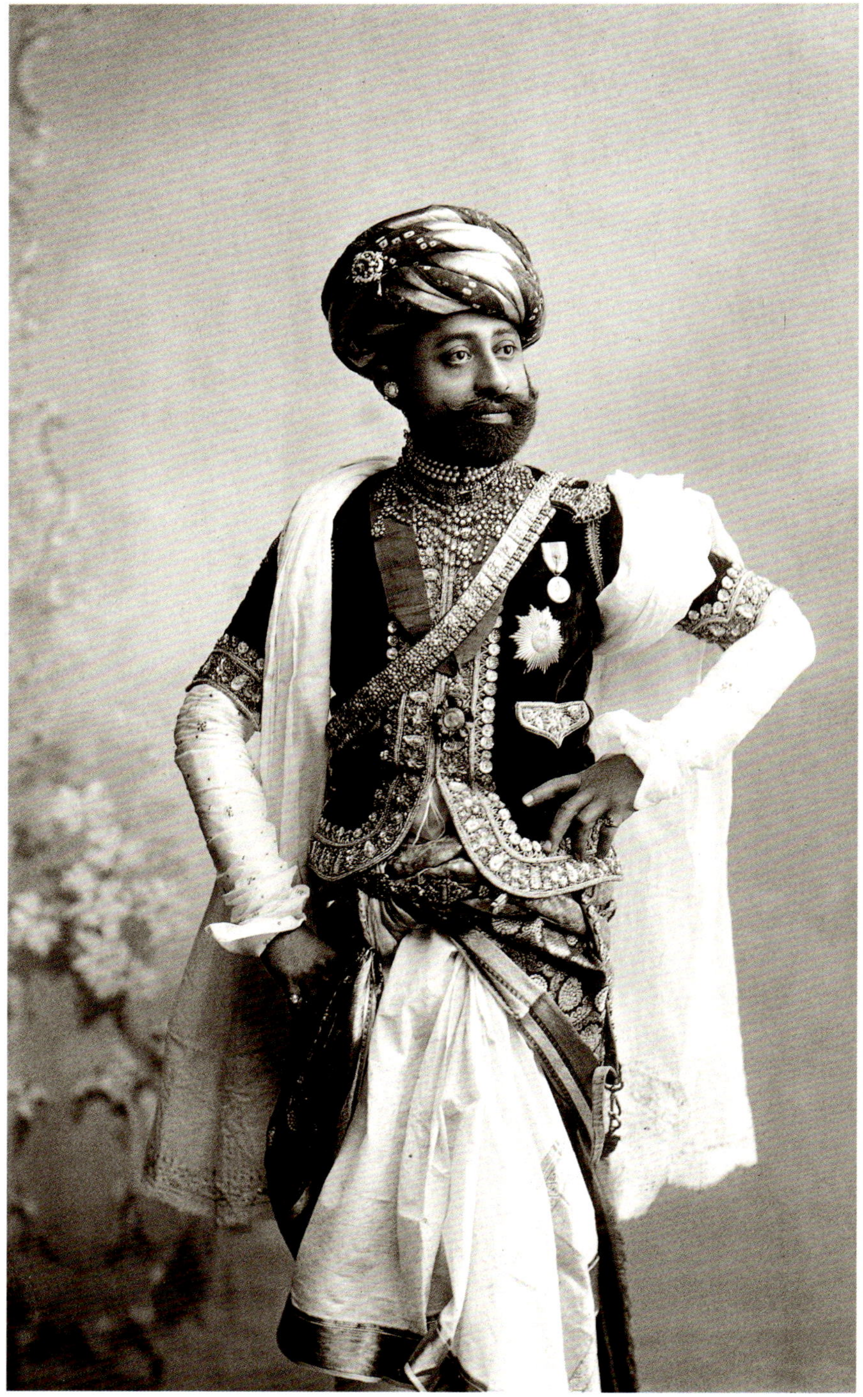

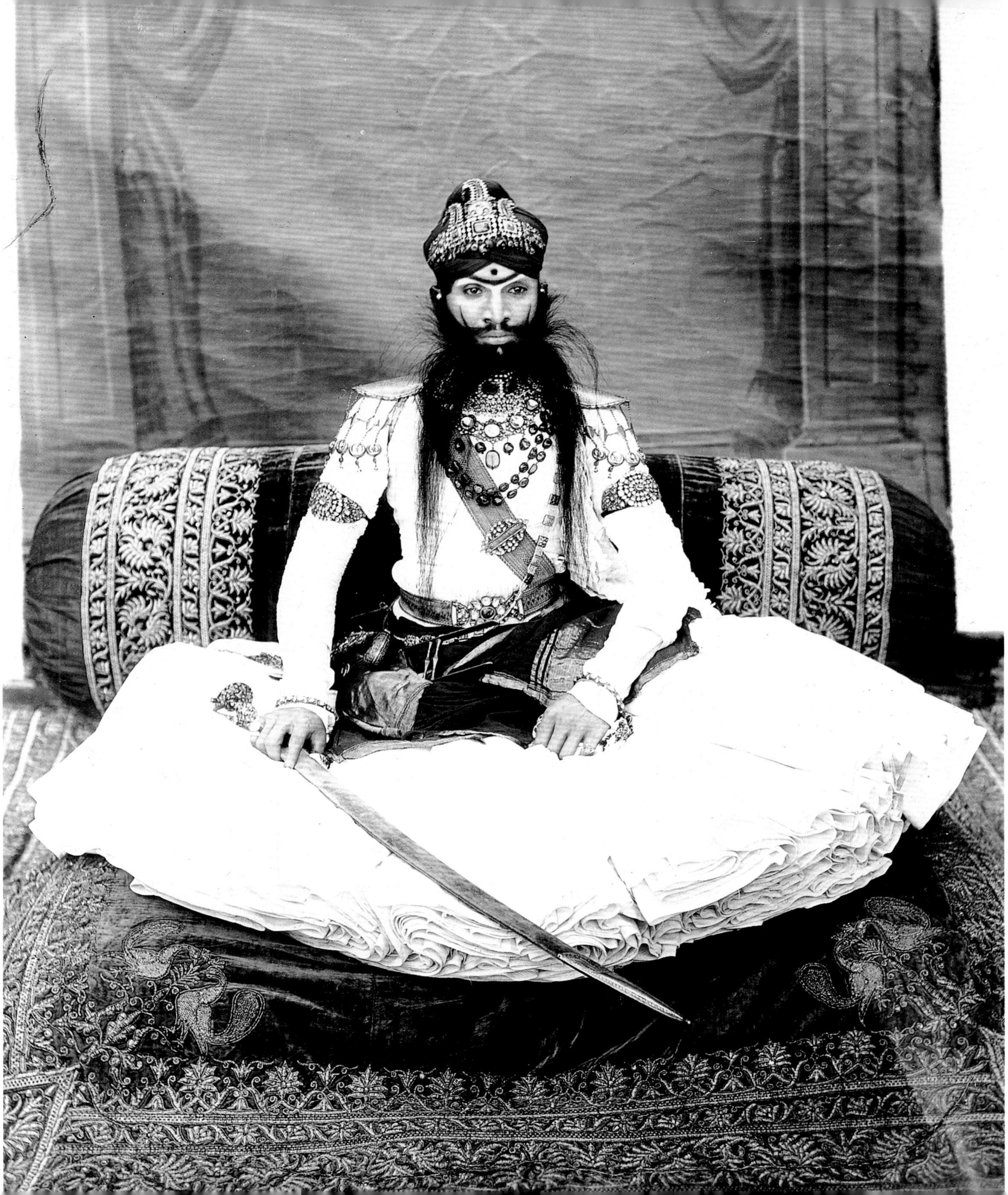

99 *Sir Madan Singh, Maharaja of Kishangarh* (1884–1926)

Herzog & Higgins

ca. 1911, hand-colored photograph, 62 x 48

The British Library, Oriental & India Office Collection photo 100 (48)

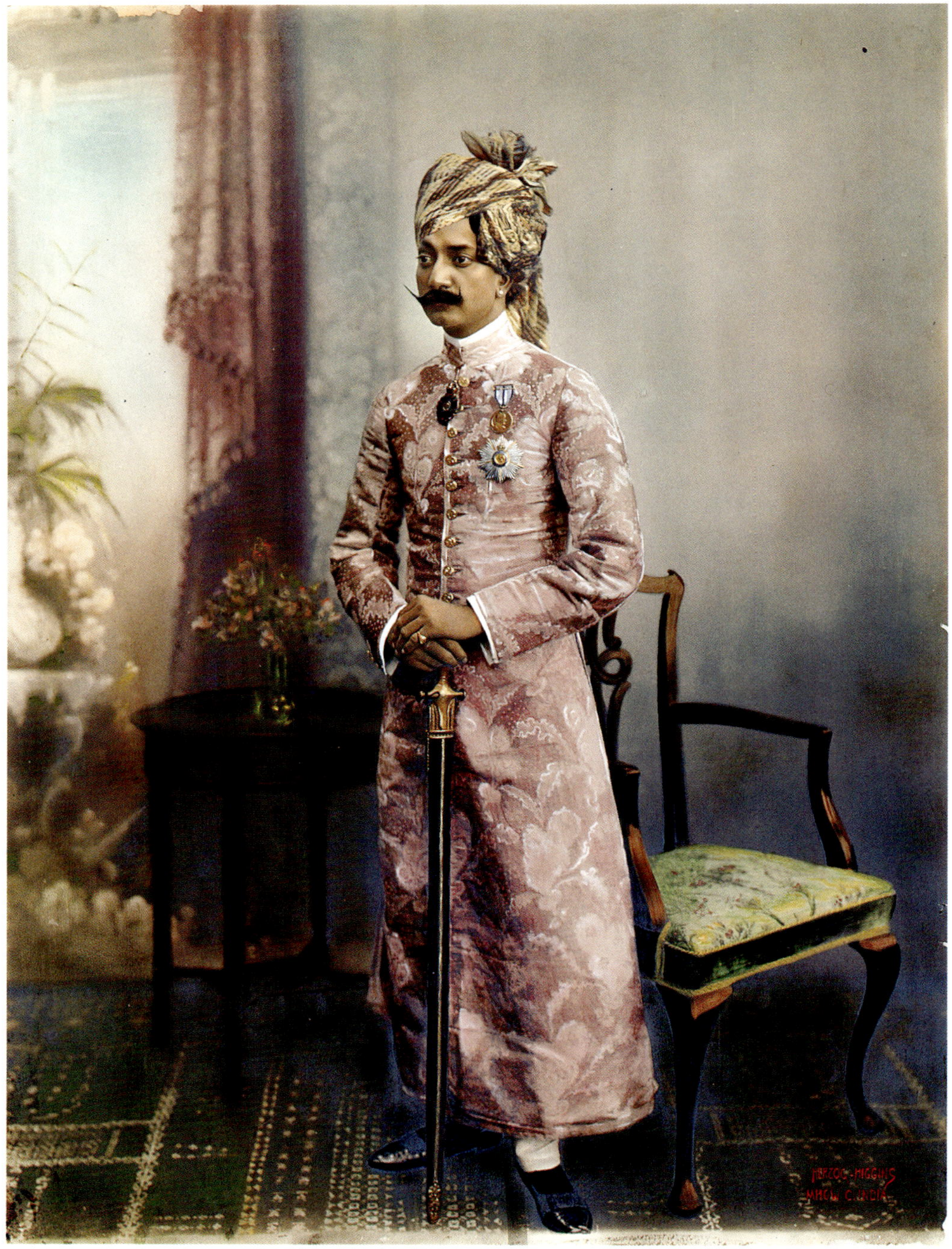

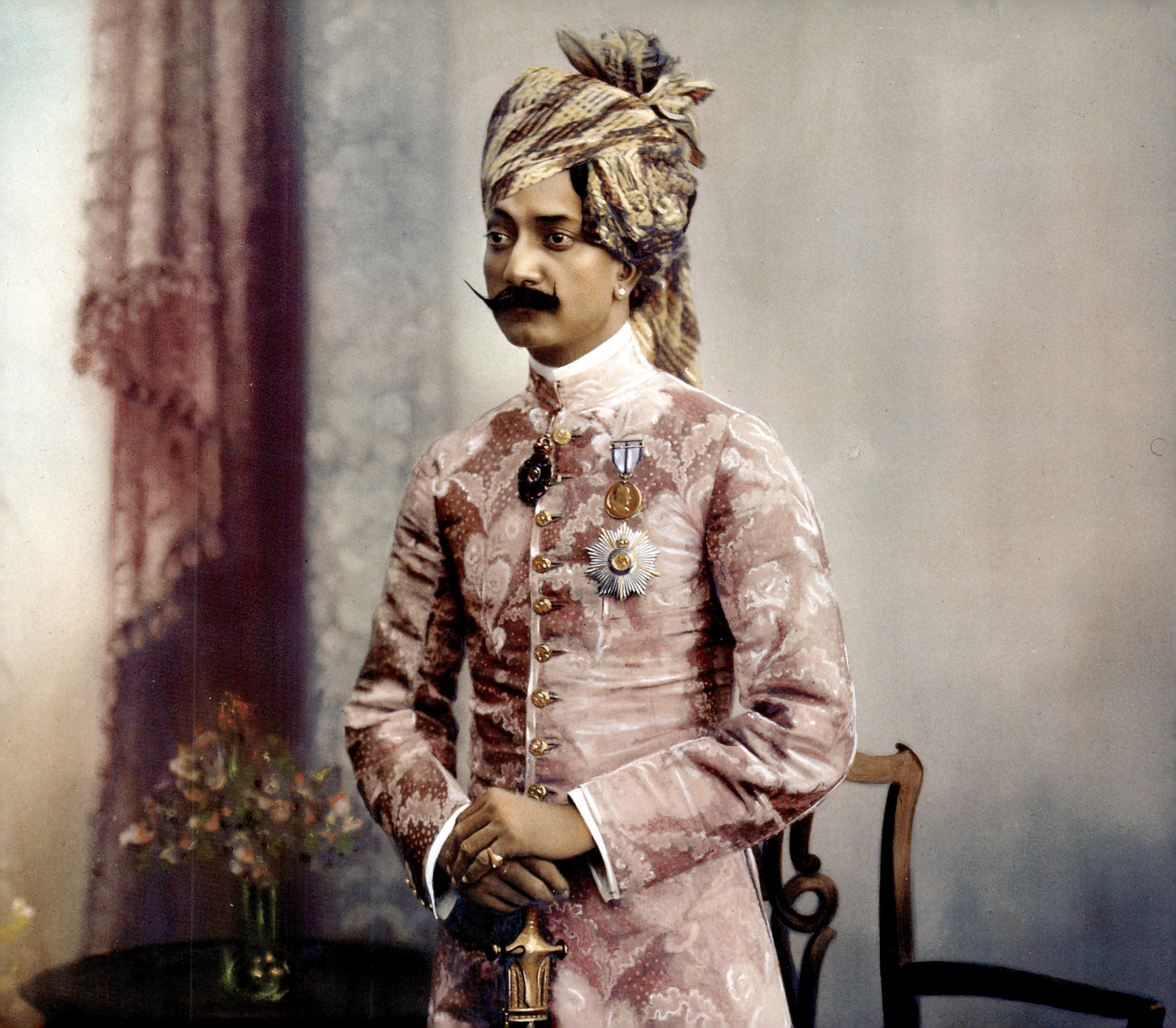

MAHARAJAS AS PHOTOGRAPHERS

Vidya Dehejia

NOT SURPRISINGLY, the new and prestigious art of photography attracted the attention of the maharajas, who were always on the lookout for the latest diversion. Some, like the raja of the hill state of Chamba, indulged in the purchase of an array of cameras, lenses, and the chemical paraphernalia known as *masalas* (spices), but did not distinguish themselves as photographers.[1] Others, like Bhawani Singh of Jhalawar, a small principality in Saurashtra, displayed a high level of competence. Bhawani Singh, in fact, published a book titled *Travel Pictures: The Record of a European Tour,* illustrated with ninety-six of his own photographs.[2] Yet others, in particular Ram Singh of Jaipur, and more than one generation of the rajas of the eastern hill state of Tripura, acquired some fame in the field of photography.

Maharaja Sawai Ram Singh II (1835–1880) of Jaipur was a member of the Bengal Photographic Society from its inception, in 1856. He bought his first camera in 1862, purchased several more cameras and an entire range of lenses from the Calcutta firm of Shib Churn Dutt & Co., finally amassing as many as two hundred pieces of photographic equipment.[3] A volume on India's princes published in 1975 contains the first account of Ram Singh's interest in photography. French photographer and author Louis Rousselet (1845–1929) wrote thus of his encounter with the maharaja: "The conversation then turns to photography (he is not only an admirer of the art, he is himself a skillful photographer)."[4] In recent years over twenty-five hundred glass plate negatives belonging to Ram Singh have been recovered from a room known as *foto ka karkhana,* or photography workshop. A guide to Jaipur published in 1876 located such a room in a mansion named Madho Nivas; it overlooked a miniature garden with winding marble paths and was situated directly above the room for drawing—an art that retained its importance at court.

Ram Singh photographed several of the women in his zenana, or women's, studios—something no other man would have been allowed to do in the context of the nineteenth century. These photographs, a fascinating social record of the times, comprise studies of women from varying parts of India, dancing girls and those who acted in popular plays (*tamashas*), and the dwarf who was the zenana superintendent. Ram Singh also photographed British men, women, and children, whom he frequently posed in front of a classical backdrop. A diary entry for 1 January 1870, written in the local Rajasthani dialect, confirms that he himself photographed the duke of Edinburgh, who was on royal visit to India. Ram Singh also made photographic portrait studies of several nobles at his court. His photographs usually display his monogram either on the mount or on the photographic paper, accompanied by the words: Photographed by H. H. Maharaja Sewai Ram Singh Bahadoor, K. G. C. S. I. of Jeypore.

Maharajas of the tiny hill state of Tripura in northeastern India were also accomplished photographers. Maharaja Birchandra Manikya started taking daguerreotypes in the mid-1850s, but kept abreast of new techniques, switching over to the wet-collodion process and later to the platinum print. He founded a camera club in his capital of Agartala and held annual photographic exhibitions in the palace.[5] On occasion, Birchandra sent examples of his work to Calcutta, and the June 1891 issue of the *Journal of the Indian Photographic Society* reports that his platinum prints arrived too late to be entered in that year's competition. It adds that this was "a fortunate circumstance for some who got them [medals]—for assuredly, had they been in time, they would have carried off a medal in the classes they represented. . . . They were all of very high merit, exceptionally so indeed, and their execution reflects the greatest credit on His Highness' skill as photographer."[6]

Birchandra's son Shamarendra Chandra Deb Burman, known generally as Bara Thakur, was an equally avid photographer who won great acclaim for his talent. Bara Thakur was an accomplished chemist; he modified existing chemical formulas to prepare his own photographic papers to compensate for the extreme damp in the northeast, one of the wettest regions of India. He read a paper on the

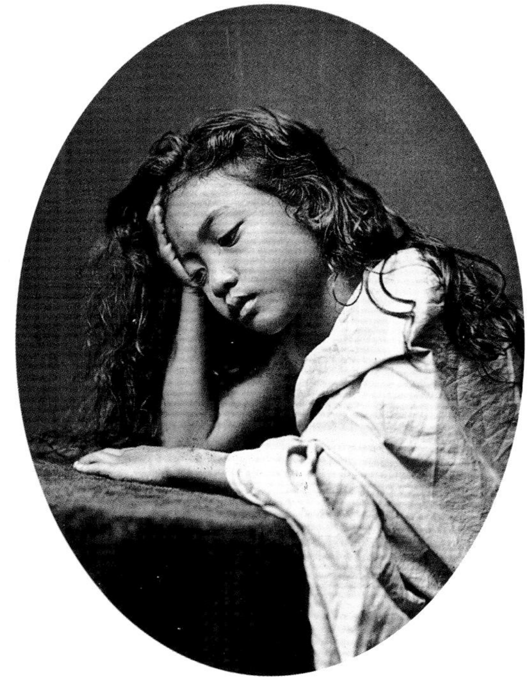

FIGURE 1 Shamarendra Chandra Deb Barman, *Portrait of a Young Girl from Hill Tippera*, ca. 1893, albumen print, 22.1 x 28. The British Library, Oriental & India Office Collection

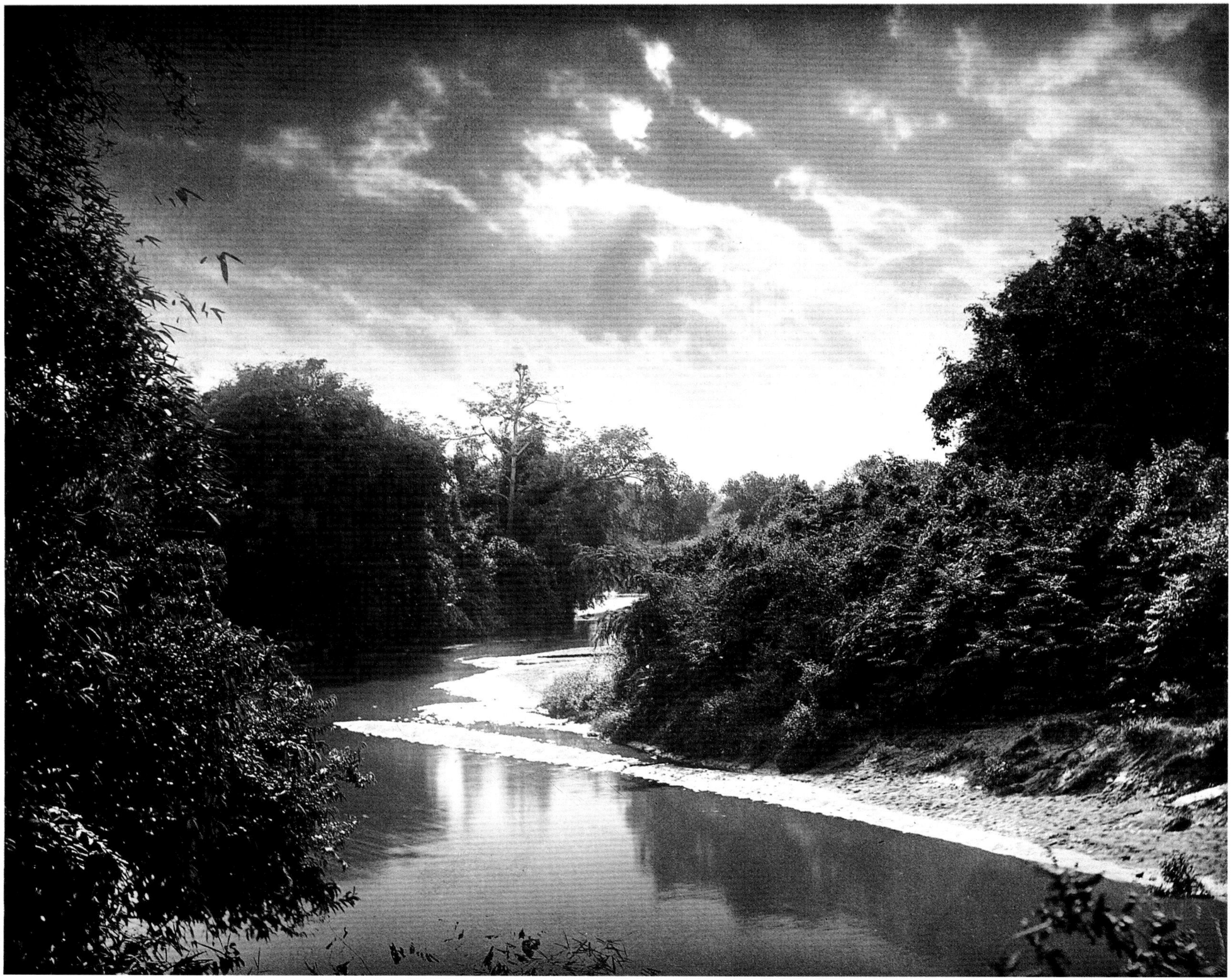

Pizzighelli Platinotype Process to the January 1982 meeting of the Bengal Photographic Society, proposing its use as an alternative chemical procedure. Bara Thakur won three medals in England—a silver medal in the landscape category in 1890 and again in 1895, and a gold medal in portraiture in 1895—as well as five medals back home in Calcutta (figs 1, 2). One of his photographs was well-enough admired to be reproduced as *Composition of Wood and Water* in an 1896 London publication titled *Artistic Landscape Photography.*[7]

NOTES

1. Samuel Bourne, "Narrative of a Photographic Trip to Kashmir (Cashmere) and Adjacent Districts," *British Journal of Photography* (2 November 1866): 524.

2. Bhawani Singh, Raj Rana Bahadur of Jhalawar, *Travel Pictures: The Record of European Tour* (London: Longmans, Green & Co., 1912).

3. Asok Kumar Das, *The Photographer Prince Maharaja Sawai Ram Singh II* (Jaipur: Maharaja Sawai Man Singh II Museum, 1985), an eight-page booklet to accompany an exhibition of the same title, is the source for much of the information on Ram Singh. See also Yaduendra Sinha, *Maharaja Sawai Ram Singh II of Jaipur: The Photographer Prince* (Jaipur: Dr. Durga Sahi Foundation, 1996).

4. Louis Rousselet, *L'Inde des rajahs: voyage dans L'inde centrale et dans les presidences de Bombay et du Bengale* (Paris: Hachette et cie, 1875).

5. Siddhartha Ghosh, "Early Photography in Calcutta," in Pratapaditya Pal, ed., *Changing Visions, Lasting Images: Calcutta through 300 Years* (Bombay: Marg Publications, 1990), 143–58.

6. Siddhartha Ghosh, *Chobi Tola: Bangalir Photographi Charcha* (Calcutta: Ananda Publishers Pvt. Ltd., 1988). See also *Journal of the Photographic Society of India* (June 1891).

7. Alfred H. Wall, *Artistic Landscape Photography: A Series of Chapters on the Practical and Theoretical Principles of Pictorial Composition* (Bradford, London: P. Lund & Co. Ltd., 1896).

FIGURE 2 Shamarendra Chandra Deb Barman, *Howrah River, Old Agartala, Hill Tippera* [Silver Medal, Calcutta], 1890, albumen print, 22.1 x 28. The British Library, Oriental & India Office Collection

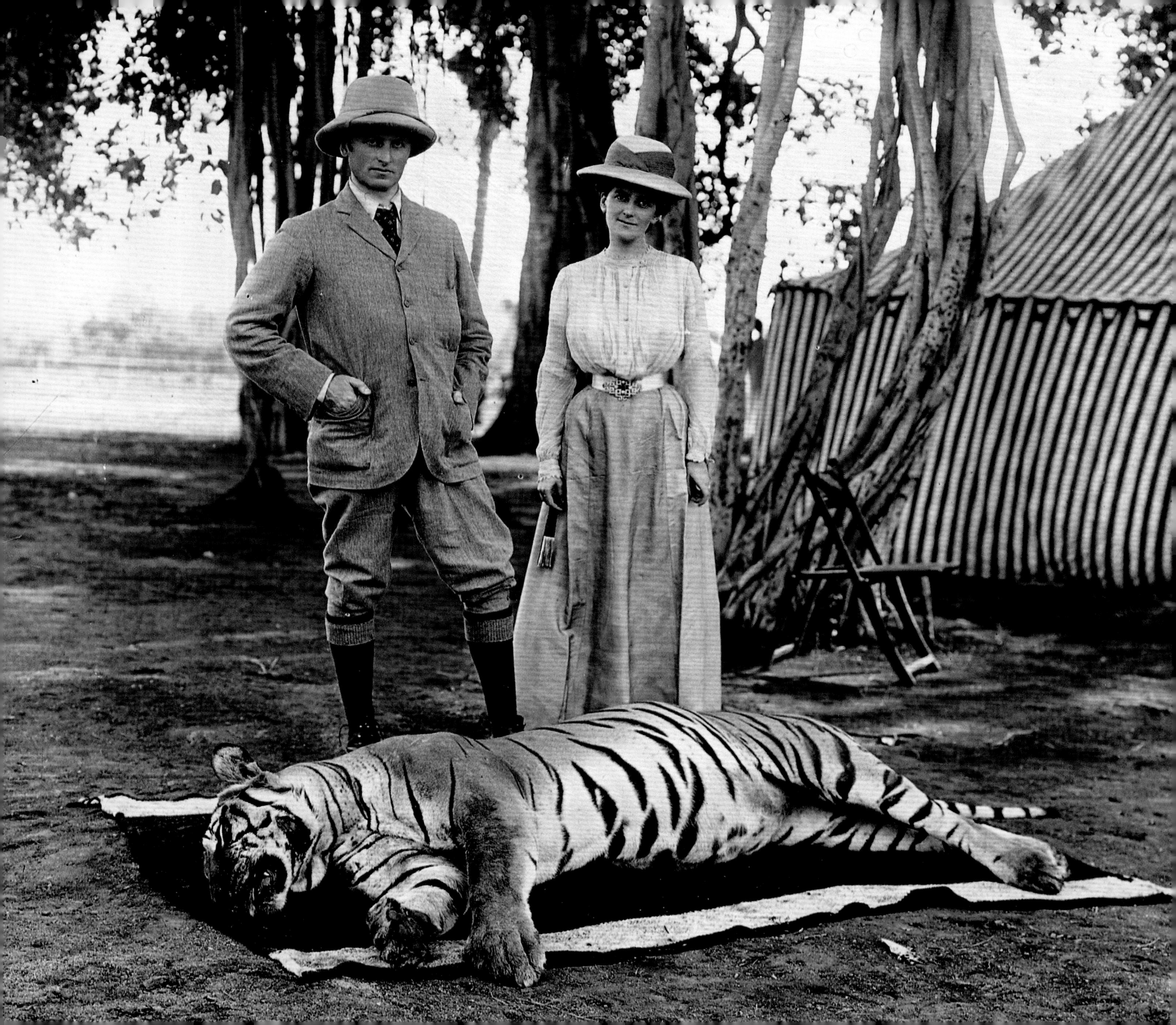

Charles Allen

Imperial Image: The Grand Durbars of 1903 and 1911

The notion that image was an essential component in advancing the cause of British rule in India was first promoted by Lord Mornington, governor-general from 1798 to 1805. In keeping with his expansionist aims, he established a style of government that was deliberately intended to impress on both subjects and rivals the awful majesty of the new ruling power. Outward magnificence was expected of their rulers by Asian peoples and the British should follow suit, he reasoned. India, he declared, must be governed "from a palace, not from a counting house; with the ideas of a Prince, not with those of a retail dealer in muslins and indigo."[1] For a palace he built himself at huge expense Government House in Calcutta, modeled on one of the largest country homes in England, wherein he entertained lavishly.

Mornington's ambitions eventually brought about his recall to England and a less ostentatious style of government by his successors. However, the rebellion of 1857 brought an end to company rule and its replacement by direct crown rule. On 1 November 1858, the new viceroy, Lord Canning, proclaimed the order by which Queen Victoria assumed direct sovereignty over her eastern possessions. He then set out on a series of image-building exercises, turning for a model to the great Mughal emperors of the past, who had made much of public displays in the form of durbars and imperial tours.

The Persian term *darbar* had been introduced to India many centuries earlier and covered a range of meanings associated with the court of a ruler, his government, and the ceremony at which his leading subjects publicly offered tokens of their submission. It was this last form of durbar—the public act of submission—that Lord Canning seized upon. Over two succeeding "cold weathers" (the winter months in India from October to March, in this case from 1858 to 1860) he embarked on extended tours across northern India interrupted by a number of grand assemblies at which all the local rulers and leading landowners were required to tender their allegiance to the viceroy as the representative of Queen Victoria (see fig. 1). The cross-country progress of what was known as the viceroy's "camp" was like the advance of an army. The viceroy and his staff alone occupied 150 large tents, requiring 80 elephants and 500 camels for its transport. Another 500 camels, 500 bullocks, and 100 bullock carts transported their equipage, with 527 porters to carry the glass windows of the larger tents, 100 water carriers to keep down the dust of the streets in their camp, and 40 sweepers to keep them clean. Including military escort and camp-followers the attendant human population amounted to no fewer than twenty thousand, and on the line of march it spread out from advance guard to rear guard along twenty-four miles of road.[2]

Two decades later, the British Prime Minister Benjamin Disraeli joined forces with Viceroy Lord Lytton to devise a political spectacle that would both reinforce Queen Victoria's imperial claims and demonstrate to the world the permanence of British rule (known to all as "the Raj") in India. An "imperial assemblage" was devised to be held outside Delhi on 1 January 1877, at which Queen Victoria's assumption of the title of *kaiser-i-hind,* or empress of India, would be proclaimed before the greatest in the land. The site for this assembly was carefully selected for its symbolic value: a barren plain just north of Delhi that had formed the site of the British camp in the summer of 1857 prior to the storming and recapture of the city. Here a series of tented camps were laid out, with a large, semicircular "throne-pavilion" as the focal point.

A spectacle was devised to evoke—and surpass—the splendors of India's Mughal past and to suggest that the British monarch was the natural heir. It commenced with a grand procession of elephants, each bearing one of the sixty-three so-called ruling princes of India but preceded by Lord and Lady Lytton on the largest elephant. "Delhi must have witnessed many splendid pageants," wrote Field-Marshall Lord Roberts, who had played a major role in organizing the event, "when the Rajput, the Moghul, and the Mahratta dynasties, each in its turn, was at the height of its glory; but never before had Princes and Chiefs of every race and creed come from all parts of Hindustan, vying with each other as to the magnificence of their entourage, and met together with the same object—that of acknowledging and doing homage to one supreme Ruler."[3]

Page 242: Detail, no. 100. *Their Excellencies Lord and Lady Curzon with First Day's Bag in Camp near Nekonda, Warangal District, Hyderabad,* Lala Deen Dayal

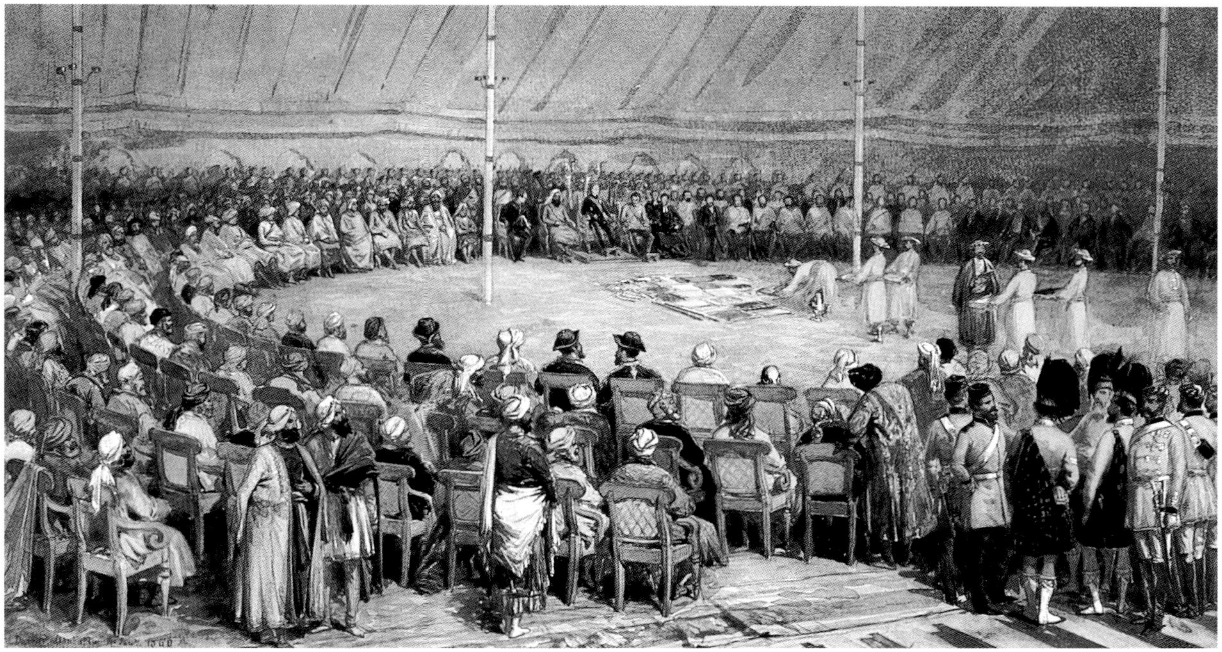

FIGURE 1 *Lord Canning's Durbar at Amballa,* by William Simpson (British, 1823–1899), 19 January 1860. Watercolor on paper. This was the fourth of a series of assemblies held during the viceroy's six-month tour of northern India, designed to impress upon local rulers and landowners the might of the British Raj in the wake of the uprising known as the Indian Mutiny of 1857. Gifts of shawls are being laid out before the viceroy. From the Lady Canning Albums, Harewood House, by kind permission of the Earl and Countess of Harewood and the Trustees of the Harewood House Trust

After several days of ceremony the assemblage moved to its climax: the proclamation by the chief herald of Queen Victoria as empress of India. The only hiccup to these impressive proceedings came when the fifteen thousand troops gathered for the occasion began the ripple of rifle fire known as the *feu de joie* (fire of joy). "This was too much for the elephants," recounts Roberts. "As the feu de joie approached nearer and nearer to them they became more and more alarmed, and at last scampered off, dispersing the crowd in every direction. When it ceased they were quietened and brought back by their *mahouts*, only to start off again when the firing recommenced."[4]

A series of measures, including royal visits, new orders of knighthood, and European-style coats of arms, bound the Indian princes ever closer to the British monarchy while at the same time raising Queen Victoria to the status of a quasi-divine cult figure. The death of the queen-empress in January 1901 provided Lord Curzon, viceroy of India from 1899 to 1905, with a marvelous opportunity to preserve what he believed to be Queen Victoria's mystique, her "overpowering effect on the imagination of the Asiatic,"[5] in the form of a memorial, rather as the remains of the Mughal emperors were immured in marble mausoleums. The outcome was the Victoria Memorial, a museum in Calcutta, defiantly Italianate in style with just a hint of the Saracenic in its four corner domes, and filled with British trophies of their conquest of India.

No viceroy before or since had a greater sense of India's worth to Britain than Curzon, who once memorably declared: "The sacredness of India haunts me like a passion. It is only when you get to see what India really is, that she is the strength and greatness of England; it is only then that you realise that every nerve, every sinew a man may bring should be used to draw even tighter the cords that bind us to India."[6] Curzon decided that the new sovereign should help the binding process by coming out to India for a special coronation, but King Edward VII did not share his mother's enthusiasm for India and declined to do so. Instead, it was decided that a coronation durbar should be staged in India attended by a minor royal, the duke of Connaught, but with the king's representative in India, the viceroy, as the central figure.

Dubbed "the Curzonisation" by Curzon's many enemies, the coronation durbar of January 1903 bore the mark of George Nathaniel Curzon in every detail, large and small. He was determined that it should be "the biggest thing ever seen in India" and spent almost two years in meticulous planning to ensure that this was so. His detractors declared that the event would cost millions of pounds sterling but deft creative accounting produced a declared expenditure amounting to no more than £180,000, much of which Curzon believed could be recovered by reusing some of the purchases. Facing his critics at a meeting of the legislative council held in Simla on 5 September 1902, Curzon gave his reasons for staging the durbar on the scale he proposed. It was to be a celebration of Britain's imperial achievement in uniting India: "Here, in India, it is for the first time under the British Crown that . . . the entire continent has acknowledged a single ruler." That celebration would be "no mere pageant" but "an act of supreme public solemnity, demonstrating to ourselves our union, and to the world our strength."

The site selected was the same upon which the 1877 durbar had been staged, and for the same reasons. Under the eyes of an Indian engineer, a "howling wilderness of jungle scrub"[7] was cleared and leveled, roads were tarred, water pipes laid, and a series of generators set up to provide electric power for lighting. A field railway borrowed from the Indian army and laid down by the sappers and miners was used to bring in the building materials and stores for what was to all intents a city under canvas, capable of housing some 150,000 people (no. 108). At its heart was the central camp, established parallel to the Delhi Ridge (no. 109), with more than a dozen lesser satellite camps—one for each of the Indian provinces and the regional political agencies that dealt with India's 565 princely states—scattered about the plain. At the heart of the central camp was the viceroy's camp, consisting of no less than 1,400 tents and requiring a staff of 1,190 servants, together with 266 rickshaw pullers and 283 policemen, to look after 138 guests. Lesser camps within the central camp provided accommodation for the commander-in-chief, the lieutenant-governors of the presidencies, the governors of the provinces, and the chief commissioners. The smallest of these subcamps was that of the durbar's royal guests, the duke and duchess of Connaught, who had to be content with a mere eight tents.

The view of this sea of tents, as seen from Flagstaff Hill on Delhi Ridge, reminded one correspondent of the central avenue of Versailles. It was divided by a fifty-foot-wide avenue that cut through the camp for almost a mile, bounded on each side by hundred-foot-wide lawns decked with palms, potted ferns, flowerbeds, and by side streets named after British proconsuls or heroes of the Raj. The tents themselves were draped in white and gold, the "royal" colors selected by Curzon as the central motif for the event. Within each tent every item of furniture was "of native manufacture," laid on floors that were first paved with wood and then carpeted. All contained glass doors, and the largest had fireplaces to take the chill out of Delhi's winter evenings.

The most impressive of all the buildings was the vast, horseshoe-shaped durbar amphitheater, built to seat 13,500 people (nos. 110, 111). It was faced by a series of delicate pillars and Saracenic arches and crowned by scores of white and gold Mughal-style cupolas. What appeared to be *pukka,* or masonry domes, were actually constructed of bamboo with a layer of gypsum on the inside and plaster of Paris on the outside. Similarly, the ornate twenty-four-foot pillars that held up the amphitheater were made up of pairs of railway tracks borrowed from the railway authorities. Bolted together and also encased in bamboo and plaster of Paris, they presented an air of strength and durability that was entirely illusory. Curzon was delighted by the effect. "Painted a creamy white," he wrote, "it shone like some fairy palace of marble in the fierce light of the Indian sun."[8]

The proceedings opened on 29 December 1902, with a state entry into Delhi, one complicated by the fact that India's rulers now arrived by train at a railway station rather than on elephant-back through the city's main gate. The solution was to receive the viceroy and his royal guests at the station within the city and then conduct them on elephants through the city streets and then out through a gate. Many weeks before, the largest elephants from the princely states of northern India had set off for Delhi. Some two hundred of these now paraded before Delhi railways station to await the arrival first of Lord and Lady Curzon and then, exactly fifteen minutes later, of the duke and duchess of Connaught. Just before noon the viceroy and vicereine mounted the largest elephant, Lachman, lent by the maharaja of Benares (Varanasi) and said to be the same elephant upon which Lord and Lady Lytton had made their state entry into Delhi in 1877 (no. 104). Seated in a silver howdah (the ceremonial seat atop the elephant) made for that earlier durbar, with a scarlet-clad attendant standing behind holding over them the royal parasol and with a score of other attendants and mace-bearers escorting them on foot, they led off the cavalcade of elephants. They were preceded by a cavalry escort that included the viceroy's bodyguard and a small detachment of the imperial cadet corps—a body devised by Curzon to encourage the princes to develop their military talents. Led by the famous chevalier of Jodhpur, Sir Pertab Singh, it was made up of thirty young princes including the young maharajas of Jodhpur, Kishangarh, Jaora, Ratlam, and Dholpur. All rode black chargers and were dressed in a uniform devised by Lord Curzon: blue turbans carrying the corps's motto "For the King," blue cummerbunds, and white frock coats faced with the Star of India.

Following the viceroy and vicereine came the Connaughts, seated upon the maharaja of Jaipur's largest elephants, and then a long line of richly caparisoned elephants bearing the so-called salute princes: those Hindu maharajas and Muslim nawabs entitled to gun salutes (no. 105). First the nizams (Muslim rulers) of Hyderabad and Berar, then the maharajas (Hindu rulers) of Mysore, Gwalior, Jammu, and Kashmir, and Baroda—all entitled to 21-gun salutes—followed by the 19-gunners and the 17-gunners and so on all the way down to the 9-gunners. To the sound of half a dozen military bands, this magnificent procession made its ponderous way through cheering crowds past Red Fort and Delhi's famous "Friday Mosque," the Jami Masjid (nos. 106, 107) and then out through the Mori gate. Here the riders dismounted to make their way by car to their various camps.

The next few days were taken up with a series of public events and receptions. The viceroy declared open a major exhibition of Indian art designed as a showcase of Indian craftsmanship—and took the opportunity to lecture the Indian princes, telling them in his speech to abandon their predilections for "Tottenham Court Road furniture" and "Brussels carpets" and purchase Indian wares instead. All this was a prelude to the durbar day itself, held on 1 January 1903 at the great amphitheater.

Lord Curzon set the tone of the day by commencing with a parade of mutiny veterans: a march-past by four hundred veterans, mostly Indian, who had fought on the British side during the bloody rebellion of 1857–58 known to the British as the "Indian Mutiny," and to the Indians as the first war of independence. The idea had been his and had been criticized for "reviving memories that ought to be forgotten." However, according to Lord Curzon, their entry into the arena to the strains of "See the Conquering Hero Comes" "brought tears to the eyes of strong men and a choking in every throat." Many of the Indians present, he later wrote, "declared it to be the supreme moment of the Durbar."[9]

In fact, however, the high point of the durbar came when the herald, a giant of a man named Captain Maxwell, advanced to a peal of trumpets to proclaim the coronation of King Edward VII as His Majesty the king-emperor (nos. 110, 111). The royal standard was raised on the hundred-foot-high flagstaff in the center of the arena, the British national anthem was played, an imperial salute of 101 guns was fired and then a feu-de-joi by the troops massed outside the arena—this time without any accompanying stampede of elephants. The viceroy then read a speech from the king, as well as his own. Again, the twin themes of "allegiance to the common queen" and the unification of India under the British were reiterated.

To round things off, the native princes were led from their seats, in strict order of precedence, to pledge their continuing allegiance to their sovereign in the person of his viceroy, Lord Curzon, now seated before the assembly on a raised dais. A state banquet that evening completed what had been for Lord Curzon a most satisfactory day. What the thoroughly eclipsed duke of Connaught made of it is not recorded.

The last major ceremony of the durbar was a grand durbar review of some forty thousand troops, at which Lord Curzon took the salute mounted on a magnificent chestnut horse named

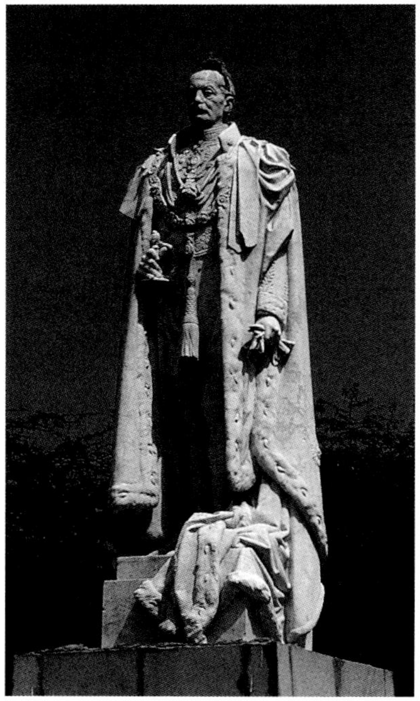

FIGURE 2 *Graveyard of Empire.* A statue of Lord Hardinge, viceroy of India from 1910 to 1916, surrounded by thornbushes at the scene of the three great durbars of 1877, 1903, and 1911, formerly the site of the British camp outside Delhi in 1857. Photograph by Aditya Patankar

Coronation. However, the occasion was marred for the viceroy by the behavior of the crowd of largely British spectators, who cheered long and hard when the 9th Lancers rode past. The senior officers of this smart British cavalry regiment had earlier covered up the murder of an Indian cook by two of its troopers. News of this incident had eventually reached Curzon, who had demanded that a public example be made of the regiment, which had its winter leave canceled. This action had further alienated the majority among the British in India, who regarded Curzon as a man bent on self-aggrandizement. "As I sat alone and unmoved on my horse," Curzon wrote to his deputy after the parade, "conscious of the implication of the cheers, I could not help being struck by the irony of the situation. There rode before me a long line of men, in whose ranks were most certainly two murderers."[10]

On the final night of the durbar week a group of drunken soldiers from a Welsh infantry regiment kicked to death an Indian policeman on duty outside the central camp. "It is a pity," the viceroy observed in a sardonic note to his wife, "we cannot have another Review for them to receive a popular ovation."[11] Nevertheless, he professed himself extremely satisfied at the success of the durbar, declaring that it would have a profound effect both in India and abroad. *The New York Journal* did not share his sentiments and denounced the "cruelty of Lord Curzon's craze for imperialistic display." The "starving Indians" had "asked for bread and had been given a durbar."[12] The Curzon durbar not only marked the zenith of Lord Curzon's career but can also be seen in retrospect as the high noon of the British Raj in India and the British Empire.

The great Delhi durbar of King George v followed in December 1911. Despite the fact that it celebrated the first visit to India by a reigning monarch, it failed to match the Curzon durbar in both grandeur and panache. No attempt was made to match the scale of the pageantry of the earlier occasion. The king broke with tradition by making his entry into Delhi on horseback, and, although a durbar ceremony was once again performed on that same patch of waste ground that had witnessed the two earlier assemblies, it was organized by a viceroy—Lord Hardinge—who had been selected because he was an able diplomat rather than a proconsul (nos. 113, 114, 115).

The one novel feature of this last imperial durbar was the effort made to show the new ruler not just to his princes and chiefs but to the people. On the day following the durbar, King George v and

Queen Mary, both with imperial crowns on their heads, appeared on the walls of Delhi's Red Fort before a huge crowd assembled in the open ground beside the Jumna River. Here, according to a government of India booklet on the 1911 durbar, "a vast troubled sea of humanity swept forward with banners waving and bands playing, a great concourse of Moslems, Sikhs and Hindoos to salute the Padishah [a Persian term for emperor]."[13]

The occasion of the King's speech at the 1911 durbar was used to announce that India's capital was to be moved from Calcutta to Delhi and that a new city to be named New Delhi was to be built. It would be sited out here to the northwest of the old city, in that same wilderness of jungle scrub where all three durbars had been held. But when the surveyors began to plot out the foundations of the city they discovered that the soil was too salty. The site was abandoned and a new location found south of old Delhi. The land reverted once more to barren scrub.

Four decades later, in the wake of India's independence as a free republic, the authorities began to look about for a central repository wherein the now redundant statues of monarchs, viceroys, governors, generals, and other heroes of the British in India still littering their streets might be safely stored. So it came about that the scene of the Raj's greatest glory and self-glorification became the resting place of some of its greatest icons. No more fitting burial ground or epitaph for an empire could possibly have been found (see fig. 2).

NOTES

1. Viscount Valentia, *Voyages and Travels to India, Ceylon in the Years 1802–6* (London: William Miller, 1810), 1: 192.

2. Charles Allen, *A Glimpse of the Burning Plain: Leaves from the Indian Journals of Charlotte Canning* (London: Michael Joseph, 1986), 125.

3. Field-Marshall Lord Roberts of Kandahar, *Forty-One Years in India from Subaltern to Commander-in-Chief* (London: Richard Bentley and Son, 1897) 2: 93.

4. Ibid., 96.

5. Lord Curzon in a letter written shortly after the Queen's death, Curzon Papers 111/160, Oriental and India Office Collection, British Library.

6. Lord Curzon in a speech delivered at Oxford, reproduced in his *Subjects of the Day* (London, 1915).

7. *Delhi Durbar Souvenir 1902–3: A Concise Illustrated History* (Madras: Spencer, 1903).

8. Lord Curzon, *Leaves from a Viceroy's Note-book* (London: Macmillan, 1926).

9. Ibid.

10. Lord Curzon in a letter to Lord Ampthill, Curzon Papers 111/162, Oriental and India Office Collection, British Library.

11. Lord Curzon to Mary Curzon in a letter dated 12 January 1903, Lady Alexandra Metcalfe Papers, quoted in David Gilmour, *Curzon* (London: John Murray, 1994), 245.

12. Leader in the *New York Journal*, January 1903.

13. Government of India, *The Great Delhi Durbar of 1911* (Calcutta: Government of India, 1911).

IMPERIAL IMAGE: THE GRAND DURBARS OF 1903 AND 1911

100 *Their Excellencies Lord and Lady Curzon with First Day's Bag in Camp near Nekonda, Warangal District, Hyderabad*

Lala Deen Dayal

April 1902, albumen print, 25.8 x 20.5
The British Library, Oriental & India Office Collection photo 556/3 (62)

101 *Her Excellency Lady Curzon Crossing a Nullah during Hunting Trip near Nekonda, Warangal District, Hyderabad*

Lala Deen Dayal

April 1902, albumen print, 19.7 x 28.1
The British Library, Oriental & India Office Collection photo 556/3 (74)

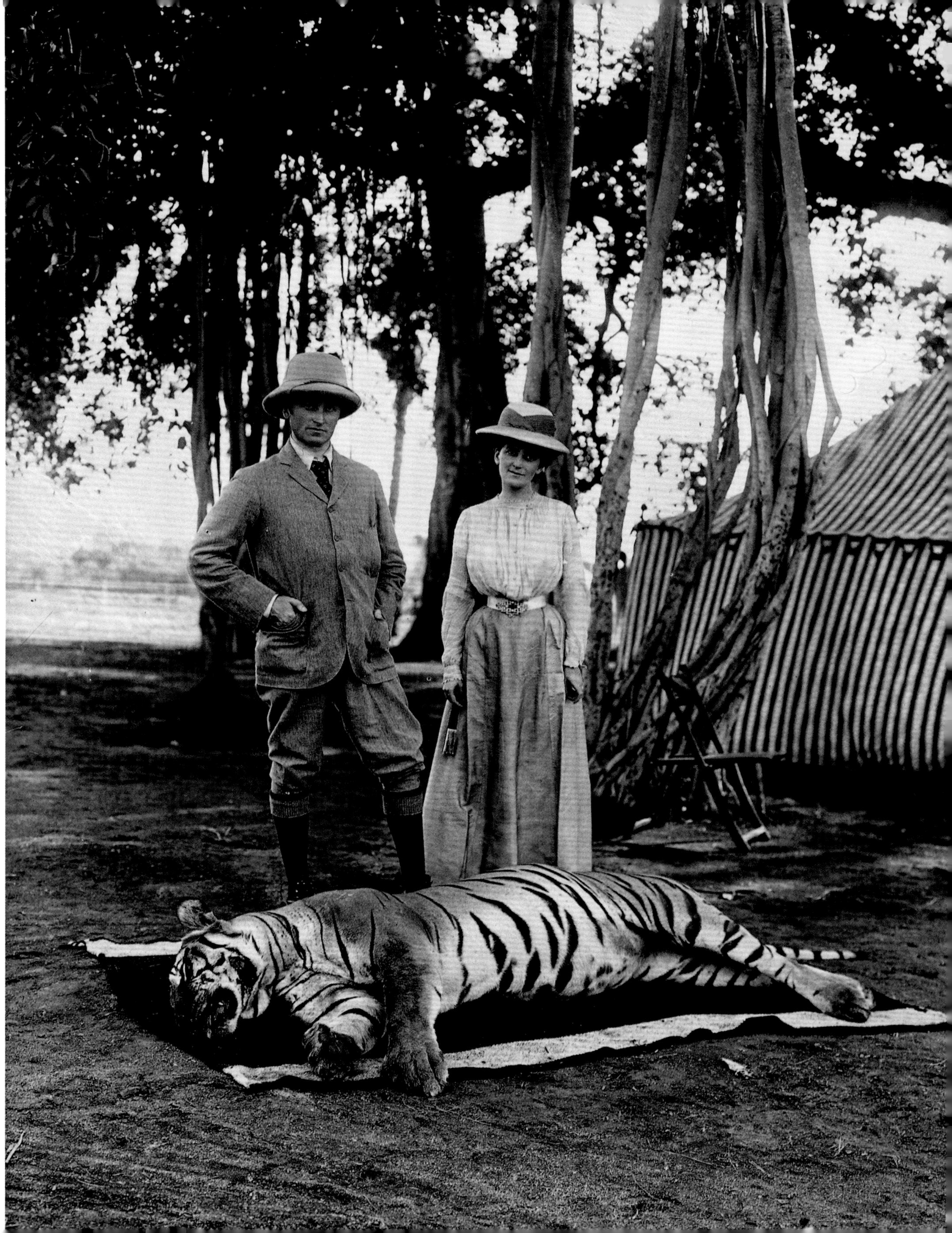

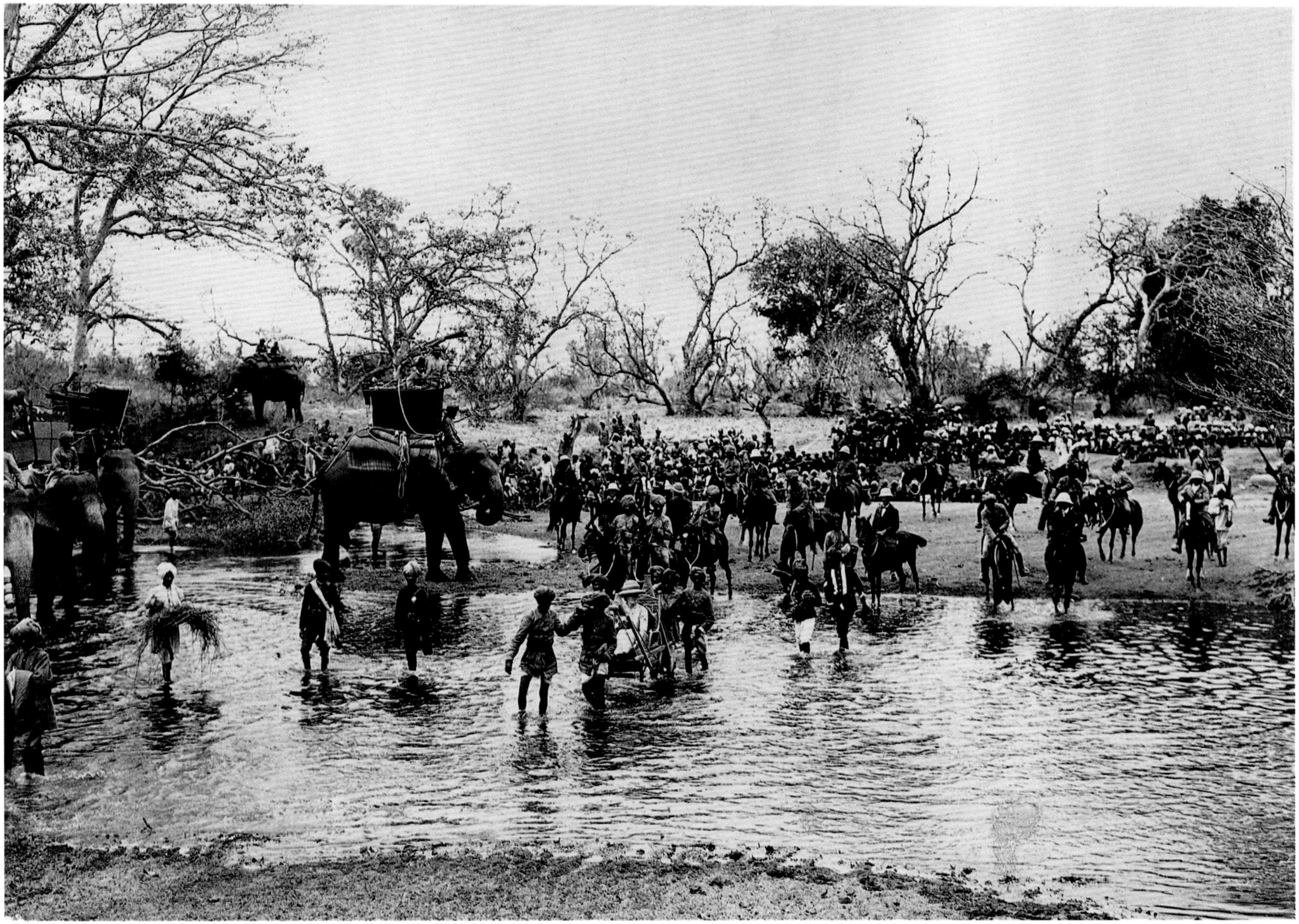

102 *Lord and Lady Curzon and Party Posed with Dead Tiger beneath Shooting Platform near Nekonda, Warangal District, Hyderabad*

Lala Deen Dayal

April 1902, albumen print, 26.5 x 21.7
The British Library, Oriental & India Office Collection photo 556/3 (67)

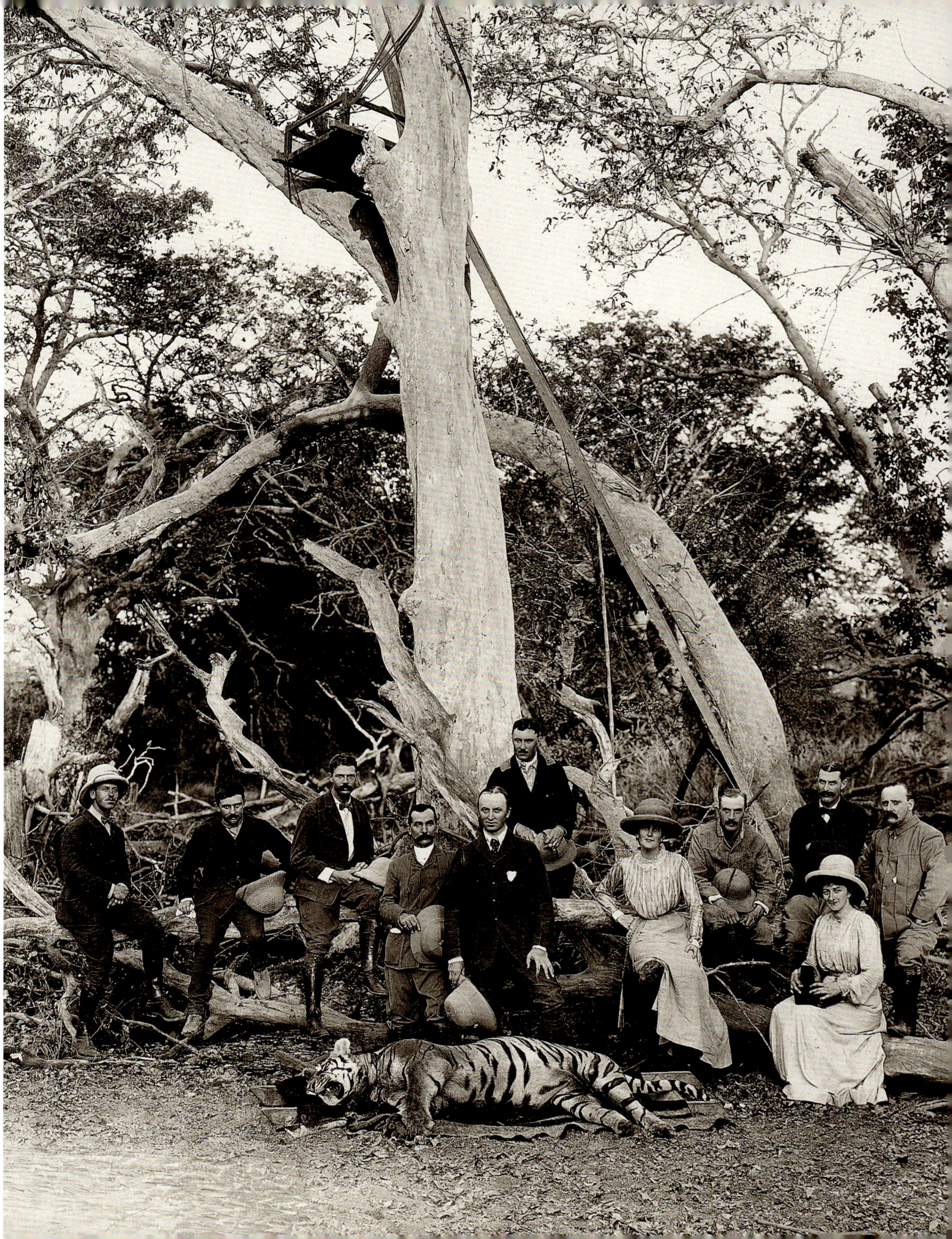

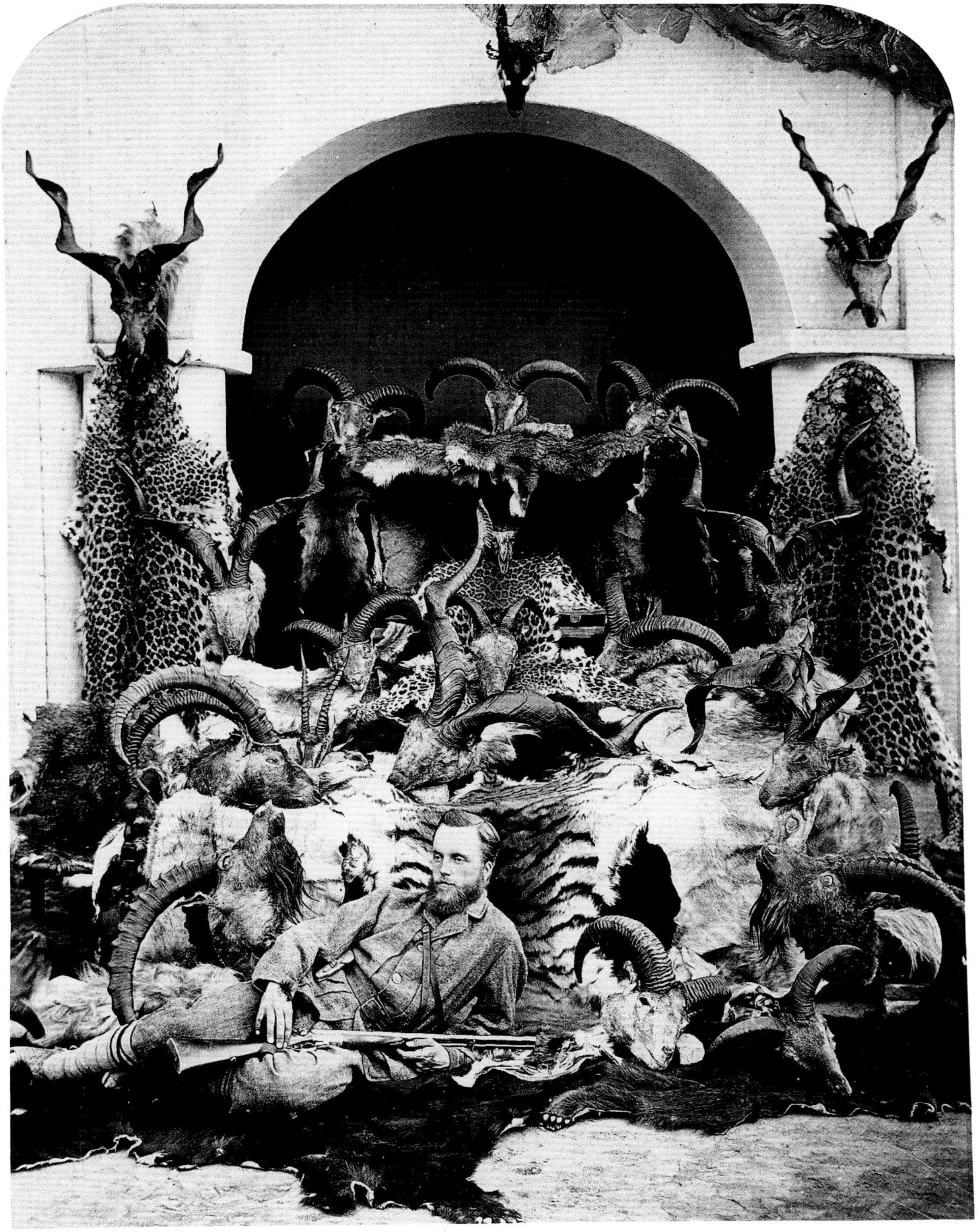

103 *Self and Some Trophies Shot in 1875*

Unknown photographer

1875, albumen print, 27.6 x 22
Smithsonian Institution, Freer Gallery of Art and Arthur M. Sackler Gallery Archives

104 *State Entry into Delhi: Viceroy and Lady Curzon and the Duke and Duchess of Connaught Mounting Their Elephants in Front of Delhi Railway Station*

Wiele & Klein

29 December 1902, albumen print, 22.4 x 28
The British Library, Oriental & India Office Collection MSS EUR F111/270 (5)

105 *State Entry into Delhi: Procession of the Ruling Chiefs*

Thomas A. Rust

29 December 1902, albumen print, 21.4 x 29.7
The British Library, Oriental & India Office Collection MSS EUR F111/270 (12)

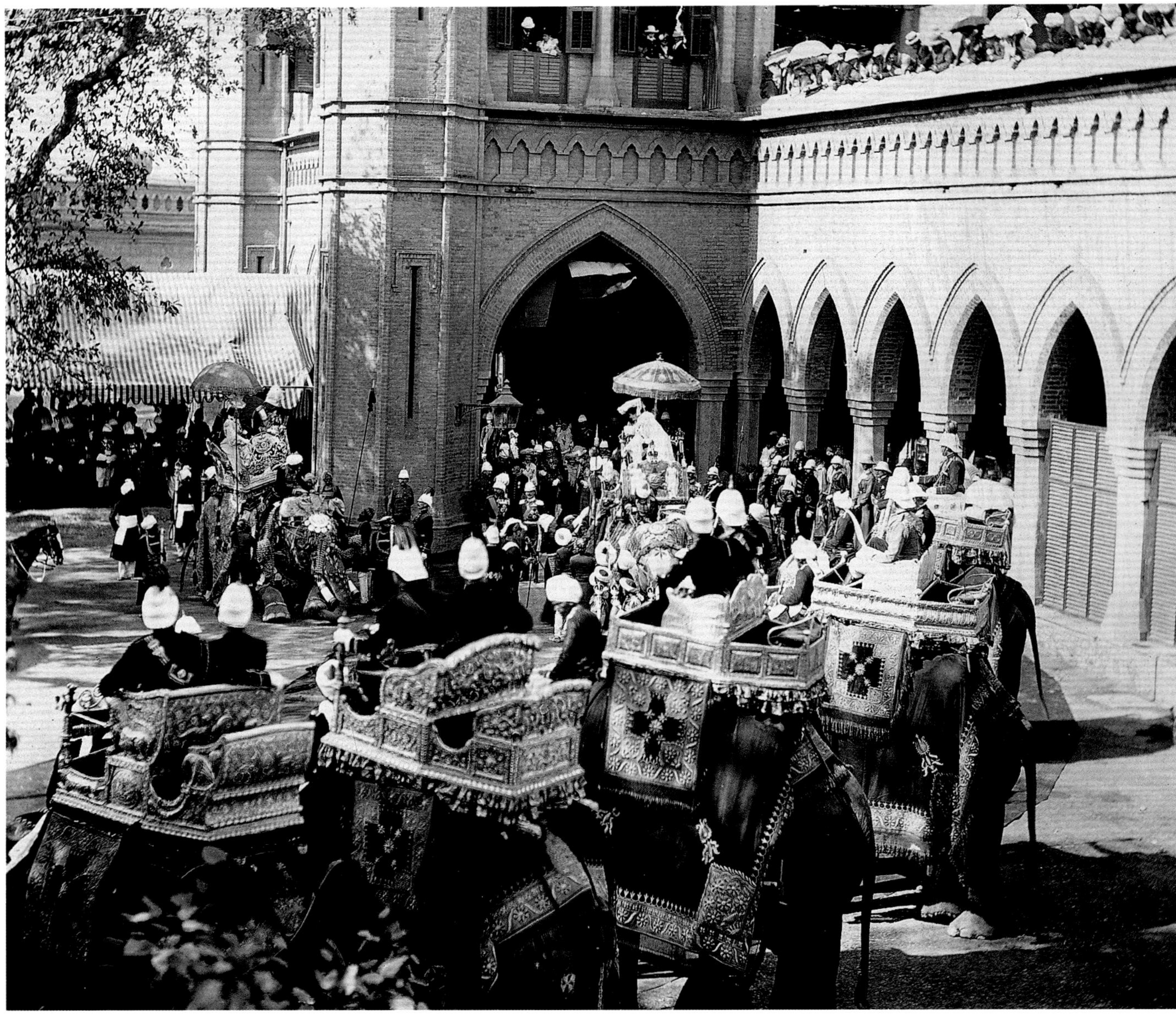

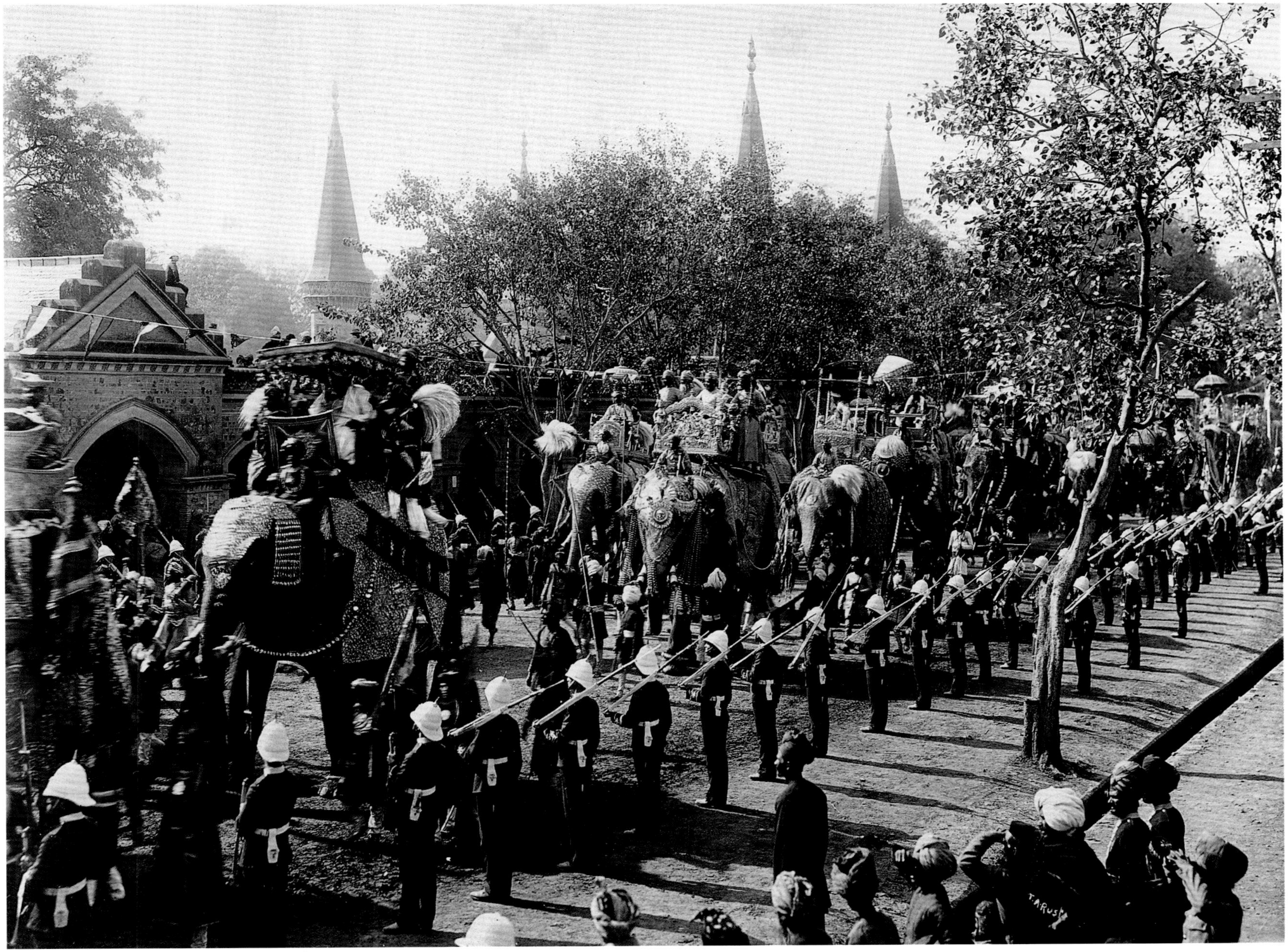
T.A.Rust

106 *State Entry into Delhi, Approaching Jami Masjid: The Procession of Indian Rulers Passing*

S. H. Dagg

29 December 1902, albumen print, 20.5 x 25.1

The British Library, Oriental & India Office Collection MSS EUR F111/270 (19)

107 *State Entry into Delhi, Rounding the Corner of Jami Masjid: Elephant Procession of the Viceroy's Staff*

Wiele & Klein

29 December 1902, albumen print, 20.2 x 28.2

The British Library, Oriental & India Office Collection MSS EUR F111/270(33)

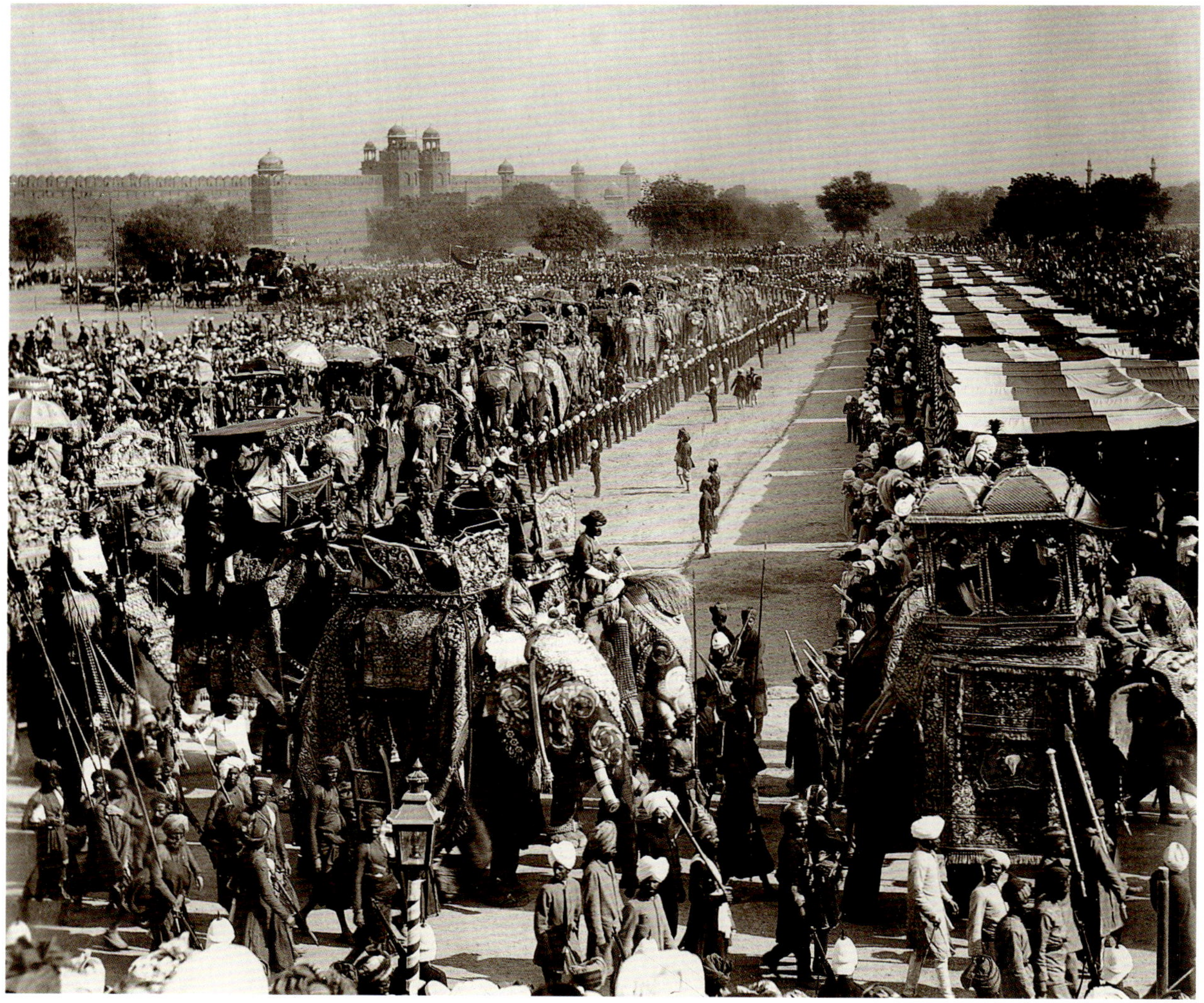

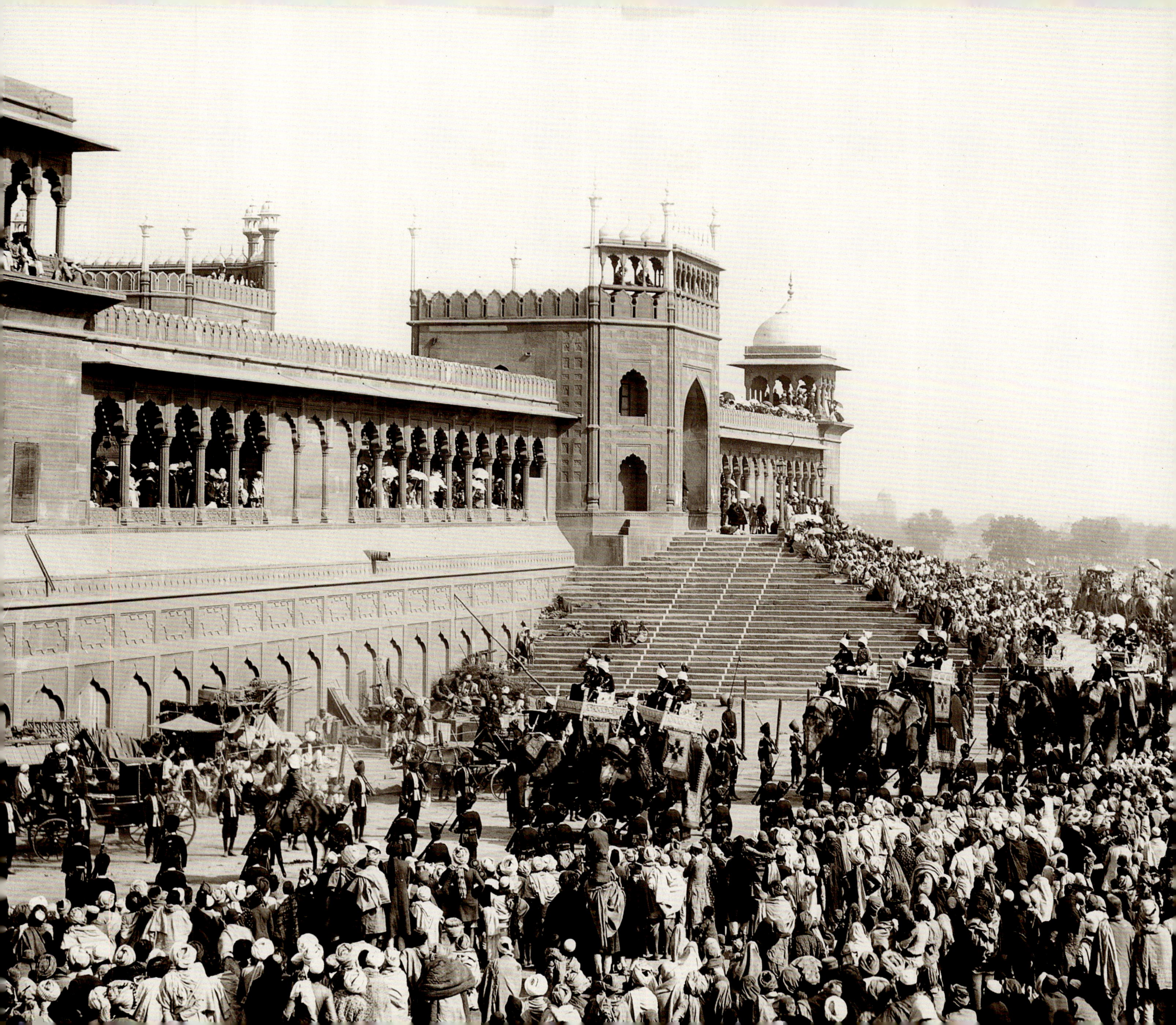

108 *View of the Durbar Camp from the Ridge, Delhi*

Frederick Bremner

30 December 1902, albumen print,
20.4 x 28.4
The British Library, Oriental & India Office Collection MSS EUR F111/270 (51)

109 *The Durbar Camp, Delhi: Main Street of the Camp from the Roof of Circuit House*

Wiele & Klein

30 December 1902, albumen print,
20.4 x 28.2
The British Library, Oriental & India Office Collection MSS EUR F111/270 (55)

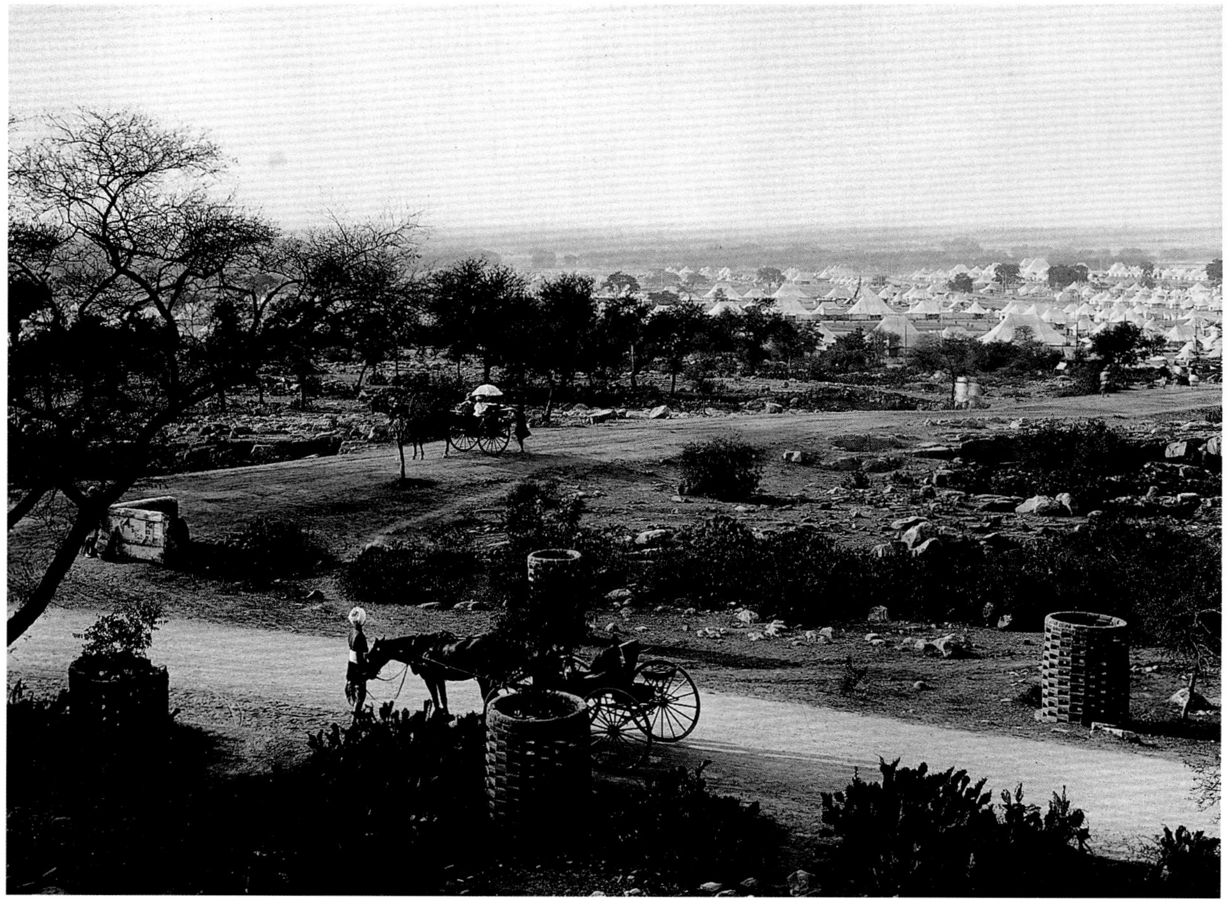

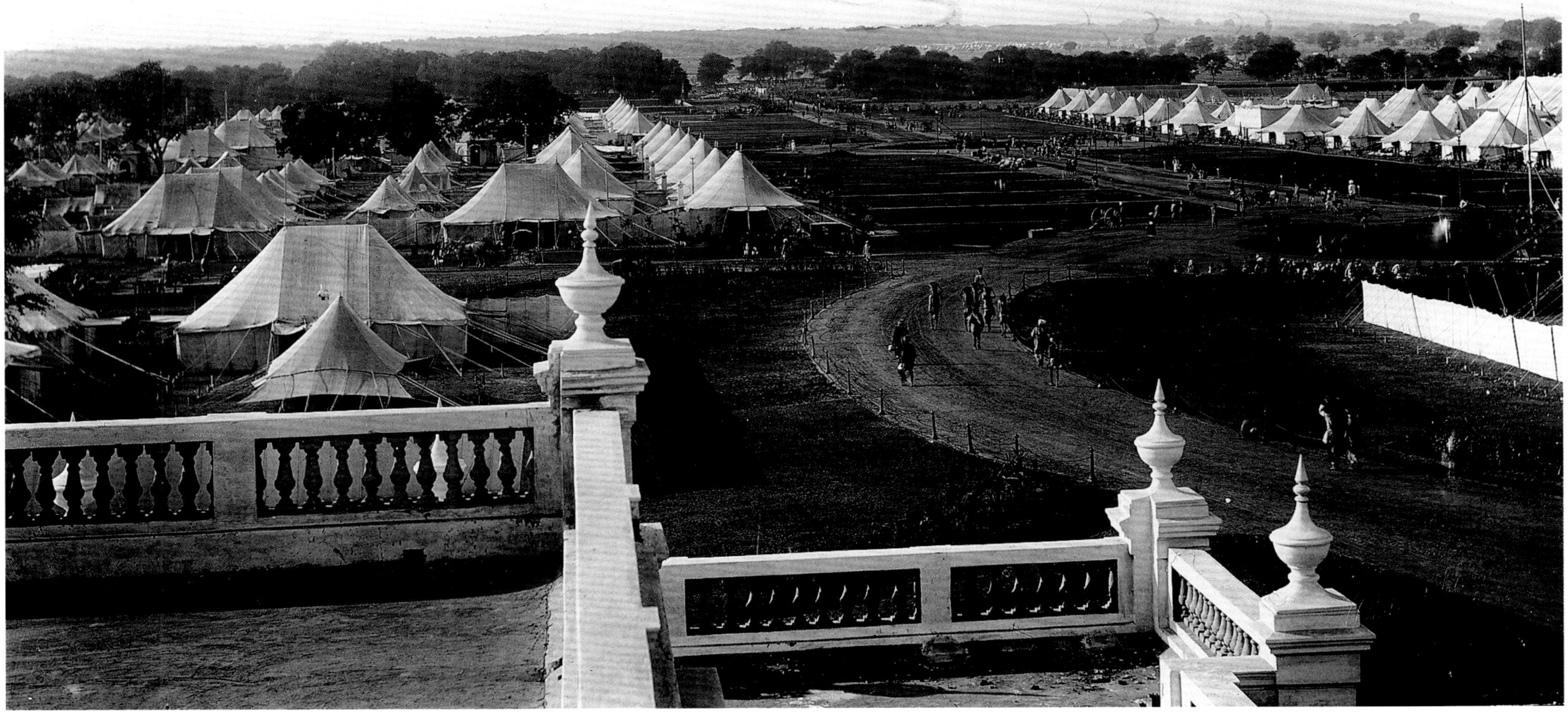

110 *Delhi Durbar: The Chief Herald, Major Maxwell, at the Viceregal Dais*

Herzog & Higgins

1 January 1903, albumen print, 19.3 x 25.5
The British Library, Oriental & India Office Collection MSS EUR F111/270 (100g)

111 *Delhi Durbar: The Chief Herald, Major Maxwell, Reading the Royal Proclamation*

Unknown photographer

1 January 1903, albumen print, 20.2 x 28.7
The British Library, Oriental & India Office Collection MSS EUR F111/270 (97b)

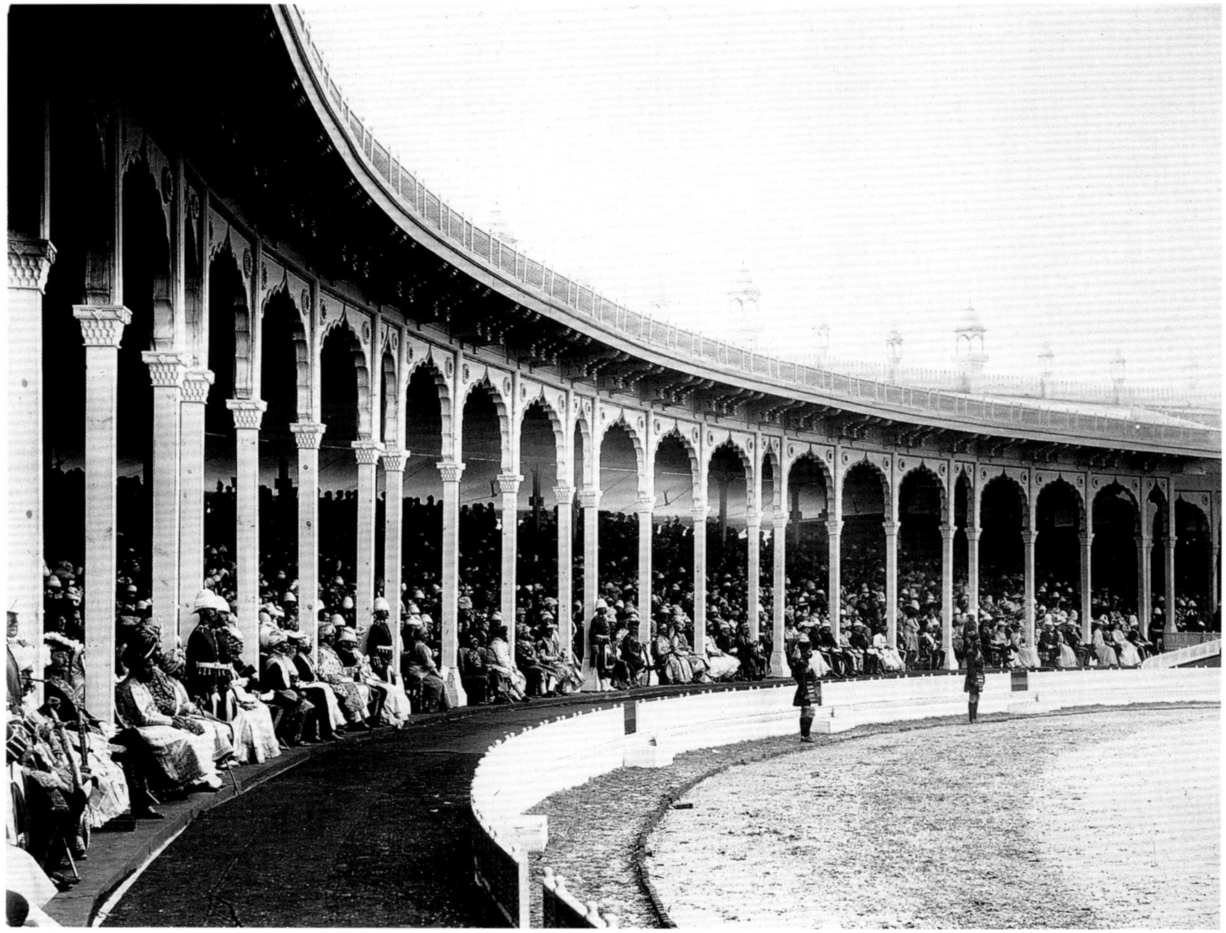

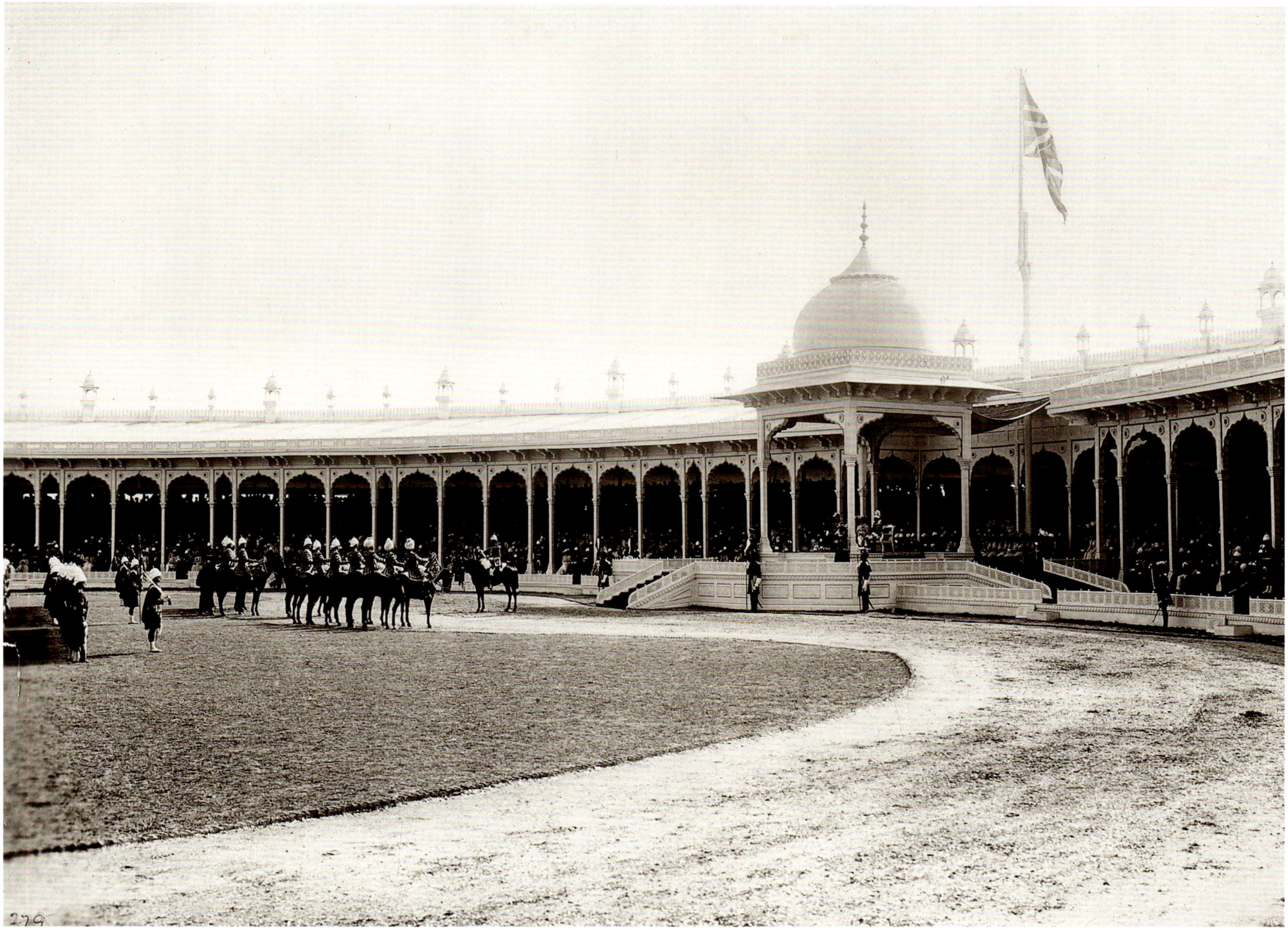
279

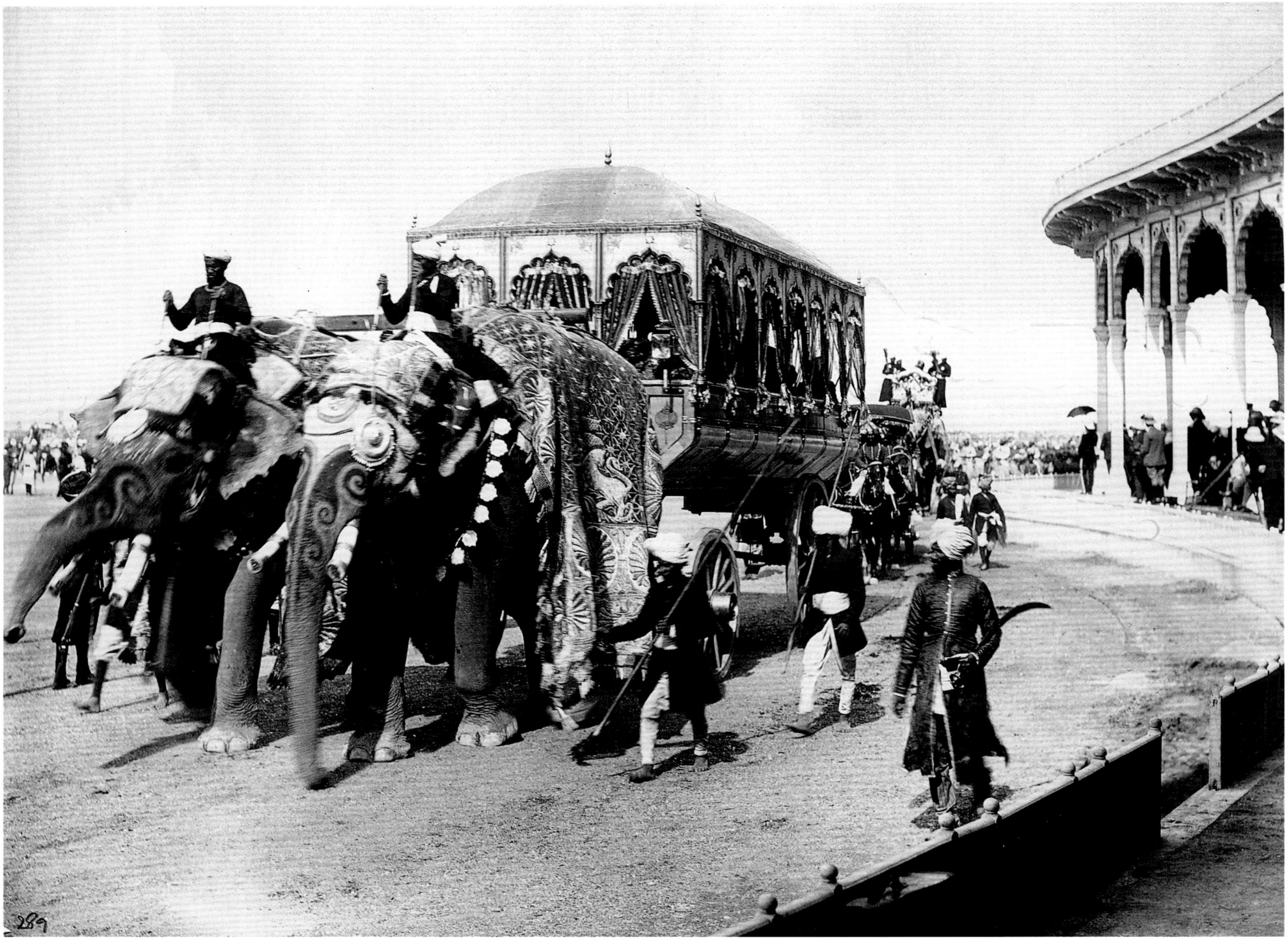

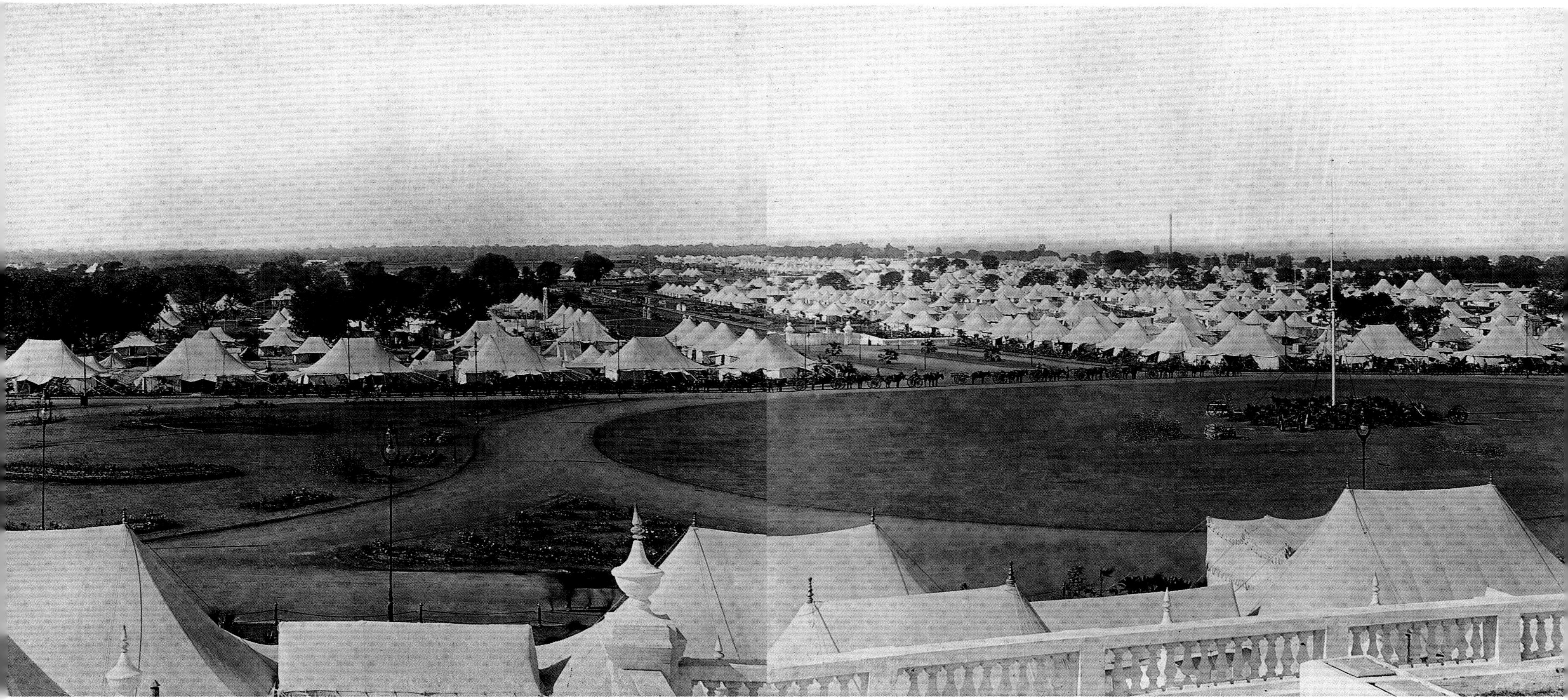

112 *Delhi Durbar, Retainers Review in the Arena: Elephant Carriage from Rewa*

Herzog & Higgins

7 January 1903, albumen print, 20.5 x 28.4

The British Library, Oriental & India Office Collection MSS Eur F111/270 (163b)

113 *View of Camp from the King's Camp*

G. W. Lawrie

2-part panorama, 1911, silver print, 23.5 x 54.5

Howard and Jane Ricketts Collection

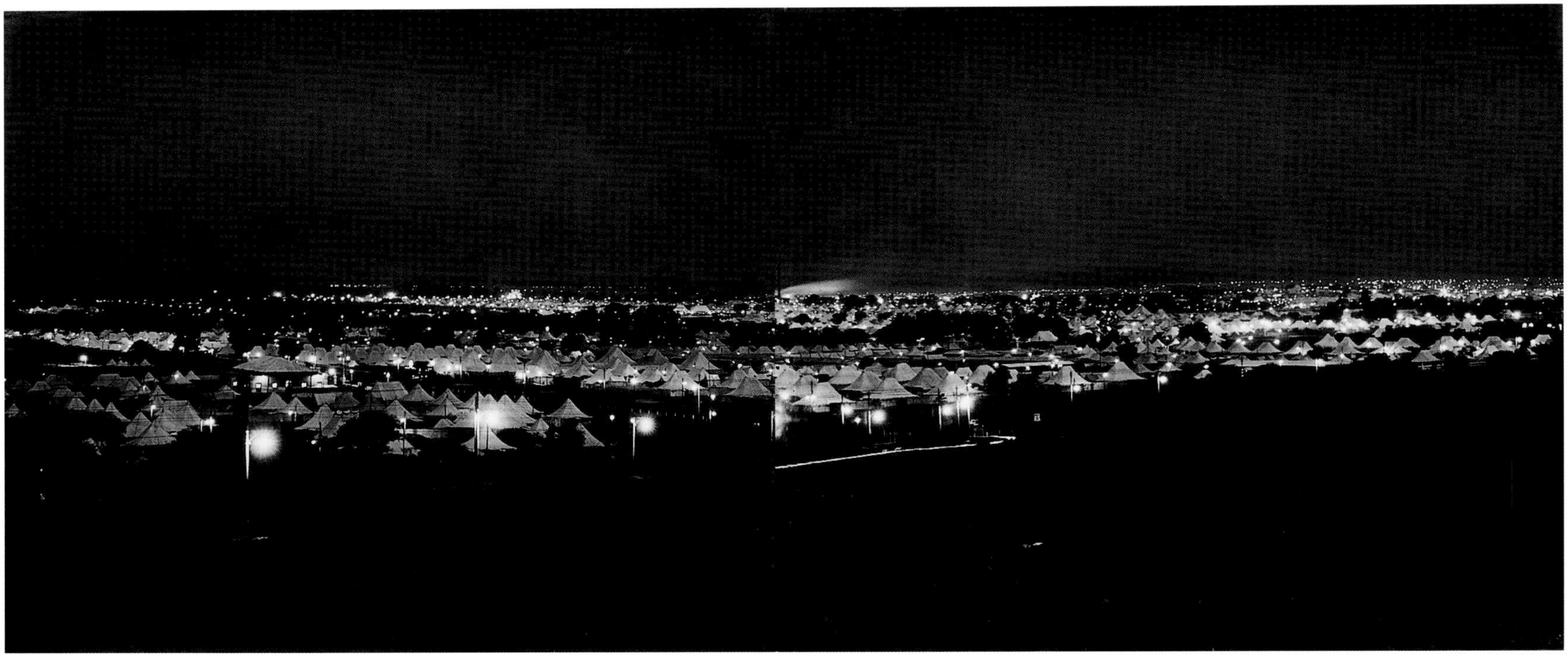

114 *View of Camp from Ridge by Night*

G. W. Lawrie

2-part panorama, 1911, silver print

24.4 x 58.8

Howard and Jane Ricketts Collection

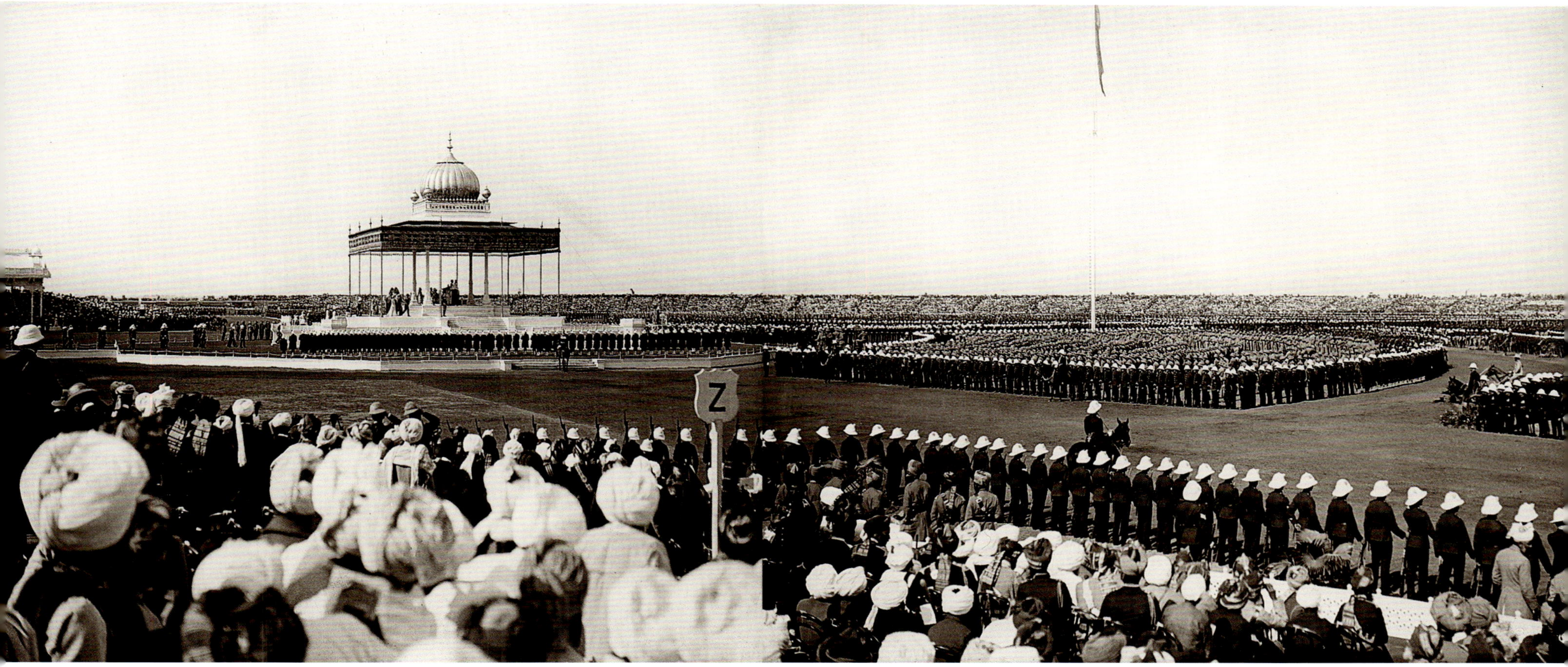

115 *Their Imperial Majesties Enthroned in the Royal Pavilion*

G. W. Lawrie

2-part panorama, 1911, silver print

24.1 x 59.2

Howard and Jane Ricketts Collection

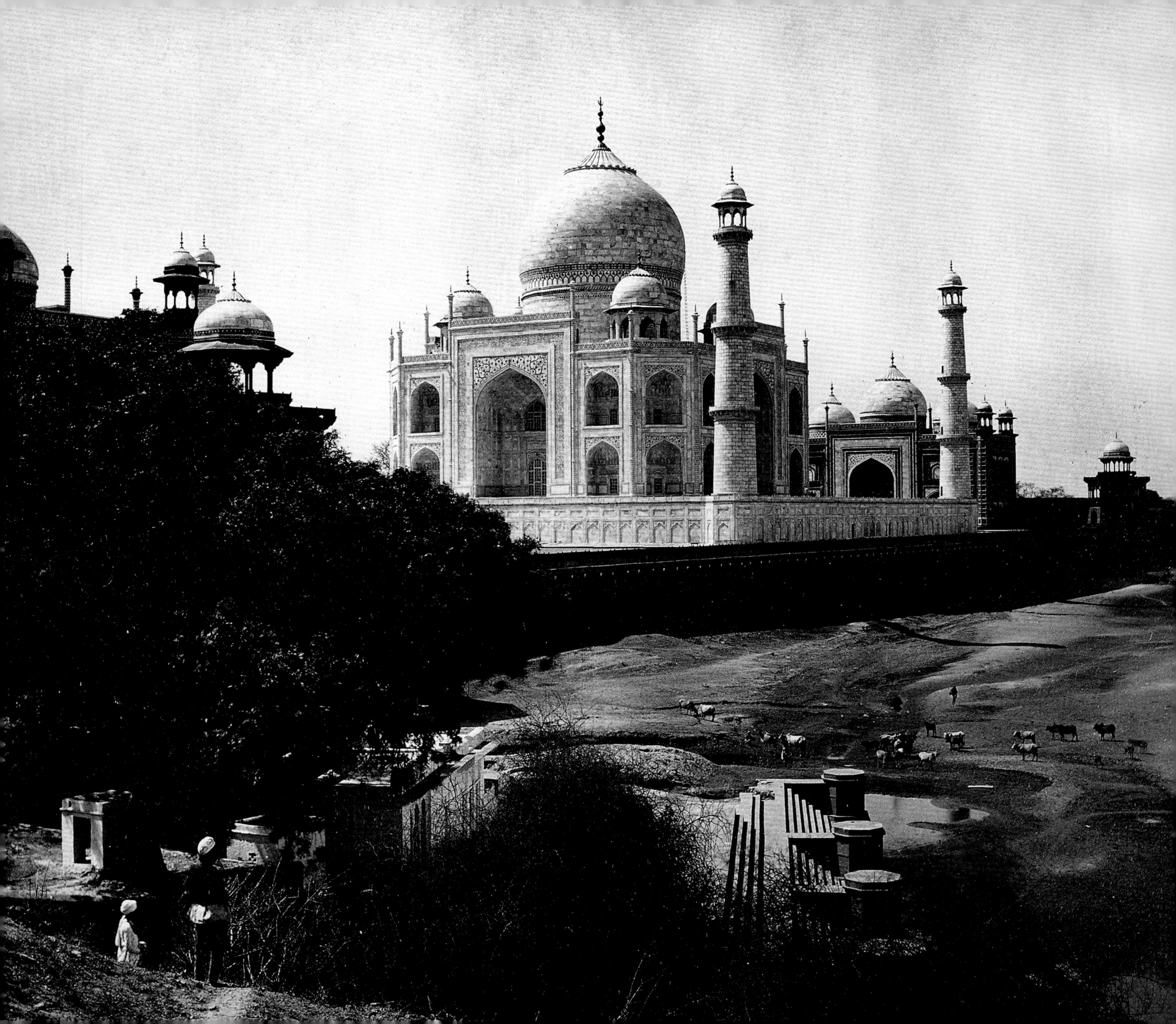

Gary D. Sampson

Lala Deen Dayal: Between Two Worlds

As the world of the princes of India gave way to British rule, one Indian photographer rose to a place of great prominence and esteem. His name was Lala Deen Dayal (1844–1910), and by 1874 he had taken up the medium and soon thereafter established himself as the leading Indian professional on the subcontinent. His work was lauded by British and Indian contemporaries alike and remains exemplary and important today.

A perusal of the names of photographers and places in *A List of Photographic Negatives of Ancient Buildings, Statues and Inscriptions, Belonging to the India Office,* London indicates that by 1900 the British government had committed itself to documenting a staggering number of Indian monuments.[1] This pictorial record, a response to serious discussions regarding the preservation of antiquities dating as far back as the 1860s, represents a high period of zealous activity in the field by both professional and amateur practitioners of proven ability with the camera. The majority of those identified in the list were European, save for one "native"—Deen Dayal—who had distinguished himself in the area of architectural views and portraits of prominent Indian and British contemporaries and events of empire. Among Deen Dayal's (alternately known as Din Dayal) immediate predecessors were Samuel Bourne, who departed India in 1870 but had left a tremendous legacy in a catalogue of images and a model establishment for future entrepreneurs. Bourne's firm continued in the capable hands of Charles Shepherd, Colin Murray, and others, whose collective example stimulated numerous professional practices that continued to expand the repertory of subjects determined to be of certain value to tourists, residents, government officials, and scientists. A big difference existed, however, between Deen Dayal and his Western counterparts. Unlike the latter, he found himself squarely situated between the two worlds of Anglo-India and "princely India." Deen Dayal's hundreds of images from the late 1870s through 1890s underscore his unabashed association with the British ruling and military elite, but concurrently much of his professional success and social station—emphasized by having the title of "raja" bestowed upon him—was owing to the patronage of one of the most powerful remaining rulers of India, the sixth nizam of Hyderabad. Such support opened the door to courtly traditions inaccessible to the photographer's European competitors, thus enabling Deen Dayal to excel in the best of circumstances with privileged patrons from both British and Indian officialdom. The implications of this point are enormous; here we can give only a concise interpretive glimpse of Deen Dayal's production of architectural and landscape views and their significance for his contemporaries.

Originally from Sardhana, near Meerut, Deen Dayal had apparently risen by his wits to enroll in the respected Roorkee College for civil engineering. The school had been established by a Mr. Thomason, lieutenant governor of the North Western Provinces (present-day Indian Punjab and Pakistan), and was open to both Indians and Europeans. For the young Deen Dayal, it would have provided an excellent introduction to British Indian civil administration. After this initial training, he gained a position as "head estimator and draftsman" with the public works department at Indore, and thus his career was launched.[2] Roorkee College played a formative role in its teaching of photography as an important new tool for recording Indian subjects.[3] Though his training was not in photography per se, it is not too surprising that Deen Dayal applied himself to the medium as well. Even at this early stage he found support from the upper classes of British as well as Indian society while stationed at Indore, including Sir Henry Daly, whom Deen Dayal credits in a memoir as having encouraged him in his first efforts with the camera.[4] By the late 1870s his reputation as a photographer had grown among civil and military authorities. One of his earliest photographic campaigns was in Simla, the summer residence of the British government in the lower Himalayas; Simla was of course a prime location for the launching of budding careers, a perfect place to establish connections with men of influence, as we have seen earlier in the case of Samuel Bourne. Ease with official India, Western and native alike, seems to have been one of Deen Dayal's specialties.

Page 258: Detail, no. 119. *The Taj from the River at Agra,* Lala Deen Dayal

One would be hard pressed to say whether the photographer actually took a specifically "Indian" approach to his subjects—landscape or otherwise—as some have tried to prove.[5] A great portion of his pictures were sensitive portraits of Indians, many of whom were affiliated with the nizam or other members of the aristocracy of central India, such as the maharaja of Indore, Tukoji Rao II, who was also instrumental in launching Deen Dayal's career. The question of an "Indian" vision, in which instead of looking to European standards of pictorial taste, the artist would presumably seek to match the aesthetic elements of the traditional court painter in his photographic compositions, is not of primary concern for this essay. We can say, however, that given his unique position, Deen Dayal was exposed to the art of Hindu and Mughal family dynasties. His portraits suggest that he gave a measure of dignity and grace to his sitters as befitting their social station, as one might well expect from an artist whose livelihood depended on pleasing his patronage. The chief ruler of Hyderabad carried the special title of "nizam," following a line of Mughal princes dating back to the previous century. He was apparently eighteen years old (and extremely wealthy) when Deen Dayal was invited to his court in 1884. The photographer was thus provided a place of honor equivalent to the court painters of Islamic India—and he was accordingly provided a "nobleman's house."[6]

The British were ever keen on keeping the maharajas and princes of India reasonably happy, as long as their internal activities were not perceived as compromising the former's strategic hold on the subcontinent. The balance of power was of course in favor of the new Raj, but it could ill afford to upset the symbolic and political stability in areas such as central India, where treaties acknowledged the authority of the Indian rulers.[7] The cultural and emblematic alliance between this double-edged patronage of Deen Dayal is witnessed in the grand buildings of Hyderabad.[8] The city and its environs became a separate kingdom by proclamation of the Mughal governor of the Deccan in 1724. The governor's successors were the nizams, and like his forebears, the sixth nizam enjoyed fantastic wealth and privilege. He was Deen Dayal's family benefactor until his death in 1911. It is indicative of Hyderabad's importance that so many pictures of the city and its monuments appear in numerous extant albums of the period, many of which in fact are exclusively dedicated to Hyderabad and areas in its immediate vicinity. Deen Dayal's commitment to supplying views to the upper echelon of Indian society and the Raj is

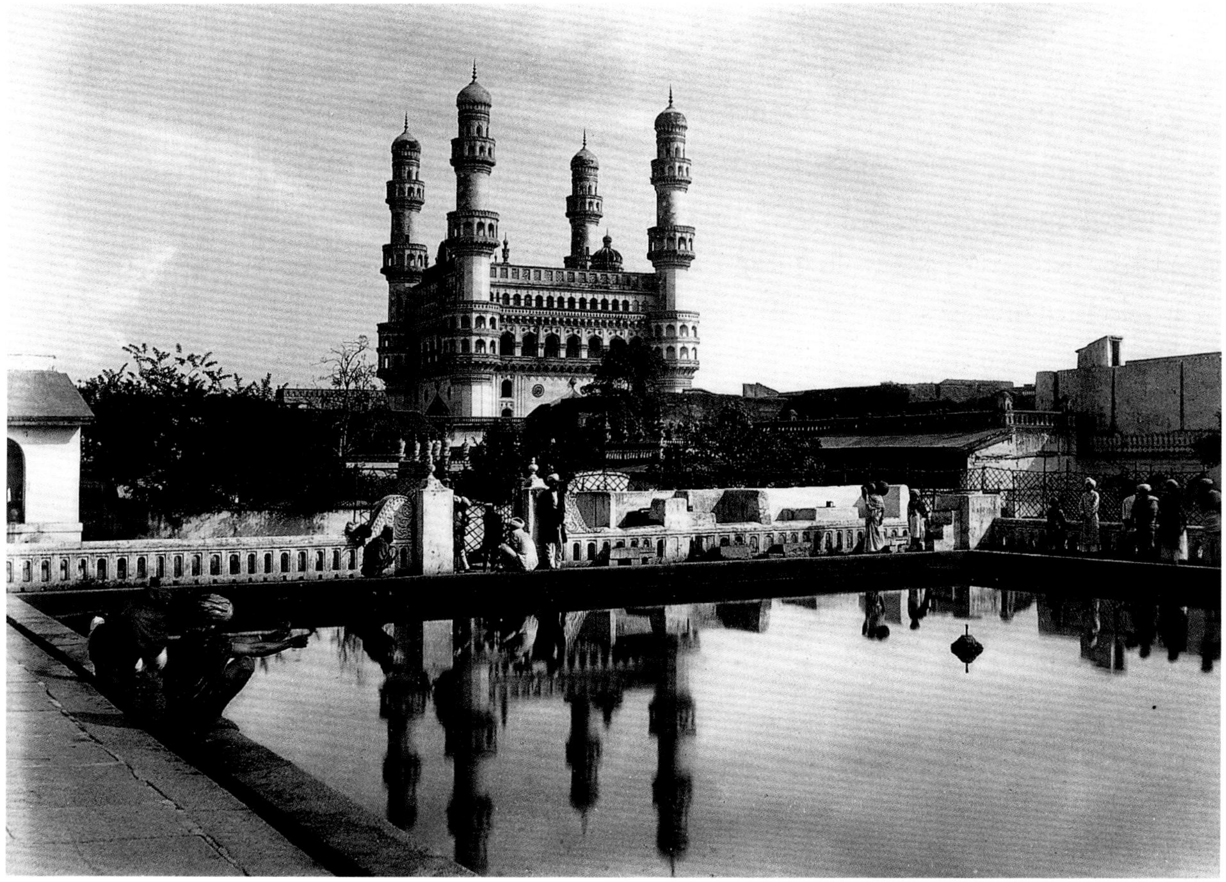

FIGURE 1 Lala Deen Dayal, *Char Minar, Hyderabad,* ca. 1884–88, albumen print, 19.4 x 26.8, Deen Dayal cat. no. 3685, private collection

tangibly evinced in the buildings inhabiting his pictures as the central objects of attention.

The European influence on the built environment of the subcontinent was profound. Since the appearance of British civil authority in the eighteenth century, the preferred style for public edifices large and small was neoclassical.[9] True, the Gothic Revival was also influential in nineteenth-century urban construction, reflecting new directions in taste back in Britain; and there emerged as well a curious hybrid of "Saracenic" (a term generally relating to medieval Islamic architecture) and Hindu features.[10] Nonetheless, classicizing tendencies in the design of government and other civic buildings continued throughout the century on the subcontinent. The later Mughal and Hindu rulers understood that the language of imperial power could be equally conveyed through the Greco-Roman tradition; the Indian aristocracy of Hyderabad, for instance, appropriated a classical architectural vocabulary for the Chowmahela Palace (really a group of four palaces), duly recorded by Deen Dayal in a two-part panorama (no. 117), and various related views. An overwhelming physical and symbolic expression of the tremendous extravagance of the court can be seen especially in the photographer's interior view of a grand salon within the palace walls (no. 118). A more recent demonstration of conspicuous expense, obviously calculated to impress the beholder, was the Faluknama Palace, or "Mirror of the Sky." The Faluknama was designed by English architects after the refined Italian villas of the Renaissance architect Palladio. Having been constructed on a prominent point in the city by the prime minister of Hyderabad for his wife in the early 1890s, the would-be owners went bankrupt upon its completion. Deen Dayal made a sweeping view of the environs of Hyderabad from the high vantage point of the palace (no. 116). While commonly working in several medium and large formats, as in the above case of the Chowmahela Palace, he had clearly learned to use multiple plates to advantage in order to extend the scope of a photographic representation of place.

Hyderabad had its share of monuments within the Islamic tradition of Mughal India. The great Char Minar (Four Minarets) was among the more significant of these, with an upper superstructure of mosque with four imposing minarets. But the same building also served as a massive gateway to one of the principal streets of the city, which Deen Dayal photographed with the Char Minar in the background and in a complementary frame more directly centered within the field of view (fig. 1). As noted in our chapter concerning Samuel Bourne's photography, the Mughal world held a particular fascination for the British intelligentsia and scientific community. Just as the Mughals had dominated India prior to the arrival of the British, official Britain now viewed itself as having risen to similar splendor as the Raj. Victoria was the benevolent queen and her viceroys were appointed to oversee India and its peoples. The power of the Raj was symbolized by the queen's own image, by the imposition of regalia, honors, and titles, by public displays of wealth and military might, and by the establishment of political hierarchy through symbolic acts of obeisance—all of which was embodied in the form of the "durbar," a spectacular event intended to impress the Indian peoples with Britain's terrifying might. Durbars became frequent occurrences in the late nineteenth and early twentieth century, not only performed by the British before their "subjects," but also by the native princes, including the nizam of Hyderabad, who apparently was having three per week at the height of his rule; Deen Dayal photographed the nizam's durbars, and at the same time made studies of Lord and Lady Curzon at the hunt near Hyderabad (nos. 100–102).[11] The connection of the durbar and the former might of the Mughal emperors was explicit in their performance. Viceroy Lytton invited "over 400 Indian princes and their retinues" to Delhi in 1876 "for a dazzling display of imperial theatre, devised to show them the majesty, permanence and sheer strength of the Raj." As Lawrence James notes, the Delhi Durbar "emphasized the unity of India as well as resurrecting the grandeur of the Mughals. . . .The Maharaja of Indore saw the durbar as a symbol of international cohesion."[12]

Even in such a seemingly benign activity as the preservation of India's legacy in architecture and antiquities, in which photography was to play an important role, not-so-subtle ideological biases were prevalent. Thus, Lord Curzon, viceroy of India between 1899 and 1905, could assert that the Taj Mahal, tomb of Mumtaz, the wife of Shah-Jahan (reigned 1628–58), was "a vision of eternal beauty." The historian Thomas R. Metcalf observes, however, that Curzon castigated the local artisans as unfit to undertake any of its restoration, which he "then supervised with a single-minded devotion to detail."[13] Curzon was an indefatigable zealot for spreading the paternalistic face of empire, which he saw extending to the preservation of India's architectural heritage. A large part of Deen Dayal's operations were devoted to exhaustive coverage of what was then considered the more noteworthy instances of this past. Some of these photographs actually duplicated the work of previous operators, as witnessed for example in various views of the Taj Mahal. Deen Dayal's compelling view of the Taj from the banks of the Jumna River (no. 119) may have been prompted by Bourne's photo from nearly the exact spot. Such reprises suggest that the photographer was motivated by a competitive spirit and a professional investment in India's legacy, but the larger impetus must have been to produce a body of work whose subjects continued to capture the imagination of the Western public. While not discounting the possibility of a personal resonance with India's architectural past, Deen Dayal surely embraced Western cultural perceptions of the more famous buildings, which is to say that he benefited both artistically and economically from the colonialist encroachment and civilizing efforts of the British. Images such as his superb Taj series, his picture of the "Water Palace" at Deeg (no. 121), and similar views demonstrate artistic and technical skills equivalent to those of his immediate predecessors. He also provided exquisite details of select ornamented buildings, as seen for instance in *Interior of Tomb of Shumshuddeen at the Kutub, Delhi* (no. 120).

Much study still remains in order to ascertain Deen Dayal's precise contribution to the official documentation of Indian monuments. The mid-1880s marks the culmination of his first ten years or so in photography, during which he traveled around central India producing the images that appear in many albums and publications related to the archaeological investigation and recognition of important buildings. This cumulative body of evidence suggests that aside from their desirability as mementos for the touring public, Deen Dayal's work of this period was intricately bound to an increasingly determined effort to comprehend the subcontinent in visual terms. An extract from his firm's 1895 catalogue, reprinted in Clark Worswick's useful introduction to Deen Dayal's work, indicates that by this time it covered a variety sites in Bundelkhand, Rajputana, and especially central India.[14] Among the specific photographically illustrated volumes in which his pictures appeared are Henry Hardy Cole's album series entitled "Col. Cole's Places of Interest in India," and the same author's *Preservation of National Monuments in India,* published in 1884–85. Cole, director of the Archaeological Survey of India, had earlier recruited for his projects Samuel Bourne's former partner Charles Shepherd in the early 1870s, as well as James Burke, who was noteworthy for his operations in the North Western Provinces and in Afghanistan.[15] The Archaeological Survey records show that no fewer than 250 pictures were obtained from Dayal's firm. The appearance of his pictures in these important compilations of albums and books testifies to his having become practically indispensable to his British associates out in the field.

Deen Dayal became affiliated with another important government agent, Sir Lepel Henry Griffin, who had previously been undersecretary to the government of Punjab, where he had studied the rajas. Like Lord Curzon at the turn of the century, Griffin adopted a typically imperial policy toward the "natives," specifying in the introduction to his *The Rajahs of the Punjab* (1870), that the "English example has done much, but its work is not yet complete, and, were its influence withdrawn, India would once relapse into anarchy and misery from which the British government has rescued it."[16] Griffin's proclivity for administering the affairs of state was tempered by a genuine interest in the people and monuments of India, but even here one senses a not uncommon desire to know India in order to produce the result of making it conform to a Western concept of civil order. In its capacity to record, photography was a superior means of cataloging places and peoples; Griffin had utilized the medium to illustrate his later tome, *Famous Monuments of Central India,* published in London in 1886, by which time he had become attached to the government of the region. Eighty-six of Deen Dayal's photographs were converted into autotype and reproduced in the book together with descriptive text. (Autotype is a permanent print resulting from a carbon process, thus no longer subject to the deterioration of photographs made with silver's impurities.) The photographer is not credited on the title page, but he is mentioned in the introduction as the photographer and an employee of the British government and secretarial office in Indore, a position surprising to find he maintained in light of the concurrent favor he enjoyed in the nizam's court. A photograph that includes a relaxed Sir Griffin with other "party" members at the Chichai Waterfall near Rewa (dated 1882 by Worswick), establishes the photographer's association with a fellow operative out in the field, leading one to speculate on the extent of Deen Dayal's travels with other officials of empire in his capacity of government employee.

Griffin's *Famous Monuments* included a number of views that Deen Dayal took of the great Buddhist stupa, or "tope," at Sanchi. This enormous mass, one of several ancient sites containing relics of the Buddha's disciples, had been a focus of Western fascination for many years and one of the key objects of study in the early days of the Archaeological Survey of India, which had been headed in the 1860s by Alexander Cunningham (Samuel Bourne had mentioned Cunningham's report on another stupa at Sarnath). Deen Dayal made at least three visits to Sanchi, thus compiling a thorough photographic account of not only the imposing central form of the shrine, but the elaborately carved gates, or *torana,* which marked the cardinal points along the stone railing surrounding the stupa itself. In an unusual distant view of the stupa, executed in the last known of Deen Dayal's campaigns at Sanchi, the hemispherical mound appears centered on the horizon, dramatically backlit against a partially cloudy sky at either sunrise or sunset (no. 123). The scene is so poetically conceived that one can easily fathom the photographer—though not Buddhist but Jain in faith—attempting to interpret the monument for the viewer by evoking the radiance of the enlightened Buddha, who was considered to be spiritually present in the stupa itself.

Still other instances of Deen Dayal's forays into India's remote past resulted in equally engaging, if not quite so evocative, representations of well-known Hindu and Jain temples, such as *The Sas Bahu Temple* (no. 124), located within the compound of the more recently constructed fortress at Gwalior, and *Interior of Dilwara Temple* (no. 125) at Mount Abu. As in the case of Sanchi, both of these were well known in the literature of Indian antiquities by the time of Deen Dayal's visits in the early 1880s. He secured splendid details of the imposing and richly carved interiors of these temples in photographs that rival in composition and exposure the similar efforts of his predecessors in the use of the demanding process of glass-plate photography. These and many other depictions of Indian monuments raise the critical question of the photographer's alliance with those who held certain theories regarding the architectural history of non-Western cultures. Contemporaneous scholars of Indian antiquities such as James Fergusson and Alexander Cunningham tended to be biased in their analysis of architecture and were particularly inclined to see the influence of India's conquering forces throughout history as having a favorable impact on the more staid edifices of its indigenous peoples. Hindu architecture was also thought to have fallen into decline, for example, until the Muslims in the late middle ages began to introduce building forms that served to infuse new life into the built environment of the subcontinent.[17] This is not to suggest that Deen Dayal had adopted a personal stance on such issues, yet as an agent for the Raj and its various colonialist activities—including the documentation and preservation of antiquities—he unavoidably shared a limited perspective of the historic landscape that has since been addressed as being too narrow in scope and inaccurate in the critical analysis of architectural sources and influences.

The vast archive of Deen Dayal's photographs also suggests that he was not beholden to any particular aesthetic persuasion, in contrast, for instance, to Samuel Bourne's obsessive pursuit of the picturesque. Still, he could not fail to have responded to the aesthetic taste of his European and upper-class Indian patrons, who often sought to emulate the British in their social and cultural aspirations. Reviews printed in the Anglo-Indian press of the annual shows of the Bengal Photographic Society in the 1860s provide a useful measure of the skill and sensitivity to tonal gradation, composition, and resolution that were considered the hallmarks of pictorial judgment by amateurs and professionals alike. Though one would have to search similar records in the newspapers of the 1880s and 1890s to fully garner the critical reception of Deen Dayal's landscapes and architectural views, the proliferation and collection of his pictures in albums, official archives, and publications are formidable proof that they were considered exceptional in their capacity to appeal to the tangible facts of place. One can also argue that the "requisites" for fine photography were consistent with many of the artist's views, especially owing to the strong standards that had been set prior to Deen Dayal's entry into the trade. A consistent quality of exposure and a well-composed framing of landscape features, calculated to appeal to eyes accustomed to the best of professional work, ensured that the Indian professional would be competitive with the best of his Western counterparts. One can observe such elements in the previous architectural views, in which the subjects have been placed carefully within the visual field with respect to the alignment of selected features: take for example a view of the palace at Deeg, in which the reflective body of water serves to move our eye swiftly to the resplendent façade of the palace (no. 121), or a street view in Alwar, in which the eye is drawn down a dramatic perspective of the busy town, terminating in a glimpse of the nearby mountains with turbulent sky overhead (no. 122). At Indore in the late 1870s and early 1880s Deen Dayal photographed periodically around the British Residency. The surrounding palm tree grove clearly appealed to the picturesque side of the artist's imagination, as evinced in several fine landscapes (no. 128). *River View at Indore* (no. 129) incorporates the graceful attenuated trunks of the palms as the principal feature of the composition, but the overall effect of the scene succeeds because the artist was so adept at seizing the light at just the right moment, thereby committing to the negative a delicate translation of fronds, dense ground cover, and water through exquisite nuance and detail. During a visit to the Chichai Waterfall near Rewa (no. 130), Deen Dayal produced another series of pictorially refined images, including the group portrait mentioned above featuring his associate Sir Lepel Griffin.

One final category of imagery that emphasizes again the photographer's almost adjutantlike role in recording the imperial presence of the British is his work which directly reflects military power. If the durbar was all ceremony tied to the establishment of political hierarchy in order to reinforce the stability of power, then the representation of actual military maneuvers was its heightened expression of physical enforcement through violent means—the "teeth" behind the Raj. Sizable divisions of sepoys, or Indians serving the army, were a significant component of this organization. Though Indian loyalty to colonialist enterprise had been at times put to the severest of tests (witnessed especially in the Indian Mutiny of 1857), the sepoys continued to be in a distinctive relationship with their British officers. It was in fact Deen Dayal's photographs of the nizam's troops on display and saluting their chief that had gained for him his station at court. But Deen Dayal was already familiar with such exhibitions of military strength. Some years earlier he had carefully recorded the British troops on the move, as for instance in catalogue number 133, in which a great contingent of soldiers is shown marching from a point far in the distance, making its way into Delhi. In a later series of striking views taken outside the Mughal fort at Jhansi, a great mass of humanity and beasts of burden rallied together for military exercises. The site itself, as seen in at least three related images, reveals a barren landscape surrounding the fort. The latter appears imposingly on the horizon, its hulking stone bulwarks a distinguishing feature of the building type. These colossal volumes, looming presences that symbolize the glory of the former Mughal empire, contrast with numerous clusters of men, bullock-drawn artillery, and elephants seen throughout the grounds in *Elephant Battery in Action at Fort Jhansi* (no. 132). A cloud of smoke from cannonade appears in the right middle ground, perhaps evidence of a practice siege in progress. A companion image was taken just moments before or possibly after the shot was fired, judging from the incidence of light and cast shadow plainly visible within the pictures. Another view taken by Deen Dayal, which shows a close-up of the "east scarp" of Daulatabad Fort, makes us especially aware of the heights upon which many of these strategic battlements were built (no. 131). These remarkable images, neither picturesque landscape nor architectural documentation, fall within their own class of reportorial photography related to early war imagery. As such they must be counted among the earliest of images to include genuine action, exposure times having been reduced by this time in the history of the medium. Thus Deen Dayal takes us into the field for a poignant glimpse of the privilege of force claimed by imperial presences in India, both past and present. Pride of force is engendered explicitly in no uncertain terms by his numerous photographs of artillery as central subject, as in *Gold and Silver Guns at Baroda* (no. 134).

The place of Deen Dayal in the scheme of dual powers, one nearly at an end, the other dominant, is embodied in the title bestowed on the photographer by the nizam, Raja Musawir Jung, which translates roughly as "Bold Photographic Warrior." Deen Dayal was not the only Indian professional in operation in the late nineteenth century—this was far from the case as the public record indicates.[18] But because of the superior body of work that he accomplished for both the Raj and the nizam, he was assured a place in the canon of names we will continue to remember as having profoundly shaped the way early modern India would continue to be visualized. Problems do exist in pinpointing the chronology of his photographs, which only further scholarship may clarify. Furthermore, one cannot be certain, after the mid-1890s, and perhaps even earlier, whether many of the images attributed to Deen Dayal were actually produced by him, by an assistant, or by one of the photographer's progeny. By 1896 he had studios in Indore, Secunderabad, and Bombay, and two sons—Raja Gyan Chand and Lala Dharam Chand—who came on as partners; Deen Dayal himself continued to undertake major commissions until his death in 1910. A case has been made that Gyan Chand had the more "native vision,"[19] and perhaps future analysis will assist us in making these distinctions. Yet however one sees it, Lala Deen Dayal was fully in charge in the early years of the 1870s and '80s. During this initial period he produced a pictorial archive unusual for its portrayal of an India that was rapidly passing and a new India that would realize even greater change in the decades to come.

NOTES

1. *A List of the Photographic Negatives of Indian Antiquities in the Collection of the Indian Museum: With Which Is Incorporated a List of Similar Negatives in the Possession of the India Office, Published by Authority of the Government of India, Department of Revenues and Agriculture* (Calcutta: Office of the Superintendent of Government Printing, 1900), 123ff.

2. For an introduction to the life of Deen Dayal, see Clark Worswick, ed. *Princely India: Photographs by Raja Deen Dayal, 1884–1910* (New York: Knopf, 1980). Also see Christopher Pinney, *Camera Indica: The Social Life of Indian Photographs* (Chicago: University of Chicago press, 1997). Worswick and Pinney have each located memoirs by Deen Dayal. See Pinney, *Camera Indica,* 223, n.23, who cites "Short Account of My Photographic Career," "typescript of manuscript dated 18 July 1899, in possession of his descendant, Prabas Chand, Secunderabad"; and Worswick, *Princely India,* 19.

3. See also Ray Desmond, *Photography in India during the Nineteenth Century* (London: India Office Library and Records Report, 1974), 31, who notes that in "1864 the Thomason College at Roorkee conducted classes in photography for Indians who were to be employed in the progress of works projects."

4. Worswick, *Princely India,* 19; Pinney, *Camera Indica,* 83.

5. Judith Mara Gutman, *Through Indian Eyes: 19th and Early 20th Century Photography from India* (New York: Oxford University Press, and International Center of Photography, 1982), 27–28, 95–96. Cf. Pinney, *Camera Indica,* 77.

6. Worswick, *Princely India,* 19.

7. For an excellent introduction to the topic, see Lawrence James, *Raj: The Making and Unmaking of British India* (New York: St. Martin's Press, 1998), especially 301–63. For a more general introduction to British imperialism, see *The Cambridge Illustrated History of the British Empire,* ed. P. J. Marshall (Cambridge: Cambridge University Press, 1996).

8. For Hyderabad and its architecture, see Shehbaz H. Safrani, ed., *Golconda and Hyderabad* (Bombay: Marg Publications, 1992).

9. See Philip Davies, *Splendours of the Raj: British Architecture in India, 1660 to 1947* (London: John Murray, 1985), 23–102, and passim.

10. The notion of "Saracenic" influence in India is discussed at length in Thomas R. Metcalf, *An Imperial Vision: Indian Architecture and Britain's Raj* (Berkeley: University of California Press, 1989), 55–140.

11. Worswick, *Princely India,* 20.

12. James, *Raj,* 316–17.

13. Thomas R. Metcalf, *Ideologies of the Raj,* part 3, vol. 4, *The New Cambridge History of India* (Cambridge: Cambridge University Press, 1994), 153.

14. Worswick, *Princely India,* 150.

15. Henry Hardy Cole, *The Architecture of Ancient Delhi, Especially the Buildings Around the Kutb Minar* (London: published by the Arundel Society for Promoting the Knowledge of Art, 1872) [photographs by Charles Shepherd]; and *Illustrations of Ancient Buildings in Kashmir. Prepared Under the Authority of the Secretary State for India in Council from Photographs, Plans, and Drawings Taken by Order of the Government of India* (London: India Museum, 1869) [photographs by James Burke].

16. Lepel Henry Griffin, *Rajahs of the Punjab* (1870), vii.

17. See especially Metcalf, *Ideologies of the Raj,* 148–159; and his lengthier treatment of the topic in *An Imperial Vision,* 24–54.

18. Gutman, *Through Indian Eyes,* xi–xii, includes a listing of "major Indian photographers of the nineteenth and early twentieth century" with corresponding dates of activity.

19. Ibid., 26, 95–96.

LALA DEEN DAYAL: BETWEEN TWO WORLDS

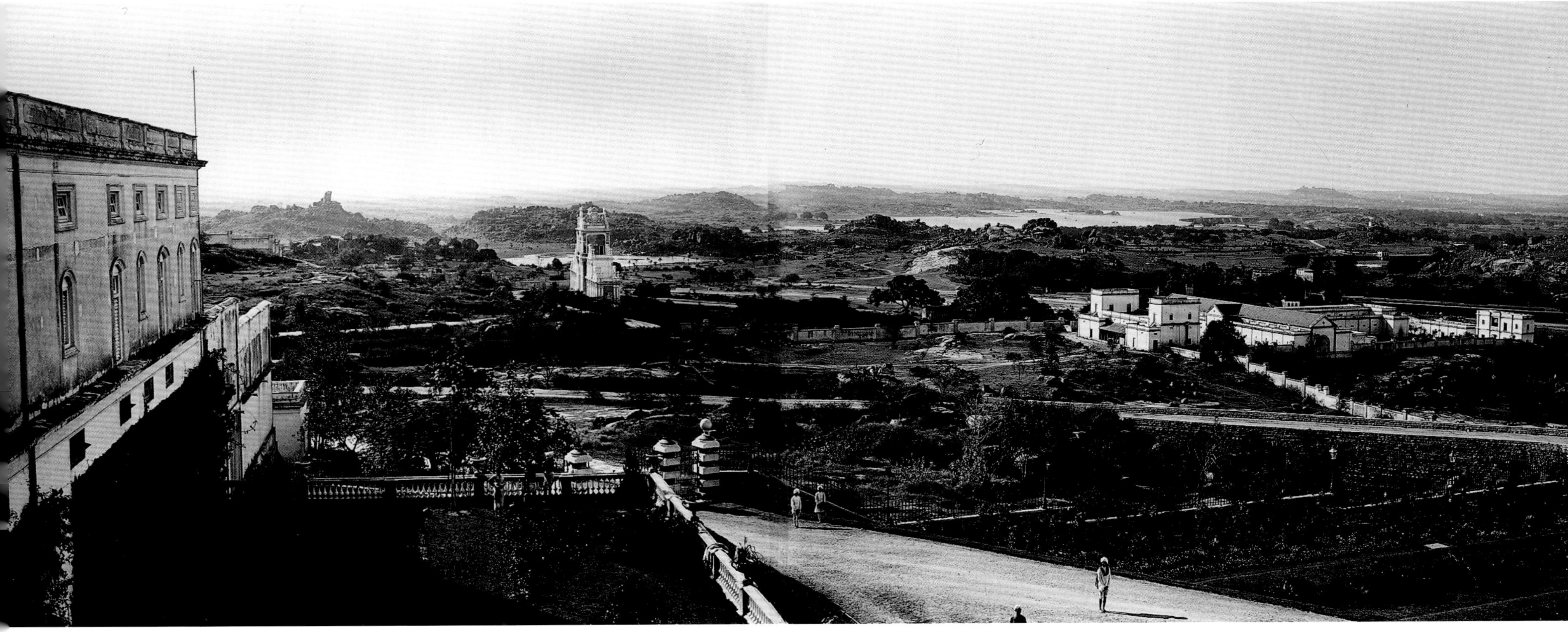

116 *Panoramic View from the Faluknama Palace* [Hyderabad]

Lala Deen Dayal

2-part panorama, ca. 1890–95, albumen print, 19.7 x 51

The British Library, Oriental & India Office Collection photo 761/1 (210)

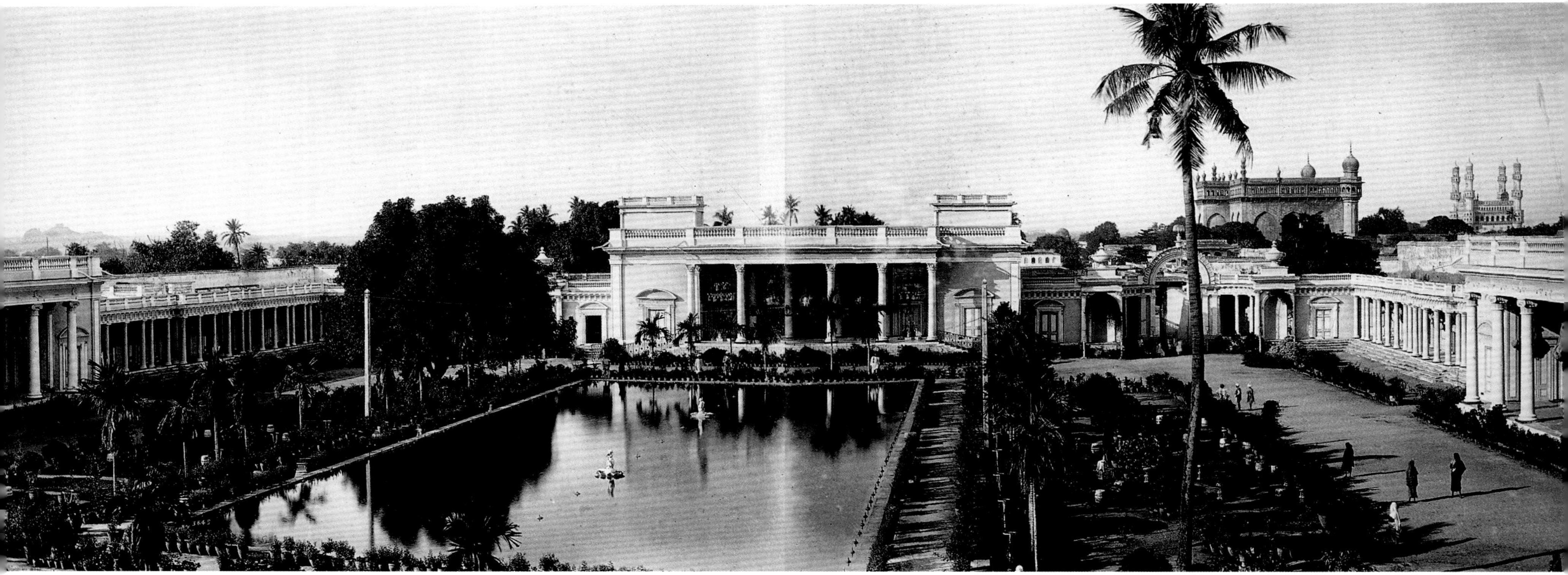

117 *HH the Nizam's Chowmahela Palace, Hyderabad*

Lala Deen Dayal

2-part panorama, ca. 1884–88, albumen print, 18.4 x 52.8. Deen Dayal cat. nos. 3645–46
The British Library, Oriental & India Office Collection photo 430/6 (2)

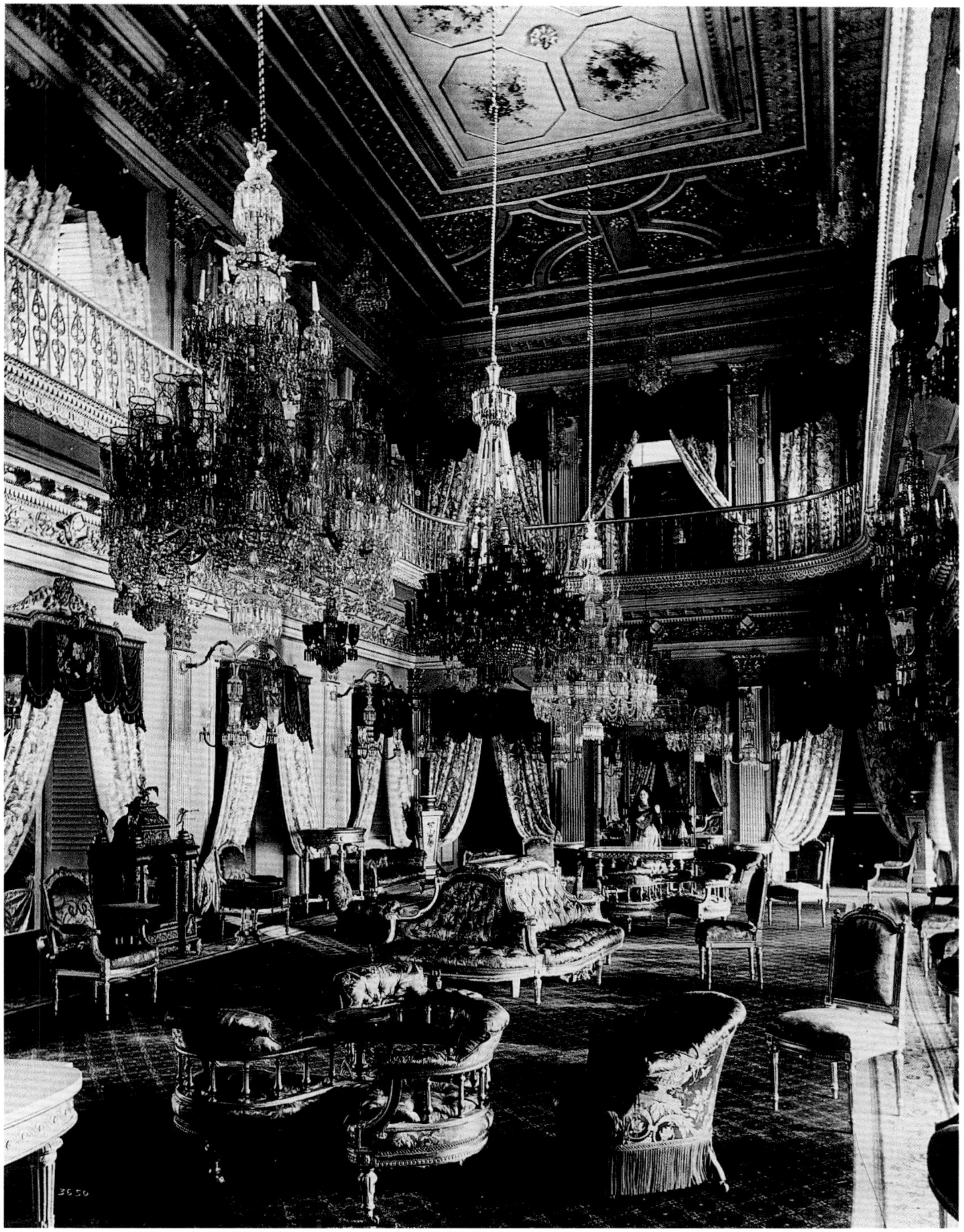

118 *Interior of Nizam's Palace, Hyderabad*

Lala Deen Dayal

albumen print, ca. 1884–88, 26.2 x 20.4

Deen Dayal cat. no. 3650

Howard and Jane Ricketts Collection

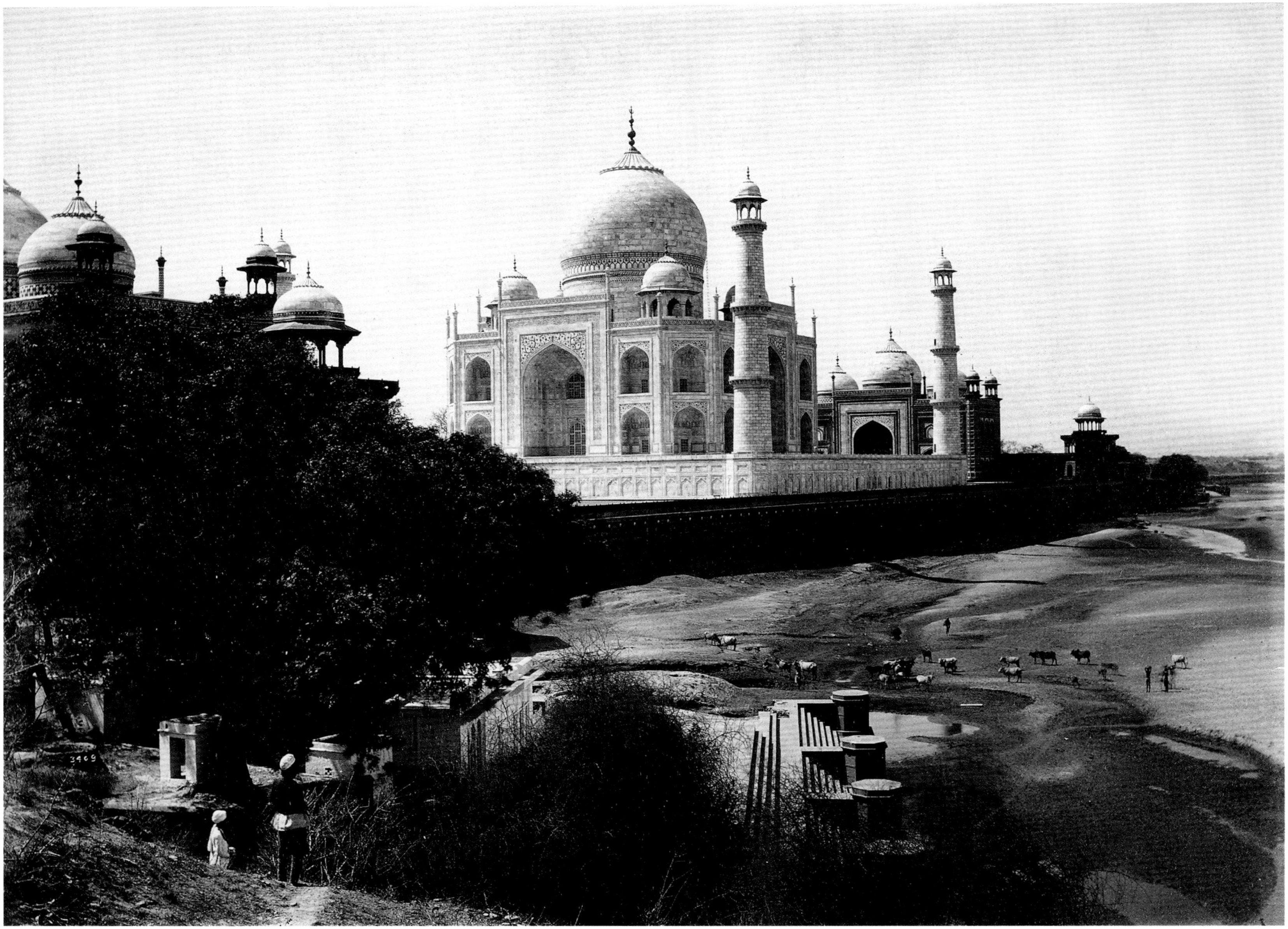

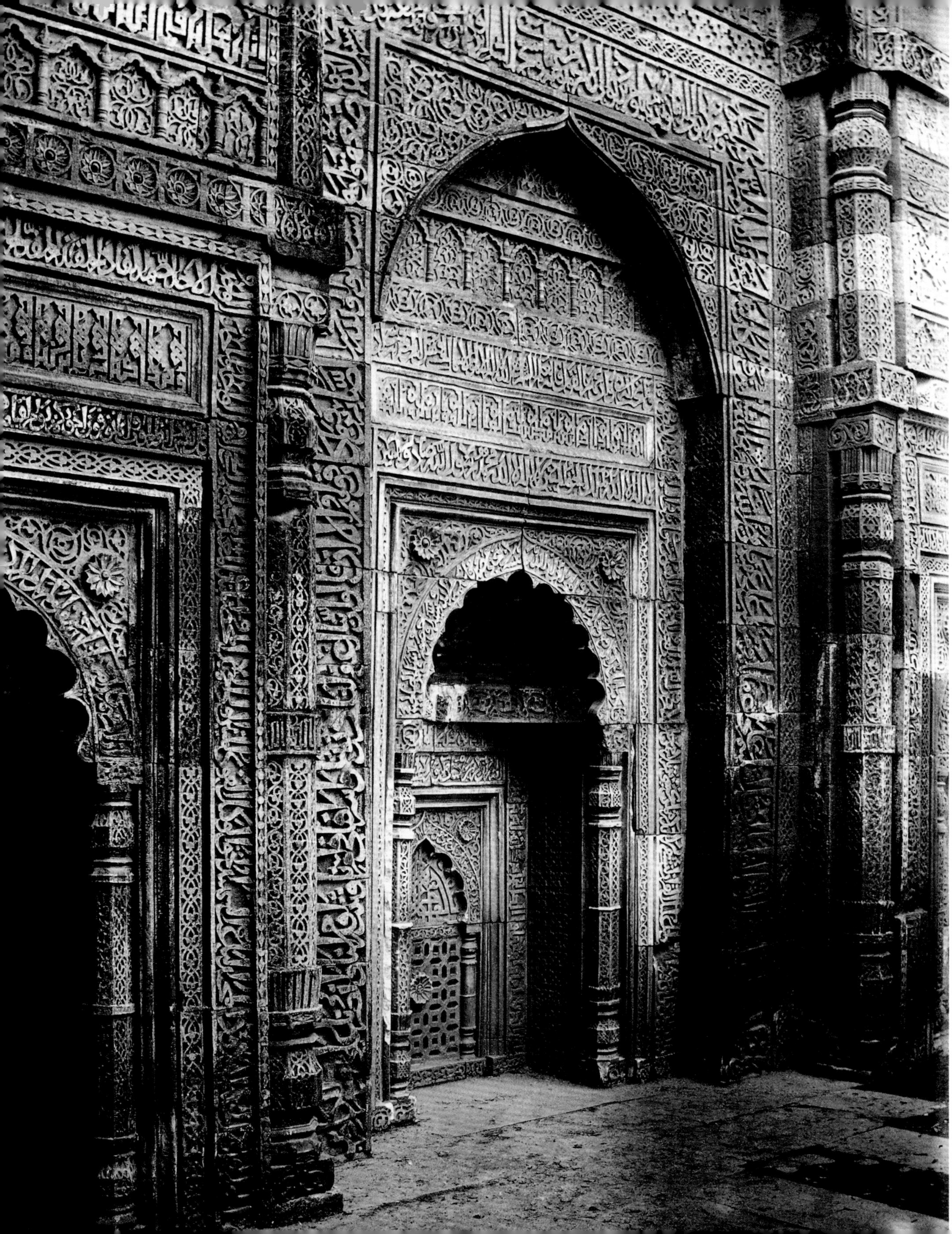

119 *The Taj from the River at Agra*

Lala Deen Dayal

ca. 1884–88, albumen print, 19.4 x 27.4

Deen Dayal cat. no. 3409

Dr. Siddharth Bhansali

120 *Interior of Tomb of Shumshuddeen at the Kutub, Delhi*

Lala Deen Dayal

ca. 1882–86, albumen print, 26.4 x 19.9

Deen Dayal cat. no. 1990

Dr. Siddharth Bhansali

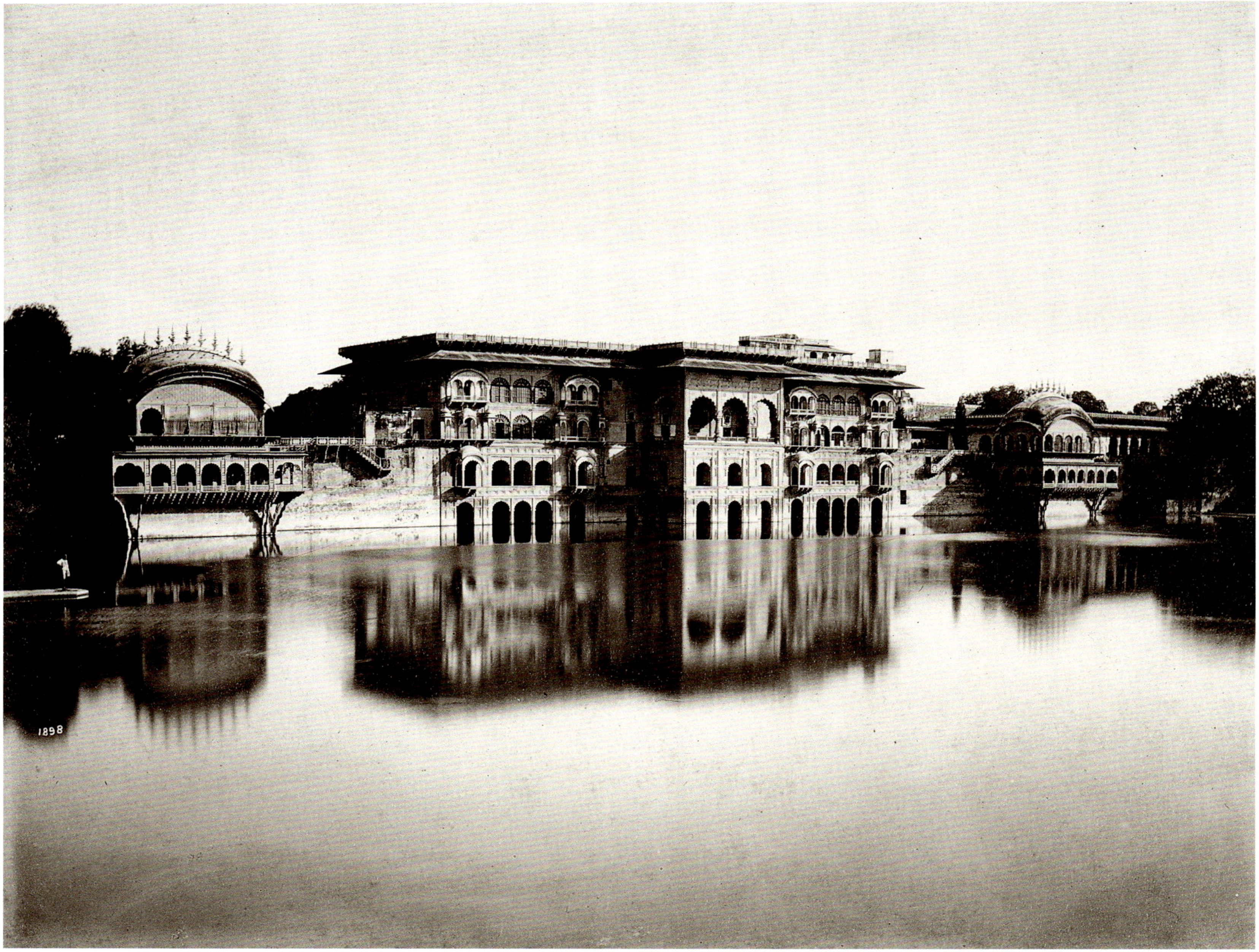
1898

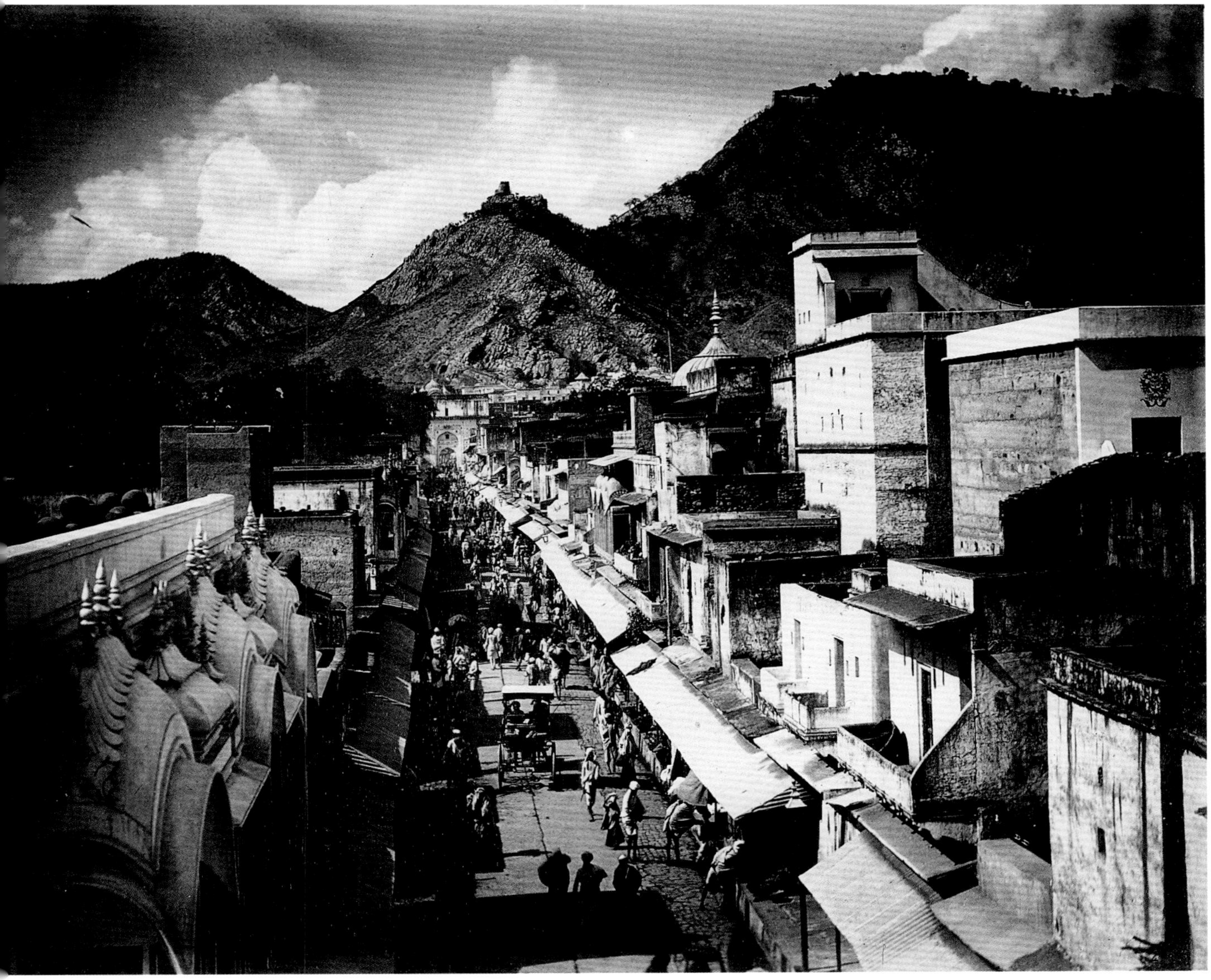

121 *Water Palace at Deeg*

Lala Deen Dayal

ca. 1882–86, albumen print, 20 x 26.8

Deen Dayal cat. no. 1898

Dr. Siddharth Bhansali

122 *Street View of Ulwar*

Lala Deen Dayal

ca. 1882–86, albumen print, 20.6 x 26.7

Deen Dayal cat. no. 1837

Dr. Siddharth Bhansali

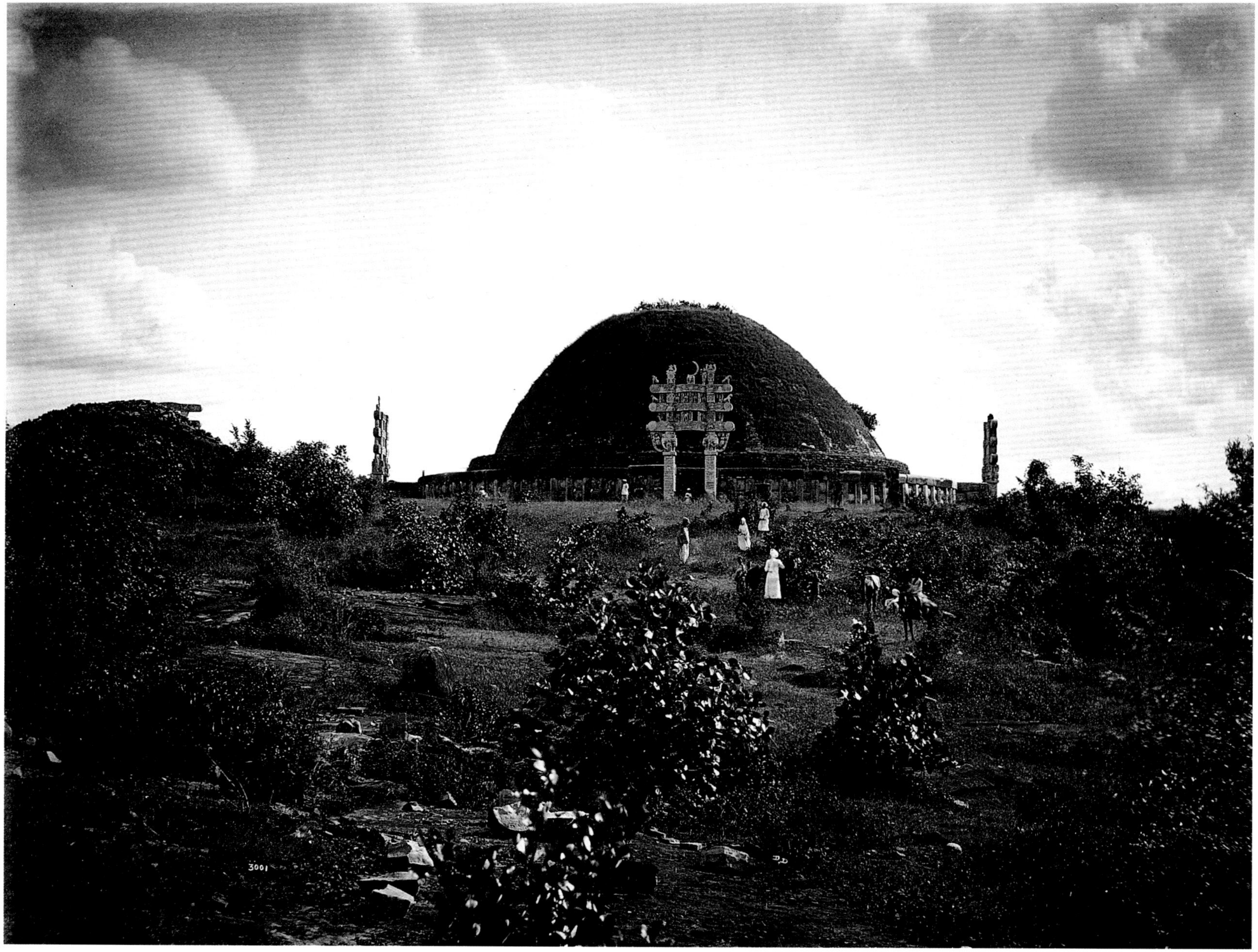
3001

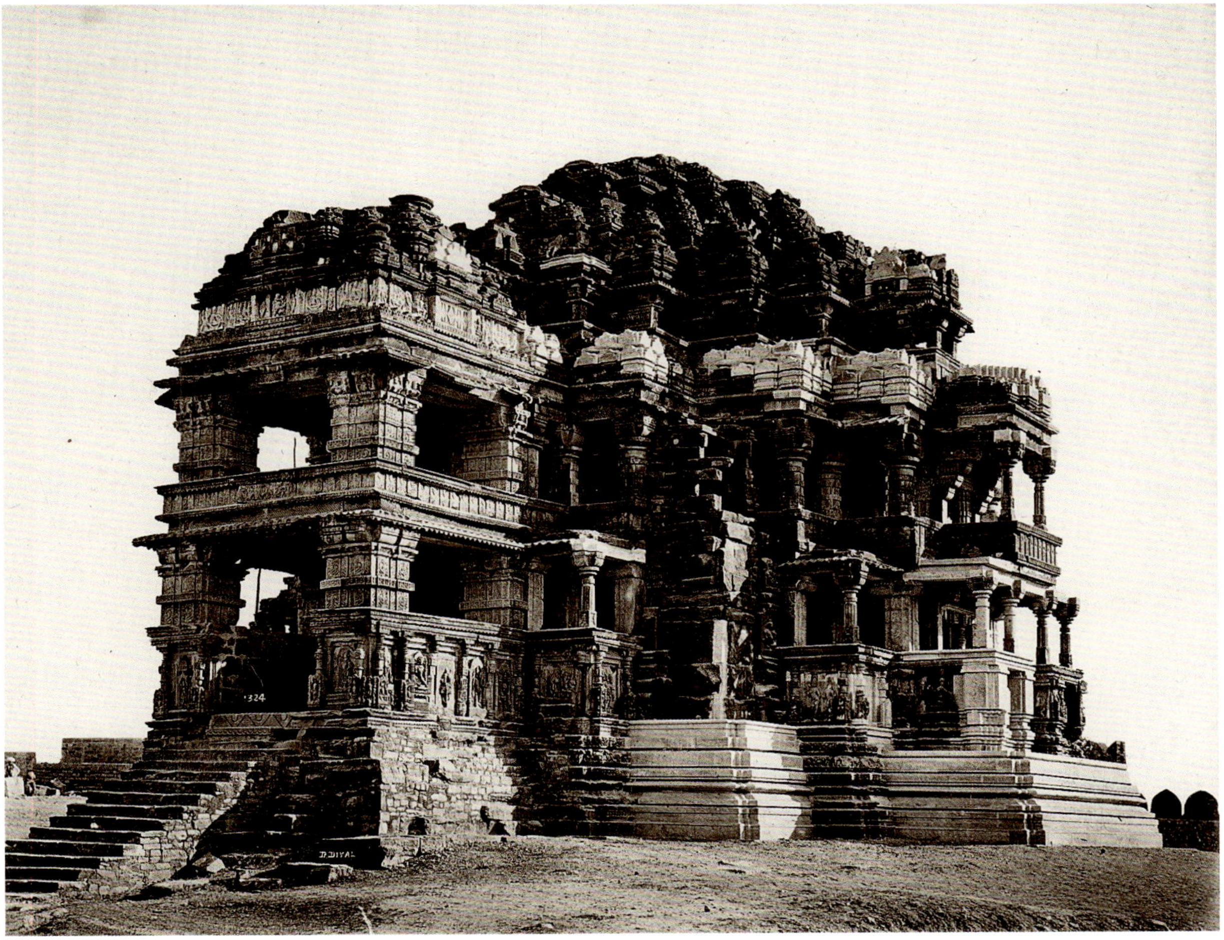

123 *The Great Buddhist Tope at Sanchi*

Lala Deen Dayal

ca. 1882–86, albumen print, 20.3 x 26.7
Deen Dayal cat. no. 3001
Dr. Siddharth Bhansali

124 *The Sas Bahu Temple in Gwalior Fort*

Lala Deen Dayal

ca. 1882–86, albumen print, 20.2 x 26.8
Deen Dayal cat. no. 1324
Dr. Siddharth Bhansali

125 *Interior of Dilwara Temple, Mount Abu*

Lala Deen Dayal

ca. 1882–86, albumen print, 26.3 x 20.4

Deen Dayal cat. no. 1186

Dr. Siddharth Bhansali

126 *Onkarjee Mandhata Temple and Ghat*

Lala Deen Dayal

ca. 1882–86, albumen print, 20.7 x 26.7

Deen Dayal cat. no. 1614

Dr. Siddharth Bhansali

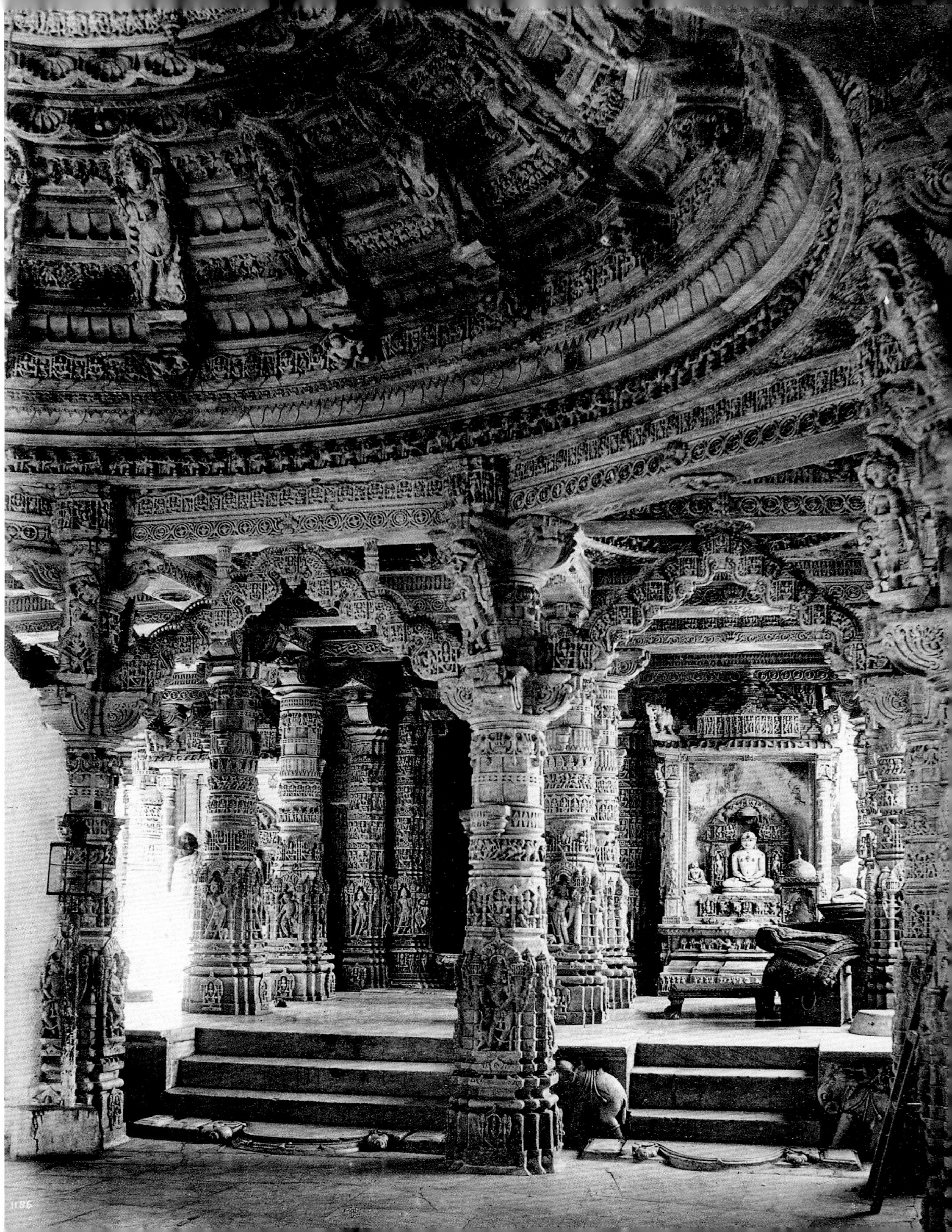

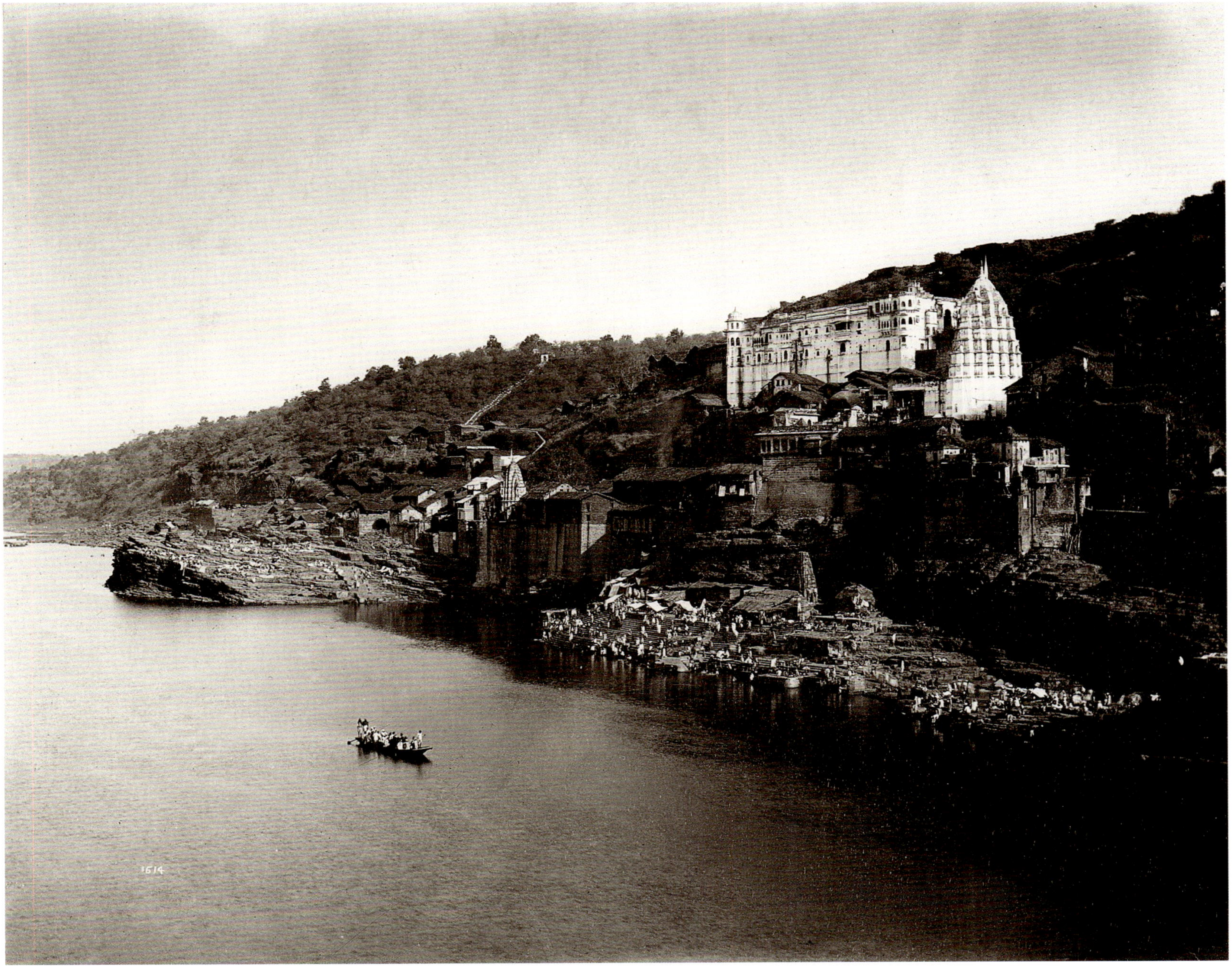

127 *Palace in Orchha Fort*

Lala Deen Dayal

ca. 1882–86, albumen print, 19.5 x 27.4
Deen Dayal cat. no. 1395
Dr. Siddharth Bhansali

128 *The Residency Bridge at Indore*

Lala Deen Dayal

ca. 1882–86, albumen print, 20.6 x 27.5
Deen Dayal cat. no. 1587
Dr. Siddharth Bhansali

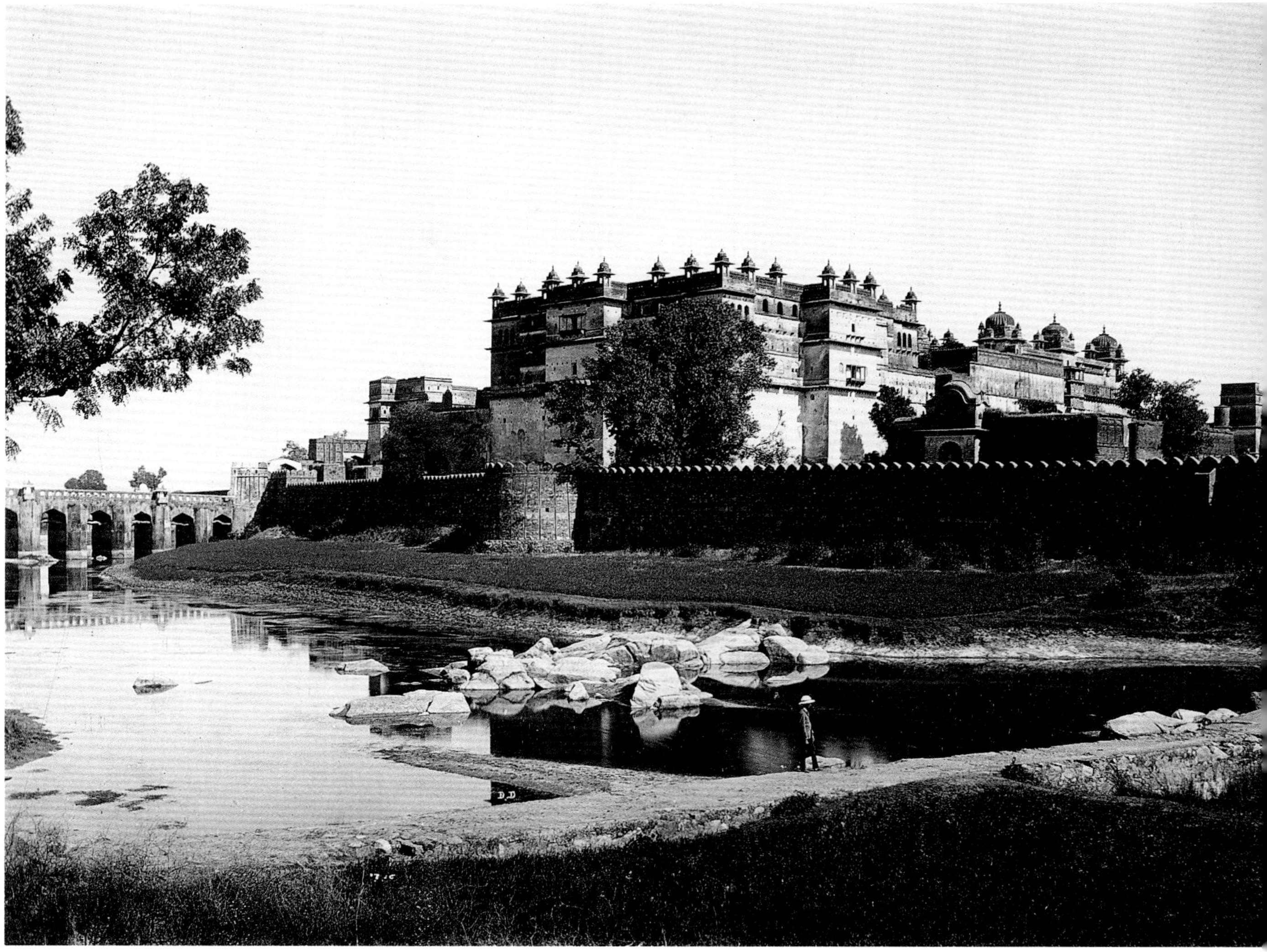

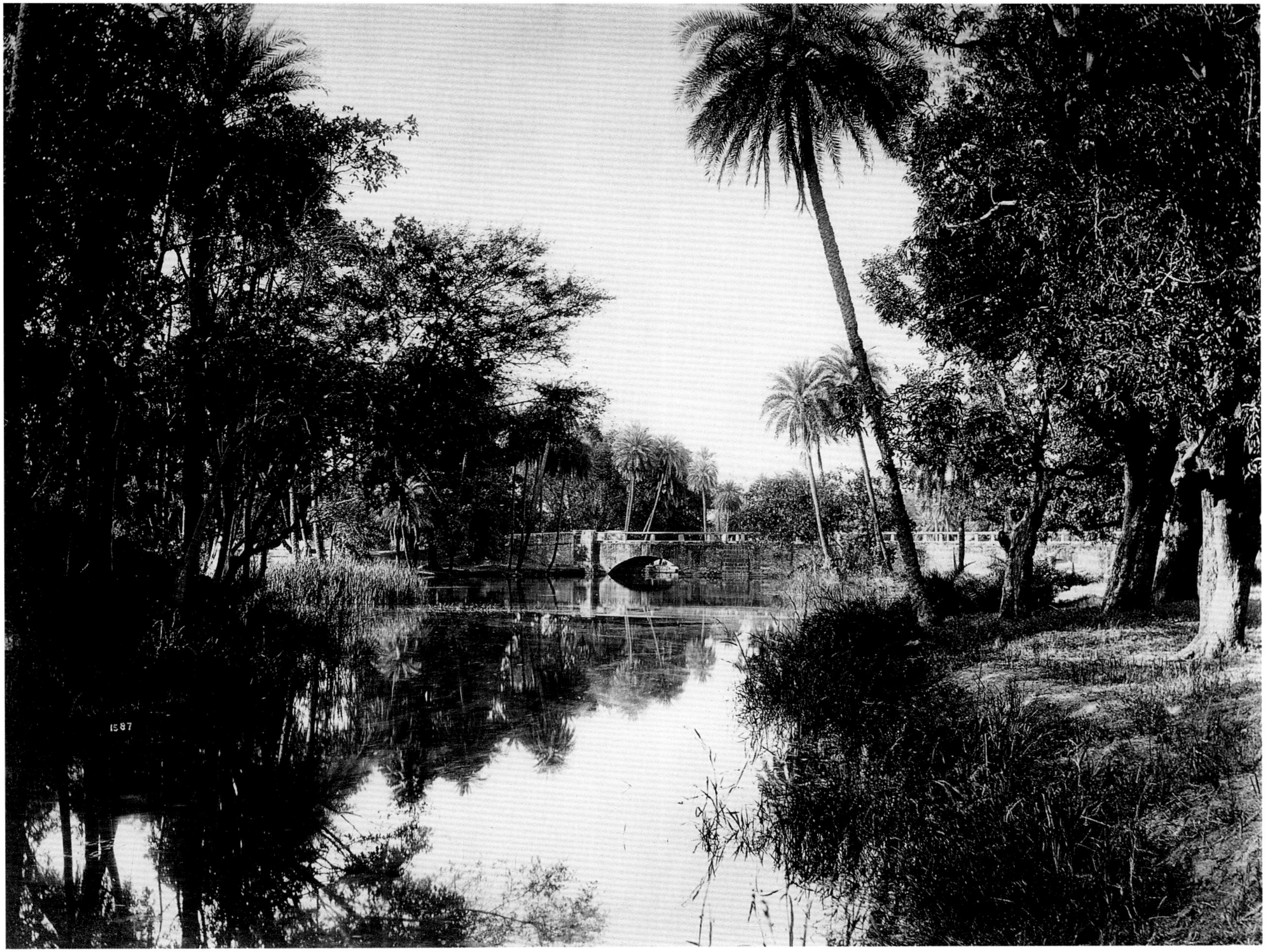
1587

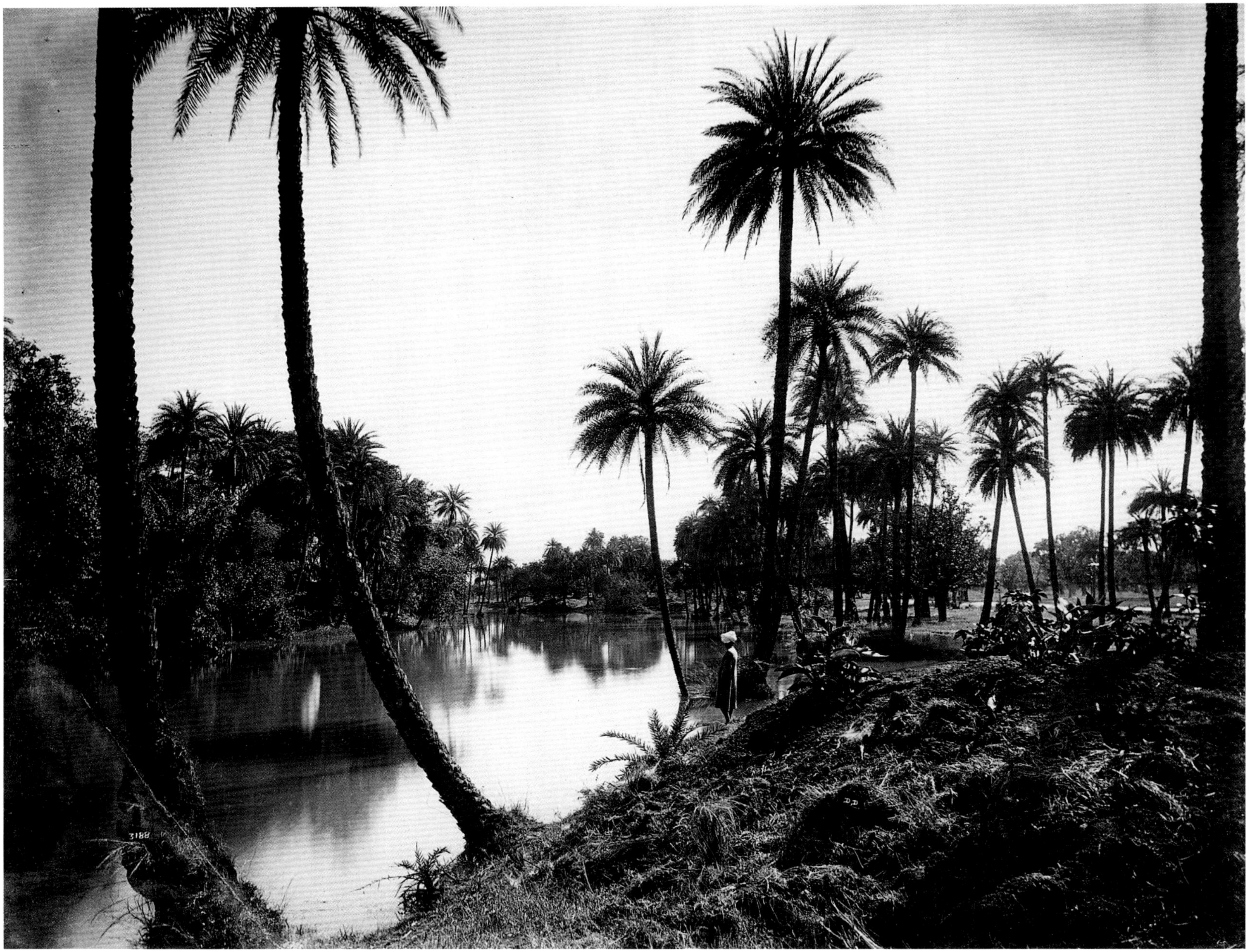
3188

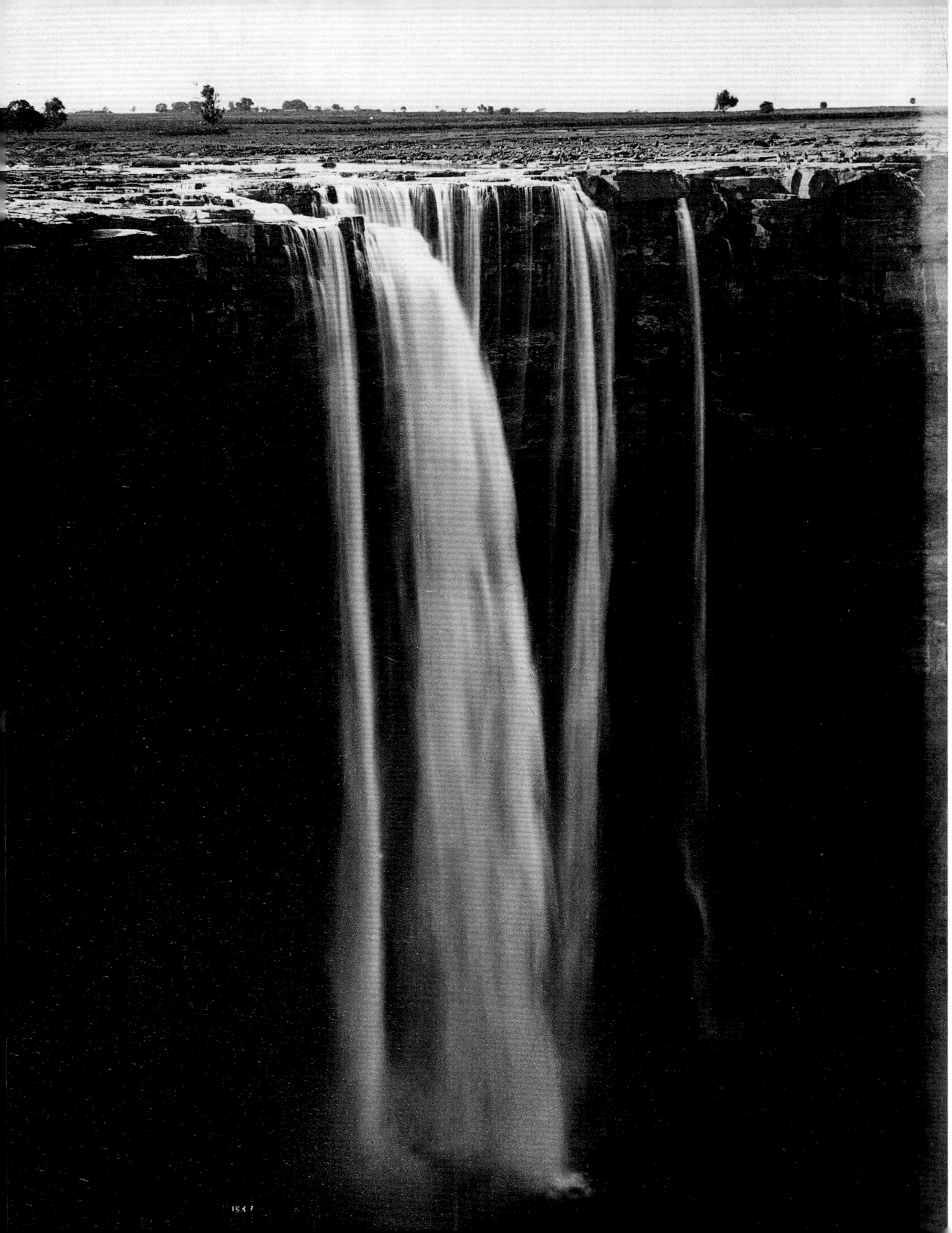

129 *River View at Indore*

Lala Deen Dayal

ca. 1882–86, albumen print, 20.7 x 27.4

Deen Dayal cat. no. 3188

Dr. Siddharth Bhansali

130 *Chichai Waterfall near Rewa*

Lala Deen Dayal

1882, albumen print, 26.3 x 20.8

Deen Dayal cat. no. 1537

Dr. Siddharth Bhansali

131 *East Scarp of Daulatabad Fort*

Lala Deen Dayal

ca. 1884–88, albumen print, 26.8 x 19.9

Deen Dayal cat. no. 3861

Howard and Jane Ricketts Collection

132 *Elephant Battery in Action at Fort Jhansi*

Lala Deen Dayal

ca. 1882–84, albumen print, 16 x 23.5

Deen Dayal cat. no. 2803

Smithsonian Institution, National Museum of Natural History NMNH 045702.00

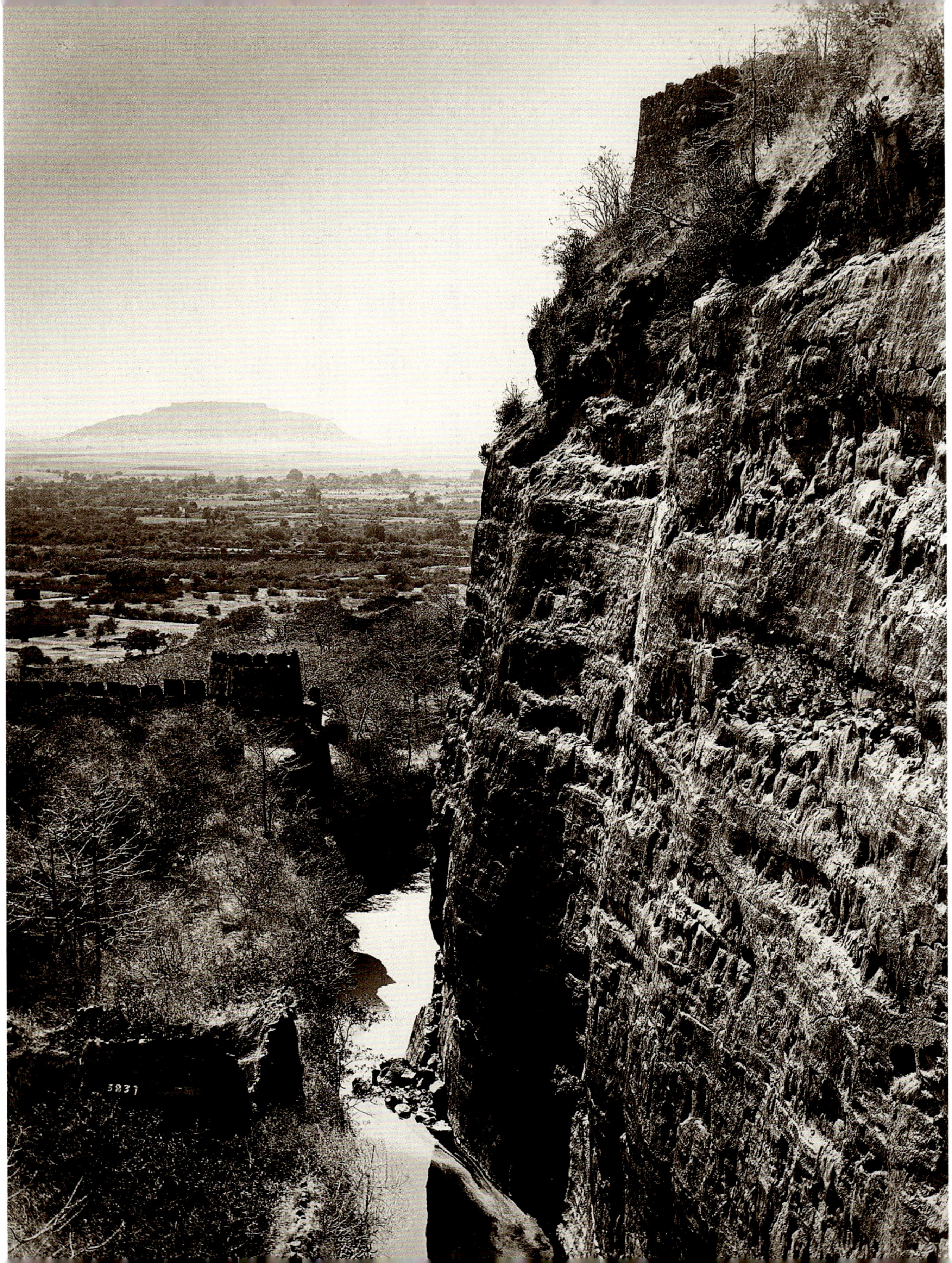

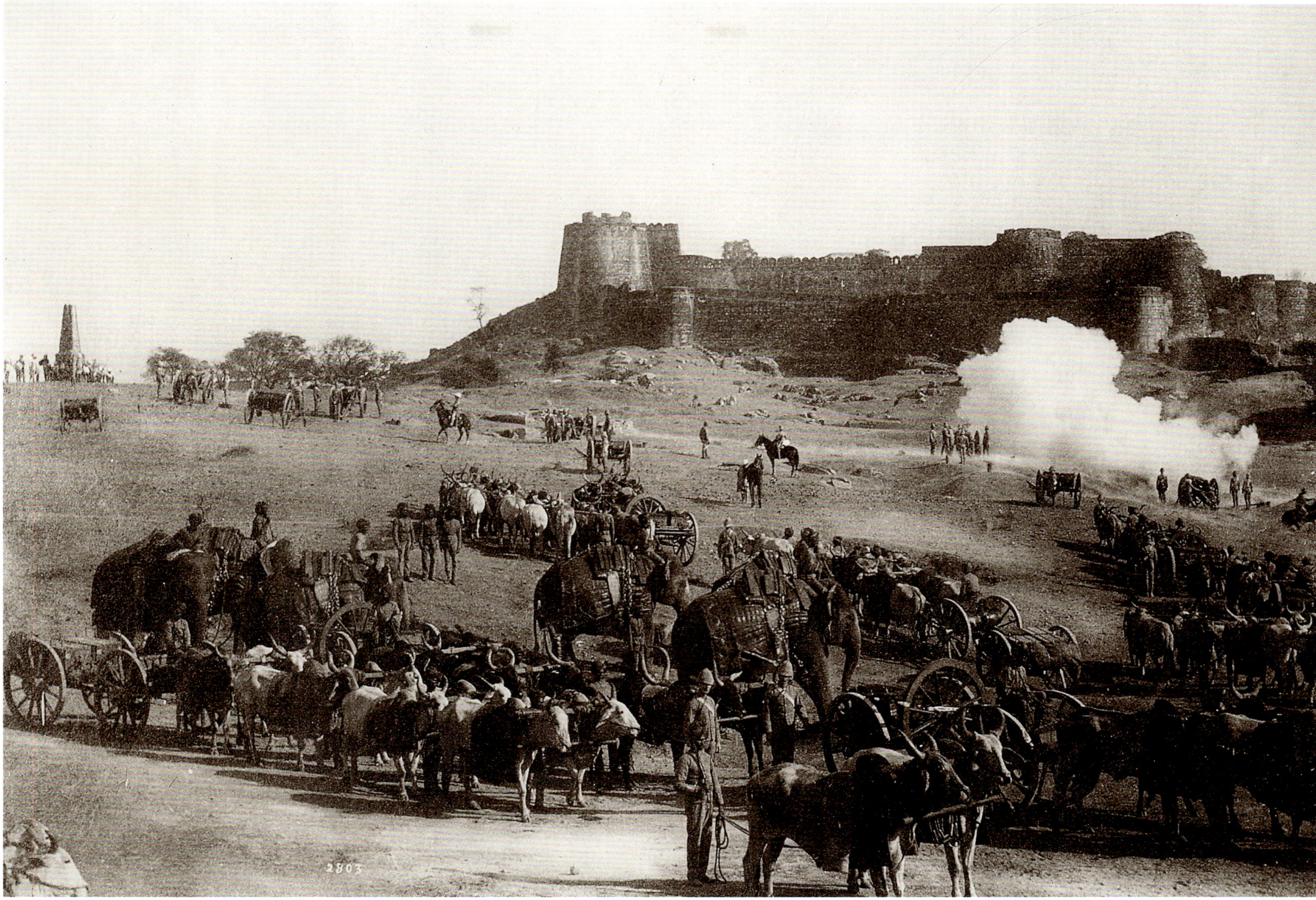
2803

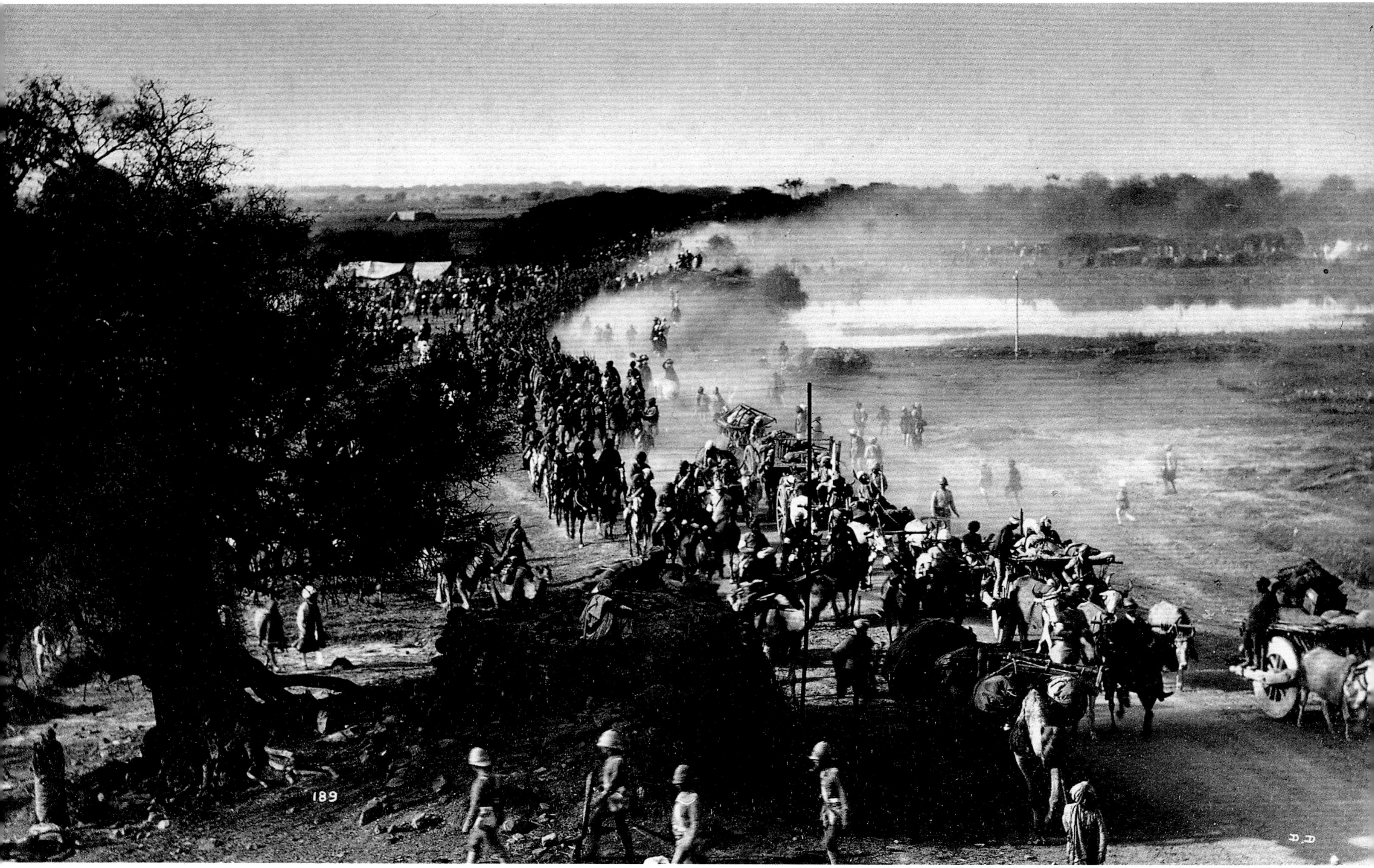
189
D.A

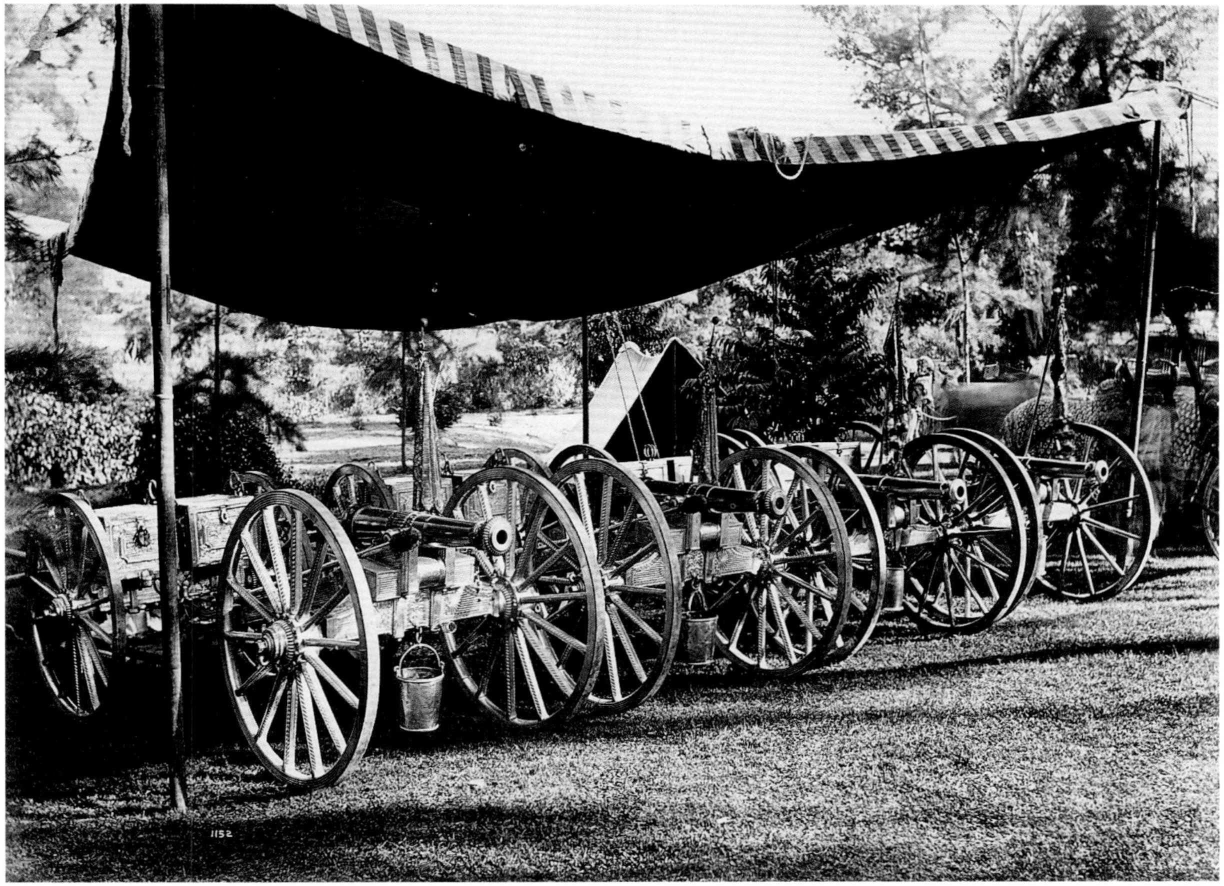

133 *Troops Returning to Delhi*

Lala Deen Dayal

ca. 1882–84, albumen print, 13.4 x 21.5

Deen Dayal cat. no. 189

Dr. Siddharth Bhansali

134 *Gold and Silver Guns at Baroda*

Lala Deen Dayal

ca. 1882–84, albumen print, 19.4 x 27

Deen Dayal cat. no. 1152

Dr. Siddharth Bhansali

SHADES OF SEPIA: PHOTOGRAPHIC PROCESSES

Michael Gray

AS PAGE AFTER page turns in this "album," differences emerge in shade, tone, texture, and surface quality. By now the reader has encountered the names of the various early processes used by Daguerre and Talbot, as well as those who were working in India, including Beato, Macfarlane, Bourne, and Deen Dayal, and to capture their first images on sheets of metal, glass, or paper. To many, the terms "silver gelatin" and "platinum" may conjure up cool blue, gray, or soft whitish silver tones, just as "albumen," (egg white), may suggest sepia, brown, or other warm colors. Not so. Color is not determined by the photographic process, and a carbon print, for instance, may have a rich brown hue. During the late nineteenth century in India, color was affected as much by humidity, temperature, purity of chemicals, and paper quality as it was by the photographer's wishes. The photographer or printer has a range of techniques from which to choose in order to create the most stable and beautiful image. A vast range of substances and metals—from eggs to gold—lends particular shades and tones (as well as stability) to every print. Many of the results seem counterintuitive; an albumen print, for example, if toned with a solution containing gold, changes from a reddish brown hue to a rich purple. Gold toning was extremely popular in India, and virtually all the photographers working in the subcontinent followed Captain Linneas Tripe's reported advice to spare no sovereigns in the quest for sources of gold.[1] Similarly, the range of surface texture depends on the photographer's preference and not on the photographic process. An albumen print can be matte, semimatte, semiglossy, glossy, glossy-burnished or double-coated; a salt paper print can be plain (matte) or albumenized, and either can receive additional coatings of gelatin, arrowroot, or resin to enhance their appearance. Perhaps the only universal assumption that can be made with reference to early photographic images is that if they survive in good condition then it is virtually certain that they must have been toned with gold salts (chloride of gold). I trust this appendix will provide some help and general guidance regarding the processes that typify the era.

Direct Positive Process

THE DAGUERREOTYPE: A MIRROR WITH A MEMORY

The daguerreotype was the first practical photographic process to be publicly announced, and the precision and exactitude of the photographic image produced on a burnished, silver-plated copper sheet created a sensation when it was revealed to members of the French Academy of Science, Paris, in the first quarter of 1839.

Daguerre had initially collaborated with Nicéphore Niépce, who, in 1826, had made the earliest known surviving photographic representation using a camera obscura, a view from the window of his house at Gras made on a pewter sheet coated with light-sensitive bitumen of Judea. Niépce died in 1833, but Daguerre continued their joint research, and in 1837 made his first successful photographic image.

The daguerreotype process involved the deposit of a thin layer of pure silver onto a copper plate, which was then polished until a perfect finish was obtained. The plate was next exposed to iodine vapor in a small box, resulting in the creation of a thin layer of light-sensitive silver iodide on the surface of the plate. This was exposed in the camera and then removed to a second box. Here the image was developed in mercury fumes (produced by heating a small bowl of mercury within the box), forming a white amalgam of silver and mercury on those parts of the image that had been exposed to light. The plate was then stabilized or "fixed" and mounted behind glass to protect the delicate surface from abrasion and chemical contamination. Almost certainly the first photographic image taken on the Indian subcontinent would have been a daguerreotype; as early as 1844 a Mr. M. L. Montairo announced that he was "Prepared to take likenesses by the Daguerreotype process in Calcutta."[2]

While the daguerreotype produced an image of startling precision and great beauty, it had a number of disadvantages that ultimately led to its demise. First, it was literally a mirror image, that is, laterally reversed. For portraiture there were obvious disadvantages, and for landscape and architectural work it produced a laterally inverted representation.[3] The highly reflective image was also difficult to view in certain lights. But the fatal drawback was that every daguerreotype was unique: if more copies were required it was necessary to expose additional plates. The paper processes, which were ultimately destined to provide the foundation of modern photographic practice, initially were less perfect and precise, but they possessed certain factors that in the end proved to be crucial. In India daguerreotype studios survived into the 1860s, but by this time photography on paper was in the ascendant and the dominance of "the mirror with a memory" was at a close.

Negative Processes

THE CALOTYPE

The calotype was the first practical negative-positive process on paper. William Henry Fox Talbot had made his first and to date the earliest-known surviving photographic negative in England by August 1835. Having achieved this breakthrough, Talbot abandoned his experiments and only resumed his researches in the light of Arago's announcement on behalf of Daguerre. By September 1840, after a period of intense work, he had made the most significant of the discoveries that formed the basis of his calotype or Talbotype process. This was the developing-out of the latent or invisible image formed in camera on a sheet of paper coated with light-sensitive silver iodide. This "developed-out" negative was then fixed in a chemical called sodium thiosulphate (known popularly as hypo) to remove the unexposed and undeveloped silver compounds in the nonimage areas and thus stabilize the resultant image. Talbot then printed his negative images by contact, using the salt print process (described below), to make a theoretically infinite number of identical copies. While the chemicals and materials used in photography have been refined over the last 160 years, Talbot's procedures for printing positive images from a negative produced in the camera are essentially the same as those in use today.[4]

The calotype process itself was subject to many modifications during the fifteen or so years during which it dominated the practice of photography in India. Of these the most important was perhaps Gustave le Gray's waxed paper process,[5] in which the negative was made more translucent before exposure by impregnating the paper with heated wax prior to sensitization with silver iodide, resulting in increased definition and a change in tonal values. Many photographers, such as John Murray and Thomas Biggs, combined the virtues of both processes by waxing their negatives after development to facilitate printing; examples of their masterful achievements are included in the exhibition this book accompanies. By the mid- to late 1850s the calotype process had reached a level of aesthetic and technical sophistication that today is difficult to believe. But by this time, both fashion and technology had moved on. Toward the end of the 1850s, although a few of the older school of photographers remained faithful to the beautiful tonal values produced from paper negatives, photography on glass was displacing it. While in India especially, the portability and convenience of the paper negative processes were major advantages, the photographic journals both in the subcontinent and in Europe had switched their allegiances to the sharpness and precision of the wet-collodion negative process on glass.

THE WET-COLLODION NEGATIVE PROCESS ON GLASS

Frederick Scott Archer had made his first negative on glass by the end of 1849, but his new process was not announced until 1851.[6] In the wet-collodion process the light-sensitive silver iodide salts were formed and held within a thin layer of collodion, which was carefully poured and "flowed" over a sheet of glass (collodion is gun cotton dissolved in ether and alcohol).[7] Chemically the process differed from that of calotype in that a more energetic developer was used and the fixing bath was the more lethal potassium cyanide rather than sodium or ammonium thiosulphate.

Whereas in Talbot's process the chemical compounds were held within the cellulose fibers of a sheet of paper, in Archer's they were retained within a permeable stratum of collodion spread on a sheet of glass. Thus, while the paper negative processes transferred not only the photographic image but impressions of the cellulose fibers from which the paper was formed, the collodion negative, supported on a completely transparent glass base, produced a textureless image of remarkable quality with a degree of sharpness that is still hard to surpass today.

The wet-plate process (so-called because the glass plate had to be coated, exposed, and developed as part of a continuous sequence before the collodion dried out) required great manipulative skill and experience to master, but its advantages of sensitivity and sharpness of definition meant that for the next decade and a half it was by far the most widely used of all the photographic processes.

SILVER GELATIN BROMIDE (NEGATIVE) EMULSION ON GLASS AND FILM

By 1872, a photographer notified the *British Journal of Photography* that he had successfully taken a series of images using a new emulsion—one of silver gelatin. Further experimentation by others led to its commercial marketing as a dry gelatin negative plate. It was essentially the same emulsion as that used for the coating of silver gelatin print paper. This process remains in use today.

Print Processes and Photographic Papers

SALT PAPER PRINT PROCESS

The first photographic printing process was a method discovered by William Henry Fox Talbot[8] between 1834 and 1839, used to make his "shadows" by contact directly from collected botanical specimens. By the early 1840s various improvements made this a convenient and practical way of making contact prints from photographic negatives.

A sheet of good quality drawing paper was floated or submerged in a bath of sodium chloride, dried, and then refloated on a second bath of silver nitrate. By a process known as double decomposition, light-sensitive silver chloride was thus formed in the top surface of the paper. The sheet was dried and then placed in a frame in contact with the negative image and exposed to sunlight for printing-out. In this process no chemical development takes place: the positive image is brought out using the sun's power alone to reduce the silver salts in the paper to their pure metallic state. The surface has no gloss or shine, and the image is retained in the top layers of the paper, giving characteristics that often resemble earlier graphic processes such as aquatints or lithographs.

The late 1840s to the early 1860s was a time when experimentation was the norm rather than the exception. The original salt paper print evolved through trial and error over a period of several years, until the albumen print emerged, which enabled more consistent results. During this time an enormous variety of animal and vegetable sizings were utilized for the preparation of the basic paper to keep the silver salts close to the surface of the paper, and these provide a wide and varied repertoire of finishes ranging from a deep matte neutral surface to a deep rich gloss and tone. These early prints, with their broad and subtle tonal range, are at their finest capable of a delicacy and expressiveness that remain unsurpassed.

THE ALBUMEN PRINT PROCESS

Introduced by the Frenchman Louis-Desire Blanquart-Evrard[9] in the mid-1850s, the albumen print process had largely ousted the salt print process by the early 1860s. Although both types of print were "printing-out processes," the albumen print is most often characterized by having a deep gloss finish when double coated. Albumen paper was used by most photographers from the 1850s up to the late 1890s, when it was replaced by a variety of papers that were capable of being produced by automated systems.

As with the salt print, the first step was to lay down an even coating or application of either sodium or ammonium chloride. This was achieved by floating a sheet of paper in a bath containing a mixture of albumen (egg white) and salt. The sheet was then floated on a bath of silver nitrate, thus forming the light sensitive layer of silver chloride. The first bath, in the salting solution, gave the paper its characteristic gloss and by sealing the pores of the paper also kept the silver sensitizing layer on the surface of the paper. As with the salt print process, the paper was then exposed to sunlight in a frame in contact with a negative. Prior to fixing, the finished print was passed through an alkaline gold toning bath to preserve the whites and maintain good coloration in the shadow areas. Some printers preferred to use a more diluted salting bath, which produced a good range of tones but without the very high gloss that many photographers and prospective purchasers considered to be "vulgar and inartistic."[10]

SILVER EMULSION PRINT PAPERS

There were two types of silver emulsion print papers, the collodio-chloride and the chloro-bromide. The collodio-chloride could have either a high gloss finish or a beautiful matte finish, but it was extremely brittle. The chloro-bromide did not have as high a gloss as the collodio-chloride, but it was more flexible and less brittle over time.

THE CARBON PROCESS

In this process a thin layer of pigmented gelatin is spread on an intermediary surface or "temporary support," which, when exposed to light under a photographic negative, hardens in direct proportion so that the unexposed parts can be washed away. The image is then transferred to the final paper support and dried. The result is a carbon print. Carbon was initially the substance used to make the pigment, but the substance held in suspension was not always 100 percent carbon black and not always a pigment. Thus the term "carbon print" eventually became generic.

Close examination of a carbon print under raking light shows a small but definite "relief" along any edge of high contrast. Generally this is the most reliable method of distinguishing carbon prints from others.

PLATINUM PRINT PROCESS

Discovered by Richard Willis in 1873, this process was based upon the light-sensitive properties of iron salts forming an image made visible by conversion into metallic platinum; the result was highly stable and permanent. It is a direct contact process; the print, exactly the same size as the negative, is made by pressing the negative directly against the paper. No enlarger is used. It was first made commercially available to photographers by the Willis Platinotype Company of London. Good quality paper was first floated on a platinum solution (ferric oxalate and potassium chloroplatinate) and then dried; the sheet was next placed, sensitive side up, in a printing frame against a glass negative, emulsion side down and exposed for a short time to direct sunlight. The image was then bought out by further immersion in a solution of potassium oxalate developer and then washed in a weak solution of hydrochloric acid, which removed all traces of the salts of iron. Using platinum alone, the resultant image became a cold neutral blue-black. Today most platinum printers more often than not use a combination of platinum and palladium with gold to gain a greater degree of control over the resultant color.

SILVER GELATIN PRINT MADE WITH THE SILVER BROMIDE PRINT PROCESS

Silver gelatin is a generic name or classification that includes all photographic papers based upon the light-sensitive properties of the silver bromide and silver chloride salts, either used together or in combination and held within an emulsive layer formed on the surface of a sheet of white, high-quality machine-produced paper. The first paper made for enlargements for rapid printing using an artificial light source appeared around 1880, and by 1884, Eastman & Co built the first really efficient emulsion-coating machine to coat both paper and film. This date marks the first appearance of the modern silver gelatin photographic print, which together with its variant, the (silver) chloro-bromide print, supplanted and replaced virtually all other types of photographic paper over the next fifty years.

Within this category there are two distinct types; silver gelatin "printing-out" paper and the one that today is most common and called silver gelatin paper, the image being "brought out" with a normal chemical developing agent rather than sunlight. By the 1880s both the production of photographic plates and of paper was gradually being industrialized; it became possible to achieve a much higher degree of consistency with the light-sensitive salts held within a protective gelatin layer irrespective of whether on paper, glass, or later film. Up to the end of the nineteenth century the majority of images were still created by the process of "printing-out"—the most popular and common were gelatin based. Silver gelatin is still the process used by today's photographers.

NOTES

1. Found by author in Tripe correspondence, whereabouts now unknown.

2. See Ray Desmond, "The Indian Scene," in *Victorian India in Focus* (London: Her Majesty's Stationery Office, 1982), 2. Mentioned in passing but giving no sources.

3. It was, of course, possible to use a front-silvered mirror to correct the inversion, however, there was a least a twenty percent loss of light. This, together with loss of image sharpness, dust, and scratches associated with the use of this, an additional attachment to the basic apparatus, ensured that this device was rarely employed.

4. The effect and influence of Talbot's calotype process on the practice of photography in the United States was virtually nonexistent, apart from a small surviving number of prints produced by Cooke, Whipple, and later on the Langenheim brothers. So when in 1851 Frederick Scott Archer published details of his wet-collodion process to most photographers who were familiar and skilled in the operation of the daguerreotype, the negative-positive process appeared as if out of the blue. Taft was somewhat puzzled as to why Talbot took out a patent for his process in 1841, so was unaware that Daguerre had somewhat deviously patented his process via Miles Berry only in England; this after having magnanimously declared that he would donate his invention to the world. Talbot was left with little or no option other than to take out a patent to protect his invention. (See Robert Taft, *Photography and the American Scene* (New York: Dover Publications, 1964), 102. (Unfortunately the author of the passage relating to Talbot's discoveries failed to mention that the Englishman's first negative photographic image was made in August 1835, therefore making it appear that he made no contribution to the development and evolution of photography until the registration of his patent in February 1841.)

5. The waxed paper process of Le Gray was a variant of Talbot's calotype negative process on paper. Le Gray waxed his negative paper prior to its impregnation with the sensitizing solution, whereas Talbot applied the wax after all his chemical manipulations had been carried out. The basis chemical additions made by Le Gray to his negatives was firstly to prevent the wax's rejecting the sensitizing solutions and to compensate for the paper's poor wet strength.

6. Published in *The Chemist,* London, March 1851. Quoted by Joseph Maria Eder in *History of Photography,* (New York: Dover Publications, 1978) 343–47.

7. Gun cotton is an explosive prepared by saturating cotton with nitric and sulfuric acid.

8. For a general overview of his life and work see A. J. P. Arnold, *William Henry Fox Talbot: Photographic Pioneer and Man of Science* (London: Hutchinson Benham, 1977).

9. Isobelle Jammes, *Louis Desire Blanquart Evrard et les Origines de L'edition Photographie Francais* (Geneva: Librairie Droz, 1981).

10. Unfortunately, it is difficult to distinguish the albumen print from the salt print. Photographic prints from this period do not always fall neatly into the two categories, and it was still unclear at the time exactly which direction photography would follow. Experimentation was the order of the day.

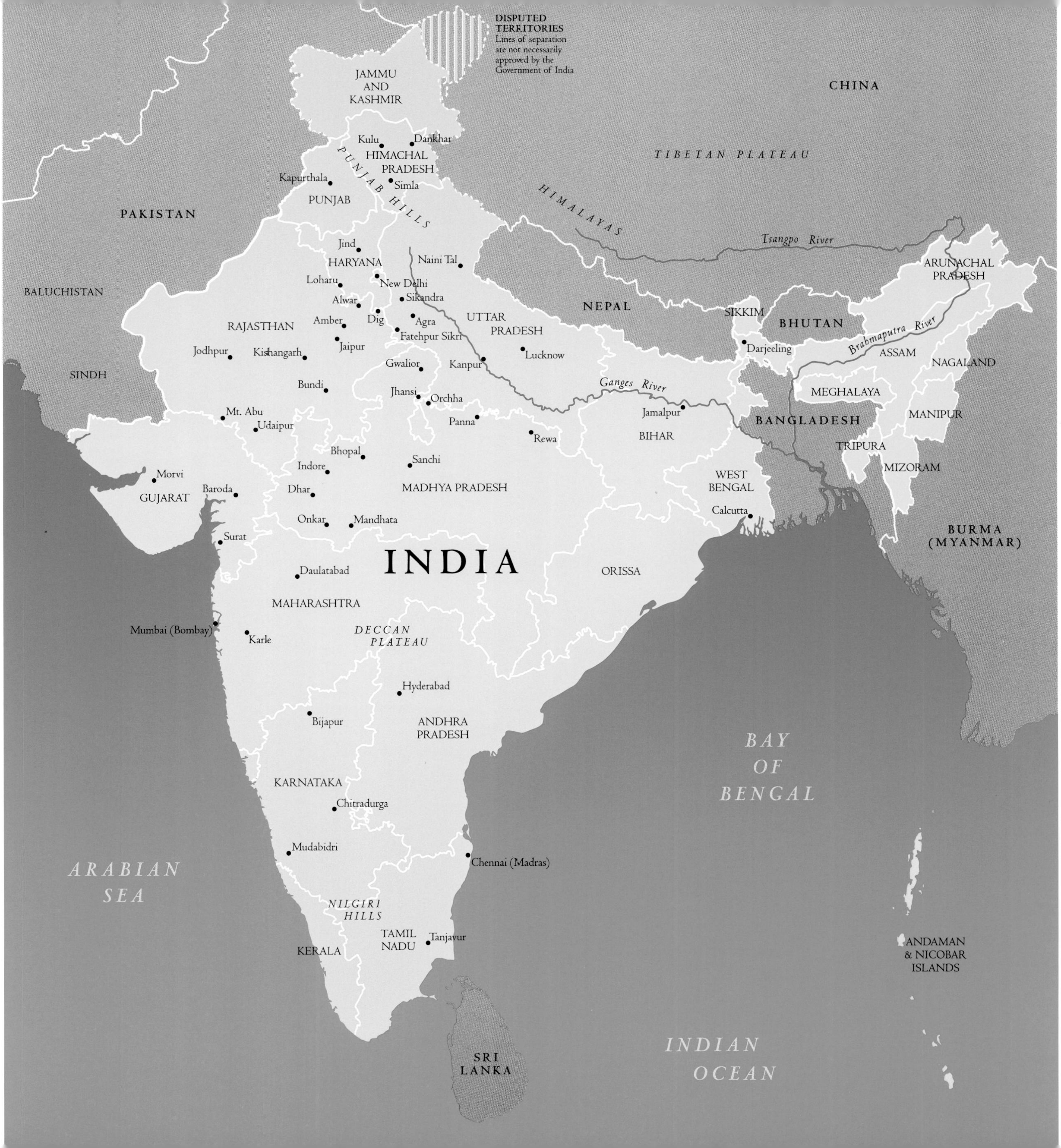

DISPUTED TERRITORIES
Lines of separation are not necessarily approved by the Government of India
CHINA
JAMMU AND KASHMIR
TIBETAN PLATEAU
Kulu
Dankhar
HIMACHAL PRADESH
PUNJAB HILLS
Kapurthala
Simla
PUNJAB
PAKISTAN
HIMALAYAS
Tsangpo River
Jind
Naini Tal
HARYANA
ARUNACHAL PRADESH
BALUCHISTAN
Loharu
New Delhi
Alwar
Sikandra
NEPAL
SIKKIM
BHUTAN
Amber
Dig
Agra
UTTAR PRADESH
RAJASTHAN
Fatehpur Sikri
Brahmaputra River
Jodhpur
Kishangarh
Jaipur
Lucknow
Darjeeling
ASSAM
NAGALAND
SINDH
Gwalior
Kanpur
Bundi
Ganges River
MEGHALAYA
Jhansi
Orchha
Jamalpur
Mt. Abu
BANGLADESH
MANIPUR
Udaipur
Panna
Rewa
BIHAR
TRIPURA
Bhopal
Sanchi
MIZORAM
Indore
Morvi
WEST BENGAL
Baroda
Dhar
MADHYA PRADESH
GUJARAT
Calcutta
Onkar
Mandhata
BURMA (MYANMAR)
Surat
INDIA
Daulatabad
ORISSA
MAHARASHTRA
Mumbai (Bombay)
Karle
DECCAN PLATEAU
Hyderabad
Bijapur
ANDHRA PRADESH
BAY OF BENGAL
KARNATAKA
Chitradurga
Mudabidri
Chennai (Madras)
ARABIAN SEA
NILGIRI HILLS
ANDAMAN & NICOBAR ISLANDS
TAMIL NADU
Tanjavur
KERALA
SRI LANKA
INDIAN OCEAN

SELECT BIBLIOGRAPHY

Allen, Charles. *Raj: A Scrapbook of British India, 1877–1947.* London: New Leaf, 1977.

———. *A Glimpse of the Burning Plain.* London: Michael Joseph, 1986.

———. *Plain Tales from the Raj.* London: Andre Deutsch, 1975. Reprint, London: Little Brown, 1998.

Allen, Charles, and Sharada Dwivedi. *Lives of the Indian Princes.* London: Century, 1984. Reprint, revised, Mumbai: Eshwar, 1998.

Bayly, C. A., ed. *The Raj: India and the British, 1600–1947.* London: National Portrait Gallery, 1990.

The Bengal Hurkaru and India Gazette, 1856–1864.

Bourne, Samuel, and Charles Shepherd. *Photographic Views in India.* London: Howard Ricketts Limited, n.d.

British Journal of Photography, 1863–1870

Brothers, Caroline. *War and Photography: A Cultural History.* London: Routledge, 1997.

Charlesworth, Michael. "Fox Talbot and the 'White Mythology' of Photography." *Word and Image* 2, no. 3 (July–September 1995): 207–15.

Clark, John, John Fraser, and Colin Osman. "Chronology of Felix (Felice) Beato (1825?–1908?)." In John Clark, *Japanese-British Exchanges in Art, 1850–1930s: Papers and Research Material.* Canberra, Australia: Department of Art History, Australian National University, 1989.

Crombie, Isobel. "China, 1860: A Photographic Album by Felice Beato." *History of Photography* 11, no. 1 (1987): 25–37.

Desmond, Ray. *Photography in India during the Nineteenth Century.* London: India Office Library and Records Report, 1974.

———. "19th Century Indian Photographers in India." *History of Photography* 1, no. 1 (1977): 313–17.

———. *Victorian India in Focus: A Selection of Early Photographs from the Collection in the India Office Library and Records.* London: Her Majesty's Stationery Office, 1982.

———. "Photography in Victorian India." *Royal Society of Arts Journal* 84, no. 5353 (December 1985): 48–61.

Dewan, Janet, and Maia-Mari Sutnik. *Linnaeus Tripe: Photographer of British India, 1854–1870.* Toronto: Art Gallery of Ontario, 1986.

Dilks, David. *Curzon in India.* 2 vols. London: Hart-Davis, 1969, 1970.

Edwards, Elizabeth, ed. *Anthropology & Photography, 1860–1920.* New Haven: Yale University Press in association with the Royal Anthropological Institute, London, 1992.

Fabian, Rainer, and Hans-Christian Adam. *Masters of Early Travel Photography.* New York: Vendome Press, 1983.

Falconer, John. "Ethnographical Photography in India 1850–1900." *Photographic Collector* 5, no. 1 (1984): 16–45.

———. *A Shifting Focus: Photography in India, 1850–1900.* London: British Council, 1995.

Fergusson, James. *History of Indian and Eastern Architecture.* London: John Murray, 1876.

Fraser, John. "Some Pre-Mutiny Photograph Portraits." *Journal of the Society for Army Historical Research* 58, no. 235 (Autumn 1980): 134–47.

———. "Beato's Photograph of the Interior of the Sikandarbagh at Lucknow." *Journal of the Society of Army Historical Research* 64, no. 237 (1981): 51–55.

Ghosh, Siddhartha. *Chabi Tola* [in Bengali]. Calcutta: Printed Circuits International Limited, 1988.

———. "Early Photography in Calcutta." In *Changing Visions, Lasting Images: Calcutta through 300 Years*, ed. Pratapaditya Pal, Bombay: Marg Publications, 1990.

Gilmour, David. *Curzon.* London: John Murray, 1994.

Goldberg, Vicki, ed. *Photography in Print: Writings from 1816 to the Present.* New York: Simon & Schuster, 1981.

Goldsmid, Sir Frederic John. *James Outram: A Biography.* 2 vols. London: Smith, Elder & Co., 1880.

Government of India. *The Great Delhi Durbar of 1911.* Calcutta: Government of India, 1911.

Gubbins, Martin Richard. *An Account of the Mutinies in Oudh, and of the Siege of the Lucknow Residency.* London: Richard Bentley, 1858.

Gutman, Judith Mara. *Through Indian Eyes: 19th and Early 20th Century Photography from India.* New York: Oxford University Press and International Center of Photography, 1982.

Hambourg, Maria Morris, et al. *The Waking Dream: Photography's First Century—Selections from the Gilman Paper Company Collection.* New York: Metropolitan Museum of Art, 1993.

Harris, David. *Of Battle and Beauty: Felice Beato's Photographs of China.* Santa Barbara: Santa Barbara Museum of Art, 1999.

Harris, David, and Eric Sandweiss. *Eadweard Muybridge and the Photographic Panorama of San Francisco, 1850–1880.* Montreal: Centre for Canadian Architecture, 1993.

Haworth-Booth, Mark, ed. *The Golden Age of British Photography: Photographs from the Victoria and Albert Musuem, London.* Millerton, N.Y.: Aperture in association with the Philadelphia Museum of Art, 1984.

Heathcote, Pauline F. "Samuel Bourne of Nottingham." *History of Photography* 6, no. 2 (April 1982): 99–112.

Hyde, Ralph. *Panoramania! The Art and Entertainment of the "All-Embracing" View.* London: Trefoil Publications in association with Barbican Art Gallery, 1988.

Innes, Lieutenant-General James McLeod. *Lucknow and Oudh in the Mutiny: A Narrative and Study.* London: A. D. Innes and Company, 1895.

James, Lawrence. *Raj: The Making and Unmaking of British India.* New York: St. Martin's Press, 1998.

Kaye, John W. *A History of the Sepoy War in India, 1857–1858.* 5th ed. 2 vols. London: W. H. Allen, 1870.

Llewellyn-Jones, Rosie. *A Fatal Friendship: The Nawabs, the British, and the City of Lucknow.* Delhi: Oxford University Press, 1985.

Macfarlane, Donald Horne, "Landscape Photography in India." *Journal of the Bengal Photographic Society* 1, no. 2 (September 1862), and no. 3 (December 1862).

Maharaja Sawai Man Singh II Museum. *The Photographer Prince: Maharaja Sawai Ram Singh II.* Jaipur: Maharaja Sawai Man Singh II Museum, 1985.

Metcalf, Thomas R. *An Imperial Vision: Indian Architecture and Britain's Raj.* Berkeley and Los Angeles: University of California Press, 1989.

———. *Ideologies of the Raj.* Cambridge: Cambridge University Press, 1994.

Mitter, Partha. *Much Maligned Monsters: History of European Reactions to Indian Art.* Oxford: Clarendon Press, 1977.

Museum of Modern Art. *A Personal View: Photography in the Collection of Paul F. Walter.* New York: Museum of Modern Art, 1985.

Newhall, Beaumont. *The History of Photography from 1839 to the Present Day.* rev. ed. London: Secker and Warburg, 1972.

Oetterman, Stephan. *The Panorama: History of a Mass Medium.* Trans. Deborah Schneider. New York: Zone Books, 1997.

Ollman, Arthur. *Samuel Bourne: Images of India.* Carmel, Calif.: Friends of Photography, 1983.

Osman, Colin. "The Later Years of Felice Beato." *Photographic Journal* 128, no. 11 (1988): 511–14.

———. "Antonio Beato, Photographer of the Nile." *History of Photography* 14, no. 2 (1990): 101–11.

———. "Invenzione e Verità sulla vita di Felice Beato." In *Felice Beato: Viaggio in Giappone, 1863–1877,* ed. Claudia Gabriele Philipp et. al., 17–23. Milan: Federico Motta Editore, 1991.

———. "The Later Years of James Robertson." *History of Photography* 16, no. 1 (1992): 72–73.

———. "Another Piece of a Jigsaw." *The Photo Historian* 105 (1994): 20–21.

Pal, Pratapaditya, and Vidya Dehejia. *From Merchants to Emperors: British Artists and India, 1757–1930.* Ithaca and London: Cornell University Press, 1986.

Pare, Richard, ed. *Photography and Architecture, 1839–1939.* Montreal: Canadian Centre for Architecture, 1982.

Pemble, John. *The Raj, The Indian Mutiny, and the Kingdom of Oudh, 1801–1859.* Rutherford, N.J.: Fairleigh Dickinson University Press, 1977.

Photographic Journal, Being the Journal of the Photographic Society, no. 138 (15 October 1863), no. 157 (15 May 1865), and no. 159 (15 July 1865).

Pinney, Christopher. *Camera Indica: The Social Life of Indian Photographs.* Chicago: University of Chicago Press, 1997.

Ricketts, Jane. "Donald Macfarlane: A New Name in Indian Photography." *Photographic Collector* 3, no .1 (Spring 1982).

Ryan, James R. *Picturing Empire: Photography and the Visualization of the British Empire.* London: Reaktion Books, 1997.

Sampson, Gary David. "Samuel Bourne and 19th-Century British Landscape Photography in India." Ph.D. diss., University of California, Santa Barbara, 1991.

———. "The Success of Samuel Bourne in India." *History of Photography* 16, no. 4 (Winter 1992): 336–47.

Sontag, Susan. *On Photography.* New York: Penguin Books, 1979.

Stapp, William F. "Souvenirs of Asia: Photography of the Far East, 1840–1920." *Image* 37, nos. 3–4 (Fall/Winter 1994): 3–53.

Steer, Valentia. *The Delhi Durbar, 1902–03.* London: Thacker and Spink, 1904.

Taylor, P. J. O., ed. *A Companion to the "Indian Mutiny" of 1857.* Delhi: Oxford University Press, 1996.

Taylor, Roger. *Samuel Bourne, 1934–1912: Photographic Views in India.* Sheffield, England: City Polytechnic, 1980.

Thomas, G. "The First Four Decades of Photography in India." *History of Photography* 3. no. 3 (July 1979): 215–26.

———. *History of Photography in India, 1840–1980.* Pondicherry: Sri Aurobindo Ashram Press, 1981.

Tod, Lieutenant-Colonel James. *Annals and Antiquities of Rajast-han or the Central and Western Rajpoot States of India.* 1829. 2 vols. Reprint, London: G. Routledge and Sons, 1914.

Trachtenberg, Alan, ed. *Classic Essays on Photography.* New Haven: Leete's Island Books, 1980.

Wheeler, James Talboys. *History of the Imperial Assemblage at Delhi.* London: Churchill, 1878.

Williams, Susan I. *Samuel Bourne: In Search of the Picturesque.* Williamstown, Mass.: McClelland Press, 1981.

Worswick, Clark, ed. *Princely India: Photographs by Raja Lala Deen Dayal, Court Photographer (1884–1910) to the Premier Prince of India.* New York: Knopf, 1980.

Worswick, Clark, and Ainslee Embree. *The Last Empire: Photography in British India, 1855–1911.* Millerton, N.Y.: Aperture, 1976.

INDEX

References to photographs are printed in italics.

CONTRIBUTORS

CHARLES ALLEN is an author and broadcaster best known for his social histories of the British colonial era. His publications include *The Lives of the Indian Princes* (1984) and *Plain Tales from the Raj* (1975).

VIDYA DEHEJIA, curator of the exhibition, editor of and contributor to the book, is deputy director and chief curator of the Arthur M. Sackler Gallery and the Freer Gallery of Art. Her many publications include *Devi: The Great Goddess* (Washington, D. C.: Arthur M. Sackler Gallery and Mapin, 1999) and *Impossible Picturesquenesss: Edward Lear's Indian Watercolors, 1873–1875* (Ahmadabad: Mapin, 1989).

JOHN FALCONER is curator of photographs, Oriental and India Office Collections, British Library.

MICHAEL GRAY is curator at the National Trust, Fox Talbot Museum, Lacock, England, and scientific director of IkonsCentre Imaging Project, University of Pordenone, Italy.

DAVID HARRIS is an independent curator and photographic historian specializing in nineteenth-century and contemporary architectural and landscape photography. His most recent publication is *Of Battle and Beauty: Felice Beato's Photographs of China* (Santa Barbara: Santa Barbara Museum of Art, 1999).

JANE RICKETTS is an independent scholar and collector who, with her husband, has concentrated on the work of British photographers in India in the nineteenth century.

GARY SAMPSON is associate professor of art history at the Cleveland Institute of Art. His doctoral dissertaion was entitled *Samuel Bourne and 19th-Century British Landscape Photography in India.*

ACKNOWLEDGMENTS

THIS BOOK and the accompanying exhibition, devoted to an exploration of early photography on the Indian subcontinent, is the result of the willing and enthusiastic collaboration among a team of international scholars, museum professionals, and volunteers. Special thanks are due to Milo Beach, director of the Freer and Sackler galleries, and Tom Lentz, former deputy director (now director of Smithsonian's International Art Museums Division), whose interest in the medium of photography helped shape the project.

Many scholars have contributed essays: Charles Allen, John Falconer, Michael Gray, David Harris, Jane Ricketts, and Gary Sampson. To them I owe a debt of gratitude. A number of individuals, institutions, libraries, and museums both loaned us the photographs presented here and graciously gave us permission to reproduce them.

Editor Lynne Shaner's thoughtful, sensitive, thorough work on the manuscript has greatly improved the quality of the book, while Carol Beehler's exquisite handling of design has produced an "album" that is a pleasure to view. Thanks are due also to Karen Sagstetter, editor-in-chief of the publications department. Naina Mistry gave generously of her time and provided valuable support for this project. And special thanks are due to exhibitions design, particularly Karen Sasaki, exhibition designer, and Nancy Hacskaylo, graphic designer, who made the show come to life in the gallery.

Vidya Dehejia

VISITING COMMITTEES

FREER GALLERY OF ART

Mr. Richard M. Danziger, Chair
Dr. Kurt Gitter
Mrs. Katharine Graham
Mrs. Richard Helms
Sir Joseph E. Hotung
Mr. H. Christopher Luce
Ms. Elizabeth Meyer
Mr. Frank H. Pearl
Dr. Martin Powers
Dr. Gursharan Sidhu, Vice Chair
Prof. Elizabeth ten Grotenhuis
Ms. Shelby White

ARTHUR M. SACKLER GALLERY

Dr. Siddharth K. Bhansali
Dr. Robert Feinberg, Vice Chair
Mrs. Nancy Fessenden, Chair
Mrs. Richard Helms
Mrs. Marie Lam
Mrs. Jill Hornor Ma
Mrs. Daniel P. Moynihan
Mr. Michael Sonnenreich
Mr. Abolala Soudavar
Mr. Robert C. Tang, S.C.
Mr. Paul F. Walter